SAP PRESS e-books

Print or e-book, Kindle or iPad, workplace or airplane: Choose where and how to read your SAP PRESS books! You can now get all our titles as e-books, too:

► By download and online access
► For all popular devices
► And, of course, DRM-free

Convinced? Then go to **www.sap-press.com** and get your e-book today.

SAP HANA® Advanced Data Modeling

SAP PRESS

SAP PRESS is a joint initiative of SAP and Rheinwerk Publishing. The know-how offered by SAP specialists combined with the expertise of Rheinwerk Publishing offers the reader expert books in the field. SAP PRESS features first-hand information and expert advice, and provides useful skills for professional decision-making.

SAP PRESS offers a variety of books on technical and business-related topics for the SAP user. For further information, please visit our website: *www.sap-press.com*.

Michael Pytel
Implementing SAP Business Suite on SAP HANA
2016, approx. 625 pp., hardcover
ISBN 978-1-4932-1257-6

Merz, Hügens, Blum
Implementing SAP BW on SAP HANA
2015, 467 pages, hardcover
ISBN 978-1-4932-1003-9

Haun, Hickman, Loden, Wells
Implementing SAP HANA (2nd edition)
2014, 860 pages, hardcover
ISBN 978-1-4932-1176-0

Schneider, Westenberger, Gahm
ABAP Development for SAP HANA
2013, 609 pages, hardcover
ISBN 978-1-59229-859-4

Anil Babu Ankisettipalli, Hansen Chen, Pranav Wankawala

SAP HANA® Advanced Data Modeling

Rheinwerk®
Publishing

Bonn • Boston

Editor Sarah Frazier
Acquisitions Editor Kelly Grace Weaver
Copyeditor Melinda Rankin
Cover Design Graham Geary
Photo Credit Shutterstock.com: 1578873/© Tomislav Forgo
Layout Design Vera Brauner
Production Kelly O'Callaghan
Typesetting SatzPro, Krefeld (Germany)
Printed and bound in the United States of America, on paper from sustainable sources

ISBN 978-1-4932-1236-1
© 2016 by Rheinwerk Publishing, Inc., Boston (MA)
1st edition 2016

Library of Congress Cataloging-in-Publication Data
Ankisettipalli, Anil Babu, author.
SAP HANA advanced data modeling / Anil Babu Ankisettipalli, Hansen Chen, Pranav Wankawala. -- 1st edition.
pages cm
Includes index.
ISBN 978-1-4932-1236-1 (print : alk. paper) -- ISBN 1-4932-1236-2 (print : alk. paper) -- ISBN 978-1-4932-1238-5 (print and ebook : alk. paper) -- ISBN 978-1-4932-1237-8 (ebook) 1. Computer simulation. 2. Databases . 3. SAP HANA (Electronic resource) I. Chen, Hansen, author. II. Wankawala, Pranav, author. III. Title.
QA76.9.C65A55 2015
003'.3--dc23
2015030306

We would like to thank all of our colleagues at the SAP Innovation Center – Silicon Valley, USA. All of our knowledge and findings have come from several projects that we have worked on together over the years. This book would not have been possible without all the knowledge sharing, brainstorming, and problem solving that we did together. Our attempt with this book is to extend our culture of collaboration, thought leadership, and innovation to a wider community. We would like to dedicate this book to this fantastic team with whom we are privileged to work with.

Contents at a Glance

Dear Reader,

Congratulations! By purchasing this book, you've taken the first step in advancing your career as an SAP HANA developer. As you know, beginner's basics only go so far in tackling the real world obstacles of SAP HANA data model design. Business breeds complexity, and it's your job to keep up. From modeling complex logic to building predictive models to calculating trends, the world of SAP HANA is bigger and more intricate than ever.

However, fear not! Having worked closely with Anil Babu Ankisettipalli, Hansen Chen, and Pranav Wankawala, I can tell you, personally, that you are in good hands. There's a difficulty and craft involved in teaching complicated topics in a comprehensive and thoughtful way. Anil, Hansen, and Pranav navigate these waters masterfully, providing in-depth examples and sample code to guide you through advanced data modeling use cases. So, what are you waiting for? It's time to take your career to the next level!

What did you think about *SAP HANA Advanced Data Modeling*? Your comments and suggestions are the most useful tools to help us make our books the best they can be. Please feel free to contact me and share any praise or criticism you may have.

Thank you for purchasing a book from SAP PRESS!

Sarah Frazier
Editor, SAP PRESS

Rheinwerk Publishing
Boston, MA

sarahf@rheinwerk-publishing.com
www.sap-press.com

Contents

5   Advanced Predictive Modeling 319

6   Simulations and Optimizations 341

Preface

SAP HANA is a database and, as such, stores data. For that data to have any meaning, it must be arranged into *data models*, maps that describe how specific elements of data relate to each other. Once arranged, the data should be used by applications. The operations on this data structure could be simple calculations, complex machine learning techniques, or anything in between. Most often, the design of a data model and joins on the tables in a data model relate to the performance of a query or function processing in any database. SAP HANA can enable application requirements like business function calculations through logical models used on top of data models. These requirements can range from simple to complex calculations in distributed, scaled-out environments with billions of rows to process.

With these calculation models, applications can also find meaningful data insights by executing machine learning or predictive algorithms. SAP HANA has both natively embedded predictive algorithms and integrations with R to offer flexibility. As we move from predictive to simulation and optimization problems, the challenge of the database is to be versatile in order to perform various complex data structure operations.

Target Audience

This book expects the reader to be aware of in-memory databases and column-oriented databases, and have basic exposure to and hands-on experience with SAP HANA development artifacts. Preferably, the reader will also have basic SQL and data modeling knowledge. Advanced data modeling topics here start from basic calculations in straightforward data models and move to performing complex calculations and machine learning or predictive analytic tasks. This book expects readers to have basic knowledge of and experience with data science-oriented activities and to use such techniques in their regular activities.

Objective

The purpose of this book is to teach developers working in SAP HANA how to design complex data models that perform optimally. With a lot of flexibility in performing database tasks in SAP HANA, this book will help readers learn about the various modeling capabilities in SAP HANA, how to develop complex logic through these logical models, and how to scale for higher volumes of data. This advanced modeling book also covers predictive modeling capabilities in SAP HANA using various algorithm libraries and how to build complex modeling scenarios using multiple types of algorithms together. Finally, we will look at performing complex processes (such as simulations and optimizations) in SAP HANA.

Structure of this Book

This book is organized into two sets of three chapters. The first set will cover data modeling of both physical and logical models and scenarios from simple to complex. The second set will move to predictive modeling, starting with basic predictive modeling and concluding with performing complex operations for simulations and optimizations.

The following walks through details of the chapters ahead:

- ▶ **Chapter 1: Types of SAP HANA Models**
  This chapter gives an overview of all SAP HANA features and then explains the workflow to use SAP HANA Studio to leverage each feature. As this book is for developers who already have SAP HANA experience, we do not provide much explanation on basic concepts; instead, we focus on elements that usually confuse developers. This chapter covers the SAP HANA modeling paradigm, information views (including attribute views, analytic views, and calculation views), analytic privileges, stored procedures (including SQLScript procedures, L language procedures, and R language procedures), and the Application Function Library (including the Business Function Library and the Predictive Analysis Library). With the overall understanding gained in this chapter, developers can move on to other chapters to learn more about SAP HANA models and modeling use cases.

- ▶ **Chapter 2: Modeling Complex Logic**
  This chapter explains how to use SAP HANA data models to represent complex business logic. As it is more flexible and efficient to leverage SAP HANA mod-

eling features to depict complex logic than traditional SQL statements, developers need to learn how to think in SAP HANA to solve complex problems.

▸ **Chapter 3: Scaling for Large Datasets**
This chapter focuses on solutions for scaling large datasets in SAP HANA. Large datasets can hinder performance, which is a primary concern for many developers. SAP HANA provides many features to handle performance, especially for large tables. We will introduce these features with examples based on our experience. Developers may need to know how to set up databases and models, design reporting strategies, and troubleshoot performance issues so as to make their applications run smoothly against large tables.

▸ **Chapter 4: Basic Predictive Modeling**
In this chapter, we will introduce the predictive analytics lifecycle. We walk through how to execute lifecycle activities in SAP HANA and provide examples of how to execute correlations, autocorrelations, component analysis, time series algorithms, and forecast accuracy measurement, along with exploration and modeling in SAP HANA. The chapter then introduces various tools, such as the Application Function Modeler and predictive analytics applications in SAP HANA for performing data science-oriented tasks.

▸ **Chapter 5: Advanced Predictive Modeling**
Now that you have learned about basic predictive modeling, this chapter looks at R's integration with SAP HANA and how to design complex predictive models that need to scale out in distributed environments. We also will look at using multiple components such as PAL and R together in single use case for machine learning activities. The chapter walks through stratification and sampling examples to reduce information transfer without losing the proportional distribution of data.

▸ **Chapter 6: Simulations and Optimization**
You can use SAP HANA to design simulation and optimization models. This chapter explains how to perform random variable generation, matrix manipulation operations, and optimizations and simulations, using a case study.

We hope this book provides an advanced look at all aspects of modeling and scaling for complex processing.

References and Resources

The following resources were used by the authors in the course of writing of this book and should be referred to for continued learning:

- **SAP HANA SQL and System Views Reference**
  http://help.sap.com/hana/sap_hana_sql_and_system_views_reference_en.pdf
- **SAP HANA Master Guide**
  http://help.sap.com/hana/sap_hana_master_guide_en.pdf
- **SAP HANA Business Function Library (BFL)**
  https://help.sap.com/hana/SAP_HANA_Business_Function_Library_BFL_en.pdf
- **SAP HANA Predictive Analysis Library (PAL)**
  http://help.sap.com/hana/sap_hana_predictive_analysis_library_pal_en.pdf
- **SAP HANA R Integration Guide**
  http://help.sap.com/hana/sap_hana_r_integration_guide_en.pdf
- **SAP HANA Modeling Guide**
  http://help.sap.com/hana/sap_hana_modeling_guide_en.pdf
- **SAP HANA Troubleshooting and Performance Analysis Guide**
  http://help.sap.com/hana/sap_hana_troubleshooting_and_performance_analysis_guide_en.pdf
- **An Introduction to R**
  https://cran.r-project.org/doc/manuals/R-intro.pdf
- **SAP HANA Modeling Overview**
  http://saphanatutorial.com/sap-hana-modeling/
- **Building Advanced Data Models with SAP HANA**
  http://scn.sap.com/docs/DOC-13267
- **SAP HANA SQLScript Reference**
  http://help.sap.com/hana/sap_hana_sql_script_reference_en.pdf

Acknowledgments

We would like to thank Sarah Frazier, our editor for this book. For all three of us who set out on this journey of writing a book for the first time, rather than being just an editor, she mentored us on the nuances of authoring a book, which is very different from writing technical papers or publications that we are used to as part of the software development process. She had to understand three different writing styles and bring consistency to the content so that you, our readers, get a product of high quality.

Daisuke Tsuru is a system engineer for Nomura Research Institute in Tokyo, Japan. As part of an exchange program he has been working at SAP since 2014. He has actively worked in developing the portfolio optimization and simulation case study implementation used in Chapter 6. We would like to thank him for his efforts in developing this technique.

Anil Babu Ankisettipalli
Hansen Chen
Pranav Wankawala

Palo Alto, California — October 2015

This chapter introduces the different data models in SAP HANA that will be discussed throughout the rest of the book, along with important concepts to keep in mind.

1   SAP HANA Data Models

This chapter provides an overview of the different data models that can be built in SAP HANA. In this chapter, we describe the three SAP HANA information views and the analytic privileges that can be applied to them. We then walk through the stored procedures, which include SQLScript procedures, L language procedures, and R language procedures. Finally, we will look at the Application Function Libraries (AFLs), such as the Business Function Library (BFL) and the Predictive Analysis Library (PAL).

For each model type, the chapter defines the model in question, outlines the criteria for choosing it, and explains its benefits. Subsequent chapters will be organized based on specific use cases that require the following different types of models: complex business logic, large datasets, predictive analysis applications, and simulation and optimization applications.

To begin, we will provide a brief overview of SAP HANA's database architecture and resources for further learning offered by SAP.

1.1   SAP HANA Database Architecture Overview

SAP HANA is an in-memory technology platform that is deployable as an appliance or in the cloud. At its core is the SAP HANA database, built for high-performance applications. Relevant data is kept in the main memory, and therefore read operations can run in the main memory.

SAP HANA's database consists of the index server, name server, statistics server, preprocessor server, and XS engine. The index server is the main data management component of SAP HANA, containing both the data stores and engines for processing data. In addition to these servers, SAP HANA uses three types of engines based on the information views: the join, online analytics processing (OLAP), and calculation engines. The join engine is used for attribute views. Analytic views without calculated columns use the OLAP engine. Finally, calculation views and analytic views with calculated attributes use the calculation engine. These engines will be discussed in greater depth as we walk through the relevant models.

Because a complete look at SAP HANA's database architecture would be beyond the scope of this book, we encourage you to take a look at SAP-provided informational material. For more information on SAP HANA database architecture as it relates to administration, modeling, and developers, please see the following resources:

- **SAP HANA Administration Guide**
  https://help.sap.com/HANA/SAP_HANA_Administration_Guide_en.pdf
- **SAP HANA Modeling Guide**
  https://help.sap.com/hana/SAP_HANA_Modeling_Guide_en.pdf
- **SAP HANA Developer Guide**
  http://help.sap.com/hana/sap_hana_developer_guide_en.pdf

Next, we will dive straight into the SAP HANA modeling paradigms and the concepts that you will find throughout the book.

1.2   SAP HANA Modeling Paradigms

Modeling refers to the activity of building models against database tables by creating modeled (information) views, stored procedures, decision tables, analytic privileges, and more to depict a business scenario. Figure 1.1 shows a diagram of the relationship between these different modeling elements in SAP HANA.

In this section, we explain these different elements and how they relate to the SAP HANA model paradigm.

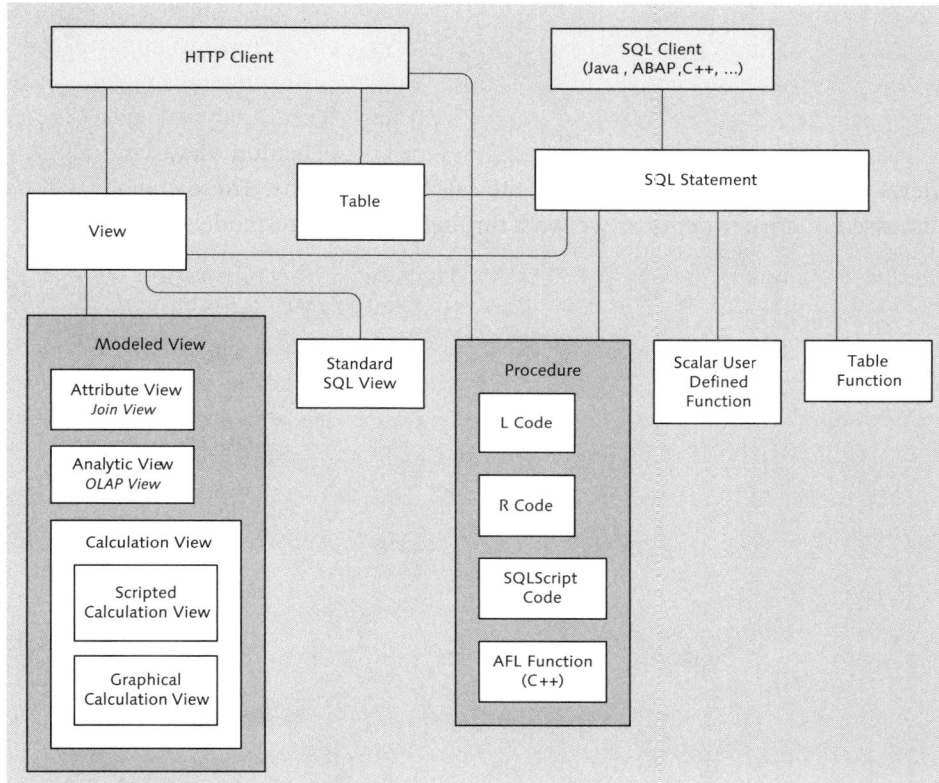

Figure 1.1 SAP HANA Models Relationship Diagram

1.2.1 Client and Data Connection

There are two types of clients in SAP HANA: HTTP and SQL. HTTP clients can connect to the XS server, and applications running in the XS server can execute SQL statements using a database API.

For the SQL clients, client applications written in C/C++ may choose the ODBC interface, those written in Java may choose the Java Database Connectivity (JDBC) interface, those written in Python may choose the Python database API, and ABAP applications hosted by the ABAP Application Server may use the SAP HANA-specific Database Shared Library (DBSL) to connect to the SAP HANA system.

1.2.2   Modeled Views

Modeled views are also called information views. We create these views with the modeling tools in SAP HANA Studio. Modeled views are stored in the repository, and actual database objects are generated from these definitions during their activation. There are three types of modeled views: *attribute views*, *analytic views*, and *calculation views*.

There are many benefits to creating modeled views, including the following:

- ▶ Modeled views are optimized to exert the power of underlying process engines; analytic views can leverage the OLAP engine and calculation views can leverage the calculation engine.

- ▶ Modeled views can be used to represent sophisticated or complex business scenarios. The execution plan of a query against the modeled view can be well optimized by removing unnecessary joins or grouping columns.

- ▶ The additional metadata generated on modeled views can be leveraged by multidimensional expression (MDX) clients, such as SAP BusinessObjects Explorer, SAP BusinessObjects Analysis for Office, and SAP Lumira.

We provide more information on modeled views (information views) in Section 1.3.

1.2.3   Stored Procedures

When information views are not enough to express complex logic or you need to update tables rather than select them, you can create *stored procedures*. Stored procedures can be created with the SQLScript, L, R, and C++ languages. SQLScript can contain SQL statements, such as SELECT or UPDATE, or calculative engine plan operators, which can result in higher performance in some cases.

More information on stored procedures can be found in Section 1.5.

Table Functions

You can use SQLScript to write a table function. This function is not very different from read-only procedures; the only limitation is that it has one single table as its output. You can use the table function in the FROM clause of queries to facilitate using the calling procedure with SELECT statements.

Scalar Functions

You can create a scalar function with SQLScript or L that returns one or more scalar values. Using a user-defined scalar function is the same as using a built-in SQL function. You can put the functions in a SELECT clause, WHERE clause, or GROUP BY clause. Scalar functions are compiled with L code, which does not support table access inside the functions.

1.2.4   C++ (Application Function Libraries)

You can execute application logic written in C++ within SAP HANA; such an application is created as an AFL. When writing C++ code, programming errors may affect the stability and availability of the whole server, so writing application logic in C++ should be restricted to privileged developers. In addition to writing procedures with C++ code, you can also install additional packages provided by SAP that are part of SAP HANA AFL, such as the BFL and PAL, both of which are written in C++ code.

1.2.5   L Language

L is a language designed by SAP for executing procedural code in SAP HANA. You can use L to express application logic that cannot be expressed with SQL or SQLScript. However, L is not officially supported. Therefore, consider using SQLScript whenever possible.

Because L procedures do not contain SQL statements, you can define input and output parameters as table types and transfer data with table objects. Using L, you can create scalar functions for which the input and output are both scalar values instead of table objects. In fact, SQLScript scalar functions and the parts in SQLScript procedures that contain the imperative code, such as WHILE and IF, are internally compiled into L code.

1.2.6   R Language

You can use *R* to create procedures to handle complex statistical computing and graphics processing. There are several benefits to using R: First, it has become popular among statisticians and data miners for developing statistical software and is widely used for advanced data analysis. Currently, you can leverage more than 4,000 packages using R. Second, the objects handled in R, such as vectors, arrays, and data frames, can be tightly bound with database objects, and the manipulation of these objects can be performed efficiently on multicore hardware.

1.3 Information Views

Information views are also called modeled views. As previously discussed, there are three types of information views: attribute view, analytic view, and calculation view. In this section, we will describe each view in detail.

1.3.1 Attribute Views

Attribute views are used to model an entity based on the relationships among the attribute data contained in multiple source tables. Attribute views can model columns, calculated columns, and hierarchies. When you perform multiple dimension analysis against a cube, you need to create an attribute view on each dimension.

For example, when you analyze the transactions of a retail company, you can make reports on sales values based on a location dimension, time dimension, and goods type dimension. For each dimension, you need to create an attribute view.

In this section, we will look at the steps that need to be performed in these dimensions.

Location Dimension

As an example, suppose you have the location dimension table LOC; the data definition language (DDL) is shown in Listing 1.1.

```
CREATE COLUMN TABLE LOC(
STORE_ID INT,
CITY VARCHAR(20));
```

Listing 1.1 DDL for Location Dimension Table

Each CITY has a corresponding STATE. The mapping information is in table LOC_CITY (see Listing 1.2).

```
CREATE COLUMN TABLE LOC_CITY(
CITY VARCHAR(20),
STATE VARCHAR(20));
```
Listing 1.2 DDL for City Dimension Table

You can create the attribute view AT_LOC for the location dimension (see Figure 1.2).

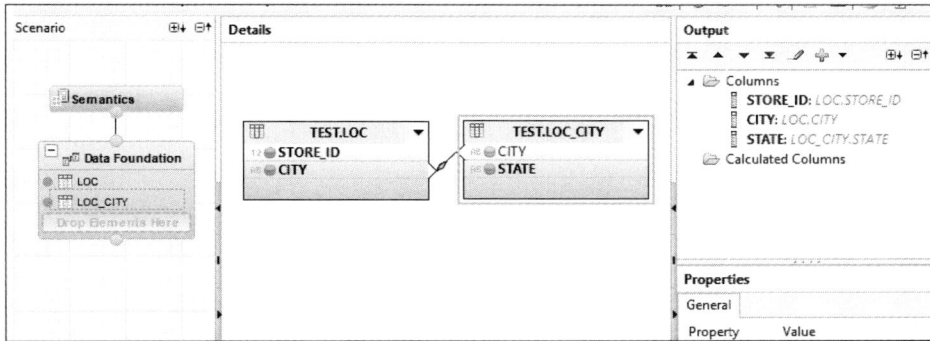

Figure 1.2 Attribute View for Location Dimension

In the attribute view, link the tables LOC and LOC_CITY on column CITY. There are three columns here: STORE_ID, CITY, and STATE. Each STORE_ID belongs to a single CITY, and each CITY belongs to a single STATE. This logic can be expressed through *hierarchies*. You can create a hierarchy object H_LOC in the attribute view (see Figure 1.3).

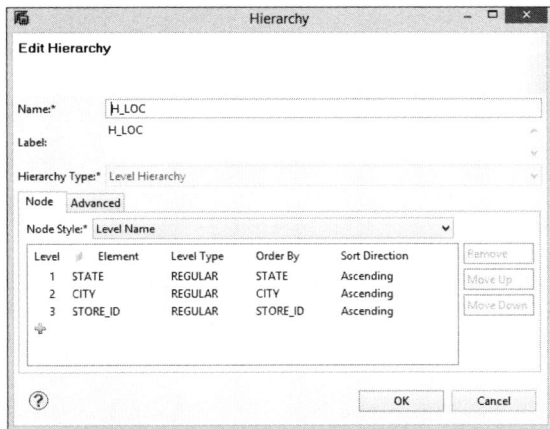

Figure 1.3 Hierarchy on Location Dimension

There are two types of hierarchies in SAP HANA that can be defined by both calculation and attribute views:

▶ **Level hierarchies**
Level hierarchies are usually for aggregation purposes. They consist of one or more levels. For example, country, province, city for a location hierarchy, and year, month, and day for a time hierarchy. Members at one level can roll up to the next higher level in a many-to-one relationship. The attributes for different levels are on different columns.

▶ **Parent–child hierarchies**
A parent–child hierarchy is a hierarchy in a standard dimension that contains a parent attribute. You usually use self-joins to represent the logic of a parent–child hierarchy. When you have two columns, the value of one column represents the child member, the value of the other column points to a parent member, and the child member of one record can be the parent member of another record.

In the example shown in Figure 1.3, the hierarchy consists of three columns, with rolling-up relations among them. Therefore, when you define the hierarchy, choose LEVEL HIERARCHY as the HIERARCHY TYPE.

For the NODE STYLE, there are three options: LEVEL NAME, NAME ONLY, and NAME PATH. The node style determines the composition of a unique node ID. The different values for the node styles are explained as follows:

▶ LEVEL NAME
The unique node ID is composed of the level name and node name—for example, [Level 2].[Austin].

▶ NAME ONLY
The unique node ID is composed of the level name alone—for example, "Austin".

▶ NAME PATH
The unique node ID is composed of the result node name and the names of all ancestors apart from the root node—for example, [Texas].[Austin].

In this example, choose LEVEL NAME based on what you know about the data. If there are identical values at different levels, assuming that Washington is a city name and also a state name, it is not appropriate to choose NAME ONLY, because using Washington as the node ID can be confusing when determining whether it is a city or a state.

If you choose LEVEL NAME, then "[Level 1].[Washington]" is the state node and "[Level 2].[Washington]" is the city node. If there are identical names for different cities, you need to choose NAME PATH. Assuming New Jersey has a city named Dover, and Minnesota also has a city named Dover, it will be confusing when you specify the node as [Level 2].[Dover]; you need to specify the path as well—for example, [Minnesota].[Dover] or [New Jersey].[Dover]. Specify the column as STATE at the first level, the CITY column at the second level, and the STORE_ID column at the third level.

The LEVEL TYPE field is used to specify the semantics for the level attributes. For example, if it shows TIMEMONTHS, this indicates that the attributes of the level contain a month, such as January. In this case, choose REGULAR, which indicates that a level does not require any special formatting.

In the MDX client tools, members will be sorted by attribute. To sort the display of the hierarchy members in ascending or descending order, select the required option from the SORT DIRECTION dropdown list.

You can set other properties of the hierarchy object in the ADVANCED tab of the EDIT HIERARCHY window (see Figure 1.4).

The following options are found under the ADVANCED tab (see Figure 1.4):

▸ AGGREGATE ALL NODES
This field indicates whether data is posted on the aggregate nodes and whether it should be shown in the user interface. If it is set to TRUE, the value of the parent will be added to the aggregation of the children when calculating the aggregate nodes. If you are sure that there is no data posted on the aggregate nodes, then set the option to FALSE; the engine will then calculate the hierarchy faster.

▸ DEFAULT MEMBER
You may set a default member for the MDX client tools to use the default node.

▸ ORPHAN NODES
Orphan nodes are nodes that do not have parents or higher levels. You can choose from one of the following options:

 ▹ ROOT NODES: Treat orphan nodes as root nodes.

 ▹ ERRORS: Stop processing and show an error.

 ▹ IGNORE: Ignore orphan nodes.

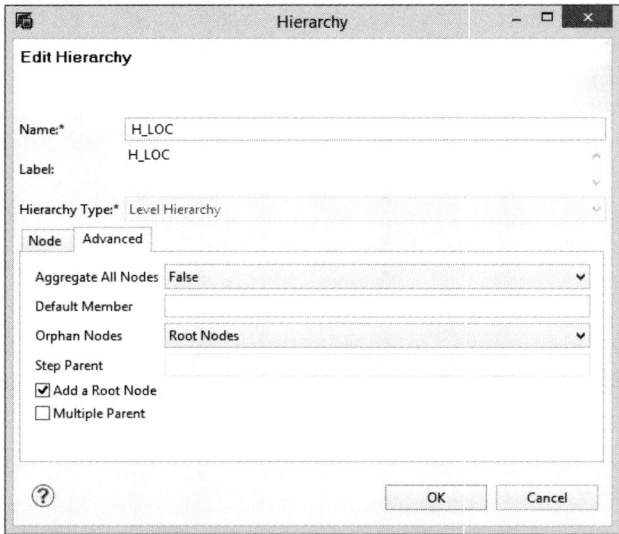

Figure 1.4 Advanced Tab to Define a Hierarchy

▶ STEP PARENT
This option is used to put a node under a stepparent node. For example, if some STORE_IDs do not have an upper level, you can add the node Unknown at the CITY column, and then specify the stepparent as [Level 2].[Unknown].

▶ ADD A ROOT NODE
This checkbox can be selected if a hierarchy does not have a root node but needs one for reporting purposes. When checked, it will create a root node with the technical name ALL.

▶ MULTIPLE PARENT
This checkbox indicates whether a hierarchy needs to support multiple parents for its elements. When checked, the hierarchy contains a node that belongs to more than one parent. For example, a STORE_ID can belong to two cities. Multiple parents can cause confusion when drilling down and drilling up.

The definition of the attribute view is stored in XML format in the SAP HANA repository. To see the XML content, export the attribute view by selecting EXPORT from the SAP HANA Studio menu bar, under FILE. You will see the EXPORT window (see Figure 1.5).

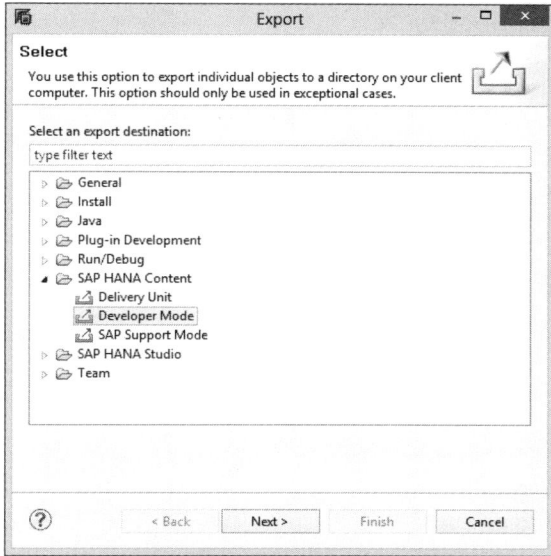

Figure 1.5 Export Window to Choose SAP HANA Content

Under the SAP HANA CONTENT folder, choose DEVELOPER MODE and then click NEXT. Then, choose the system you want to export content from and click NEXT (see Figure 1.6).

Figure 1.6 Export Window to Choose System

Next, choose the objects you want to export, specify the TARGET FOLDER on the local machine, and click FINISH (see Figure 1.7).

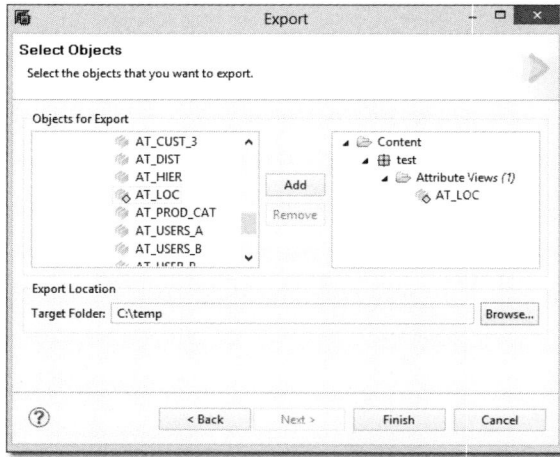

Figure 1.7 Export Window to Choose Objects

When the export finishes, you will see the XML file AT_LOC.attributeview in the specified folder. Listing 1.3 shows the content of the file.

```
<?xml version="1.0" encoding="UTF-8"?>
<Dimension:dimension
  xmlns:xsi="http://www.w3.org/2001/XMLSchema-instance"
  xmlns:Dimension="http://www.sap.com/ndb/BiModelDimension.ecore"
  schemaVersion="1.2" id="AT_LOC" defaultClient="$$client$$"
  defaultLanguage="$$language$$" visibility="internal"
  dimensionType="Standard">
<origin/>
<descriptions defaultDescription="AT_LOC"/>
<metadata changedAt="2015-05-05 14:56:36.0"/>
<attributes>
  <attribute id="STORE_ID" key="true">
    <descriptions defaultDescription="STORE_ID"/>
    <keyMapping schemaName="TEST" columnObjectName="LOC"
                columnName="STORE_ID"/>
  </attribute>
  <attribute id="CITY">
    <descriptions defaultDescription="CITY"/>
    <keyMapping schemaName="TEST" columnObjectName="LOC"
                columnName="CITY"/>
  </attribute>
  ...
  ...
<hierarchies>
  <hierarchy xsi:type="Dimension:LeveledHierarchy" id="H_LOC"
             aggregateAllNodes="true" withRootNode="true"
```

```
              nodeStyle="LEVEL_NAME">
      <descriptions defaultDescription="H_LOC"/>
      <levels>
        <level levelAttribute="#STATE"
               levelType="MDLEVEL_TYPE_REGULAR" order="1"
               orderAttribute="#STATE"/>
        <level levelAttribute="#CITY" levelType="MDLEVEL_TYPE_REGULAR"
               order="2" orderAttribute="#CITY"/>
        <level levelAttribute="#STORE_ID"
               levelType="MDLEVEL_TYPE_REGULAR" order="3"
               orderAttribute="#STORE_ID"/>
      </levels>
    </hierarchy>
  </hierarchies>
</Dimension:dimension>
```

Listing 1.3 XML Definition File of the Attribute View

In the XML file, you can see the join definition, attribute definition, and hierarchy definition. In some cases, you may edit the XML file directly. For example, when you change the schema and move the view from the development environment to the production environment, it is tedious to replace the tables one by one in SAP HANA Studio. Instead, you can make the change in the exported XML files and reimport the revised versions.

There are two internal input parameters in the XML file: `defaultClient ="$$client$$"` and `defaultLanguage="$$language$$"`. The value of the `"$$client$$"` parameter is set by the user's property. The value of `"$$language$$"` is set in the logon window. We will explain these parameters in detail in Section 1.3.2.

When you active the attribute view, you will see the column view in schema `"_SYS_BIC"`. You can run the column view with the following SQL statement:

```
SELECT * FROM _SYS_BIC."test/AT_LOC";
```

In the background, the column view is created with the SQL statement shown in Listing 1.4.

```
CREATE COLUMN VIEW "_SYS_BIC"."test/AT_LOC" WITH PARAMETERS(
indexType=6,
joinIndex="TEST"."LOC",
joinIndexType=0,
joinIndexEstimation=0,
joinIndex="TEST"."LOC_CITY",
joinIndexType=0,
joinIndexEstimation=0,
joinCondition=('JOIN_LOC_LOC_CITY_1',"TEST"."LOC","CITY",
```

```
  "TEST"."LOC_CITY","CITY",'',16,0),
joinPath=('PATH','JOIN_LOC_LOC_CITY_1'),
viewAttribute=('STORE_ID',"TEST"."LOC","STORE_ID",'PATH','V_LOC',
  'attribute','','test/AT_LOC$STORE_ID'),
viewAttribute=('CITY',"TEST"."LOC","CITY",'PATH','V_LOC',
  'attribute','','test/AT_LOC$CITY'),
viewAttribute=('STATE',"TEST"."LOC_CITY","STATE",'PATH','V_LOC',
  'attribute','','test/AT_LOC$STATE'),
view=('V_LOC',"TEST"."LOC"),
defaultView='V_LOC',
'REGISTERVIEWFORAPCHECK'='1',
OPTIMIZEMETAMODEL=0)
```

Listing 1.4 DDL of the Column View

The column view is based on the definition of the join index. There are several types of join indexes: An index type of 6 indicates an attribute view; when an index type is 5, it is an analytic view; and when an index type is 11, it is a calculation view. By understanding the syntax of the column view statement, you can create column views without using the information view tool.

However, objects created with the information view tool can be used to create other information views with the information view tool, whereas the column views that are created manually cannot. The column view is well optimized to leverage the SAP HANA engine and results in better performance than achieving the same logic with a pure SQL query. For example, to execute a simple join of two tables, it is usually faster to execute an attribute view including the join than to use a SELECT statement to make the join.

Time Dimension

In addition to the location dimension, you usually need to create a model for a time dimension. SAP HANA provides table _SYS_BI.M_TIME_DIMENSION as a calendar table. If there are no rows currently in this table, you can generate the content of the table with the GENERATE TIME DATA tool, found under the QUICK LAUNCH tab of the SAP HANA Modeler perspective of SAP HANA Studio (see Figure 1.8).

If the tab is not shown in SAP HANA Studio, click on the MODELER button to switch the perspective in the toolbar (see Figure 1.9).

If the MODELER button is not on the toolbar, click on the WINDOW dropdown menu on the toolbar and navigate to OPEN PERSPECTIVE • MODELER. The QUICK LAUNCH tab will appear (see Figure 1.10).

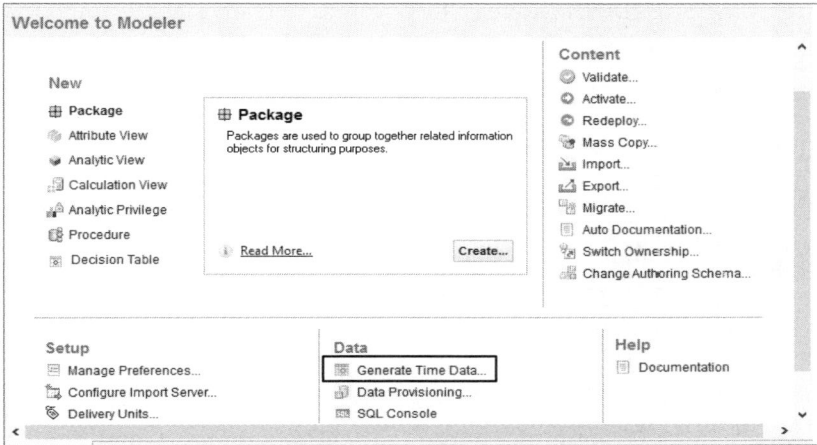

Figure 1.8 Generate Time Data Tool Under the Quick Launch Tab

Figure 1.9 SAP HANA Modeler Button in Toolbar

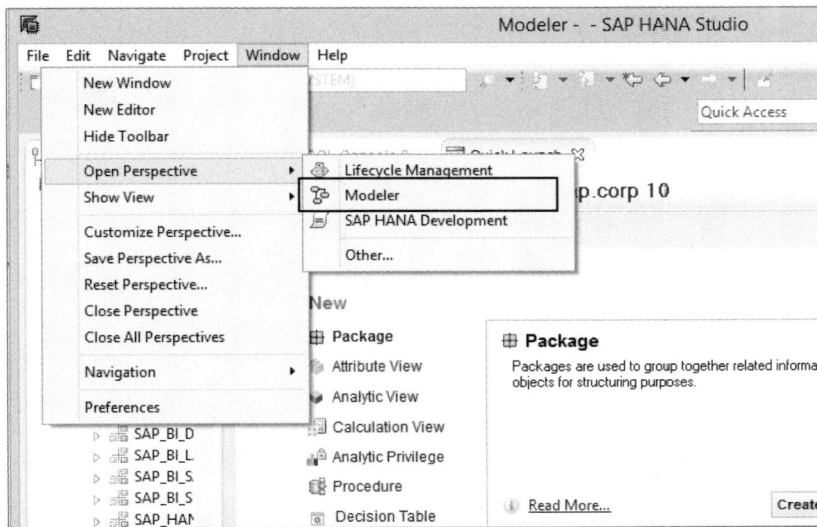

Figure 1.10 Modeler Button in Window Dropdown

Once you are in the SAP HANA Modeler tool, you can create the attribute view AT_CALENDAR against the calendar table (see Figure 1.11).

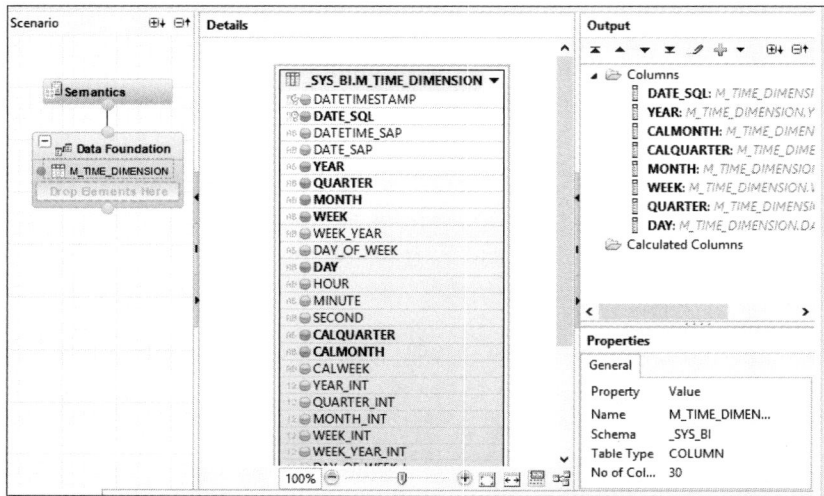

Figure 1.11 Attribute Table on Date Dimension

Also create a hierarchy for the date dimension, as shown in Figure 1.12.

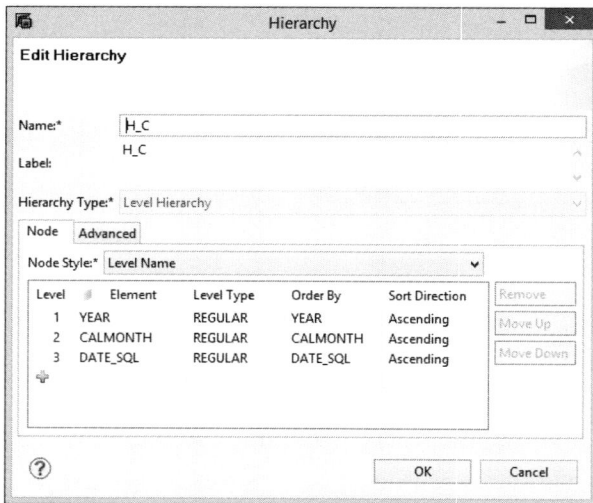

Figure 1.12 Hierarchy of the Date Dimension

In the hierarchy definition window, set the column YEAR as the first level, column CALMONTH as the second level, and DATE_SQL as the third level. The format of the CALMONTH column is a year value with a month value, such as 201312. Therefore, one value of CALMONTH only points to a single year. There is another column, MONTH, on the calendar table. If the format of the column is only the month value, then each value on this column points to multiple values of the year. If you choose the MONTH column at the second level, you need to choose LEVEL TYPE as the NAME PATH. The resulting expression will be [2013].[12], which points to a unique node.

After you activate the attribute view, you will see a new column view: _SYS_BIC. "test/AT_CALENDAR".

Other Dimensions

You can also create attribute views for other dimensions, such as goods-related dimensions, payment method dimensions, customer dimensions, and more. With attribute views, you can define joins, filters, calculated columns, and hierarchies. When you need other kinds of logic, such as aggregation or union, you can create other kinds of information views.

1.3.2 Analytic Views

Analytic views can be used to model columns, calculated and restricted columns, input parameters, and variables. Analytic views are used to model data that includes measures. For example, say that you have a transaction table TRANS that stores a transaction log, and you need to analyze the measures for quantity and price. You may choose to create an analytic view against the table (see Listing 1.5).

```
CREATE COLUMN TABLE "TRANS" (
"TRANS_DATE" DATE,
"TRANS_NO" BIGINT ,
"STORE_ID" INT,
"PROD_ID" INTEGER ,
"SALES_QTY" BIGINT ,
"PRICE" DECIMAL(18,2));
```
Listing 1.5 DDL of Fact Table TRANS

Data Foundation

To create an analytic view, you first need to define the data foundation using the information view tool (see Figure 1.13).

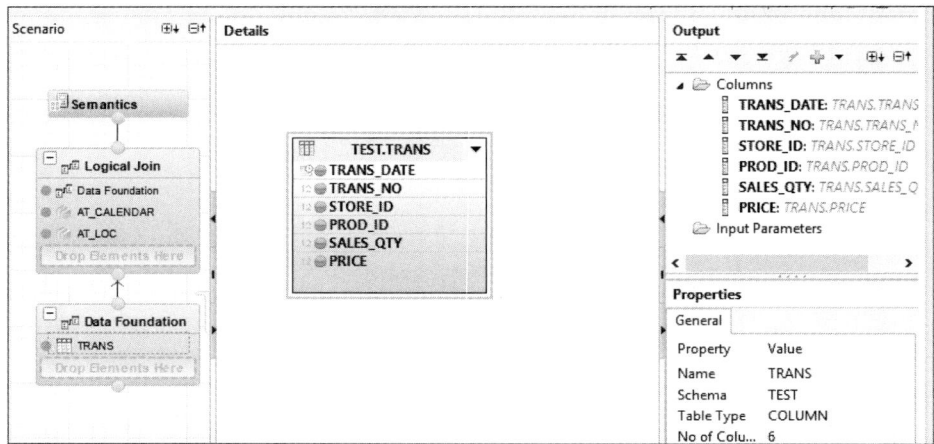

Figure 1.13 Data Foundation of the Analytic View AN_TRAN

Drag table TRANS to the data foundation. In this table, the column names are straightforward, but in other cases, the column names might be incomprehensible or misleading. In these situations, you should show the description of each column in the UI. You can run the statements shown in Listing 1.6 to add comments on each column of the table.

```
COMMENT ON COLUMN TRANS.TRANS_DATE IS 'Date of transaction';
COMMENT ON COLUMN TRANS.TRANS_NO IS 'ID of transaction';
COMMENT ON COLUMN TRANS.STORE_ID IS 'ID of store';
COMMENT ON COLUMN TRANS.PROD_ID IS 'ID of merchandise';
COMMENT ON COLUMN TRANS.SALES_QTY IS 'Quantity of sold';
COMMENT ON COLUMN TRANS.PRICE IS 'Price of merchandise';
```

Listing 1.6 Add Comments on Each Column

As shown in Figure 1.14, after adding comments for each column, when you check the table in the UI, you will find the column name and column description shown side by side.

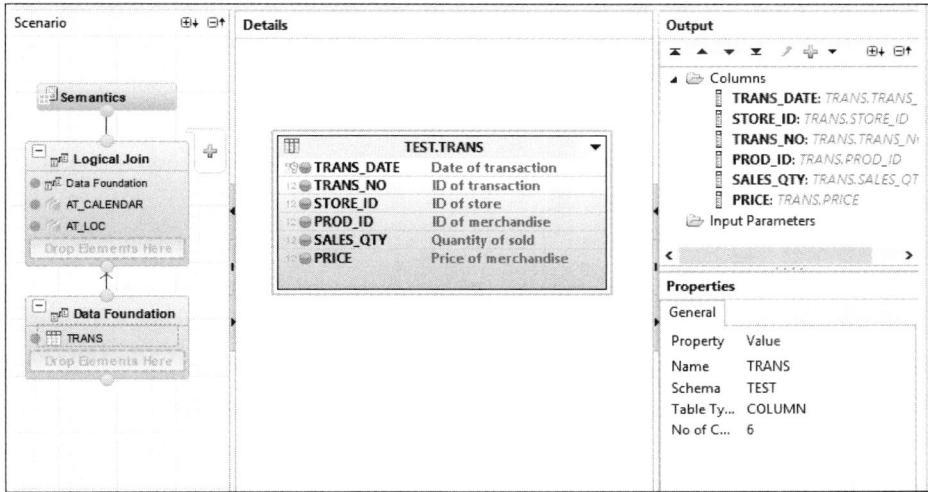

Figure 1.14 Column Name and Description Shown Side by Side

Join Definitions

Next, examine the join definition in the analytic view (see Figure 1.15). Add two attribute views, AT_CALENDAR and AT_LOC, to join with the data foundation.

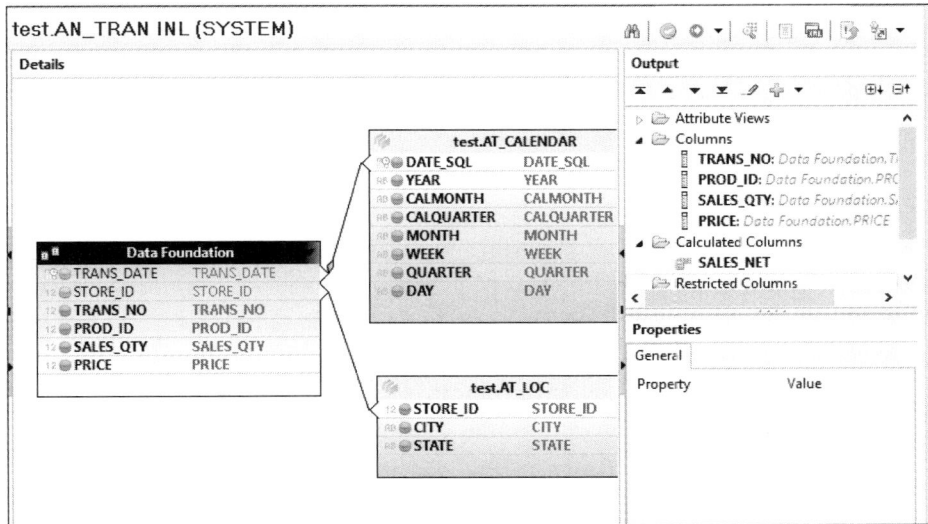

Figure 1.15 Join Definition in an Analytic View

Table `AT_CALENDAR` is for the time dimension, and table `AT_LOC` is for the location dimension. When you run reporting against the analytic view, you can leverage any column of the linked attribute views. When you use an MDX query, you can also leverage the hierarchies defined in the attribute views.

A *join* combines two or more table or view records. There are several types of joins that you should be aware of:

▶ **Inner joins**
Inner joins return records that show the mapping between two tables and filter out records without any mapping. When a join is defined as an inner join, it is always performed when a query is run against an analytic view, regardless of whatever columns exist in the query.

▶ **Outer joins**
Outer joins include *left outer joins* and *right outer joins*. The left outer join returns all the records on the left table, regardless of whether the record has mappings on the right table. Similarly, the right outer join returns all the records on the right table, regardless of whether the record has mappings on the left table. When running a query against a view containing a left outer join, the join is performed only when the query contains any column from the right table. When there is no column from the right table in the query, the join is not performed. The same is true in reverse for right outer joins. This helps the SAP HANA engine simplify its execution plan and improve performance. In the running example, if you set the join between the data foundation and `AT_LOC` as a left outer join, then when you run a query to analyze sales on the date dimension, regardless of the location dimension, the join between the data foundation and `AT_LOC` will not be performed.

▶ **Referential joins**
Referential joins behave like inner joins, when the query contains columns from both linked tables. They also behave like outer joins when the query contains columns from only one of the linked tables. For example, if you set the join between the data foundation and `AT_LOC` as a referential join, when the query does not contain the `CITY` or `STATE` column, the join is not performed; when the query contains the `CITY` or `STATE` column, the join is performed like an inner join, and the records on the data foundation that do not have a mapping row on `AT_LOC` will be filtered out. There is an exception when the underlying attribute view contains an inner join: The referential join in the analytic view will behave like an inner join regardless of whether the attribute view's columns

exist in the query or not. Therefore, if you want the referential join to behave dynamically based on the query, make sure the underlying attribute view uses a referential join or outer join instead of an inner join.

With a referential join, you can link time-dependent dimension tables. For example, a store once belonged to City 1 from 2001 to 2005, and it belonged to City 2 from 2006 to 2010. Here, you need to create a time-dependent dimension table to store the history relation between the store and the city, assuming you use DATE_FROM and DATE_TO columns to store the date range. When you define the join, you need to set the TRANS_DATE column as a temporal column, DATE_FROM as a from column, and DATE_TO as a to column.

► **Text joins**
Text joins behave like inner joins, but with a restricted language column. This join is beneficial in multilingual applications. For example, suppose you have a location dimension table that supports multilingual usage, and for each store ID there are two records pointing to two languages. Use the LANG column to specify the language type with value E or D. Then, you can define the join as a text join and set LANG as the language column. When you log on to SAP HANA, specify the language value for the logon session. The value is sent to the analytic view with the internal input parameter $$language$$. A filter based on the value will be applied to the LANG column, and the analytic view will return the records that match the language setting of the session.

When you make a join between the data foundation and the attribute view, the join columns on the data foundation are grayed out. When you need the columns in the query, you have to use the linked column on the attribute view. For example, when you need to use the TRANS_DATE column, you have to use the DATE_SQL column. For an inner join, there is no difference between TRANS_DATE and DATE_SQL, because they return only the mapping records; the mapping records have the same values on the columns.

For a referential join, using DATE_SQL and using TRANS_DATE works differently; if you use DATE_SQL, the join is performed, and the record of the transaction table without mapping will be filtered out on the transaction table. If you use TRANS_DATE, the join is not performed, and the records without mapping will be kept.

For a left outer join, the logic becomes more complex. DATE_SQL no longer points to the AT_CALENDAR column, but to the TRANS_DATE column on the data foundation. When the DATE_SQL column is used in the query, it returns the value of

TRANS_DATE, and the join is not performed. In order to perform the join, you need to add another column of AT_CALENDAR to the query.

To avoid confusion on the join column, it is better to create separate columns for joins. In attribute view AT_LOC, create an additional column, STORE_ID_J, which points to STORE_ID. In the attribute view AT_CALENDAR, create an additional column, DATE_SQL_J, which points to DATE_SQL.

As shown in Figure 1.16, in the analytic view we created additional columns for STORE_ID_1 and TRANS_DATE_1. The data foundation joins to AT_CALENDAR on columns TRANS_DATE and DATE_SQL_J. The data foundation then joins to AT_LOC on columns STORE_ID_1 and STORE_ID_J. Given that the STORE_ID columns for attribute view AT_LOC and the data foundation have duplicate names, add an alias of STORE_ID on AT_LOC as AT_LOC_STORE_ID, then you can use the name STORE_ID to point to the data foundation and use the name AT_LOC_STORE_ID to point to AT_LOC.

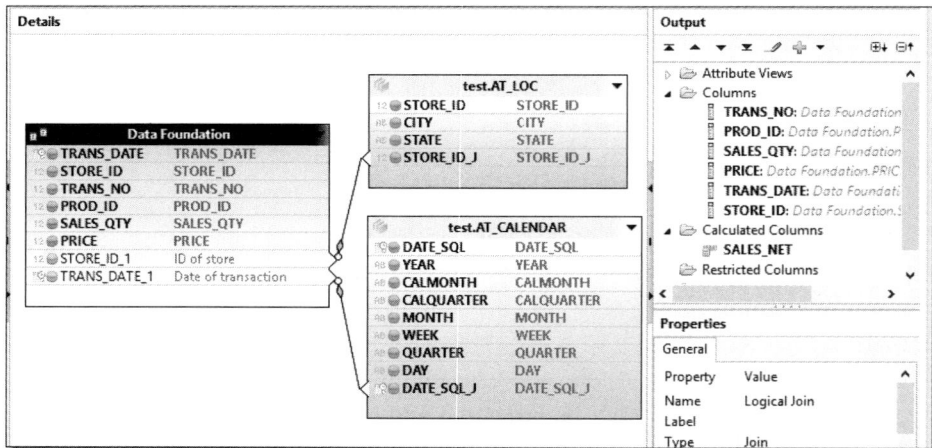

Figure 1.16 Join to Separate Columns

With this approach, the join columns between tables are explicitly separated, and can be referenced separately in queries. For example, if the join for the data foundation and AT_CALENDAR is an inner join, then you can use either DATE_SQL or TRANS_DATE, as they return the same result. However, for a referential join or left outer join, if you do not want to perform the join, choose column TRANS_DATE in the query; if you do want to perform the join, choose DATE_SQL. The solution is to avoid confusion about the owner of the join column. If the query doesn't need the join column, you do not have to apply it. For example, in an analytic view, if you want to aggregate data at the month, quarter, or year level instead of at the day level, you will not run into this confusion.

You can set the *cardinality* when defining joins. Appropriate cardinality settings can help the optimizer choose an optimal execution path. For fact tables, when joined to a dimension table on the primary key, the cardinality is usually N:1. The cardinality setting should respect the actual data relation; otherwise, it may lead to errors or low performance. When the cardinality information is unknown, you can leave the cardinality setting empty; the system will diagnose the best-suited cardinality and execute the join.

Calculated Columns

You can also create a calculated column on an analytic view. In the following example, you have the quantity and price. To calculate the total sales of each transaction, you need to create the calculated column SALES_NET (see Figure 1.17).

In the CALCULATED COLUMNS window, you can set the column as an ATTRIBUTE or MEASURE in the COLUMN TYPE field according to the nature of the column. In this case, set it as MEASURE, because its expression is "PRICE"*"SALES_QTY", and the value will be aggregated with SUM() in the query. If you select the CALCULATE BEFORE AGGREGATION checkbox, then the calculation is performed for each row. This can be time-consuming with volume data. When this checkbox is not selected, the calculation is performed on the aggregation result to improve performance. In this case, the result of SUM("PRICE" * "SALES_QTY") is not equal to SUM("PRICE")*SUM("SALES_QTY"), so select the checkbox. Alternatively, you can create a calculated column on the fact table with the following statement:

```
ALTER TABLE TRANS ADD (SALES DECIMAL(18,2) GENERATED ALWAYS AS
PRICE*SALES_QTY);
```

You can use the calculated SALES column in the analytic view as well, and it behaves like a physical column. The performance is better than when defining the calculation in the analytic view. If the columns of the expression are from different tables, you have to define the calculated column in the analytic view.

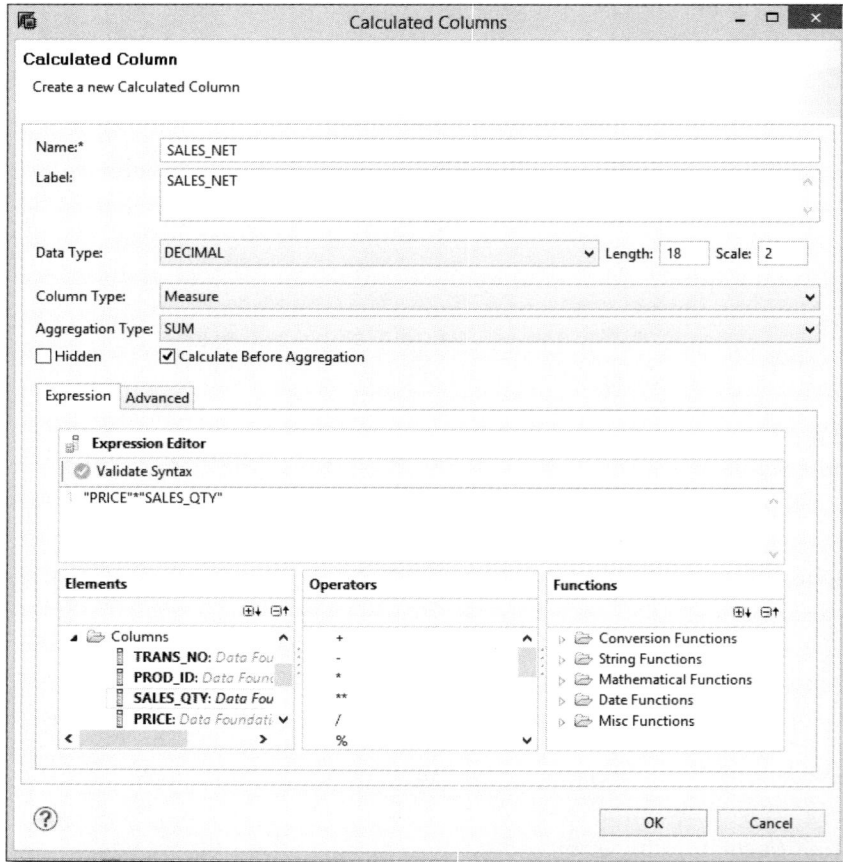

Figure 1.17 Calculated Columns

Semantics Nodes

After defining the joins and calculated columns, you can enter the semantics node. There, you can define the column type, aggregation type, and some peripheral settings (see Figure 1.18).

Define the columns TRANS_DATE, STORE_ID, and so on as attributes, because you can use the columns in the GROUP BY clause or WHERE clause. Define SALES_QTY and SALES_NET as measures, because you can use the SUM() function on them.

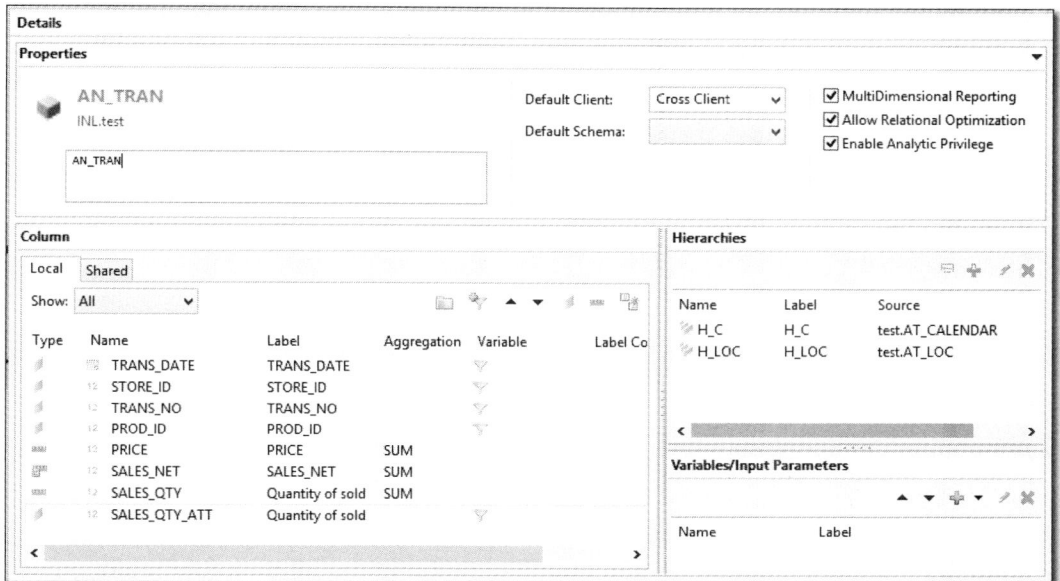

Figure 1.18 Semantics Node of an Analytic View

> **Measures**
>
> In some cases, you may also need a column for measures in the WHERE clause. For example, suppose you use a positive value on SALE_QTY for goods sold and a negative value for goods returned. You need a filter like "WHERE SALE_QTY>0" in the query when you analyze the goods sold. When using a measure as a filter, some client tools may filter it after aggregation and return the wrong result.
>
> To avoid this problem, create separate columns in the data foundation: SALES_QTY and SALE_QTY_ATT, which both point to one column. Define SALES_QTY as a measure and SALES_QTY_ATT as an attribute. In an SQL query or other client tools, when the column is needed in an aggregation function, use SALES_QTY. For a GROUP BY clause or WHERE clause, use the SALES_QTY_ATT column.

As shown in Figure 1.18, there are three checkboxes in the PROPERTIES section: MULTIDIMENSIONAL REPORTING, ALLOW RELATIONAL OPTIMIZATION, and ENABLE ANALYTIC PRIVILEGE. When MULTIDIMENSIONAL REPORTING is selected, the view can be consumed with MDX to perform multidimensional reporting; otherwise, it cannot be consumed with MDX.

The Allow Relational Optimization checkbox relates to the calculation engine's behavior. To understand its use, you need to know how the view is structured on the backend. If an analytic view has complex logic, such as calculated attributes, currency conversion, or input parameters, then when it is activated, it generates a column view with index type 5, a calculation scenario based on the column view, and another column view with index type 11, which is based on the calculation scenario. In Listing 1.7, the column view with index type 5 is _SYS_BIC. "test/AN_TRAN/olap".

```
CREATE COLUMN VIEW "_SYS_BIC"."test/AN_TRAN/olap"
  WITH PARAMETERS (indexType=5,
  joinIndex="TEST"."LOC",
  joinIndexType=2,
  joinIndexEstimation=0,
  joinIndex="TEST"."LOC_CITY",
 ...
 ...
 ...
  characteristic=('PROD_ID',
    keyAttribute="PROD_ID",''),
    characteristic=('SALES_QTY_ATT',
    keyAttribute="SALES_QTY_ATT",''),
    'REGISTERVIEWFORAPCHECK'='1',
    OPTIMIZEMETAMODEL=0);
```
Listing 1.7 DDL of Column View Based on an Analytic View Definition

The column view does not contain calculated attributes. Those attributes are defined in another kind of object called a *calculation scenario* (see Listing 1.8).

```
CREATE CALCULATION SCENARIO "_SYS_BIC"."test/AN_TRAN" USING
  '[{"__CalculationNode__": true,"name": "dataSource","operation":
  {"__OlapDSNodeData__": true,"source": "_SYS_BIC:test/AN_TRAN/olap",
  "dataSourceFlags": 0},"attributeVec": [{"__Attribute__": true,
  "name": "DATE_SQL","role": 1,"datatype": {"__DataType__": true,
  "type": 101,"sqlType":
...
...
...
true,"name": "row.count","role": 2,"datatype": {"__DataType__": true,
"type": 66,"length": 18},"kfAggregationType": 2,"attributeType": 4,
"specialAttrType": 4}]}]';
```
Listing 1.8 DDL of a Calculation Scenario

A column view _SYS_BIC. "test/AN_TRAN" with index type 11 is generated based on the calculation scenario (see Listing 1.9).

```
CREATE COLUMN VIEW "_SYS_BIC"."test/AN_TRAN" WITH
  PARAMETERS (indexType=11,
  'PARENTCALCINDEXSCHEMA'='_SYS_BIC',
  'PARENTCALCINDEX'='test/AN_TRAN',
  'PARENTCALCNODE'='finalAggregation');
```

Listing 1.9 DDL of a Column View Based on a Calculation Scenario

When you create calculation views, they create similar calculation scenarios. The calculation scenario is executed in the calculation engine. At runtime, the calculation engine executes an instantiation process, which transforms a stored calculation model into an executed calculation model based on a query on top of a calculation view.

The ALLOW RELATIONAL OPTIMIZATION checkbox affects the optimization of an executed calculation model. When it is selected, redundant columns will be removed from the execution plan and the performance is improved.

Because the calculation engine does not behave relationally, the relational optimization of a query in the calculation engine may cause unexpected results in some cases. For example, when calculating COUNT(*), it does not specify a projection list of columns that should be counted. Due to the instantiation process, the result set of the executed calculation model can vary. To address the potential problem with COUNT(*), you may use an internal column row.count, which will return the correct result. Therefore, the query to calculate COUNT(*) can be revised as follows:

```
SELECT SUM("row.count") FROM _SYS_BIC."test/AN_TRAN;
```

Alternatively, you may create a calculated column on the fact table and assign it the value of constant 1:

```
ALTER TABLE TRANS ADD (ONE INT GENERATED ALWAYS AS 1);
```

To calculate the value of COUNT(*), calculate SUM(ONE):

```
SELECT SUM(ONE) FROM _SYS_BIC."test/AN_TRAN";
```

However, if you create a calculated attribute—for example, ONE_A with constant value 1—on the analytic view instead of on the table, it sometimes may behave in a different way. When we run following query, it returns null:

```
SELECT SUM(ONE_A) FROM _SYS_BIC."test/AN_TRAN";
```

The calculated column in an analytic view is different from that in a table. This is due to the calculation engine's instantiation process. Because there are no other columns in the query except the calculated column, the calculated attribute is not instantiated, and so it returns null. To fix this, you may change the calculated attribute to a calculated measure with the CALCULATED BEFORE AGGREGATION flag.

The ALLOW RELATIONAL OPTIMIZATION setting in Figure 1.18 doesn't impact optimization at the SQL query level. Therefore, whether the checkbox is selected or not, when we run the following query,

```
SELECT SUM(C) FROM (SELECT CITY,COUNT(*) C FROM _SYS_BIC."test/AN_
TRAN" GROUP BY CITY);
```

it will be optimized as follows:

```
SELECT COUNT(*) FROM _SYS_BIC. "test/AN_TRAN";
```

Optimization Strategy	
Optimization strategies may change with SAP HANA releases. To stay current, refer to the release notes.	

As introduced previously, there is a column view of index type 5 based on a cube definition and a column view of index type 11 based on a calculation scenario. These two kinds of column views behave in different ways in some cases. Examine the following query:

```
SELECT COUNT(*) FROM (SELECT * FROM _SYS_BIC."test/AN_TRAN");
```

If the column view is of index type 5, it is executed as follows:

```
SELECT COUNT(*) FROM _SYS_BIC."test/AN_TRAN";
```

If the column view is of index type 11, it is executed as follows:

```
SELECT COUNT(*) FROM (
SELECT DISTINCT DATE_SQL, YEAR, CALMONTH, CALQUARTER, MONTH, WEEK,
   QUARTER, DAY, AT_LOC_STORE_ID, CITY, STATE, TRANS_DATE, STORE_ID,
   TRANS_NO, PROD_ID
FROM _SYS_BIC."test/AN_TRAN");
```

Because the execution plans are different, the queries against the different types of views perform differently and return different results. It is important to check the execution plan when troubleshooting SQL query issues, because similar queries against different kinds of views can lead to significant differences in the execution plan.

When optimization is performed and some columns are removed from the optimized query, it might impact the joins. If a join between the data foundation and AT_LOC is a referential join, then when the CITY column is in the query, the join will be executed; otherwise, it is not executed. To enforce the execution of the join, you may add a filter, such as "WHERE CITY IS NOT NULL", in the query.

With newer revisions of SAP HANA, more features have been introduced, and the UI has also changed. Examine the semantics node definition window of SAP HANA Studio version 2.0.15, shown in Figure 1.19.

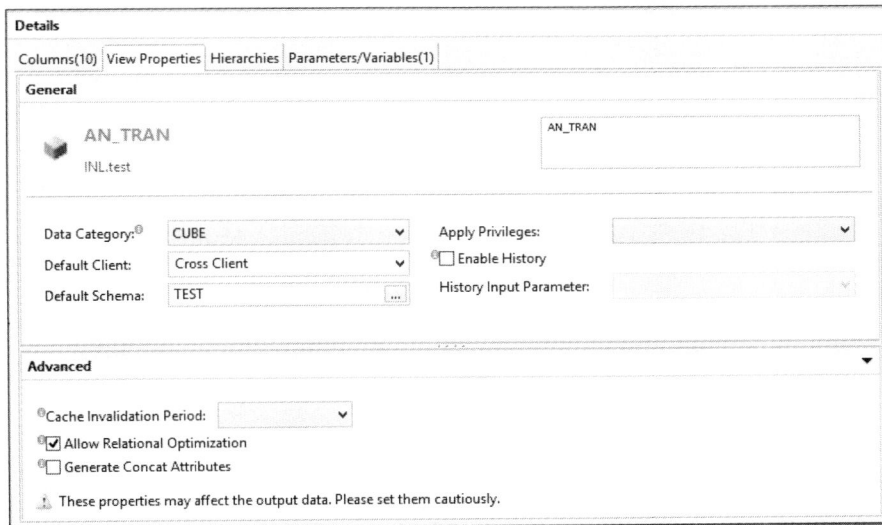

Figure 1.19 Semantics Node Definition Window in SAP HANA Studio Version 2.0.15

In Figure 1.19, note the following elements:

▶ DATA CATEGORY
This field has two dropdown options: CUBE and EMPTY. When you choose CUBE, the analytic view is multidimensional and can be used in an MDX query.

▶ DEFAULT CLIENT
This setting has three options:

▹ SESSION CLIENT
Controls the behavior of the restriction based on the user's session client number. When you create a user, you can specify the user's SESSION CLIENT number (see Figure 1.20).

49

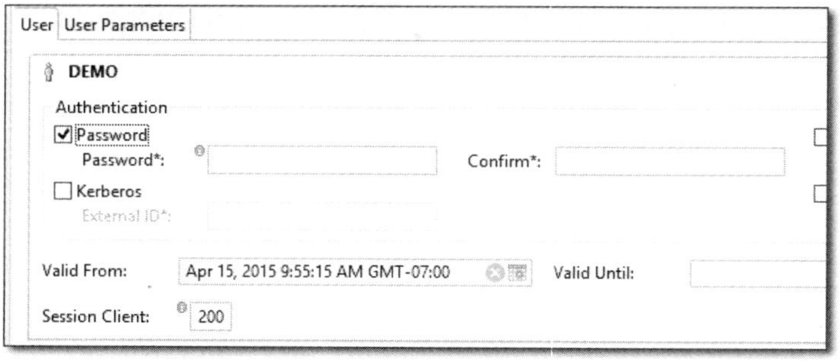

Figure 1.20 User's Session Client Setting

In the table, you can define a column with the name MANDT or CLIENT and use it to separate the records of datasets from different clients. The client number can be used to share the same database resource with multiple groups, while letting each group has a dedicated dataset. For example, you can set a value of 200 for MANDT for company A, and 300 for company B.

If you set DEFAULT CLIENT to SESSION CLIENT, when you run a query against the analytic view, it applies a filer on the column MANDT or CLIENT according to the user's client number. For example, when the user's client is 200, it applies the filter as WHERE MANDT='300'. As a result, users with different client numbers will consume different datasets even with the same query against the same analytic view. If the client number is not defined on the user, the filter will not be applied.

The client number of the user will be overridden if you explicitly assign a value to the internal input parameter $$client$$. For example:

```
SELECT SUM(SALES) FROM _SYS_BIC."test/AN_VIEW1"
(PLACEHOLDER."$$client$$"=>'300');
```

The filter will be created with the explicitly assigned value of the parameter, regardless the actual client number of the user. The client setting doesn't guarantee implementation of authorization; a user with one client value can access a dataset belonging to a different client value by explicitly assigning a value to the internal parameter.

▶ CROSS CLIENT
If this is selected, no filter based on a user's client number will be applied.

▶ FIXED VALUE
Another option is to set a fixed value, such as 300, on the field. As a result,

any query against the analytic view will internally combine a filter such as `MANDT='300'` or `CLIENT='300'`, and the internal parameter `$$client$$` will no longer exist.

▶ DEFAULT SCHEMA
This setting is for scripted calculation views and has no effect on the analytic view.

▶ ENABLE HISTORY
This checkbox is used to achieve time travel within a history table. When it is selected, you need to specify an input parameter to retrieve the data version at a history point.

▶ CACHE INVALIDATION PERIOD
You can enable or disable the cache feature with this checkbox. If it is not selected and the cache feature is disabled, every time you run a query against the analytic view, the SAP HANA engine will access the underlying tables, retrieve the data, and execute the joins. This process can be time-consuming when tables are large.

As shown in Figure 1.19, you can set the CACHE INVALIDATION PERIOD field to DAILY or HOURLY. Then, the query result is cached in-memory for the specified period of time, and other queries will get results from the cache directly instead of accessing the underlying tables. This will enable better performance. However, the downside is that the result is not quite up-to-date. The life of the cache is one day or one hour, according to the field setting. When the cache expires, the cached result is removed; a query fired after that point will reaccess the underlying tables, and the new result will be cached.

▶ GENERATE CONCAT ATTRIBUTES
This checkbox can be used to improve join performance. When it is selected, it creates additional calculated columns for the joins based on multiple columns. For example, when two tables are joined on `T1.A=T2.A` and `T1.B=T2.B`, the column `$A$B$` will be created on two tables, and the join will be changed to `T1.$A$B$=T2.$A$B$`. Apply this feature with caution, because it may lead to incorrect results in some cases. Assuming the values of the columns on T1 are 12 and 3 and on T2 are 1 and 23, when they are concatenated, they both become 123 and the join condition based on the concatenated column is satisfied; but this is not the desired behavior.

Analytic views are executed in the OLAP engine and perform well, especially with larger tables. When you have to address various reporting requirements, an analytic view should be the first option to come to mind. Only when there is logic that cannot be achieved with an analytic view should you use calculation views or stored procedures.

1.3.3 Calculation Views

Calculation views are used to provide composites of other views, including attribute views, analytic views, or other calculation views. With calculation views, you can perform more complex data manipulations, such as making joins or unions of two data flows or adding filters on top of aggregation results.

You can create two types of calculation views: *graphical calculation views* and *scripted calculation views*. In this section, we will look at how to create each type in turn.

Graphical Calculation View

Graphical calculation views are modeled using the graphical modeling features of the SAP HANA Modeler. To walk through how to create a graphical calculation view, suppose you have two fact tables; one is TRANS (mentioned in the previous section and contains sales records), and the other is PURCHASE, which contains the purchase records (see Listing 1.10).

```
CREATE COLUMN TABLE "PURCHASE" (
"PURCHASE_DATE" DATE,
"PURCHASE_NO" BIGINT ,
"STORE_ID" INT,
"PROD_ID" INTEGER ,
"PURCHASE_QTY" BIGINT ,
"PRICE" DECIMAL(18,2));
```
Listing 1.10 DDL of the PURCHASE Table

Also create the analytic view AN_PURCHASE in the same way as AN_TRAN. When you want to make a report to show the sales and purchases data side by side, you need to union the outputs of the two analytic views AN_TRAN and AN_PURCHASE. You can use a calculation view to achieve this (see Figure 1.21).

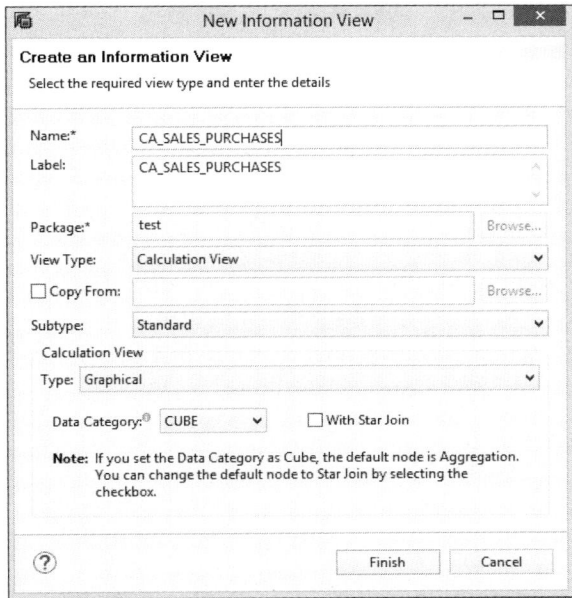

Figure 1.21 Calculation View of CA_SALES_PURCHASE

When you create a calculation view, you can choose what to enter for the Calcu-lation View Type. There are two option: Graphical and SQL Script. As shown in Figure 1.21, choose Graphical.

The Subtype field has two options: Standard and Time. Time means that the view is based on the system calendar table. For all other views, choose Standard. The Data Category field defines the last node of the view. When set to Dimension or blank, the last node is a projection; when set to CUBE, the last node is an aggregation, and the view can be consumed with MDX on multidimensional reporting tools. When you choose CUBE, you can also select the With Star Join checkbox. This feature is used to simulate an analytic view in a calculation view.

In the calculation view, create a union node and drag the two analytic views AN_TRAN and AN_PURCHASE to the node (see Figure 1.22). When managing the mapping columns between the tables, map the attributes of the same dimension of the two tables. For example, map the STORE_ID column between the two tables, and then map the CITY column between the two tables. For measures, create separate target columns. You will have separate target columns for SALES_QTY and PURCHASE_QTY and separate target columns for SALES_NET and PURCHASE_NET.

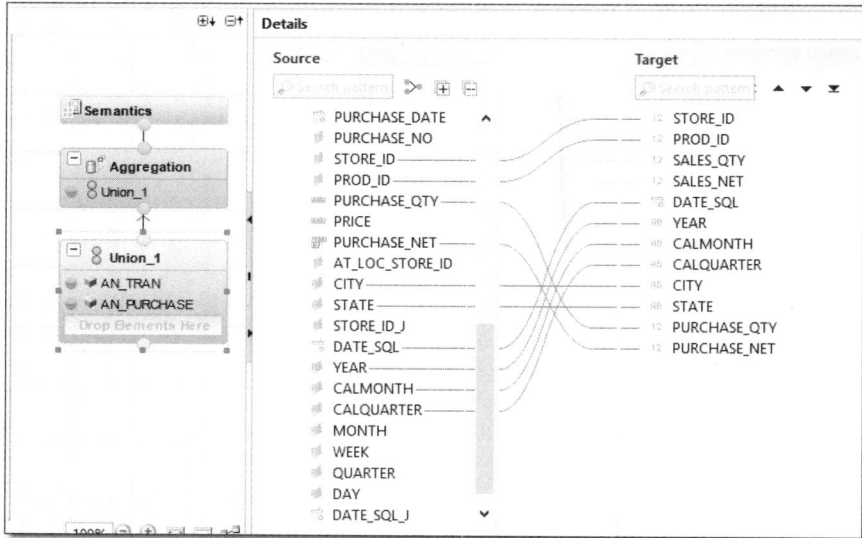

Figure 1.22 Union Node Definition in a Calculation View

After defining the union node, enter the aggregation node (see Figure 1.23). For each column that has an attribute, you can click the column or choose ADD TO OUTPUT from the context menu to add it as an attribute column. For each column that is a measure, you can choose ADD AS AGGREGATED COLUMN from the context menu to add it as a measure column.

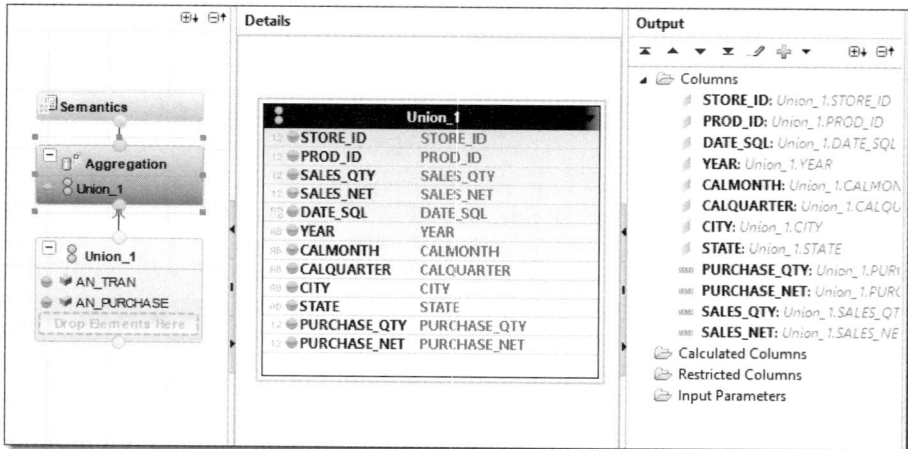

Figure 1.23 Aggregation Node Definition in a Calculation View

The semantics node window of a calculation view is similar to that of an analytic view (see Figure 1.24). You can select the DATA CATEGORY and DEFAULT CLIENT just as you did for the analytic view.

The EXECUTE IN field is specifically for calculation views. When it is blank, the view is executed in the calculation engine. When it is set to SQL ENGINE, the view is executed in the SQL engine. Each engine has its own strength. For example, the calculation engine is good at calculating currency conversion, whereas the SQL engine is good at optimizing join order. The EXECUTE IN field should be customized on a case-by-case basis to determine which engine should be chosen. Some native functions are supported only with the column engine and not convertible such as with date(). When the view contains such functions, you cannot set it to be executed in the SQL engine.

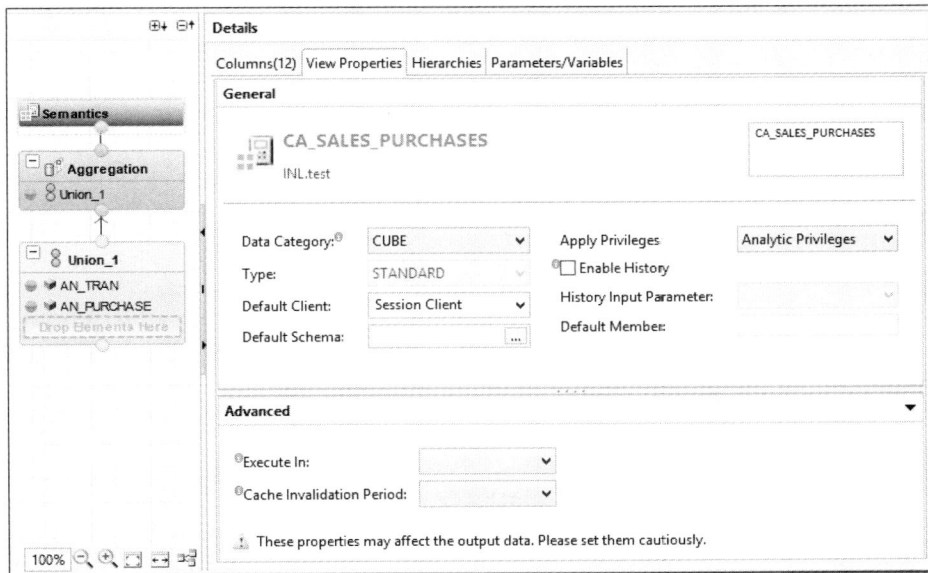

Figure 1.24 Semantics Node Definition of a Calculation View

Some expressions are handled in different ways. In a calculation engine, the expression 1+null returns 1, but it returns null in the SQL engine. Therefore, you can expect to see different results when you switch engines. When the view contains other graphical views that can be executed in different engines or contains scripted calculation views, different types of views will be optimized separately.

After the calculation view is activated, you will see the column view CA_SALES_PURCHASES created in the _SYS_BIC schema. The view is based on a calculation scenario (see Listing 1.11).

```
CREATE CALCULATION SCENARIO "_SYS_BIC"."test/CA_SALES_PURCHASES"
  USING '[{"__CalculationNode__": true,"name": "AN_TRAN","operation":
  {"__OlapDSNodeData__": true,"source": "_SYS_BIC:test/AN_TRAN",
  "dataSourceFlags": 0},"attributeVec": [{"__Attribute__":
  true,"name":
...
...
"Aggregation"}},{"__Variable__": true,"name": "$$language$$",
  "typeMask": 512,"usage": 0,"isGlobal": true},{"__Variable__": true,
  "name": "$$client$$","typeMask": 512,"usage": 0,"isGlobal": true},
  {"__CalcScenarioMetaData__": true,"externalScenarioName":
  "test::CA_SALES_PURCHASES"}]'
;
CREATE COLUMN VIEW "_SYS_BIC"."test/CA_SALES_PURCHASES" WITH
  PARAMETERS (indexType=11,
  'PARENTCALCINDEXSCHEMA'='_SYS_BIC',
  'PARENTCALCINDEX'='test/CA_SALES_PURCHASES',
  'PARENTCALCNODE'='finalAggregation')
```
Listing 1.11 DDL of a Column View Based on the Calculation View Definition

Graphical calculation views support the following types of calculation nodes:

▶ **Projection node**
This node is used to define filters and select columns. Usually, you put each data source, such as an embedded table or view, into a projection node and apply a filter to cut down data size as early as possible.

▶ **Join node**
This node is to define joins. If one table needs to join multiple tables, you need to join them one by one in separate nodes. Alternatively, you can create a star join node and then join from one table to multiple tables at one node. With a star join, all the tables need to be wrapped into calculation views. Star joins are like analytic views except they allow you to create measures from different tables.

You can make inner joins, outer joins, referential joins, and text joins on a calculation view as well, but there is a limitation on text joins. The filter on the WHERE clause of a query will not be pushed down to the table level when there is a text join in the calculation view. If this causes performance issues, then you need to consider a different approach than using a text join.

On the join node, SAP HANA also supports the spatial join, which enables you to handle calculations between 2-D geometries performed using predicates, such as intersects, contains, and more.

▸ **Aggregation node**
This node is used to define aggregation. You can define the aggregation type as SUM, MIN, MAX, or COUNT. You also can create a counter, which is used to calculate COUNT DISTINCT.

▸ **Rank node**
With a rank node, you can filter data based on rank. As shown in Figure 1.25, you can set the SORT DIRECTION as DESCENDING (TOP N) or ASCENDING (BOTTOM N). The THRESHOLD field is to set the value of N. PARTITION BY COLUMN sets the columns to partition the records into multiple windows. In each window, it returns the top N or bottom N records. The DYNAMIC PARTITION ELEMENTS checkbox allows you to choose the columns dynamically from the list under PARTITION BY COLUMN in case some of these columns do not exist in the query.

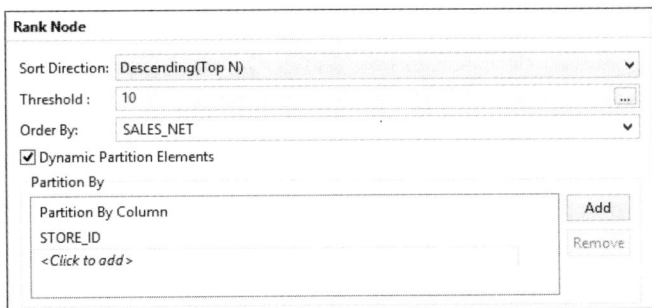

Figure 1.25 Rank Node Definition in a Calculation View

Among these nodes, the counter measure in the aggregation node is the most troublesome. Therefore, you need to use it with caution. Because the calculation of a counter is impacted by the GROUP BY column, when the workflow is complex, a query may return different results with different execution paths. For example, when a view contains a stacked view, if a query has a filter on columns on a stacked view, then there are different options to calculate the counter. One option is to push down the filter to a stacked view; another is to apply the filter to the output of the stacked view. The TRANSPARENT FILTER option controls the behaviors filter in the calculation view (see Figure 1.26).

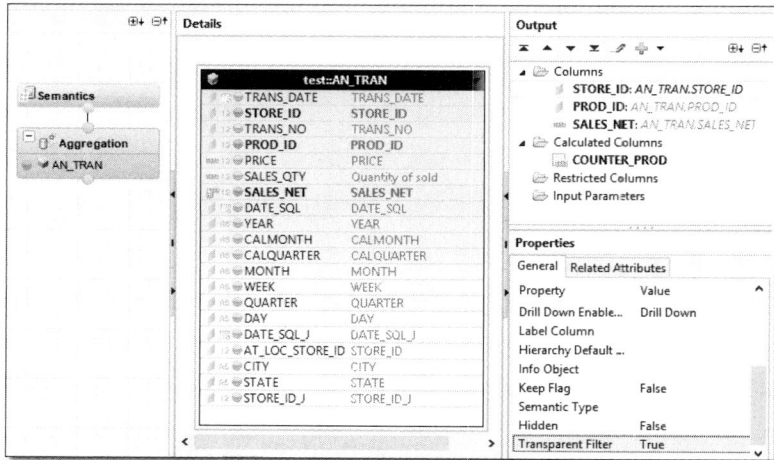

Figure 1.26 Transparent Filter Flag in a Calculation View

Suppose you want to check the count distinct of PROD_ID in two specific stores with a query against CA_TRAN2 in which CA_TRAN2 embeds another calculation view called CA_TRAN. In the CA_TRAN calculation view, add the COUNTER_PROD counter to calculate the distinct count of PROD_ID. You can set the TRANSPARENT FILTER field on the column STORE_ID to TRUE. Also, in the CA_TRAN2 calculation view, set TRANSPARENT FILTER on the STORE_ID column to TRUE (see Figure 1.27).

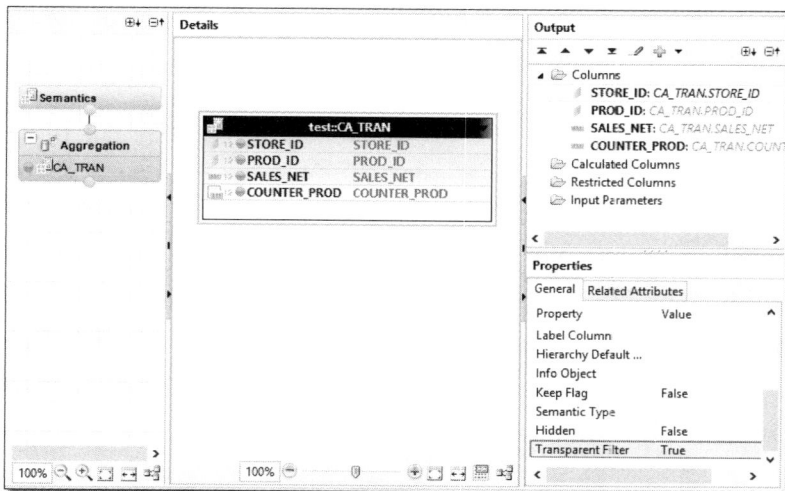

Figure 1.27 Transparent Filter Setting on a Calculation View

When you run the query in Listing 1.12, it will push down the filter of STORE_ID IN (2,3) to the CA_TRAN stacked view.

```
SELECT SUM(COUNTER_PROD)
FROM _SYS_BIC."test/CA_TRAN2"
WHERE STORE_ID IN (2,3);
```
Listing 1.12 Query with a Column Filter on a Stacked View

The query in Listing 1.12 will be executed as shown in Listing 1.13.

```
SELECT SUM(COUNTER_PROD)
FROM
(SELECT SUM(COUNTER_PROD) COUNTER_PROD
FROM _SYS_BIC."test/CA_TRAN"
WHERE STORE_ID IN (2,3));
```
Listing 1.13 Query with the Filter Pushed Down

Otherwise, if you set Transparent Filter to False, the filter will be applied to the output of the stacked view, and the query will be executed, as shown in Listing 1.14.

```
SELECT SUM(COUNTER_PROD)
FROM
(
SELECT STORE_ID,SUM(COUNTER_PROD) COUNTER_PROD
FROM _SYS_BIC."test/CA_TRAN2"
GROUP BY STORE_ID
)
WHERE STORE_ID IN (2,3);
```
Listing 1.14 Query without the Filter Pushed Down

As a result, the common values on the PROD_D column in stores 2 and 3 will both add up to the measure COUNTER_PROD, returning the wrong count distinct. Based on your business requirements, you should make the appropriate setting on the flag.

In addition, you can also enforce a column existing in the execution plan with the Keep option (see Figure 1.28). The CA_TRAN3 calculation view has a stacked analytic view called AN_TRAN, which contains a referential join between the data foundation and AT_LOC. When you set the Keep flag of the CITY column as True, the CITY column will exist in the execution plan regardless of whether it exists in the query, and when the CITY column exists, the referential join will be executed.

Run the following query against the view that has the column with the Keep option set to True:

```
SELECT SUM(SALES_NET),COUNT(PROD_ID)
FROM _sys_bic."test/CA_TRAN3";
```

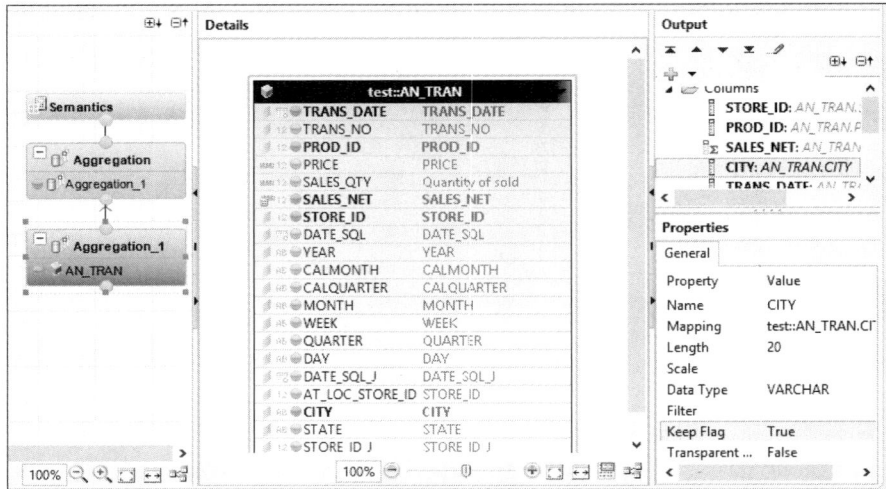

Figure 1.28 Keep Flag in a Calculation View

It is parsed as the query shown in Listing 1.15, which has an additional column in the inner query. The inner query will be executed first, and the final aggregation will be applied on top of the output. The results might be different because an underlying referential join is executed.

```
SELECT SUM(S),SUM(C)
FROM
(
SELECT CITY,SUM(SALES_NET) S,COUNT(PROD_ID) C
FROM _sys_bic."test/CA_TRAN3"
GROUP BY CITY
);
```

Listing 1.15 Query with Additional Column with the Keep Flag

The output of one node can be the input of another node. With the node-by-node building approach, you can build complex processing logic. The topology view of the data flow is like a tree. With SAP HANA's multiple core engine, the calculation of data flows can be split into multiple cores and the execution can be in parallel. If you define a node for which the output points to multiple nodes, then the calculation engine fails to separate input data flows between Join_1 and Join_2, causing performance issues (see Figure 1.29).

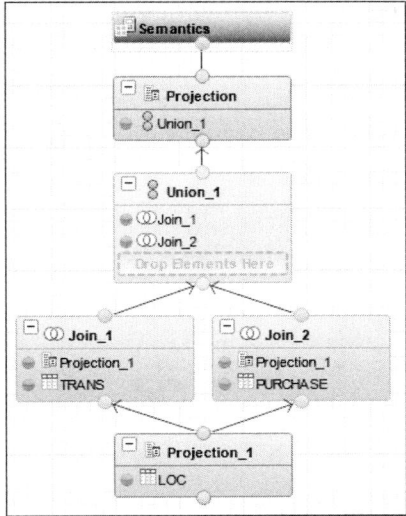

Figure 1.29 Calculation View with an Output of a Node Pointing to Multiple Nodes

To address the issue, create a different projection node so that each node points to a dedicated join node. When the topology view data flow is like a tree, the execution can be well optimized in the calculation engine (see Figure 1.30). If there is a filter in the query, the filter can be pushed down to the table level.

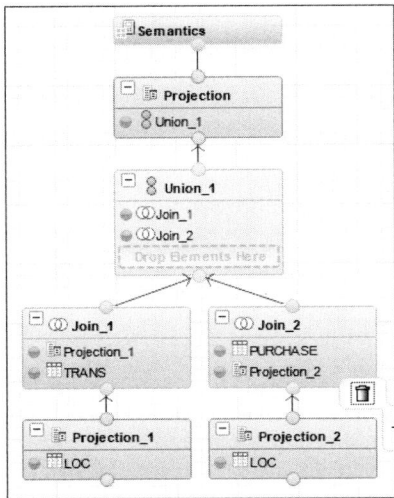

Figure 1.30 Calculation View with an Output of Every Node Pointing to a Single Node

Scripted Calculation View

Another type of calculation view is a scripted calculation view. Such a view is written using SQLScript. To create this type of calculation view, choose SQL SCRIPT in the TYPE field in the CREATE AN INFORMATION VIEW window (see Figure 1.31).

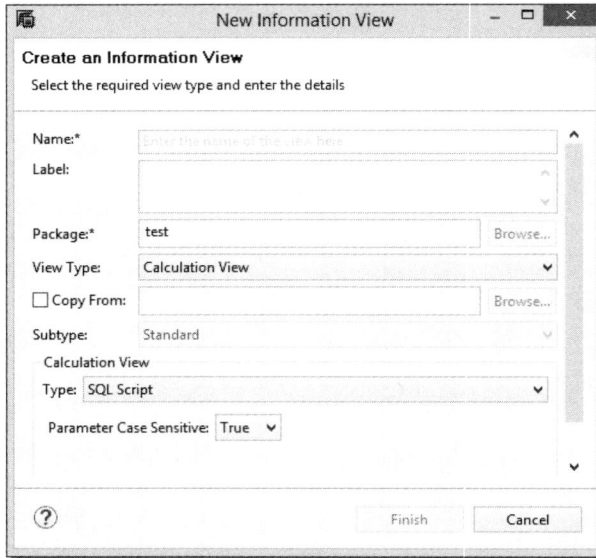

Figure 1.31 Scripted Calculation View

For example, if you create a view called CA_TRAN4 to union the output of AN_TRAN and AN_PURCHASE, you can edit the script as shown in Figure 1.32. var_out is the table variable used to define the output of the view. You need to define the columns at the output panel. The name, sequence, and data type should be exactly the same as the columns in the SELECT clause of the var_out variable.

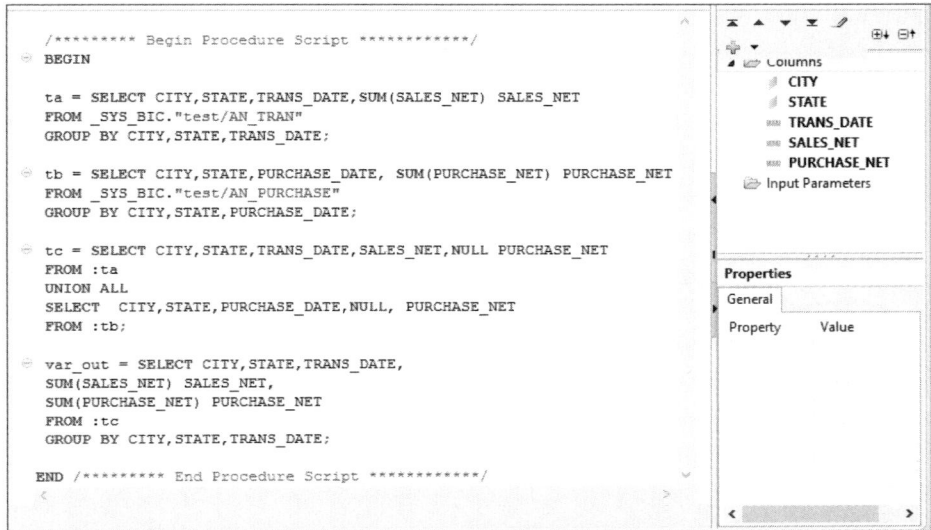

```
/********* Begin Procedure Script ************/
BEGIN

  ta = SELECT CITY,STATE,TRANS_DATE,SUM(SALES_NET) SALES_NET
FROM _SYS_BIC."test/AN_TRAN"
GROUP BY CITY,STATE,TRANS_DATE;

  tb = SELECT CITY,STATE,PURCHASE_DATE, SUM(PURCHASE_NET) PURCHASE_NET
FROM _SYS_BIC."test/AN_PURCHASE"
GROUP BY CITY,STATE,PURCHASE_DATE;

  tc = SELECT CITY,STATE,TRANS_DATE,SALES_NET,NULL PURCHASE_NET
  FROM :ta
  UNION ALL
  SELECT  CITY,STATE,PURCHASE_DATE,NULL, PURCHASE_NET
  FROM :tb;

  var_out = SELECT CITY,STATE,TRANS_DATE,
  SUM(SALES_NET) SALES_NET,
  SUM(PURCHASE_NET) PURCHASE_NET
  FROM :tc
  GROUP BY CITY,STATE,TRANS_DATE;

END /********* End Procedure Script ************/
```

Columns
- CITY
- STATE
- TRANS_DATE
- SALES_NET
- PURCHASE_NET

Input Parameters

Properties

General

Property	Value

Figure 1.32 SQLScript Statements in a Scripted Calculation View

After editing the scripts of the view, you can define the VIEW PROPERTIES at the semantics node (see Figure 1.33). There are two fields specific to scripted calculation views:

▶ RUN WITH
This defines the user's authorization behavior. When it is set to DEFINER'S RIGHTS, users who run the view will be applied as the definer of the view. For example, user A creates the view and has select rights on the underlying table. If user B has the rights on the view, then user B can run the view even though user B doesn't have select rights on the underlying tables. When RUN WITH is set to INVOKER'S RIGHTS, user B should have rights on both the view and underlying tables before running the view.

▶ DEFAULT SCHEMA
You can specify a schema name in the DEFAULT SCHEMA field when there is an unqualified table name in the script. SAP HANA will search the table in the specified schema.

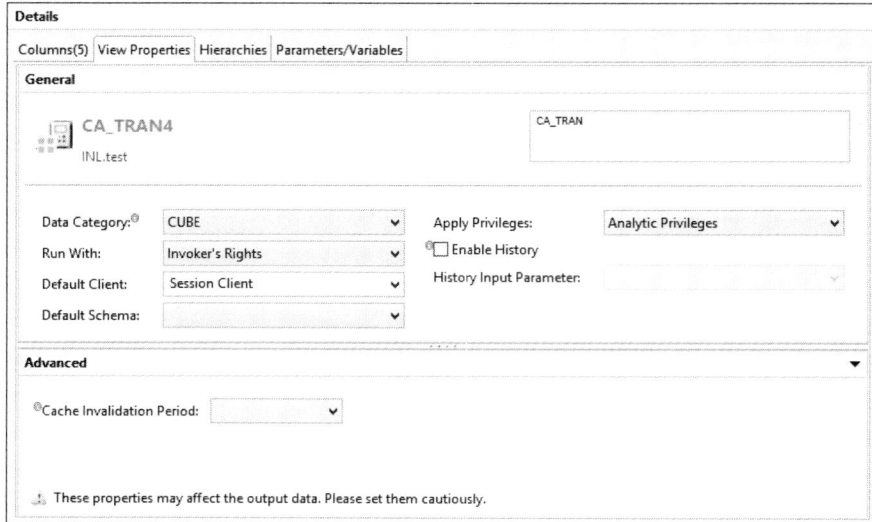

Figure 1.33 View Properties of the Scripted Calculation View

When the scripted calculation view is activated, you will see the `"_SYS_BIC"`. `"test/CA_TRAN4/proc"` procedure generated (see Listing 1.16).

```
create procedure "_SYS_BIC"."test/CA_TRAN4/proc" ( OUT var_out "_SYS_
BIC"."test/CA_TRAN4/proc/tabletype/VAR_
OUT" ) language sqlscript sql security invoker reads sql data as
/********* Begin Procedure Script ************/
BEGIN
ta = SELECT CITY,STATE,TRANS_DATE,SUM(SALES_NET) SALES_NET
FROM _SYS_BIC."test/AN_TRAN"
GROUP BY CITY,STATE,TRANS_DATE;
tb = SELECT CITY,STATE,PURCHASE_DATE,SUM(PURCHASE_NET) PURCHASE_NET
FROM _SYS_BIC."test/AN_PURCHASE"
GROUP BY CITY,STATE,PURCHASE_DATE;
tc = SELECT CITY,STATE,TRANS_DATE,SALES_NET,NULL PURCHASE_NET
FROM :ta
UNION ALL
SELECT  CITY,STATE,PURCHASE_DATE,NULL, PURCHASE_NET
FROM :tb;
var_out = SELECT CITY,STATE,TRANS_DATE,
SUM(SALES_NET) SALES_NET,
SUM(PURCHASE_NET) PURCHASE_NET
FROM :tc
GROUP BY CITY,STATE,TRANS_DATE;
END /********* End Procedure Script ************/
```

Listing 1.16 DDL of Procedure Generated with the Calculation View Design Tool

Based on the procedure, the "_SYS_BIC"."test/CA_TRAN4" view is generated as shown in Listing 1.17.

```
CREATE COLUMN VIEW "_SYS_BIC"."test/CA_
TRAN4" WITH PARAMETERS (indexType=11,
'PROCEDURE_SCHEMA'='_SYS_BIC',
'PROCEDURE_NAME'='test/CA_TRAN4/proc');
```

Listing 1.17 DDL of the Column View Based on the Procedure

Behind the scenes, the scripted calculation view is a read-only procedure. Therefore, you should not have DDL and data manipulation language (DML) statements in the script except SELECT.

In this example, each statement is a declaration of a table variable, which we refer to as *declarative logic*. When all the statements in the scripted view are declarative logic, it gives SAP HANA the freedom to optimize the data flow thoroughly, resulting in better performance. When this kind of scripted view is used in other graphical views or scripted views, optimization can go into the view, filters are pushed down to table level, and columns which do not contribute to the final results are pruned.

For example, suppose you have the view embedded in another graphical view, CA_TRAN5. If the query is as follows,

```
SELECT CITY,SUM(SALES_NET) FROM "_SYS_BIC"."test/CA_TRAN5"
WHERE TRANS_DATE='2015-01-01' GROUP BY CITY;
```

then the filter is pushed down into CA_TRAN4, and the columns STATE and PURCHASE_NET are removed from the execution plan.

If a scripted view contains statements such as IF/THEN, WHILE/DO, CURSOR, or so on, we call that *imperative logic*, and the result set will be materialized before it is optimized. For example, suppose we have a CA_TRAN4 view with imperative logic embedded in another graphical view, CA_TRAN5. We then run the following query:

```
SELECT CITY,SUM(SALES_NET) FROM "_SYS_BIC"."test/CA_TRAN5"
WHERE TRANS_DATE='2015-01-01' GROUP BY CITY;
```

The filter will not be pushed down into CA_TRAN4, but will apply to the result set of the embedded view. The columns STATE and PURCHASE_NET are also materialized in the result set.

In a scripted calculation view, you can use the calculation engine plan operators, which allow you to bypass the SQL processor during evaluation to directly inter- act with the calculation engine. To use the calculation engine plan operators, revise the scripted view as shown in Listing 1.18.

```
/********* Begin Procedure Script ************/
 BEGIN
 ta = CE_OLAP_VIEW("_SYS_BIC"."test/AN_TRAN",["CITY","STATE","TRANS_
DATE",SUM("SALES_NET")]);
 tb = CE_OLAP_VIEW("_SYS_BIC"."test/AN_PURCHASE",[
"CITY","STATE","PURCHASE_DATE",SUM("PURCHASE_NET")]);
 ta1= CE_PROJECTION(:ta,["CITY","STATE","TRANS_DATE","SALES_NET",CE_
CALC('NULL', decimal(18,2)) AS "PURCHASE_NET"]);
 tb1= CE_PROJECTION(:tb,["CITY","STATE","PURCHASE_DATE" AS "TRANS_
DATE",CE_CALC('NULL', decimal(18,2)) AS "SALES_NET","PURCHASE_NET"]);
 tc = CE_UNION_ALL (:ta1, :tb1);
 var_out = CE_AGGREGATION(:tc,[SUM(SALES_NET) AS SALES_
NET,SUM(PURCHASE_NET) AS PURCHASE_NET],["CITY","STATE","TRANS_DATE"]);
END /********* End Procedure Script ************/
```

Listing 1.18 Scripted Calculation View Using the Calculation Engine Plan Operators

In the script, the CE_OLAP_VIEW() operator selects the columns from a cube. Examine the following statement:

```
ta = CE_OLAP_VIEW("_SYS_BIC"."test/AN_TRAN",["CITY","STATE","TRANS_
DATE",SUM("SALES_NET")]);
```

This returns the same result as the SQL query:

```
ta = SELECT CITY,STATE,TRANS_DATE,SUM(SALES_NET) SALES_NET
 FROM _SYS_BIC."test/AN_TRAN"
 GROUP BY CITY,STATE,TRANS_DATE;
```

It is not recommended to mix SQL queries and calculation engine plan operators, because different types of statements will be optimized separately.

So far, we have explained the three information views. To build models based on simple joins to represent dimensions, you created attribute views. To build mod- els to represent star schema and calculated measures, you created analytic views. For more complex models, you used calculation views, which includes aggrega- tion on multiple data flows, SQLScript, or other information views.

Now that you are familiar with the three information views, let's look at how we can assign analytic privileges to them for users.

1.4 Analytic Privileges

Analytic privileges control access to SAP HANA data models. Analytic privileges help you to achieve row-level security on information views. To define analytic privileges, specify the range of values that a user is permitted to access. When the user uses the view, a filter based on the analytic privilege will be applied on the view to retrieve the records that the user is permitted to access. You can define two types of analytic privileges: *classical XML-based analytic privilege* and *SQL-based analytic privilege*. In this section, we will look at examples of how to use analytic privileges to control access to SAP HANA models.

1.4.1 Classical XML-Based Analytic Privilege

An XML-based, or classic, analytic privilege allows you to assign selective access to information views to users based on data combinations.

In this section, we will look at how to create this analytic privilege with an example: Suppose a user of a store is permitted to access records of his or her own store in the analytic view AN_TRAN. In this situation, you can create the analytic privilege AP_STORE and apply it to the user. In this case, choose the underlying attribute view AT_LOC on the SELECT INFORMATION MODELS window when you create the privilege (see Figure 1.34).

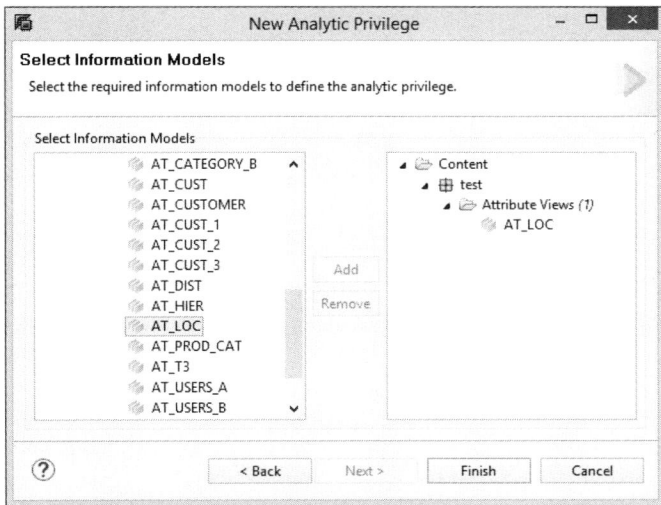

Figure 1.34 Create Analytic Privilege

In the analytic privilege definition window, you can define a date range in the PRIVILEGE VALIDITY pane (see Figure 1.35). Within that range, those users with the privilege are authorized to access the views. Otherwise, they are not authorized. This defines the privilege from a time perspective.

To define row-level security, first choose the attribute you want to add the restriction to. In this case, choose the STORE_ID column for the AT_LOC attribute view under the ASSOCIATED ATTRIBUTES RESTRICTIONS pane. Then, set a filter on the column under the ASSIGN RESTRICTIONS pane.

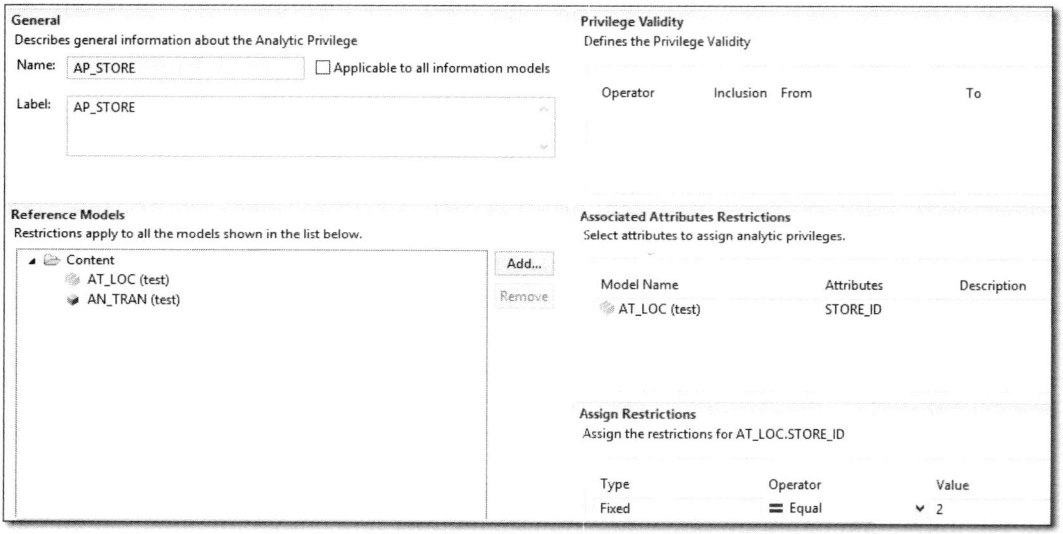

Figure 1.35 Analytic Privilege Definition Window

There is also an APPLICABLE TO ALL INFORMATION MODELS checkbox in the GENERAL pane. When this checkbox is selected, the privilege is applicable to all models. If it is not selected, then you can edit the content under the REFERENCE MODELS pane and add the models that you want to apply the privilege to. In this case, choose AT_LOC and AN_TRAN. On the view's definition, to apply the privilege, you need to set the APPLY PRIVILEGES field to ANALYTIC PRIVILEGES (see Figure 1.36).

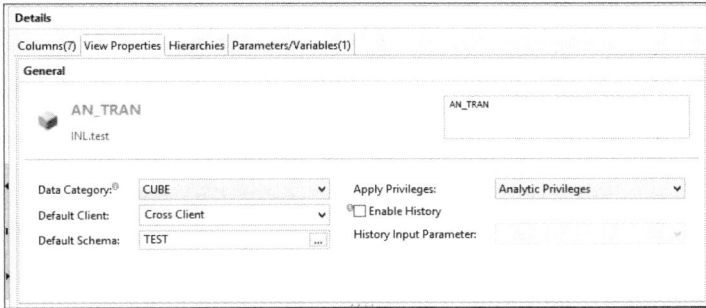

Figure 1.36 Enable Analytic Privileges in an Information View

After the analytic privilege is activated, you need to grant the privilege to users. To avoid having to grant the privilege to users one by one, you can create a role, grant the privilege to the role, then grant the role to users. First, define the role R_DEMO (see Figure 1.37). On the PACKAGE PRIVILEGE tab, add the package that you are using, and then select the REPO.READ checkbox to grant the privilege to this package.

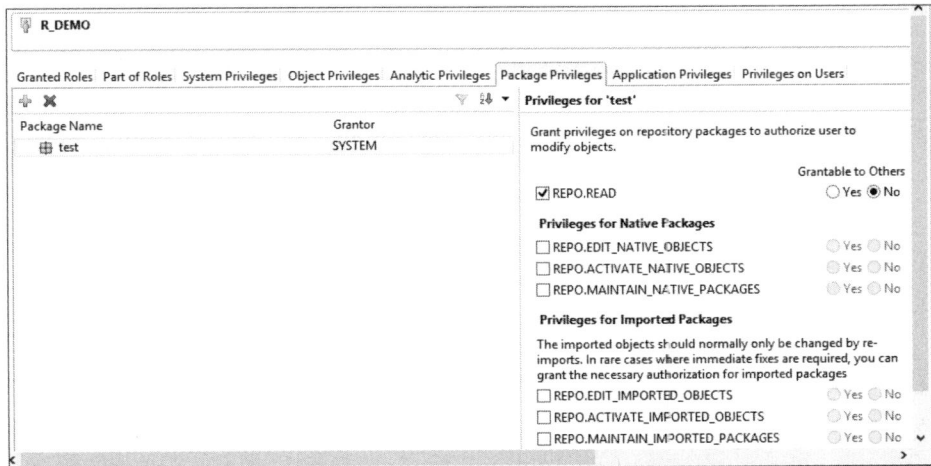

Figure 1.37 Package Privilege Definition of a Role

Next, under the OBJECT PRIVILEGES tab, add the _SYS_BI and _SYS_BIC schemas to the SELECT and EXECUTE privileges in order to access objects generated with the modeler. Then, add the REPOSITORY_REST procedure with the EXECUTE privilege in order to browse the objects of the repository (see Figure 1.38).

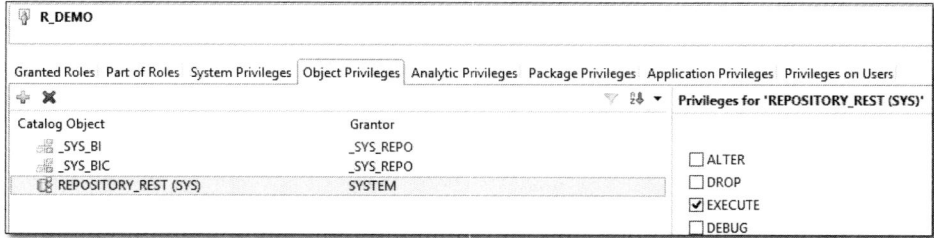

Figure 1.38 Object Privileges Definition of a Role

Next, grant the analytic privilege AP_STORE to the role under the Analytic Privileges tab (see Figure 1.39).

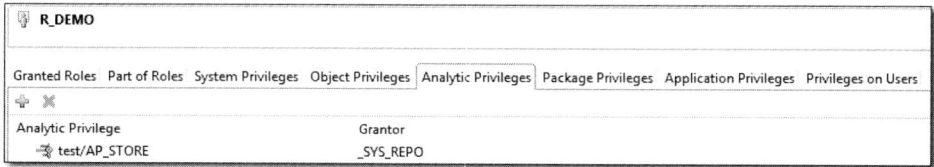

Figure 1.39 Analytic Privileges Definiton of a Role

After the R_DEMO role is created, you can grant it to a user. As shown in Figure 1.40, under the Granted Roles tab in the user's definition window, add the R_DEMO role, then activate the user U1.

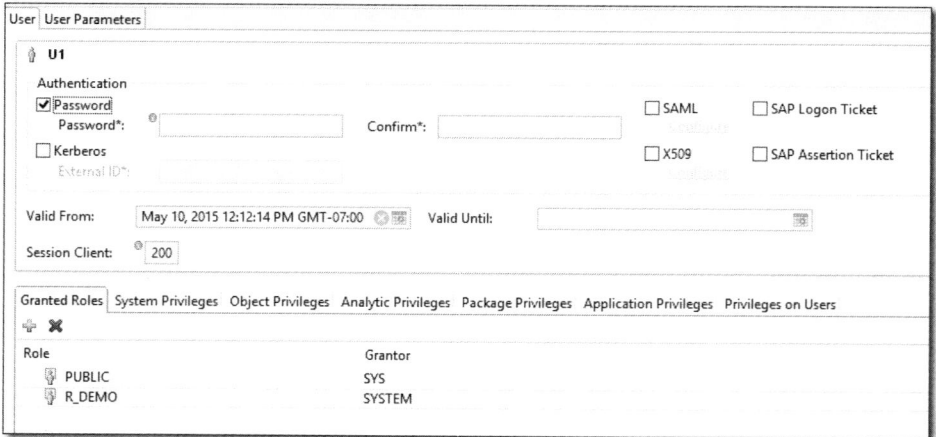

Figure 1.40 Granted Roles Definition of a User

When you log on to SAP HANA with the user U1 and run a query against AN_TRAN, it returns the results with restriction STORE_ID=2.

In addition to defining row-level security, you can leverage the analytic privilege feature for other purposes—for example, to define the preferred value of an attribute for a user. Suppose for the user U1 you want to set the preference as STORE_ID=2, and you also want the user to have access to other stores. You can define the analytic view AN_TRAN with the privilege, and another view, AN_TRAN2, without the privilege. Create a calculation view CA_TRAN_PRIVI to union the two views (see Figure 1.41).

Create an input parameter $$RANGE$$. On the node Projection_1, add a $$RANGE$$!='All' filter. On the node Projection_2, add a $$RANGE$$='All' filter. Then, run the following query:

```
SELECT SUM(SALES_NET) FROM _SYS_BIC."test/CA_TRAN_
PRIVI" (PLACEHOLDER."$$RANGE$$"=>'All');
```

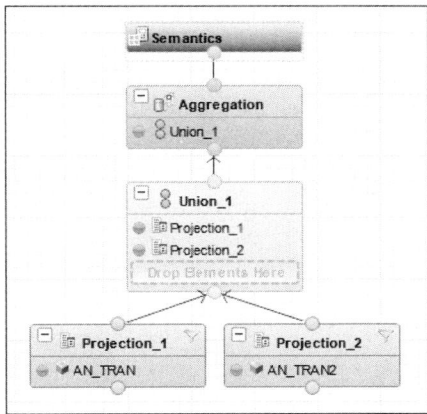

Figure 1.41 Calculation View to Switch Views

This retrieves records from the analytic view without privileges and returns the SALES_NET value for all stores. Next, run the following query:

```
SELECT SUM(SALES_NET) FROM _SYS_BIC."test/CA_TRAN_PRIVI";
```

This retrieves records from the analytic view with privileges, and returns the SALES_NET value of one store. In this view, you use the privilege to set the preferred value.

When you define restrictions in the analytic privilege window, in addition to a fixed value, you can also choose a catalog procedure or repository procedure if you want to define more complex logic for the restriction. For example, to define the repository procedure test::P_PRIVI, make it in the package of a repository with the SAP HANA Modeler tool (see Figure 1.42). According to the operator of the restriction, when the operator is "in," the output of the procedure is a single-column table.

Figure 1.42 Repository Procedure for Analytic Privileges

You can add objects for which the user has access rights to the procedure and make complex logic. Because the privilege will be set on the AT_LOC view, you should not use AT_LOC in the procedure; otherwise, it leads to recursive authorization checking and returns an error. If you need refer to the ID of the user executing the procedure, you can use the internal column SESSION_USER.

After activating the procedure, configure the ASSIGN RESTRICTIONS field of the analytic privilege and add the procedure name in the VALUE field (see Figure 1.43).

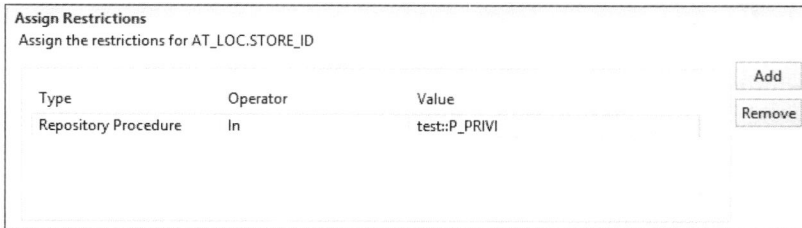

Figure 1.43 Restriction Based on the Repository Procedure

Catalog procedures are made with SQL statements directly, without the SAP HANA Modeler tool. For example, you can run the statement in Listing 1.19 to make procedure P_PRIVI2 with the same logic as test::P_PRIVI.

```
CREATE PROCEDURE TEST.P_PRIVI2 (
OUT VAL_TAB TABLE(STORE_ID INT))
LANGUAGE SQLSCRIPT
SQL SECURITY DEFINER
READS SQL DATA AS
BEGIN
 VAL_TAB = SELECT TOP 2 STORE_ID
            FROM TEST.LOC
            ORDER BY STORE_ID;
END;
```
Listing 1.19 Catalog Procedure for Analytic Privileges

Then, configure the ASSIGN RESTRICTIONS field of the analytic privileges, and add the catalog procedure name in the VALUE field (see Figure 1.44).

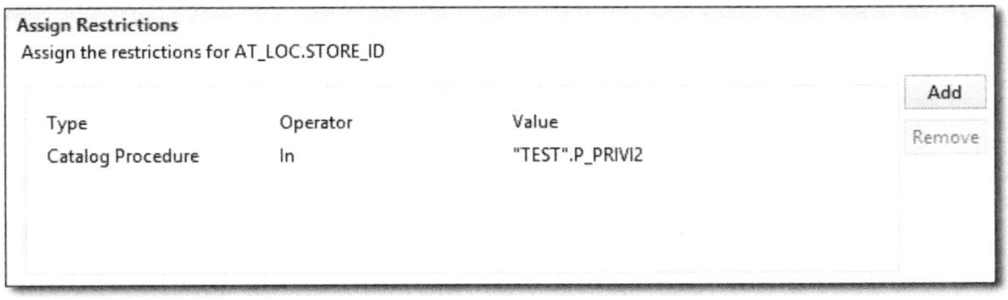

Figure 1.44 Restriction Based on Catalog Procedure

Before running a query against the view with the privileges, you need to grant the internal user _SYS_REPO with EXECUTE:

```
GRANT EXECUTE ON TEST.P_PRIVI2 to "_SYS_REPO" WITH GRANT OPTION;
```

1.4.2 SQL-Based Analytic Privilege

You can also create a SQL-based analytic privilege if the restriction has more complex logic. In an analytic view, first choose SQL ANALYTIC PRIVILEGES for the APPLY PRIVILEGES field (see Figure 1.45).

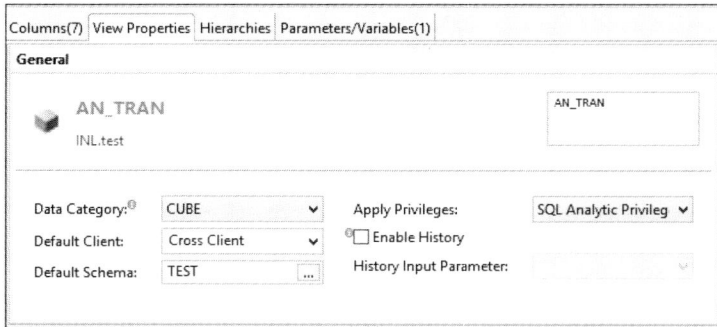

Figure 1.45 Analytic View with SQL Analytic Privileges

Second, create the SQL analytic privileges (see Listing 1.20).

```
CREATE STRUCTURED PRIVILEGE AP_LOC1 FOR SELECT
ON _SYS_BIC."test/AN_TRAN"
WHERE store_id LIKE '%2%' OR PROD_ID<5;
```
Listing 1.20 Statement to Define SQL-Based Analytic Privileges

Third, apply privilege AP_LOC1 to the role (see Figure 1.46).

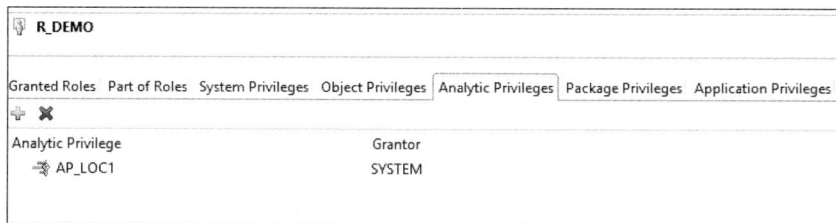

Figure 1.46 Apply the Privilege to the Role

Then, log on as the user with the R_DEMO role, and run the following query:

```
SELECT STORE_ID,PROD_ID,sum(SALES_NET)
FROM _SYS_BIC."test/AN_TRAN" GROUP BY STORE_ID,PROD_ID;
```

The attribute restriction defined in the analytic privileges will be applied on the view, and the actual query executed will be changed into what is shown in Listing 1.21.

```
SELECT STORE_ID,PROD_ID,sum(SALES_NET)
FROM _SYS_BIC."test/AN_TRAN"
```

```
WHERE STORE_ID LIKE '%2%' OR PROD_ID<5
GROUP BY STORE_ID,PROD_ID;
```
Listing 1.21 Query with the Attribute Restriction

SQL-based analytic privileges support not only modeled views, but also SQL views. Just add the key words WITH STRUCTURED PRIVILEGE CHECK when defining the view. For example:

```
CREATE VIEW V1
AS SELECT * FROM TABLE1 WITH STRUCTURED PRIVILEGE CHECK;
```

In this section, we explained how to use analytic privileges to achieve row-level security. Compared to other kinds of privileges, which are defined on a table or schema basis, an analytic privilege can be defined on a row basis. This can help you manage security at a more detailed granularity.

1.5   Stored Procedures

Stored procedures can be defined with several programming languages and executed directly in the database engine. The supported programming languages include SQLScript, L, R, and C++.

In this section, we will look at these three supported languages and how they relate to stored procedures.

1.5.1   SQLScript Procedures

SQLScript is the default programming language for stored procedures. Listing 1.22 provides a simple example of a SQLScript procedure.

```
CREATE PROCEDURE TEST.P_TRAN()
LANGUAGE SQLSCRIPT
AS
BEGIN
SELECT STORE_ID,SUM(SALES_NET) SALES_NET
FROM _SYS_BIC."test/AN_TRAN"
GROUP BY STORE_ID;
END;
```
Listing 1.22 SQLScript Procedure

This procedure uses LANGUAGE SQLSCRIPT to specify the programming language. When you call the procedure in SAP HANA Studio, it returns results to the UI. However, if you need to call the procedure in another procedure or program, then you need to add an output variable to store the result. SAP HANA supports table types in a procedure, as shown in Listing 1.23.

```
CREATE PROCEDURE TEST.P_TRAN
(OUT VAL_OUT TABLE(STORE_ID INT,SALES_NET DECIMAL(18,2)))
LANGUAGE SQLSCRIPT
AS
BEGIN
VAL_OUT = SELECT STORE_ID,SUM(SALES_NET) SALES_NET
FROM _SYS_BIC."test/AN_TRAN"
GROUP BY STORE_ID;
END;
```

Listing 1.23 Procedure with an Output Table Variable

To call the procedure, run the following statement:

```
CALL TEST.P_TRAN(?);
```

You can store the result sets of a procedure in a temporary table so that a user can browse it in a session without re-executing the procedure. To leverage this feature, call the procedure by adding the words WITH OVERVIEW:

```
CALL TEST.P_TRAN(?) WITH OVERVIEW;
```

This returns name of the temporary table, such as "SYSTEM"."VAL_OUT_ 555C799BC2E281A9E10000000A06007C", which you can refer to in the session.

When there are no DDLs or other DML statements, such as INSERT, UPDATE, or DELETE, you can mark the procedure as read-only. SAP HANA's engine can apply better optimization for read-only procedures. The identifier words for a read-only procedure are READS SQL DATA. For read-only procedures, you can generate views to refer to the result sets and access them with SELECT statements instead of using CALL. Use WITH RESULT VIEW to assign the view name. The procedure can be changed as shown in Listing 1.24.

```
CREATE PROCEDURE TEST.P_TRAN(OUT VAL_OUT TABLE(STORE_ID INT,SALES_
NET DECIMAL(18,2)))
LANGUAGE SQLSCRIPT
READS SQL DATA WITH RESULT VIEW TEST.V_TRAN
AS
BEGIN
VAL_OUT = SELECT STORE_ID,SUM(SALES_NET) SALES_NET
```

```
FROM _SYS_BIC."test/AN_TRAN"
GROUP BY STORE_ID;
END;
```

Listing 1.24 Procedure with a Result View

To call the procedure with the SELECT statement, run the following query:

```
SELECT * FROM  TEST.V_TRAN;
```

Make sure there is only one table variable as an output in the procedure. For the input, you can have multiple variables (see Listing 1.25).

```
CREATE PROCEDURE TEST.P_TRAN(
IN DATE_FROM DATE,IN DATE_TO DATE,
OUT VAL_OUT TABLE(STORE_ID INT,SALES_NET DECIMAL(18,2)))
LANGUAGE SQLSCRIPT
READS SQL DATA
WITH RESULT VIEW TEST.V_TRAN
AS
BEGIN
VAL_OUT = SELECT STORE_ID,SUM(SALES_NET) SALES_NET
FROM _SYS_BIC."test/AN_TRAN"
WHERE TRANS_DATE BETWEEN :DATE_FROM AND :DATE_TO
GROUP BY STORE_ID;
END;
```

Listing 1.25 Procedure with Input Variables

To pass values in a query, use placeholders. Make sure to add single quotes around the value, as shown in Listing 1.26.

```
SELECT * FROM  TEST.V_TRAN
('PLACEHOLDER' = ('$$date_from$$', '2011-01-01'),
 'PLACEHOLDER' = ('$$date_to$$','2015-01-01'));
```

Listing 1.26 Pass Values with Placeholders

When an embedded model has input parameters, to use a variable to pass a value to an input parameter, you need to use the => operator (see Listing 1.27).

```
CREATE PROCEDURE TEST.P_TRAN2(
IN "DATE_FROM" DATE,IN "DATE_TO" DATE,
OUT VAL_OUT TABLE(STORE_ID INT,SALES_NET DECIMAL(18,2)))
LANGUAGE SQLSCRIPT
READS SQL DATA
WITH RESULT VIEW TEST.V_TRAN2
AS
BEGIN
VAL_OUT = SELECT STORE_ID,SUM(SALES_NET) SALES_NET
```

```
FROM _SYS_BIC."test/AN_TRAN2"
(PLACEHOLDER."$$DATE_FROM$$"=>:DATE_FROM,
PLACEHOLDER."$$DATE_TO$$"=>:DATE_TO)
GROUP BY STORE_ID;
END;
```
Listing 1.27 Pass Value through an Input Parameter to an Embedded Model

Alternatively, you can create a column view based on a procedure with a separate DDL statement (see Listing 1.28).

```
CREATE COLUMN VIEW V_TRAN2 WITH PARAMETERS (
indexType=11,
'PROCEDURE_SCHEMA'='TEST',
'PROCEDURE_NAME'='P_TRAN2');
```
Listing 1.28 Column View Based on a Procedure

In addition to creating a view based on a procedure, SAP HANA provides another option to enable you to run procedures with SELECT statements: the *table function*. Listing 1.29 shows an example.

```
CREATE FUNCTION F_T1(VAR_IN VARCHAR(20))
RETURNS TABLE (TRANS_DATE DATE, SALES_NET DECIMAL(18,2))
LANGUAGE SQLSCRIPT
READS SQL DATA
AS
BEGIN
 IF :VAR_IN='MAX' THEN
 RETURN SELECT TRANS_DATE,MAX(SALES_NET) SALES_NET
        FROM _SYS_BIC."test/AN_TRAN"
        GROUP BY TRANS_DATE;
 ELSE
 RETURN SELECT TRANS_DATE,SUM(SALES_NET) SALES_NET
        FROM _SYS_BIC."test/AN_TRAN"
        GROUP BY TRANS_DATE;
 END IF;
END;
```
Listing 1.29 Table Function

Table functions are a kind of procedure. The output of a table function is a dataset in the format of a table. You can reference a table function in the FROM clause of a query—for example, see the following SQL query:

```
SELECT * FROM F_T1('SUM');
```

There is not much difference between a table function and a procedure-based column view; you can choose either based on your preference.

Regarding functions, SAP HANA provides a *scalar function* as well, which supports scalar values as an output. A limitation of the scalar function is that it cannot contain SQL statements. Listing 1.30 shows a simple scalar function example.

```
CREATE FUNCTION F_Factorial(I INT)
RETURNS F INT
LANGUAGE SQLSCRIPT
AS
BEGIN
DECLARE  N INT := 2;
F := 1;
WHILE :N <= :I DO
 F := :F * :N;
 N := :N + 1;
END WHILE;
END;
```
Listing 1.30 Scalar Funciton

You can use the scalar function in the same way as you use native functions—for example:

```
SELECT  F_Factorial(5) FROM DUMMY;
```

As previously discussed, in information views, you can define row-level security with analytic privileges. in procedures, because everything is scripted, the security configuration can be more flexible.

First, if the procedure contains information views, the analytic privileges being applied on the views is still valid inside the procedure. Second, for source tables without analytic privileges, you can define row security explicitly for users with the WHERE clause. To implement this, create a table to store the restriction information of row security; for example, see table ROLE_PRIV in Listing 1.31.

```
CREATE COLUMN TABLE ROLE_PRIV(
ROLE VARCHAR(20),
STORE_ID INT);
INSERT INTO ROLE_PRIV VALUES ('R_DEMO',1);
INSERT INTO ROLE_PRIV VALUES ('R_DEMO',2);
```
Listing 1.31 Table to Define Attribute Restriction

Again, you usually set the restriction information on the role level and then grant the role to users. In table ROLE_PRIV, you assign the values of STORE_ID, which the role needs privilege to access. To find the roles of users, use the SYS.GRANTED_ROLES system view shown in Listing 1.32.

```
CREATE PROCEDURE P_TRAN_PRIV()
LANGUAGE SQLSCRIPT SQL SECURITY DEFINER
AS
BEGIN
SELECT STORE_ID,SUM(SALES_NET)
FROM _SYS_BIC."test/AN_TRAN"
WHERE STORE_ID IN (
SELECT STORE_ID FROM ROLE_PRIV
WHERE ROLE IN (
SELECT ROLE_NAME FROM "SYS"."GRANTED_ROLES"
WHERE GRANTEE=SESSION_USER))
GROUP BY STORE_ID;
END;
```

Listing 1.32 Script to Achieve Row-Level Security

You can log on with a different user and run the following query:

```
CALL P_TRAN_PRIV;
```

If the user has a role on R_DEMO, it returns the SALES_NET for STORE_IDs 1 and 2. The security mode of the procedure is SQL SECURITY DEFINER. This means that the user who calls the procedure does not need to have access to the underlying table. When the procedure is called, the user who is the definer accesses the underlying table, and a filter is applied to the table to implement row security.

This procedure consists of several levels of nested queries:

▶ The first level is SELECT ROLE_NAME FROM "SYS"."GRANTED_ROLES" WHERE GRANTEE=SESSION_USER. This level is used to retrieve the role granted to the user. Be sure to use SESSION_USER, not CURRENT_USER. The session user is the actual user calling the procedure, and the current user is the procedure definer, whose privilege is used to access underlying tables.

▶ The second level is SELECT STORE_ID FROM ROLE_PRIV WHERE ROLE IN (). This is used to retrieve the values of STORE_ID that the role needs to access. With the two levels of nested queries, the filter is made to return the rows for which the user has privileges.

Although procedures are very flexible, we often avoid creating them when the same logics can be made with graphical modeled views, because modeled views are built to adapt to SAP HANA engines and can fully exploit the capabilities of the hardware. When the logic cannot be handled by graphical modeled views, it is fine to choose a stored procedure, but inside the stored procedure, you still have a chance to use a graphical modeled view. For example, if a part of the workflow can be performed with the OLAP engine, it is better to create an analytic view for this part and leave the other parts of the workflow as script in the procedure.

1.5.2   L Procedures

The L language is based on concepts from the C/C++ world. You can use L to write procedures for low-level, high-performance programming. When you write L procedures, you use the words LANGUAGE LLANG to specify the language. However, the language is not officially supported yet. Therefore, you need approval from the SAP HANA database development team before using it.

Listing 1.33 is a simple example of a procedure made with L.

```
CREATE PROCEDURE P_L1
      ( IN input0 table(L int,R int),
      OUT output0 table(L int,R int) )
LANGUAGE LLANG AS
begin export Void main (Table< Int32 "L" , Int32 "R" > "input0" input0,
  Table< Int32 "L" , Int32 "R" > "output0" & output0 )
  { Column<Int32> input0Column1 = input0.getColumn<Int32> ("L") ;
    Column<Int32> input0Column2 = input0.getColumn<Int32> ("R") ;
    Column<Int32> output0Column1=output0.getColumn<Int32> ("L") ;
    Column<Int32> output0Column2=output0.getColumn<Int32> ("R") ;
    Size i =0z ;
    Size j = 0z ;
    Size k = 0z ;
    Size num_rows = input0Column1.getSize () ;
    while (i < num_rows ) {
      if ( i ==
 0z ||  input0Column1.getElement(i) > input0Column2.getElement(j) ) {
        output0Column1.setElement(k, input0Column1.getElement(i));
        output0Column2.setElement(k, input0Column2.getElement(i));
       k = k.next();
       j=i;
      } i= i.next();
    }
  }
end;
```

Listing 1.33 Procedure in L

In the procedure, L does not support access to the database, so you need to transfer data between the database and the procedure through input and output variables. You can define the table type on the variables.

In this example, the line `IN input0 table(L int, R int)` is used to define the input variable `input0` as the table type. For the type `int` in the database, the corresponding type in L is `Int32`. For each input/output variable defined with the `CREATE PROCEDURE` statement, the corresponding declaration is at the L language `main` function, so you have the line `Table< Int32 "L_NO" , Int32 "R_NO" > "input0"` `input0` to map the input variable and the line `Table< Int32 "L_NO", Int32 "R_NO" > "output0" & output0` to map the output variable.

You can define a variable as column type `Column<Int32>` to bind the variable to a table column. To do so, use the `getColumn` function in the line `Column<Int32>` `input0Column1 = input0.getColumn<Int32> ("L")`. To retrieve the value from a column at a row, use the `getElement()` function. To set value on a column at a row, use the `setElement()` function.

The procedure's functionality is to generate an output table based on some row-level calculation on an input table. This specific logic can be achieved with SQLScript using an array type. There are some benefits of L that do not exist in SQLScript. For example, L supports container data types, such as `Block`, `Matric`, `Tuple`, `Dict`, and more. Those data structures can be leveraged to perform data flow execution for complex logic. L contains a math library to provide mathematic functions. Moreover, you can specify parallel execution with the `_parallel` modifier, which is useful for improving performance. Listing 1.34 shows the syntax for this modifier.

```
_parallel {
    Func1(para1);
Func2(para2);
Func3(para3);
}
```
Listing 1.34 To Call Functions in Parallel

1.5.3   R Procedures

To write R procedures, use the words `LANGUAGE RLANG` in the DDL to specify the language. You can use R for statistical computing and graphics processing. Because R is an open-source programming language and is available under a general public license, SAP does not provide support for R. In order to integrate SAP HANA with R, you need to download R from the open-source community and configure it. This is discussed in greater detail in Chapter 5, Section 5.1.1.

Let's walk through a simple example. Suppose you have two tables, TABLEA and TABLEB. You need to retrieve data from TABLEA and store the result generated in TABLEB (see Listing 1.35).

```
CREATE TABLE TABLEA(COLUMNA INTEGER);
INSERT INTO TABLEA VALUES (2);
INSERT INTO TABLEA VALUES (3);
INSERT INTO TABLEA VALUES (1);
CREATE TABLE TABLEB(COLUMNA INTEGER);
```
Listing 1.35 Definition of the Source Table and Target Table

In the R procedure, you set the type of input variable as TABLEA, and the type of output variable as TABLEB (see Listing 1.36).

```
CREATE PROCEDURE P_R1(IN var_in TABLEA, OUT var_out TABLEB)
LANGUAGE RLANG AS
BEGIN
var_out <- as.data.frame(sort(var_in$COLUMNA)^2);
names(var_out) <- c("COLUMNA");
END;
```
Listing 1.36 A Simple R Procedure Example

In this procedure, the input and output tables map to data.frame in R. If the data is not a frame, you need to use the as.data.frame() function to convert it to a frame. To call the procedure, run the following statement:

```
CALL P_R1 (TABLEA,?);
```

This statement reads data from TABLEA and sends the output as the table structure of TABLEB. To store the output data to a physical table, add WITH OVERVIEW to the statement:

```
CALL P_R1 (TABLEA, TABLEB) WITH OVERVIEW;
SELECT * FROM TABLEB;
```

For the input variable, you can use any table with the same structure as TABLEA, and for the output variable, you can use any table with the same structure as TAB-LEB. To avoid any confusion between table names and table types, when defining the procedure, declare the type of variables as table types instead of table names (see Listing 1.37).

```
CREATE PROCEDURE P_R1(IN var_in TABLE(COLUMNA INTEGER), OUT var_
out TABLE(COLUMNA INTEGER))
LANGUAGE RLANG AS
```

```
BEGIN
var_out <- as.data.frame(sort(var_in$COLUMNA)^2);
names(var_out) <- c("COLUMNA");
END;
```
Listing 1.37 R Procedure to Define Input and Output Variables as Table Types

When you call the procedure with table names as the input and output variables, the R procedure transfers data to the database tables directly. In some cases, you do not handle database objects inside R procedure; instead, you use SQLScript procedures to handle the data transfer and use table variables to transfer a dataset between R procedures and SQLScript procedures. Listing 1.38 shows an example.

```
CREATE PROCEDURE P_R2()
LANGUAGE SQLSCRIPT AS
BEGIN
ta = SELECT TOP 100 COLUMNA FROM TABLEA;
CALL P_R1(:ta,tb);
SELECT * FROM :tb;
END;
```
Listing 1.38 Call R Procedure in a SQLScript Procedure

Using R, you can leverage thousands of packages that provide a variety of statistical and graphical techniques, including linear and nonlinear modeling, classical statistical tests, time series analysis, and more. Before using a package, make sure it is installed. To install a new package, run the following command in an R session:

```
install.packages("<the package's name>")
```

In R procedures, to use a function, you need to specify the package that contains the function's definition:

```
library("<the package's name>")
```

To show all packages installed on the machine, run the following command:

```
library()
```

This command returns a table (see Table 1.1) to list all the packages installed and their corresponding package descriptions.

Package	Description
base	The R Base Package
boot	Bootstrap Functions (originally by Angelo Canty for S)
class	Functions for Classification
cluster	Cluster Analysis Extended Rousseeuw et al.
codetools	Code Analysis Tools for R
compiler	The R Compiler Package
datasets	The R Datasets Package
foreign	Read Data Stored by Minitab, S, SAS, SPSS, Stata, Systat, dBase, ...
graphics	The R Graphics Package
grDevices	The R Graphics Devices and Support for Colours and Fonts
grid	The Grid Graphics Package
KernSmooth	Functions for kernel smoothing for Wand & Jones (1995)
lattice	Lattice Graphics
MASS	Support Functions and Datasets for Venables and Ripley's MASS
Matrix	Sparse and Dense Matrix Classes and Methods
methods	Formal Methods and Classes
mgcv	Mixed GAM Computation Vehicle with GCV/AIC/REML smoothness estimation
nlme	Linear and Nonlinear Mixed Effects Models
nnet	Feed-forward Neural Networks and Multinomial Log-Linear Models
parallel	Support for Parallel computation in R
rpart	Recursive Partitioning
spatial	Functions for Kriging and Point Pattern Analysis
splines	Regression Spline Functions and Classes
stats	The R Stats Package
stats4	Statistical Functions using S4 Classes
survival	Survival analysis, including penalised likelihood.
tcltk	Tcl/Tk Interface
tools	Tools for Package Development
utils	The R Utils Package

Table 1.1 Packages Installed on the Machine

To make a specific calculation, it is better to load specialized packages than to write one from scratch. For example, you can install package `lme4` to deal with linear and generalized linear mixed-effects models, install package `car` to deal with models for applied regression, or install package `zoo` to deal with time series objects.

There are more than six thousand packages available at *https://cran.r-project.org* that you can leverage in R procedures. For detailed information, refer to the reference manual on the Comprehensive R Archive Network (CRAN) website: *https://cran.r-project.org/web/packages*.

1.6   Application Function Library

To execute complex computations without using R procedures, SAP HANA provides application functions. *Application functions* are like database procedures written in C++ and are called from outside to perform data-intensive and complex operations.

Functions for a particular topic are grouped into the AFL, which includes the BFL and the PAL.

1.6.1   Business Function Library

The BFL is one of SAP HANA's AFLs, and it focuses on common business algorithms. The functions in the library can be roughly classified into the following categories:

- **Assets-related functions**
  These functions can be used to calculate asset values. They include functions for diminishing balance depreciation, straight-line depreciation, sum-of-year depreciation, funds, and lease variable.

- **Payment-related functions**
  These functions can be used to calculate payment values. They include functions for days outstanding, delay, number of periods, payment, rate, and time sum.

- **General balance-calculation functions**
  These functions can be used to calculate balances of accounts. They include functions for feed, feed overflow, forecast, future, present value, and growth.

► **Cost-calculation functions**

These functions can be used to calculate cost. They include functions for driver, forecast dual driver, forecast driver, forecast agents, forecast mix, forecast sensitivity, seasonal simple, seasonal complex, and seasonal simulation.

► **Cash flow-related functions**

These functions can be used for cash flow management. They include functions for inflated cash flow, internal rate of return (IRR), net present value, discounted cash flow, and delay debt.

► **Supply chain-related functions**

These functions can be used for supply chain management. They include functions for Outlook, stock flow, stock flow reverse, stock flow batch, and delay stock.

► **General statistics analysis functions**

These functions are not for a specific area; instead, they can be used for general reporting. They include functions for moving average and moving sum, moving median, volume driver, year-over-year difference, year-to-date, year-to-date statistical, cycles, cumulate, decumulate, maximum value, minimum value, and linear average.

► **Miscellaneous functions**

These functions can be used to transform or prepare data for further processing. They include rounding, transform, days, lag, last, proportion, repeat, and time.

Let's see how to use the BFL with a simple example of the BFL procedure `AFLBFL_CUMULATE_DECUMULATE_PROC`. This procedure has two functions: cumulate and decumulate, controlled with an input flag. *Cumulate* is to calculate cumulated totals; that is, the first record in an output table returns the first record of an input table, the second record returns the sum of the first and second records of an input table, the third record returns the sum of the first, second, and third records of the input table, and so on. *Decumulate* means to calculate the original series from the cumulated totals. To call the BFL procedure, run the following query:

```
CALL _SYS_AFL.AFLBFL_CUMULATE_DECUMULATE_PROC (TBL_IN, TBL_OUT,1)
  WITH OVERVIEW;
```

`TBL_IN` is the input table with the source series—for example, {1, 3, 6, 4}. `TBL_OUT` is the output table. Add `WITH OVERVIEW` in the statement to save the result to physical table. The flag value is 1, which means to execute the cumulate function; 0

means to execute the decumulate function. After calling the procedure, you can see the output by browsing `TBL_OUT`:

```
SELECT * FROM TBL_OUT;
```

In this example, the output is {1, 4, 10, 14}. You can also call the BFL procedure inside a SQLScript procedure and transfer the input and output datasets by variables instead of physical tables:

```
CALL _SYS_AFL.AFLBFL_CUMULATE_DECUMULATE_PROC (:TBL_A,:TBL_B,1);
```

There are about 50 procedures in the BFL library, which helps you address the many types of business algorithms efficiently. Because the complex calculations can be done within the database, you do not have to transfer volume data from the database to the application server. The database hardware is powerful enough to handle the calculations, providing overall good performance.

1.6.2 Predictive Analysis Library

The PAL is another one of SAP HANA's AFLs, and it focuses on predictive analysis. The PAL functions can be classified into the following categories:

▶ **Clustering algorithms**
This refers to cluster analysis, which is used to group data into clusters, where similar data in each cluster is similar; the data in different clusters are different. This category includes five types of functions:

  ▷ *Anomaly detection* is used to find outliers that are discordant with the rest of the dataset.

  ▷ *Density-based spatial clustering of applications with noise (DBSCAN)* is used on density-based data to detect the points in low-density regions.

  ▷ *K-means* is used to partition points into clusters based on their positions and to determine the lowest sum of the distances between each point and each partition center.

  ▷ *Self-organizing maps* can be used to visualize high-dimensional data with low-dimensional views.

  ▷ *Slight silhouettes* can be used to validate clusters of data.

▶ **Classification algorithms**
Classification algorithms identify categories in which new observations belong. This category includes 10 types of functions:

- *Bi-variate geometric regression* models the relationship between a scalar variable (such as y) and a variable denoted as x using geometric functions.

- *Bi-variate natural logarithmic regression* is used to model the relationship between a scalar variable and a variable x using natural logarithmic functions.

- *Exponential regression* models are based on exponential functions.

- *Logistic regression* models are based on linear functions. They model the relationship between dependent and independent variables.

- *Multiple linear regression* and *polynomial regression* are used to model relationships among variables.

- *C4.5 decision tree* and *CHAID decision tree* are used to create models that predict the value of target variables based on input variables.

- *K-Nearest Neighbor* (KNN) is used to classify objects based on the majority vote of its neighbors.

- *Naive Bayes* is used to classify objects according to Bayes' theorem.

▶ **Association algorithms**
These algorithms are used for association analysis, which discovers patterns related to item-to-item association behavior among a set of items. This category includes the *apriori* function, which is used to find frequent subsets among transaction data.

▶ **Time series algorithms**
These algorithms use future value prediction based on an existing time series. They include functions based on single exponential smoothing, double exponential smoothing, and triple exponential smoothing.

▶ **Preprocessing algorithms**
These algorithms are used to preprocess data and make it ready for predictive analysis. They include several types of functions:

- *Sampling* is used to take samples from a large dataset.

- *Scaling range* is used to scale data to an appropriate range.

- *Binning* is used to transform values into bin numbers. The function to convert a category type to a binary vector is used to translate a string attribute to a numerical column.

▹ *Inter-quartile range test* is used to detect outliers outside the inter-quartile range.

▹ *Variance test* is used to detect outliers based on the standard deviation.

► **Social network analysis algorithms**

These algorithms are used for social network analysis. They include the link prediction function, which is used to predict missing links based on existing links.

► **Miscellaneous algorithms**

This category includes two functions:

▹ *ABC analysis* is used to classify objects based on percentage criteria on a particular measure.

▹ *Weighted score table* is used to evaluate a total score with added weight to represent the importance of each criterion.

Similar to the BFL, when calling a PAL procedure, you need to specify the input table, output table, and control table, as shown in the following example query:

```
CALL _SYS_AFL.PAL_ANOMALY_DETECTION(TBL_IN,CONTROL_TBL, TBL_OUT)
  WITH OVERVIEW;
```

The PAL procedure `PAL_ANOMALY_DETECTION` is used to find the existing data objects that do not comply with the general behavior or model of the data. You can define the calculation rules with the control table by specifying parameters such as `DISTANCE_LEVEL`, `OUTLIER_PERCENTAGE`, `NORMALIZATION`, and more.

PAL procedures are written in C++ and are well optimized by fully leveraging database hardware. The performance should be better than when writing the same logic with SQLScript.

1.7   Summary

In this chapter, we introduced the core features of SAP HANA data modeling. Attribute views provide master data modeling. Analytic views make the joins between the fact table and master data and define the measures. Calculation views can embed other information views and represent more complex logic. For each information view, you can apply a security setting on the view level by granting or revoking rights to or from users or roles. Furthermore, with analytic privileges you can apply row-level security.

For logic that cannot be expressed with graphical models, you can create scripted calculation views or procedures. Procedures can be made with multiple languages, such as SQLScript, L, and R. SQLScript provides database control and process control, and you can also leverage its array feature to perform complex calculations. L can be roughly characterized as a safe subset of C/C++ that is enriched by SAP HANA database data types and concepts in order to simplify the manipulation of and interaction with database objects. R is an open-source programming language and software environment for statistical computing and graphics.

For some common business algorithms, you can install AFLs on top of the SAP HANA database, which provide several libraries, including the BFL and the PAL. Without switching to R, you can call BFL or PAL functions in SQLScript procedures to perform advanced data analysis.

In the next chapter, we will begin looking at how to leverage SAP HANA data models to represent complex logic.

In this chapter, we will look at using SAP HANA data models to represent complex business logic.

2 Modeling Complex Logic

A major feature of SAP HANA is its ability to execute complex logic to accelerate application processes that would otherwise be time intensive within both the database and application server layers. Within SAP HANA, a number of modeling techniques enable developers to model complex logic in various business scenarios.

This chapter explains how to use SAP HANA data models to present complex business logic. Each section offers an example of complex logic, such as recursive logic via a hierarchy and calculating running total, and then explains how to model the logic in SAP HANA.

2.1 Achieving Recursive Logic with Hierarchies

Recursion involves repeating a process in a similar way. Many approaches can be taken to achieve recursive logic. A straightforward approach is to make self-joins as many times as the recursive levels exist. In most cases, this method might not be appropriate, due to the unknown recursive levels when you are writing the query. Another approach is to use a stored procedure and loops, but because of the coding involved, such an option might not be considered the most convenient method.

Based on these issues, we recommend expressing recursive logic through hierarchies. *Hierarchies* are used to define the relationship between attributes. SAP HANA can use recursive logic to traverse hierarchy data and provide several navigation functions based on the hierarchy view, which can help you fulfill a variety of data mining requirements. In this section, we will primarily focus on achieving recursive logic via hierarchies in SAP HANA.

2.1.1 Creating Hierarchies with Tables

The first step in achieving recursive logic is to create the hierarchies. This can be done with either tables, an attribute view, or a calculation view. This section will focus on creating a hierarchy with a table to hold the hierarchy data.

First, let's prepare some testing data. We will create a table with two columns, pred and succ, and they will have a parent-child relationship (see Listing 2.1).

```
CREATE COLUMN TABLE h_mini_src ( pred VARCHAR(2), succ VARCHAR(2) );
INSERT INTO h_mini_src VALUES ( null, 'A1' );
INSERT INTO h_mini_src VALUES ( 'A1', 'B1' );
INSERT INTO h_mini_src VALUES ( 'A1', 'B2' );
INSERT INTO h_mini_src VALUES ( 'B1', 'C1' );
INSERT INTO h_mini_src VALUES ( 'B1', 'C2' );
INSERT INTO h_mini_src VALUES ( 'B2', 'C3' );
INSERT INTO h_mini_src VALUES ( 'B2', 'C4' );
INSERT INTO h_mini_src VALUES ( 'C3', 'D1' );
INSERT INTO h_mini_src VALUES ( 'C3', 'D2' );
INSERT INTO h_mini_src VALUES ( 'C4', 'D3' );
```
Listing 2.1 Script to Generate Hierarchy Source Table

The diagram in Figure 2.1 shows the structure of the hierarchy.

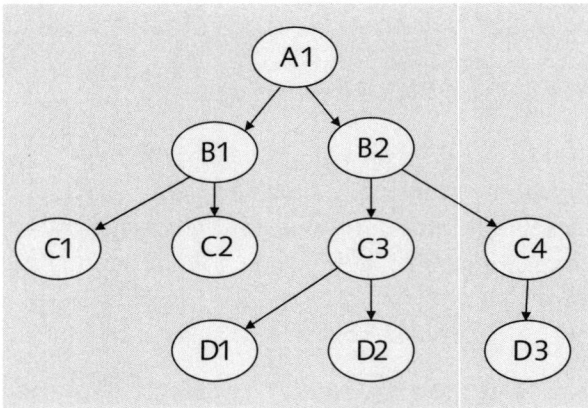

Figure 2.1 Structure of the Hierarchy

There are 10 records in the table that show the parent-child relationship between the nodes. To see the node's parent's parent, you will need to continually make self-joins, as shown in Listing 2.2.

```
SELECT PRED ANCESTOR,SUCC SUBORDINATE
FROM h_mini_src
WHERE PRED IS NOT NULL
UNION ALL
SELECT A.PRED,B.SUCC
FROM h_mini_src A, h_mini_src B
WHERE B.PRED=A.SUCC
AND   A.PRED IS NOT NULL
UNION ALL
SELECT A.PRED,C.SUCC
FROM h_mini_src A, h_mini_src B, h_mini_src C
WHERE B.PRED=A.SUCC
AND C.PRED=B.SUCC
AND A.PRED IS NOT NULL;
```
Listing 2.2 Query to Use Self-Joins to Present Hierarchy

To figure out the relationship between D3 and A1, you first must find the records of C4 and D3, then B2 and C4, then A1 and B2. The more levels in a hierarchy, the more times you have to join.

To avoid using self-joins or stored procedures, you can create a column view and choose the HIERARCHY type. The following is the data definition language (DDL) for this process:

```
CREATE COLUMN VIEW h_mini TYPE HIERARCHY AS SELECT pred, succ
FROM h_mini_src ORDER BY succ;
```

Now that the hierarchy column view is created, you can check it with the following query:

```
SELECT * FROM h_mini;
```

The output for this query can be seen in Figure 2.2.

QUERY_NODE	RESULT_NODE	LEVEL	LEVEL_NAME	ORDINAL	IS_LEAF	QUERY_NODE_NAME	RESULT_NODE_NAME
A1	A1	0	LEVEL 00	1	0	A1	A1
B1	B1	1	LEVEL 01	2	0	B1	B1
C1	C1	2	LEVEL 02	3	1	C1	C1
C2	C2	2	LEVEL 02	4	1	C2	C2
B2	B2	1	LEVEL 01	5	0	B2	B2
C3	C3	2	LEVEL 02	6	0	C3	C3
D1	D1	3	LEVEL 03	7	1	D1	D1
D2	D2	3	LEVEL 03	8	1	D2	D2
C4	C4	2	LEVEL 02	9	0	C4	C4
D3	D3	3	LEVEL 03	10	1	D3	D3

Figure 2.2 Hierarchy View Records

You will not see much useful information from the output, because there is no relation information between the nodes. However, if you add multidimensional expressions (MDX) like navigation functions on the column view, then you will get the desired output. See the following query:

```
SELECT query_node, result_node FROM h_mini( "expression" =>
  'descendants(*)' );
```

The asterisk (*) indicates all the nodes referred in the `query_node` column. The `descendants()` function returns all descendant nodes for each `query_node` in the `result_node` column. The query returns all of the nodes of the hierarchy, with every descendant of each node listed side by side. The resulting output is shown in Table 2.1.

Query Node	Result Node
A1	B1
A1	C1
A1	C2
A1	B2
A1	C3
A1	D1
A1	D2
A1	C4
A1	D3
B1	C1
B1	C2
B2	C3
B2	D1
B2	D2
B2	C4
B2	D3
C3	D1
C3	D2
C4	D3

Table 2.1 Output of a Hierarchy View

No more self-joins, no more loops in stored procedures: The recursive logic can be achieved easily using the `SELECT` statement to browse the hierarchy view.

As previously stated, you can also make hierarchies within an attribute view or calculation view with recursive logic, which we will look at next.

2.1.2   Creating a Hierarchy in an Attribute or Calculation View

In this section, we will focus on creating a hierarchy with attribute and calculation views for recursive logic. Let's begin by looking at how to do this with an attribute view.

At the semantics layer of the attribute view, you will find the HIERARCHIES pane, in which you can design the hierarchy (see Figure 2.3).

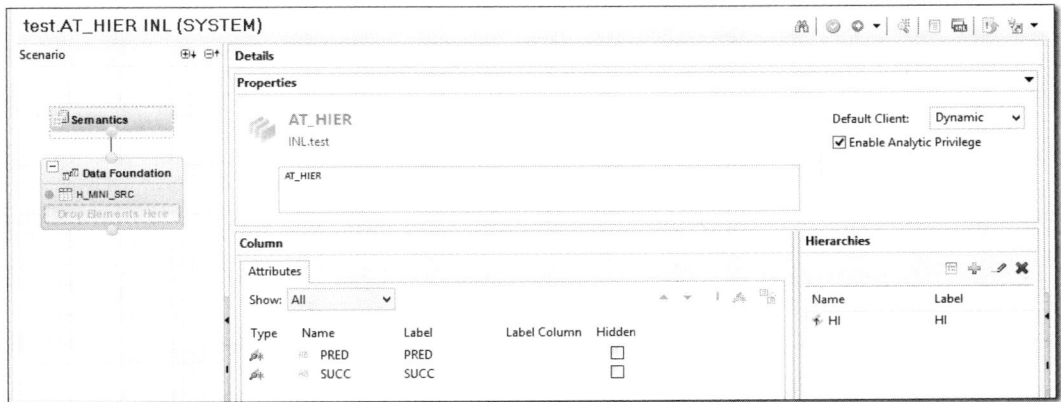

Figure 2.3 Creating a Hierarchy in the Attribute View

In the HIERARCHY definition window, specify PARENT CHILD HIERARCHY for the HIERARCHY TYPE field. In the NODES tab, set the SUCC as CHILD, and PRED as PARENT (see Figure 2.4).

You can also run a query against the hierarchy view to retrieve all of the nodes with an ancestor-descendant relationship:

```
SELECT query_node, result_node FROM _SYS_BIC."test/AT_HIER/hier/HI"
( "expression" => 'descendants(*)' );
```

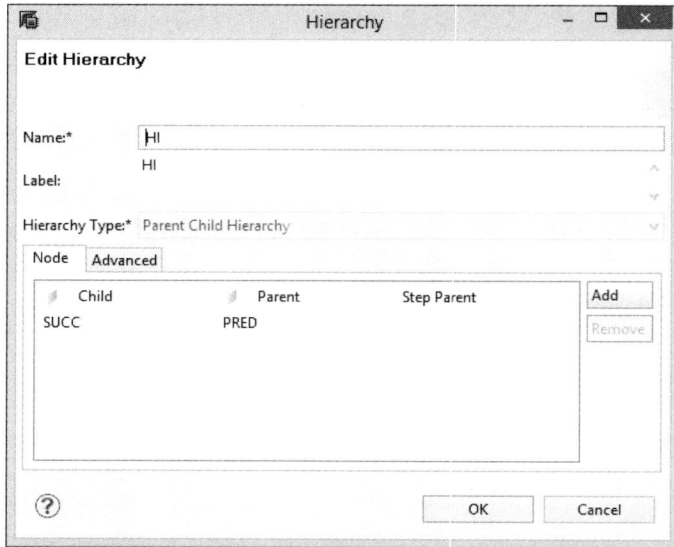

Figure 2.4 Hierarchy Definition Window

Not only can a hierarchy view be created with a table in an attribute view, it can also be created with the result sets of complex queries. To see this process in action, let's look at how to create a hierarchy in a calculation view.

In this example, suppose we have another table, h_mini_src2 (see Listing 2.3).

```
CREATE COLUMN TABLE h_mini_src2 ( pred VARCHAR(2), succ VARCHAR(2) );
INSERT INTO h_mini_src2 VALUES ( 'B1', 'E1' );
INSERT INTO h_mini_src2 VALUES ( 'B1', 'E2' );
INSERT INTO h_mini_src2 VALUES ( 'E1', 'F1' );
INSERT INTO h_mini_src2 VALUES ( 'E1', 'F2' );
```
Listing 2.3 Script to Generate Second Source Table

With a calculation view, you can merge the hierarchies defined in the two tables. This involves two steps: making a union and making a hierarchy based on the result set of that union (see Figure 2.5).

You can then run the following query to check the nodes' relationships against the merged hierarchy:

```
SELECT query_node, result_node FROM _SYS_BIC."test/CA_HIER/HI2/hier/
HI2" ( "expression" => 'descendants(*)' );
```

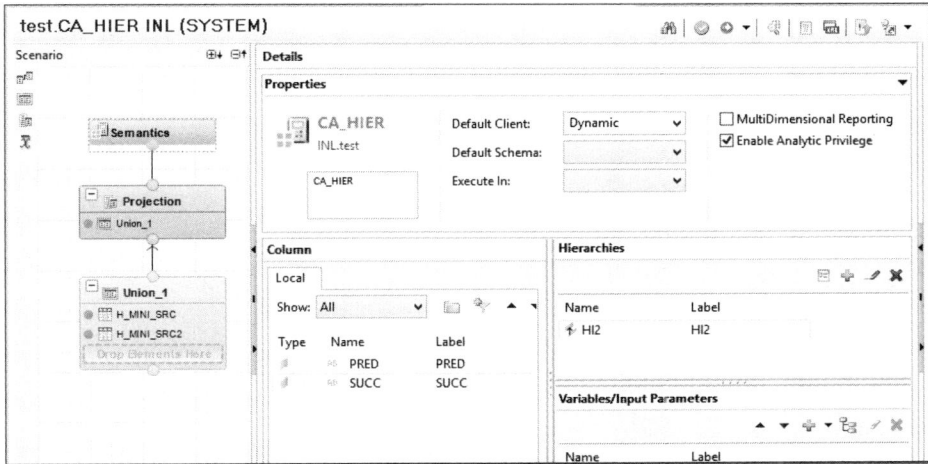

Figure 2.5 Hierarchy in a Calculation View

Hierarchy View Name

The actual name of the hierarchy view might change depending on your calculation view label. Check the objects created under the COLUMN VIEWS folder of the _SYS_BIC schema for the exact hierarchy view name.

Table 2.2 provides the output results of this query.

Query Node	Result Node
A1	B1
A1	C1
A1	C2
A1	E1
A1	F1
A1	F2
A1	E2
A1	B2
A1	C3
A1	D1

Table 2.2 Output of the Query Against the Hierarchy

Query Node	Result Node
A1	D2
A1	C4
A1	D3
B1	C1
B1	C2
B1	E1
B1	F1
B1	F2
B1	E2
E1	F1
E1	F2
B2	C3
B2	D1
B2	D2
B2	C4
B2	D3
C3	D1
C3	D2
C4	D3

Table 2.2 Output of the Query Against the Hierarchy (Cont.)

2.1.3 Hierarchy View Attributes

The hierarchy view is an important feature of SAP HANA. In this section, we will look at its attributes in detail. To begin, run the following query to check the content and bring up its attributes:

```
SELECT * FROM _SYS_BIC."test/AT_HIER/hier/HI";
```

The resulting output is shown in Figure 2.6.

The query returns the content of QUERY_NODE, RESULT_NODE, LEVEL, ORDINAL, IS_ LEAF, PATH, PARENTS, CHILDREN, and other columns. To gather a better understanding of each of these attributes, refer to Table 2.3.

QUER...	RESU...	LEVEL	LEVEL_N...	ORDINAL	IS_LEAF	QUER...	RESU...	PATH	PARENTS	CHILDREN
A1	A1	0	LEVEL 00	1	0	A1	A1	A1		B1,B2
B1	B1	1	LEVEL 01	2	0	B1	B1	A1/B1	A1	C1,C2
C1	C1	2	LEVEL 02	3	1	C1	C1	A1/B1/C1	B1	
C2	C2	2	LEVEL 02	4	1	C2	C2	A1/B1/C2	B1	
B2	B2	1	LEVEL 01	5	0	B2	B2	A1/B2	A1	C3,C4
C3	C3	2	LEVEL 02	6	0	C3	C3	A1/B2/C3	B2	D1,D2
D1	D1	3	LEVEL 03	7	1	D1	D1	A1/B2/C3/D1	C3	
D2	D2	3	LEVEL 03	8	1	D2	D2	A1/B2/C3/D2	C3	
C4	C4	2	LEVEL 02	9	0	C4	C4	A1/B2/C4	B2	D3
D3	D3	3	LEVEL 03	10	1	D3	D3	A1/B2/C4/D3	C4	

Figure 2.6 Hierarchy View Output

Attribute Name	Type	Description
QUERY_NODE	INTEGER, STRING	This is the unique name/key/ID of the node the navigation used as an origin point. For parent-child hierarchies, the value always corresponds to the node's unique key (e.g., A1, B1, C1); for leveled hierarchies, the value is a combination of the node's level and name, or its key (e.g., [YEAR].[2010], [CALMONTH].[201001], [DATE_SQL].[2010-01-25]).
RESULT_NODE	INTEGER, STRING	This is the unique name/key/ID of the query's result node. The result node is set based on the expression of the query; when there is no expression, RESULT_NODE points to QUERY_NODE itself. When the expression is, for example, Parents(), then RESULT_NODE will point to the parents of QUERY_NODE. When a single QUERY_NODE has multiple parents, it returns multiple records to show all the parents of the node. There are several navigation functions that can be used in the query expressions, which help you achieve flexible navigation operations on top of hierarchies. Again, for leveled hierarchies, the value is a combination of the node's level and name, or its key. For recursive hierarchies, the value always corresponds to the node's unique key.
QUERY_NODE_NAME	STRING	This is the name of the node the navigation used as an origin point. For recursive parent-child hierarchies, the value is always identical to QUERY_NODE. For leveled hierarchies, it contains the node's pure (potentially nonunique) name value without any level or path information (e.g., 2010, 2010-01-25).

Table 2.3 Attribute Description

Attribute Name	Type	Description
RESULT_NODE_NAME	STRING	This is the name of the query's result node. Again, for recursive parent-child hierarchies, the value is always identical to RESULT_NODE. For leveled hierarchies, it contains the node's pure (potentially non-unique) name value without any level or path information.
LEVEL	INTEGER	This represents the distance of the result node from the nearest root node above the query node. The value is 0 at root level, 1 at the first level, 2 at the second level, and so on.
LEVEL_NAME	STRING	This is the name of the result node's level. For parent-child hierarchies, the names are LEVEL 00, LEVEL 01, LEVEL 02, etc. For leveled hierarchies, the level names are similar to ALL, YEAR, CALMONTH, DATE_SQL, etc.
IS_LEAF	INTEGER	This indicates whether a result node is a branch (0) or a leaf (1).
ORDINAL	INTEGER	This refers to the ordinal number of the result node, mainly for purposes of displaying query results. The exact meaning of the ordinal depends on the query. For example, if a query involves no navigation expression, the output ordinal reflects the natural hierarchy node order.

Table 2.3 Attribute Description (Cont.)

You can create SQL queries including the attributes described in Table 2.3 to browse the data of a hierarchy view. For example, when you search leaf nodes, you can run the following query:

```
SELECT QUERY_NODE FROM _SYS_BIC."test/AT_HIER/hier/HI" WHERE IS_LEAF=1;
```

You can use an MDX query to perform sophisticated cube analysis in the hierarchy view. For SQL, you can also enjoy flexible navigation capabilities based on the hierarchy navigation expressions. A *navigation expression* argument using node IDs as an input is able to evaluate the nested navigation functions as well, thus allowing for complex, multistep navigation within a single expression.

Table 2.4 provides detailed descriptions of some commonly used navigation functions.

Navigation Functions	Description	Syntax	Example	Output
Members	Selects all hierarchy member nodes from a specified level. Only one level can be selected in the function.	`Members( levelNumber )`	`SELECT result_node FROM h_mini("expression"=>'Members(0)');`	[A1]
Parents	Returns the directly superordinate nodes of a list of input nodes or of the result of nested inner expressions. To add values of multiple nodes to the function, separate them with commas.	`Parents( nodeId1 | expression1[, nodeId2 | expression2, ...])`	`SELECT query_node, result_node FROM h_mini("expression" => 'Parents("C2", "C3")');`	[(C2,B1), (C3,B2)]
Children	Returns the directly subordinate nodes of a list of input nodes or of the result of nested inner expressions.	`Children( nodeId1 | expression1[, nodeId2 | expression2, ...])`	`SELECT result_node FROM h_mini( "expression" => 'Children("A1")');`	[B1, B2]
Siblings	Returns the nodes with the same parents as a list of input nodes or of the result of nested inner expressions. To achieve the same navigation, combine the parents and children functions; the expression Siblings("C2") is equivalent to Children(Parents("C2")).	`Siblings( nodeId1 | expression1[, nodeId2 | expression2, ...])`	`SELECT result_node FROM h_mini( "expression" => 'Siblings("C2")');`	[C1, C2]
Leaves	Returns the leaves below a set of input nodes or of the result of nested inner expressions.	`Leaves( [nodeId1 | expression1][, nodeId2 | expression2, ...])`	`SELECT query_node, result_node FROM h_mini("expression" => 'Leaves("A1", "C3")');`	[(A1,C1), (A1,C2), (A1,D1), (A1,D2), (A1,D3), (C3,D1), (C3,D2)]

Table 2.4 Commonly Used Navigation Functions

Navigation Functions	Description	Syntax	Example	Output
Union	Combines the results of multiple navigation functions and individual node selections. Duplicate result nodes are eliminated from the result set. For example, you can retrieve all parents and all children of a node with one single query using the union function.	`Union( expression1 | nodeId1, expression2 | nodeId2 [, ...expression n | nodeId n] )`	`SELECT query_node, result_node FROM h_mini( "expression" => 'Union( Leaves("B1"), Parents("C3"), "D2")' );`	`[ (B1,C1), (B1,C2), (C3,B2), (D2,D2) ]`
UnionAll	Combines the results of multiple navigation functions and individual node selections. Duplicate result nodes are retained.	`UnionAll( expression1 | nodeId1, expression2 | nodeId2 [, ...expression n | nodeId n] )`	`SELECT result_node FROM h_mini( "expression" => 'UnionAll( Children("A1"), subtree("B1",0,1) )' );`	`[ B1, B2, B1, C1, C2 ]`
Intersect	Restricts the result of the navigation expression to the subset contained in one or more filter expressions result sets. Filter expressions may also be individual node IDs. This function can be used to simulate the WHERE clause of SQL queries, which links multiple filters with AND operators.	`Intersect( navigation expression, filter expression1[, ...filter expression n] )`	`SELECT result_node FROM h_mini( "expression" => 'Intersect( Members(2), subtree("B2") )' );`	`[ C3, C4 ]`

Table 2.4 Commonly Used Navigation Functions (Cont.)

Navigation Functions	Description	Syntax	Example	Output
Difference	Removes all result nodes of the filter expressions from the result of the navigation expression. Filter expressions may also be individual node IDs. This is like the NOT IN operator in SQL queries.	Difference(navigation expression, filter expression1[,..filter expression n])	SELECT result_node FROM h_mini("expression" =>'difference(subtree("D1",.-99,.-1),Members(0))');	[B2, C3]
Ancestors	Selects all ancestors at the given distance. When the distance is 1, it returns parents; when the distance is 2, it returns parents of parents; and so on.	Ancestors(nodeId, distance)	SELECT result_node FROM h_mini("expression" => 'Ancestors("D1",2)');	[B2]
Ascendants	Returns all ancestors, excluding the query nodes.	Ascendants(nodeId1 | expression1[,nodeId2 |expression2,...])	SELECT result_node from h_mini("expression"= >'ascendants("D1")') ORDER BY ordinal	[C3, B2, A1]
Descendants	Returns all descendants, excluding the query nodes.	Descendants(nodeId1 | expression1[,nodeId2 |expression2,...])	SELECT result_node from h_mini("expression"= >'descendants("B2")') ORDER BY ordinal	[C3, D1, D2, C4, D3]

Table 2.4 Commonly Used Navigation Functions (Cont.)

Navigation Functions	Description	Syntax	Example	Output
Nodes	Selects one or more hierarchy member nodes directly. If the navigation function is called without specifying a node ID, all hierarchy nodes are selected. To select a specific member, you can also not specify the function, the expression being =>'("C2")'.	nodes([nodeId1][, nodeId2,...])	▲ SELECT result_node, level, ordinal FROM h_mini("expression" => 'nodes("C2", "B2")'); ▲ SELECT result_node FROM h_mini; ▲ SELECT result_node FROM h_mini("expression" => 'nodes()'); ▲ SELECT result_node FROM h_mini("expression" => 'nodes(*)'); ▲ SELECT result_node FROM h_mini("expression" => '*');	▲ [(C2,2,1), (B2,1,2)] ▲ [A1, B1, C1, C2, B2, C3, D1, D2, C4, D3]

Table 2.4 Commonly Used Navigation Functions (Cont.)

Navigation Functions	Description	Syntax	Example	Output
Subtree	Subtree is the most generic navigation function. It allows the selection of nodes by relative distance to a given node or relative to the result set of a nested expression. It includes the selection of direct children (`distanceFrom=distanceTo =1`), parents (`distanceFrom=distanceTo = -1`), all ancestors (`distanceFrom= -999, distanceTo= -1`), etc. If `distanceTo` is not provided, `INT_MAX` is assumed; if `distanceFrom` is not provided, 0 is assumed. You can use this function to substitute some other functions, such as `Parents()`, `Descendants()`, etc., by configuring the distance value.	`subtree( nodeId | expression [, distanceFrom, distanceTo] )`	`SELECT result_node FROM h_mini ( "expression" => 'subtree("C3",-1,1)');`	[B2, C3, D1, D2]
Inputtable	Read node IDs from the given SQL table. This allows you to process the navigation only for a given set of nodes.	`inputtable([schema,] tableName [, column name 1,...,column name N] )`	`CREATE LOCAL TEMPO-RARY COLUMN table "#t1" AS ( select 'B1' succ from dummy); SELECT query_node, result_node FROM h_mini("expression"=>'leaves(inputTable("#t1"))');`	[(B1,C1), (B1,C2)]

Table 2.4 Commonly Used Navigation Functions (Cont.)

The navigation functions provide a lot of flexibility during data analysis. Some logic that is too complex to achieve with SQL queries can be performed easily with the MDX-like navigation functions.

In some use cases, the hierarchy relation is constructed in a different way. You may find it difficult to apply hierarchical features to a table that does not provide parent-child relationships for each row. Let's look at an example. Suppose you have table `HIER_SRC2P`:

```
CREATE COLUMN TABLE HIER_SRC2(EMP_ID VARCHAR(2),
N_FROM INT,N_TO INT);
```

You add some sample records, as shown in Listing 2.4.

```
INSERT INTO HIER_SRC2 VALUES ('A1',1,15);
INSERT INTO HIER_SRC2 VALUES ('B1',2,5);
INSERT INTO HIER_SRC2 VALUES ('B2',6,14);
INSERT INTO HIER_SRC2 VALUES ('C1',3,3);
INSERT INTO HIER_SRC2 VALUES ('C2',4,4);
INSERT INTO HIER_SRC2 VALUES ('C3',7,10);
INSERT INTO HIER_SRC2 VALUES ('C4',11,13);
INSERT INTO HIER_SRC2 VALUES ('D1',8,8);
INSERT INTO HIER_SRC2 VALUES ('D2',9,9);
INSERT INTO HIER_SRC2 VALUES ('D3',12,12);
```

Listing 2.4 Script to Generate the HIER_SRC2 Source Table

`N_FROM` and `N_TO` specify the authority scope of each user. If user A's scope covers user B's scope, then user A is the superior of user B. It is easy to make a join to retrieve all of the superior-subordinate or ancestor-descendant relationships (see Listing 2.5).

```
SELECT A.EMP_ID DES, B.EMP_ID ANC
FROM HIER_SRC2 A,HIER_SRC2 B
WHERE A.N_FROM>B.N_FROM
AND A.N_TO<B.N_TO;
```

Listing 2.5 Query to Show Ancestor-Descendant Relationships

The result set of the query cannot be defined as a hierarchy view yet, because all pairs for the ancestor-descendant relationships are still present, and you only need pairs that present the parent-child relationships. For example, D1 has three records: (A1,D1), (B2,D1), (C3,D1). To generate a hierarchy view, D1 should only have one record, (C3,D1), to show the parent-child relations.

To make a query show only the parent-child relations, you can use the window function to set the partition by target `Emp_ID`, and find the record with the closest scope. You can then set that record as the parent node and filter out other records for the target `Emp_ID`, as shown in Listing 2.6.

```
SELECT ANC PRED, DES SUCC
FROM
(
SELECT A.EMP_ID DES, B.EMP_ID ANC,ROW_NUMBER() OVER(PARTITION BY
A.EMP_ID ORDER BY B.N_FROM DESC) R
FROM HIER_SRC2 A,HIER_SRC2 B
WHERE A.N_FROM>B.N_FROM
AND A.N_TO<B.N_TO
)
WHERE R=1;
```
Listing 2.6 Query to Show Parent-Child Relations

The `R=1` filter in the query is to return the record that has the closest `N_FROM` value—that is, the direct parent of the node. The output shows that the hierarchy has the same structure as we have shown in previous examples (see Table 2.5). You can now create a hierarchy view based on the output of the query and union a record with the largest scope as the root node.

PRED	SUCC
A1	B1
A1	B2
B1	C1
B1	C2
B2	C3
B2	C4
C3	D1
C3	D2
C4	D3

Table 2.5 Parent-Child Relationship Output

To create the hierarchy, use the `CREATE COLUMN VIEW` statement with `TYPE HIERARCHY` (see Listing 2.7). Alternatively, you can create a scripted calculation view and define the hierarchy in the calculation view.

```
CREATE COLUMN VIEW h_mini2 TYPE HIERARCHY
AS SELECT ANC PRED,DES SUCC
FROM
(
SELECT A.EMP_ID DES, B.EMP_ID ANC,ROW_NUMBER() OVER(PARTITION BY A.EMP_
ID ORDER BY B.N_FROM DESC) R
FROM HIER_SRC2 A, HIER_SRC2 B
WHERE A.N_FROM>B.N_FROM
AND A.N_TO<B.N_TO
)
WHERE R=1
UNION (SELECT TOP 1 NULL,EMP_ID
FROM HIER_SRC2
ORDER BY N_FROM ASC
);
```
Listing 2.7 Script to Create a Hierarchy View Based on the Query Result

With the hierarchy view created, you can leverage navigation functions on this view to perform a flexible analysis.

2.2   Transposing Columns and Rows

People may have different preferences when it comes to defining table structures. Some prefer tables with many columns; others like fewer columns. When presenting data in a UI, you sometimes have to transpose columns to rows or rows to columns. In this section, we will address these kinds of transposition requirements using complex logic.

2.2.1   Column-to-Row Transposition

Let's look first at a column-to-row transposition. Suppose you have a table called MARK_R to record students' school reports (see Listing 2.8).

```
CREATE COLUMN TABLE MARK_R(
STUDENT VARCHAR(20),
ENGLISH INT,
MUSIC INT,
MATHEMATICS INT,
PHYSICS INT,
BIOLOGY INT);
```

```
INSERT INTO MARK_R VALUES ('JACK',23,54,56,76,43);
INSERT INTO MARK_R VALUES ('DAVID',73,24,96,44,51);
```
Listing 2.8 Script to Prepare the Source Table MARK_R

Table 2.6 shows the grades in all the subjects for each row.

Student	English	Music	Mathematics	Physics	Biology
Jack	23	54	56	76	43
David	73	24	96	44	51

Table 2.6 Students' School Report

To transpose the columns to rows, first create a dimension table to save the subject names (see Listing 2.9).

```
CREATE COLUMN TABLE SUBJECT(
ONE INT,
SUBJECT_NAME VARCHAR(20));

INSERT INTO SUBJECT VALUES (1,'ENGLISH');
INSERT INTO SUBJECT VALUES (1,'MUSIC');
INSERT INTO SUBJECT VALUES (1,'MATHEMATICS');
INSERT INTO SUBJECT VALUES (1,'PHYSICS');
INSERT INTO SUBJECT VALUES (1,'BIOLOGY');
```
Listing 2.9 Script to Create a Dimension Table SUBJECT

You need to join all records of the dimension table to all records of the source table in what is called a *Cartesian join*. To do so, add a dummy column to the source table:

```
ALTER TABLE MARK_R ADD (ONE INT DEFAULT 1);
```

Then, create a calculation view to make the Cartesian join between the source table and the dimension table (see Figure 2.7).

In the calculation view CA _ROW_COLUMN, define a calculated column MARK, as shown in Listing 2.10.

```
case("SUBJECT_NAME"
,'ENGLISH',"ENGLISH"
,'MUSIC',"MUSIC"
,'MATHEMATICS',"MATHEMATICS"
```

```
,'PHYSICS',"PHYSICS"
,"BIOLOGY")
```
Listing 2.10 Formula for the Calculated Column MARK

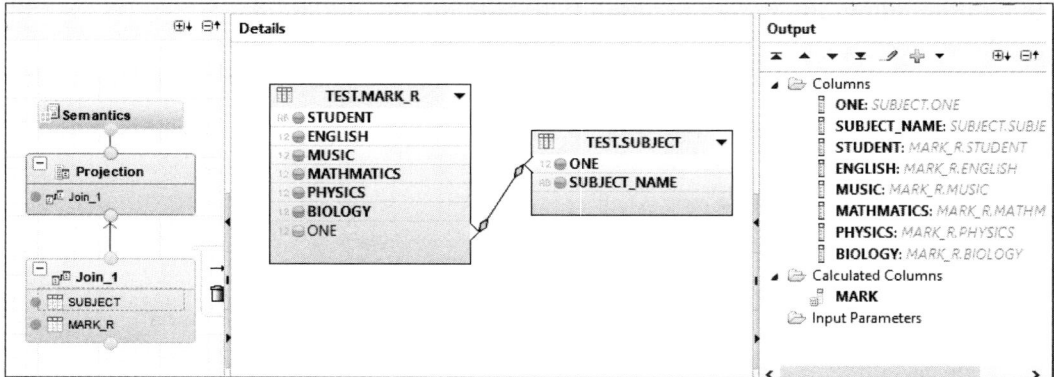

Figure 2.7 Calculation View to Transpose Columns to Rows

The idea is to first duplicate the rows of the source table with the Cartesian join, and then for each row use the case() function to return the mark or grade of the referred subject from the five optional columns:

```
SELECT STUDENT,SUBJECT_NAME,MARK FROM _SYS_BIC."test/CA_ROW_COLUMN"
ORDER BY STUDENT,SUBJECT_NAME;
```

The output of the calculation view has a subject name and the grade of the referred subject, with the different subjects in different rows (see Table 2.7).

Student	Subject Name	Mark/Grade
David	Biology	51
David	English	73
David	Mathematics	96
David	Music	24
David	Physics	44
Jack	Biology	43
Jack	English	23
Jack	Mathematics	56

Table 2.7 Output of the Calculation View

Student	Subject Name	Mark/Grade
Jack	Music	54
Jack	Physics	76

Table 2.7 Output of the Calculation View (Cont.)

You also can achieve the same result with another approach. Instead of creating the subject list table, create table SUBJECT_MATRIX, which contains the subject list within a matrix (see Listing 2.11).

```
CREATE COLUMN TABLE SUBJECT_MATRIX(
ONE INT,
SUBJECT_NAME VARCHAR(20),
ENG INT,
MUS INT,
MAT INT,
PHY INT,
BIO INT);
INSERT INTO SUBJECT_MATRIX VALUES (1,'ENGLISH'    ,1,0,0,0,0);
INSERT INTO SUBJECT_MATRIX VALUES (1,'MUSIC'      ,0,1,0,0,0);
INSERT INTO SUBJECT_MATRIX VALUES (1,'MATHEMATICS',0,0,1,0,0);
INSERT INTO SUBJECT_MATRIX VALUES (1,'PHYSICS'    ,0,0,0,1,0);
INSERT INTO SUBJECT_MATRIX VALUES (1,'BIOLOGY'    ,0,0,0,0,1);
```

Listing 2.11 Script to Create a Matrix Table SUBJECT_MATRIX

Now, create a calculation view to cross join the source table MARK_R and the dimension table SUBJECT_MATRIX. You can create a calculated column MARK with the following formula:

```
"ENGLISH"*"ENG"+"MUSIC"*"MUS"+"MATHEMATICS"*"MAT"+"PHYSICS"*"PHY"+
"BIOLOGY"*"BIO"
```

You can then browse the calculation view and get the same result. There is not much difference between these two approaches. In most cases, the first approach can be more convenient, because you do not have to maintain an additional matrix.

Grouping Sets

The two approaches discussed in the previous section are both based on joining to an additional table. This might be a convenient way to create the additional table to help you to achieve the complex logic, but depending on the use case, you may also want a way to transpose the rows without resorting to joins. One way to do this is to use a union to merge multiple queries against the same table, but this can be resource intensive. Another way is to use *grouping sets*. You can add several grouping sets to one query and have the output contain multiple copies of the same records.

To differentiate copies from different grouping sets, use the GROUPING_ID () function. GROUPING_ID returns an integer value to identify to which grouping set each row belongs. It is assigned by converting the bit vector generated from GROUPING SETS to a decimal number, by treating the bit vector as a binary number. When a bit vector is composed, 0 is assigned to each column specified in GROUPING SETS and 1 is assigned to the unspecified column. In addition, the order of the digits is the order as they appear in the GROUPING_ID (). By treating the bit vector as a binary number, this function returns an integer value as the output. Therefore, for this table, you can run the query shown in Listing 2.12 to split each row into five.

```
SELECT STUDENT,(CASE GROUPING_
ID(ENGLISH,MUSIC,MATHEMATICS,PHYSICS,BIOLOGY)
    WHEN 15 THEN 'ENGLISH'
    WHEN 23 THEN 'MUSIC'
    WHEN 27 THEN 'MATHEMATICS'
    WHEN 29 THEN 'PHYSICS'
    ELSE 'BIOLOGY' END) SUBJECT,
    SUM(ENGLISH) ENGLISH,
    SUM(MUSIC) MUSIC,
    SUM(MATHMATICS) MATHEMATICS,
    SUM(PHYSICS) PHYSICS,
    SUM(BIOLOGY) BIOLOGY
FROM MARK_R
GROUP BY GROUPING SETS(
(ENGLISH,STUDENT),
(MUSIC,STUDENT),
(MATHMATICS,STUDENT),
(PHYSICS,STUDENT),
(BIOLOGY,STUDENT));
```
Listing 2.12 Query to Split Rows with Grouping Sets

You will see the subject name for each record, which is generated according to GROUPING_ID(), and each student points to five subjects (see Table 2.8).

Student	Subject	English	Music	Math	Physics	Biology
David	English	73	24	96	44	51
Jack	English	23	54	56	76	43
David	Music	73	24	96	44	51
Jack	Music	23	54	56	76	43
David	Mathematics	73	24	96	44	51
Jack	Mathematics	23	54	56	76	43
David	Physics	73	24	96	44	51
Jack	Physics	23	54	56	76	43
David	Biology	73	24	96	44	51
Jack	Biology	23	54	56	76	43

Table 2.8 Using Grouping Sets to Split Rows

Run the query shown in Listing 2.13 on top of the result set to transpose the columns to rows.

```
SELECT STUDENT,SUBJECT,CASE SUBJECT
    WHEN 'ENGLISH' THEN ENGLISH
    WHEN  'MUSIC' THEN MUSIC
    WHEN 'MATHEMATICS' THEN MATHEMATICS
    WHEN 'PHYSICS' THEN PHYSICS
    ELSE BIOLOGY END MARK
FROM
(
SELECT STUDENT,(CASE GROUPING_
ID(ENGLISH,MUSIC,MATHEMATICS,PHYSICS,BIOLOGY)
    WHEN 15 THEN 'ENGLISH'
    WHEN 23 THEN 'MUSIC'
    WHEN 27 THEN 'MATHEMATICS'
    WHEN 29 THEN 'PHYSICS'
    ELSE 'BIOLOGY' END) SUBJECT,
    SUM(ENGLISH) ENGLISH,
    SUM(MUSIC) MUSIC,
    SUM(MATHEMATICS) MATHEMATICS,
    SUM(PHYSICS) PHYSICS,
    SUM(BIOLOGY) BIOLOGY
FROM MARK_R
GROUP BY GROUPING SETS(
(ENGLISH,STUDENT),
(MUSIC,STUDENT),
(MATHEMATICS,STUDENT),
```

```
(PHYSICS,STUDENT),
(BIOLOGY,STUDENT)
));
```
Listing 2.13 Query to Transpose Rows to Columns without a Join

In this query, you use the CASE/WHEN operator to separate the values for each sub-ject. It returns the same result as the previous approach. This approach is not as simple as the previous one, but it does provide a new way to duplicate rows without adding joins to an additional table.

2.2.2   Row-to-Column Transposition

Next, let's look at row-to-column transposition. For this example, suppose you have a source table MARK_C. To create the test playground, insert the result of CA_ROW_COLUMN into this table (see Listing 2.14).

```
CREATE COLUMN TABLE MARK_C(
STUDENT VARCHAR(20),
SUBJECT_NAME VARCHAR(20),
MARK INT);

INSERT INTO MARK_C
SELECT STUDENT,SUBJECT_NAME,MARK
FROM _SYS_BIC."test/CA_ROW_COLUMN";
```
Listing 2.14 Script to Create Table MARK_C

Then, create a calculation view CA_ROW_COLUMN3 against the table (see Figure 2.8).

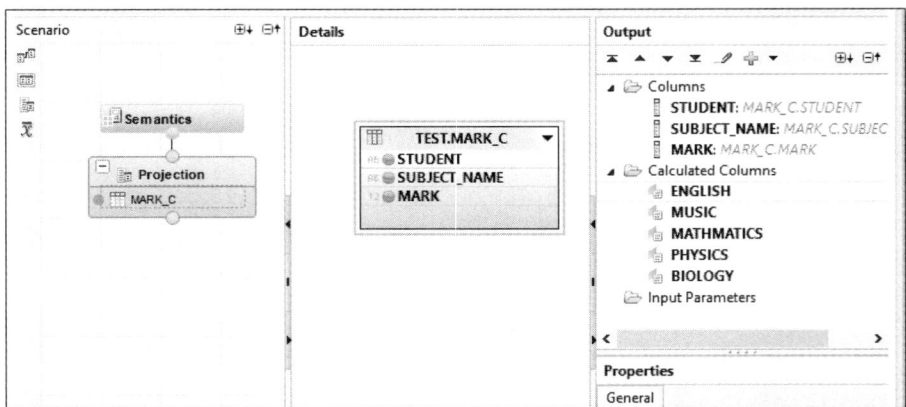

Figure 2.8 Calculation View to Transpose Rows to Columns

In Figure 2.8, in the calculation view, we created five calculated columns (see Listing 2.15).

```
"ENGLISH"→IF("SUBJECT_NAME"='ENGLISH',"MARK",NULL)
"MUSIC"→IF("SUBJECT_NAME"='MUSIC',"MARK",NULL)
"MATHEMATICS"→IF("SUBJECT_NAME"='MATHEMATICS',"MARK",NULL)
"PHYSICS"→IF("SUBJECT_NAME"='PHYSICS',"MARK",NULL)
"BIOLOGY"→IF("SUBJECT_NAME"='BIOLOGY',"MARK",NULL)
```

Listing 2.15 Formulas of the Calculated Columns

When you run the following query shown in Listing 2.16, it returns two rows. Each row has a dedicated column for each subject.

```
SELECT STUDENT,
SUM(ENGLISH) ENGLISH,
SUM(MUSIC) MUSIC,
SUM(MATHEMATICS) MATHEMATICS,
SUM(PHYSICS) PHYSICS,
SUM(BIOLOGY) BIOLOGY
FROM _SYS_BIC."test/CA_ROW_COLUMN3"
GROUP BY STUDENT;
```

Listing 2.16 Query to Transpose Rows to Columns

You can see the query output in Table 2.9. The marks/grades that were originally in different rows are now put in one row in different columns for each student.

Student	English	Music	Mathematics	Physics	Biology
Jack	23	54	56	76	43
David	73	24	96	44	51

Table 2.9 Output of Column to Row Transposition

Matrix Multiplication

You also can try a matrix multiplication approach to transpose rows to columns. To do so, first create a calculation view CA_ROW_COLUMN4 to join table MARK_C with the table SUBJECT_MATRIX on the column SUBJECT_NAME (see Figure 2.9).

In the calculation view, create five calculated columns (see Listing 2.17).

```
"ENGLISH"→"MARK"*"ENG"
"MUSIC"→"MARK"*"MUS"
"MATHEMATICS"→"MARK"*"MAT"
```

```
"PHYSICS"→"MARK"*"PHY"
"BIOLOGY"→"MARK"*"BIO"
```
Listing 2.17 Formulas of Calculated Columns

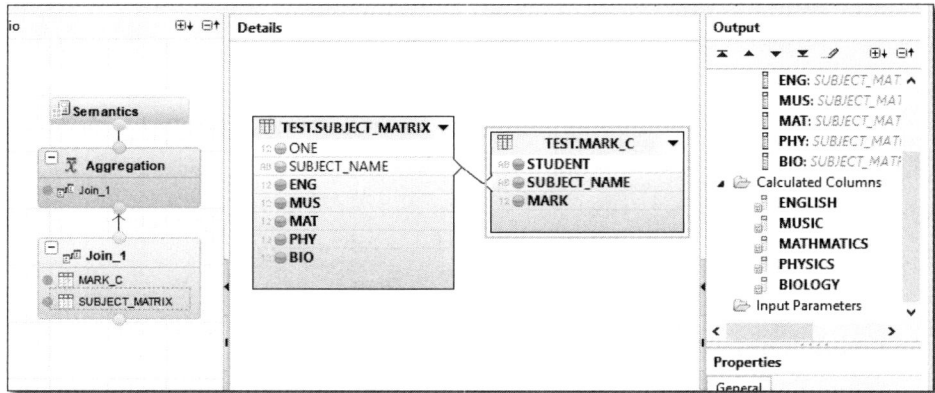

Figure 2.9 Calculation View to Transpose Rows to Columns

When you run Listing 2.18, it returns the same results.

```
SELECT STUDENT,
SUM(ENGLISH) ENGLISH,
SUM(MUSIC) MUSIC,
SUM(MATHEMATICS) MATHEMATICS,
SUM(PHYSICS) PHYSICS,
SUM(BIOLOGY) BIOLOGY
FROM _SYS_BIC."test/CA_ROW_COLUMN4"
GROUP BY STUDENT;
```
Listing 2.18 Query to Transpose Columns to Rows Based on Join Results with a Matrix Table

Again, the two approaches are similar. One uses the if() function; the other uses matrix multiplication to simulate the if() function.

2.2.3   Reversing a Matrix

Now that you understand the methods for transposing columns to rows and vice versa, we can move on to the process of reversing a matrix. For this example, suppose you have a table MARK_M to show marks/grades in five subjects from five schools (see Listing 2.19).

```
CREATE COLUMN TABLE MARK_M(
SCHOOL VARCHAR(20),
ENGLISH INT,
MUSIC INT,
MATHEMATICS INT,
PHYSICS INT,
BIOLOGY INT);
INSERT INTO MARK_M VALUES ('HARVARD',23,54,56,76,43);
INSERT INTO MARK_M VALUES ('STANFORD',23,54,44,11,67);
INSERT INTO MARK_M VALUES ('QUEEN',43,16,33,88,35);
INSERT INTO MARK_M VALUES ('BOSTON',66,98,71,25,66);
INSERT INTO MARK_M VALUES ('EDWARD',71,29,32,67,19);
```

Listing 2.19 Script to Create Table MARK_M

The output for the query is shown in Table 2.10.

School	English	Music	Mathematics	Physics	Biology
Harvard	23	54	56	76	43
Stanford	23	54	44	11	67
Queen	43	16	33	88	35
Boston	66	98	71	25	66
Edward	71	29	32	67	19

Table 2.10 Tables to Show a Matrix

If you want to compare grades from different schools in each row (see Table 2.10), you need to change the columns to rows and the rows to columns. You'll do so in two steps.

For the first step, you will again need the dimension table SUBJECT. You can create a calculation view CA_ROW_COLUMN5 to cross join the source table and the dimension table (see Figure 2.10).

In the calculation view, you can define a calculated column MARK, as shown in Listing 2.20.

```
case("SUBJECT_NAME"
,'ENGLISH',"ENGLISH"
,'MUSIC',"MUSIC"
,'MATHEMATICS',"MATHEMATICS"
```

```
,'PHYSICS',"PHYSICS"
,"BIOLOGY")
```
Listing 2.20 Formula of Calculated Column MARK

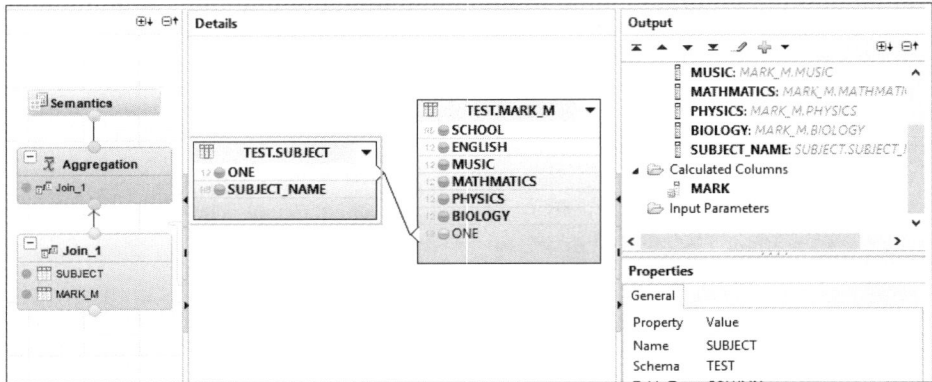

Figure 2.10 Calculation View to Transpose Columns to Rows

You can then send the result of the join node to the aggregation node, where you can transpose the rows to columns in the way we described previously (see Figure 2.11).

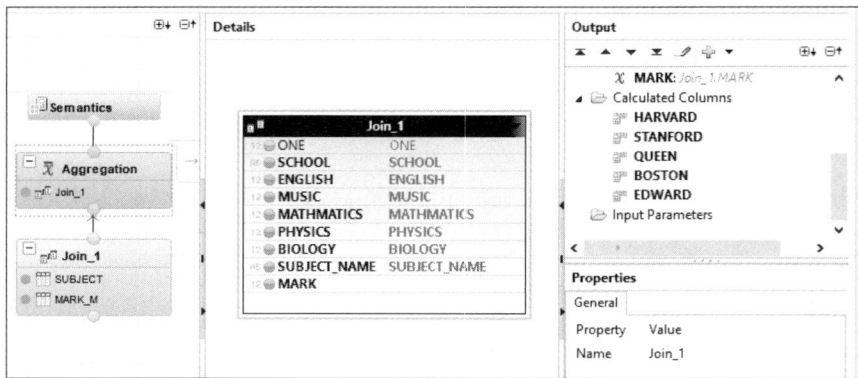

Figure 2.11 Aggregation Node in a Calculation View

At the aggregation node, create five calculated columns (see Listing 2.21).

```
"HARVARD"→IF("SCHOOL"='HARVARD',"MARK",NULL)
"STANFORD"→IF("SCHOOL"='STANFORD',"MARK",NULL)
"QUEEN"→IF("SCHOOL"='QUEEN',"MARK",NULL)
"BOSTON"→IF("SCHOOL"='BOSTON',"MARK",NULL)
"EDWARD"→IF("SCHOOL"='EDWARD',"MARK",NULL)
```
Listing 2.21 Formulas of Calculated Columns for MARK in Different Schools

With the calculation view created, you can run the query shown in Listing 2.22.

```
SELECT SUBJECT_NAME,SUM(HARVARD) HARVARD,
SUM(STANFORD) STANFORD,
SUM(QUEEN) QUEEN,
SUM(BOSTON) BOSTON,
SUM(EDWARD) EDWARD
FROM _SYS_BIC."test/CA_ROW_COLUMN5"
GROUP BY SUBJECT_NAME;
```
Listing 2.22 Query to Reverse the Matrix

In the query output shown in Table 2.11, the subject names that were column names in the source table are distributed to rows. University names that were distributed to rows become column names.

Subject Name	Harvard	Stanford	Queen	Boston	Edward
English	23	23	43	66	71
Music	54	54	16	98	29
Mathematics	56	44	33	71	32
Physics	76	11	88	25	67
Biology	43	67	35	66	19

Table 2.11 Result of the Calculation View

With these two simple steps, the rows and columns of the source table have been completely switched.

2.2.4 Merging Data from Multiple Records

Another kind of row-to-column transposition method is to merge data from multiple records. When you perform aggregation reporting, sometimes you still want to check further details. For example, when you sum based on state, you may still want to see the included cities. SAP HANA provides a useful function, STRING_AGG

(), that can help in this case. STRING_AGG() returns the concatenation of strings for each group of records.

For this example, consider the school report table MARK_S (see Listing 2.23).

```
CREATE COLUMN TABLE MARK_S(
STUDENT VARCHAR(20),
SUBJECT VARCHAR(20),
MARK INT);
INSERT INTO MARK_S VALUES ('David','Maths',23);
INSERT INTO MARK_S VALUES ('David','English',78);
INSERT INTO MARK_S VALUES ('David','Physics',18);
INSERT INTO MARK_S VALUES ('Mike','Maths',53);
INSERT INTO MARK_S VALUES ('Mike','French',38);
INSERT INTO MARK_S VALUES ('Mike','Biology',98);
INSERT INTO MARK_S VALUES ('Alice','Music',83);
INSERT INTO MARK_S VALUES ('Alice','German',68);
INSERT INTO MARK_S VALUES ('Alice','Chemistry',78);
```
Listing 2.23 Script to Create Table MARK_S

Because each student may have learned different subjects, it is worth listing the subject names when showing average grades. To do so, run the following query:

```
SELECT STUDENT,AVG(MARK),STRING_AGG(SUBJECT,',') SUBJECTS
FROM MARK_S GROUP BY STUDENT;
```

This results in the output shown in Table 2.12.

Student	Avg(mark)	Subjects
David	39.666666	Maths, English, Physics
Mike	63	Maths, French, Biology
Alice	76.333333	Music, German, Chemistry

Table 2.12 Example of STRING_AGG()

The subject names are merged as a new column, SUBJECTS. This method allows you to concatenate strings with a behavior similar to aggregation functions.

2.2.5 Splitting Strings

In some cases, you also may need to split a string into multiple strings. For example, when using a stored procedure, you include a list of values in one string and then pass the string to the stored procedure through an input parameter. In the stored procedure, you may want to parse the concatenated string back to separated values.

The logic is not complex, and you can achieve it with the script shown in Listing 2.24.

```
CREATE PROCEDURE SPLIT(SOURCE_STR VARCHAR(500),DELIMITER VARCHAR(10))
AS
BEGIN
  DECLARE R nvarchar(100) ARRAY;
  DECLARE S nvarchar(500);
  DECLARE I integer;
  S := :SOURCE_STR;
  I := 1;
  WHILE LOCATE(:S,:DELIMITER) > 0 DO
  R[:I] := SUBSTR_BEFORE(S,:DELIMITER);
  S := SUBSTR_AFTER(S,:DELIMITER);
  I:= :I + 1;
  END WHILE;
  R[:I] := :S;
  T = UNNEST(:R) AS ("ITEM");
  SELECT * FROM :T;
END;
```

Listing 2.24 Stored Procedure to Split String

In the stored procedure, the SOURCE_STR variable is the source string, and the DELIMITER variable is the delimiter character. When you call the stored procedure, it returns split rows. You can then use the result set as a table in the stored procedure to join to other tables—for example:

```
CALL SPLIT('Boston,New York,Seatle,San Fransisco',',')
```

2.3   Using cube() with Hierarchies

To analyze data based on all dimension combinations, you can leverage the cube() function.

Let's begin by looking at an example. Suppose you have table FACT_3 with one measure and several dimensions (see Listing 2.25).

```
CREATE COLUMN TABLE FACT_3(
YEAR INT,
CALMONTH INT,
DTE DATE,
```

```
COUNTRY VARCHAR(20),
CITY VARCHAR(20),
SIZE VARCHAR(20),
MODEL VARCHAR(20),
SALES DECIMAL(18,2));
INSERT INTO FACT_3 VALUES (2010,201001,'2010-01-
02','Canada','Toronto','Large','DJ201',25);
INSERT INTO FACT_3 VALUES (2011,201101,'2011-01-
02','US','DC','Small','DJ5',33);
INSERT INTO FACT_3 VALUES (2012,201201,'2012-01-
02','UK','London','Large','DJ44',22);
INSERT INTO FACT_3 VALUES (2010,201003,'2010-03-
02','Canada','Vancouver','Small','DJ201',99);
INSERT INTO FACT_3 VALUES (2010,201001,'2010-03-
02','US','DC','Large','DJ201',33);
INSERT INTO FACT_3 VALUES (2012,201201,'2012-01-
02','Canada','Toronto','Small','DJ201',88);
```
Listing 2.25 Script to Create Table FACT_3

To analyze SALES from all the combinations of dimensions, you can use the function cube(), as in Listing 2.26.

```
SELECT YEAR,CALMONTH,DTE,COUNTRY,CITY,SIZE,MODEL,SUM(SALES)
FROM FACT_3
GROUP BY CUBE(YEAR,CALMONTH,DTE,COUNTRY,CITY,SIZE,MODEL);
```
Listing 2.26 Use cube() Function

This function returns the results of all possible grouping sets. You can then simulate the feature with grouping sets, but you first need to write more lines, like those shown in Listing 2.27.

```
GROUP BY GROUPING SETS(
(YEAR,CALMONTH,DTE,COUNTRY,CITY,SIZE,MODEL),
(YEAR,CALMONTH,DTE,COUNTRY,CITY,SIZE),
(YEAR,CALMONTH,DTE,COUNTRY,CITY,MODEL),
(YEAR,CALMONTH,DTE,COUNTRY,SIZE,MODEL),
(YEAR,CALMONTH,CITY,SIZE,MODEL),
(YEAR,COUNTRY,CITY,SIZE,MODEL),
```
Listing 2.27 Code Example of Grouping Sets

When there are seven dimensions, the grouping set amount is 128. The cube() feature looks powerful, but when there are hierarchies among the dimensions, there will be a lot of redundancy in the grouping sets.

In this example, there are two hierarchies: (YEAR, CALMONTH, DTE) and (COUNTRY, CITY). A value of DTE always points to a single CALMONTH, and a value of CALMONTH always points to a single YEAR. Also, a value of CITY always points to a COUNTRY. When grouping set (YEAR, CALMONTH, DTE) has been calculated, the grouping sets (DTE), (YEAR, DTE), and (CALMONTH, DTE) become redundant and should be removed. To make the query more efficient, use the cube() function at the leaf level of the hierarchies.

The first step is to run the query, as follows:

```
SELECT DTE,CITY,SIZE,MODEL,SUM(SALES) SALES
FROM FACT_3 GROUP BY CUBE(DTE,CITY,SIZE,MODEL) ;
```

To show the upper level of the hierarchies, make the join between the result set and the hierarchy dimension tables. For a date hierarchy, use table _SYS_BI.M_TIME_DIMENSION. For a location hierarchy, create the dimension table CITY (see Listing 2.28).

```
CREATE COLUMN TABLE CITY(
COUNTRY VARCHAR(20),
CITY VARCHAR(20));
INSERT INTO CITY VALUES('Canada','Toronto');
INSERT INTO CITY VALUES('UK','London');
INSERT INTO CITY VALUES('US','DC');
INSERT INTO CITY VALUES('Canada','Vancouver');
```

Listing 2.28 Script to Create Table CITY

You can make a view to present the logic for the join between the result set and the dimension tables (see Listing 2.29).

```
CREATE VIEW V_CUBE_HI AS
SELECT YEAR,CALMONTH,DTE,COUNTRY,F.CITY,SIZE,MODEL,SALES
FROM
(
SELECT DTE,CITY,SIZE,MODEL,SUM(SALES) SALES
FROM FACT_3
GROUP BY CUBE(DTE,CITY,SIZE,MODEL)
) F
LEFT OUTER JOIN CITY C
ON F.CITY=C.CITY
LEFT OUTER JOIN _SYS_BI.M_TIME_DIMENSION T
ON F.DTE=T.DATE_SQL;
```

Listing 2.29 Script to Create a View Against the Result of the Query with cube()

The view does not yet cover all valid dimension combinations. On the date hierarchy, you have (YEAR, CALMONTH, DTE), but miss (YEAR, CALMONTH) and (YEAR). On the location hierarchy, you have (COUNTRY, CITY), but miss (COUNTRY). We will add the missing combinations separately. For the missing date hierarchy, use the query in Listing 2.30 with a filter on DTE.

```
SELECT YEAR,CALMONTH,NULL,COUNTRY,CITY,SIZE,MODEL,SUM(SALES)
FROM V_CUBE_HI
WHERE DTE IS NOT NULL
GROUP BY GROUPING SETS(
(YEAR,CALMONTH,COUNTRY,CITY,SIZE,MODEL),
(YEAR,COUNTRY,CITY,SIZE,MODEL));
```
Listing 2.30 Query to Add Calendar Hierarchy

For the missing location hierarchy, use the query shown in Listing 2.31 with a filter on CITY.

```
SELECT YEAR,CALMONTH,DTE,COUNTRY,NULL,SIZE,MODEL,SUM(SALES)
FROM V_CUBE_HI
WHERE CITY IS NOT NULL
GROUP BY YEAR,CALMONTH,DTE,COUNTRY,SIZE,MODEL;
```
Listing 2.31 Query to Add Location Hierarchy

For the missing combinations of the two hierarchies, use the query shown in Listing 2.32 with a filter on both DTE and CITY.

```
SELECT YEAR,CALMONTH,NULL,COUNTRY,NULL,SIZE,MODEL,SUM(SALES)
FROM V_CUBE_HI
WHERE DTE IS NOT NULL
AND CITY IS NOT NULL
GROUP BY GROUPING SETS(
(YEAR,CALMONTH,COUNTRY,SIZE,MODEL),
(YEAR,COUNTRY,SIZE,MODEL));
```
Listing 2.32 Query to Add a Combination of the Calendar and Location Hierarchies

The final query merges result sets from all four queries (see Listing 2.33).

```
SELECT YEAR,CALMONTH,DTE,COUNTRY,CITY,SIZE,MODEL,SALES
FROM V_CUBE_HI
UNION ALL
SELECT YEAR,CALMONTH,NULL,COUNTRY,CITY,SIZE,MODEL,SUM(SALES)
FROM V_CUBE_HI
WHERE DTE IS NOT NULL
GROUP BY GROUPING SETS(
(YEAR,CALMONTH,COUNTRY,CITY,SIZE,MODEL),
```

```
(YEAR,COUNTRY,CITY,SIZE,MODEL)
)
UNION ALL
SELECT YEAR,CALMONTH,DTE,COUNTRY,NULL,SIZE,MODEL,SUM(SALES)
FROM V_CUBE_HI
WHERE CITY IS NOT NULL
GROUP BY YEAR,CALMONTH,DTE,COUNTRY,SIZE,MODEL
UNION ALL
SELECT YEAR,CALMONTH,NULL,COUNTRY,NULL,SIZE,MODEL,SUM(SALES)
FROM V_CUBE_HI
WHERE DTE IS NOT NULL
AND CITY IS NOT NULL
GROUP BY GROUPING SETS(
(YEAR,CALMONTH,COUNTRY,SIZE,MODEL),
(YEAR,COUNTRY,SIZE,MODEL));
```
Listing 2.33 Final Query with All Valid Combinations

This final query will include all the valid dimension combinations and no redundancies.

2.4   Calculating Running Total

A *running total* is the *summation* based on a sequence of numbers, usually a calendar sequence, for which the total at each point covers a fixed range of the sequence. The ranges at different points can overlap. In this section, we will look at the steps needed to model this complex logic.

For example, suppose you wanted to perform an analysis to check the sales by month, and each month you need the amount for not only this month but also the month before and the month after. That is, the running total of month 2 is the sum of months 1, 2, and 3; the running total of month 3 is the sum of months 2, 3, and 4; and so on. Let's explore this solution further. Suppose you have the transaction table Trans_DTL (see Listing 2.34).

```
CREATE COLUMN TABLE Trans_DTL(
Trans_DATE DATE,
Trans_No INT,
Prod_ID BIGINT,
Sales_Qty BIGINT,
Sales_Net DECIMAL(18,2));
INSERT INTO Trans_DTL VALUES ('2014-01-01',1243,1,234,23);
INSERT INTO Trans_DTL VALUES ('2014-01-01',132,2,234,23);
INSERT INTO Trans_DTL VALUES ('2014-01-01',133,2,4353,345);
```

```
INSERT INTO Trans_DTL VALUES ('2014-02-01',1243,1,2222,2222);
INSERT INTO Trans_DTL VALUES ('2014-03-01',1243,1,3333,3333);
INSERT INTO Trans_DTL VALUES ('2014-04-01',1243,1,4222,4222);
INSERT INTO Trans_DTL VALUES ('2014-05-01',1243,1,5222,5222);
INSERT INTO Trans_DTL VALUES ('2014-06-01',1243,1,6222,6222);
INSERT INTO Trans_DTL VALUES ('2014-07-01',1243,1,7222,7222);
INSERT INTO Trans_DTL VALUES ('2014-08-01',1243,1,8222,8222);
INSERT INTO Trans_DTL VALUES ('2014-11-01',13243,1,11,1);
INSERT INTO Trans_DTL VALUES ('2014-12-01',13243,1,1,1);
```

Listing 2.34 Script to Create Table Trans_DTL

In Figure 2.12, you can see the join between transaction table `Trans_DTL` and attribute view `AT_CALENDAR`, based on the calendar table `_SYS_BI"."M_TIME_DIMENSION` introduced in Chapter 1.

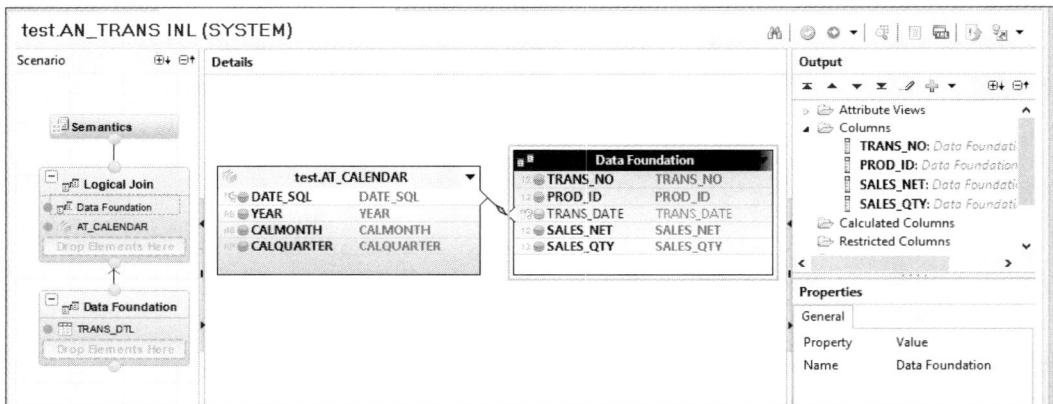

Figure 2.12 Analytic View to Join the Transaction Table with the Calendar Table

From here, you can run a query to retrieve the sum of sales on a monthly basis (see Listing 2.35).

```
SELECT CALMONTH,SUM(SALES_NET) SALES
FROM _SYS_BIC."test/AN_TRANS"
GROUP BY CALMONTH;
```

Listing 2.35 Query to Browse the Analytic View AN_TRANS

To have the sum of each month include one month before and one month after, use the window functions `LEAD` and `LAG`. The `LEAD` function returns values of the offset rows after the current row. The offset should be non-negative with a default of 1. The LAG function returns the value of the offset rows before the current row. The offset should be non-negative with a default of 1.

In this case, base the sequence of records on the order of CALMONTH. The formula for the running total is as follows:

current value + value in one record before + value in one record after

Then, run the query shown in Listing 2.36 to calculate the running total.

```
SELECT CALMONTH,
SUM(SALES_NET)
+LEAD(SUM(SALES_NET)) OVER(ORDER BY CALMONTH)
+LAG(SUM(SALES_NET)) OVER(ORDER BY CALMONTH)
RUNNING_TOTAL
FROM _SYS_BIC."test/AN_TRANS"
GROUP BY CALMONTH;
```
Listing 2.36 Query to Calculate the Running Total

The month range of the running total is three months. If the range was 12 months, the formula would be much longer.

Let's try another approach. You can create a table called CALENDAR_RUNNING_TOTAL to have each month value point to three related month values, then join it with the output of the analytic view (see Listing 2.37).

```
CREATE COLUMN TABLE CALENDAR_RUNNING_TOTAL(
CALMONTH INT,
CALMONTH_S INT);
INSERT INTO CALENDAR_RUNNING_TOTAL
SELECT A.CALMONTH,B.CALMONTH
FROM _SYS_BI.M_TIME_DIMENSION A,_SYS_BI.M_TIME_DIMENSION B
WHERE A.DAY=1
AND B.DAY=1
AND B.DATE_SQL>='1999-12-01'
AND A.DATE_SQL>='2000-01-01'
AND A.DATE_SQL BETWEEN ADD_MONTHS(B.DATE_SQL,-1) AND ADD_MONTHS(B.DATE_
SQL,1);
```
Listing 2.37 Script to Generate a Table for the Running Total

In the table, each value at column CALMONTH points to three values at column CALMONTH_S. For example, the value 200403 points to 200402, 200403, and 200404 (see Table 2.13).

CALMONTH	CALMONTH_S
200403	200402
200403	200403
200403	200404
200404	200403
200404	200404
200404	200405
...	...

Table 2.13 Sample Records

Then, run the query shown in Listing 2.38 to get the running total.

```
SELECT B.CALMONTH,SUM(SALES_NET) RUNNING_TOTAL
FROM _SYS_BIC."test/AN_TRANS" A, CALENDAR_RUNNING_TOTAL B
WHERE A.CALMONTH=B.CALMONTH_S
GROUP BY B.CALMONTH;
```

Listing 2.38 Query to Calculate the Running Total Based on the Join Result

You can put the logic into a graphical calculation view (see Figure 2.13).

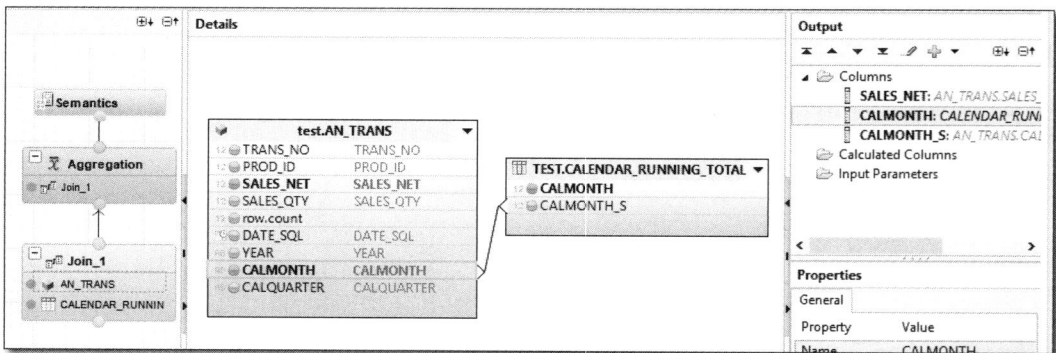

Figure 2.13 Calculation View for the Running Total

The query against the calculation view is shown in Listing 2.39.

```
SELECT CALMONTH,SUM(SALES_NET)
FROM _SYS_BIC."test/CA_RUNNING_TOTAL"
GROUP BY CALMONTH;
```

Listing 2.39 Query to Calculate the Running Total Against the Calculation View

In this example, we made table CALENDAR_RUNNING_TOTAL join to the output of the analytic view and made the join happen in the calculation view. Joining table CALENDAR_RUNNING_TOTAL in the calculation view will perform better than joining it inside the analytic view. Because the output of an analytic view is aggregated data and the row count is fewer than that of the source data, a join applied on fewer rows will run faster.

2.5   Calculating Cumulative Sum

There may be times when you will need to perform a year-to-date (YTD) analysis. Doing so requires you to calculate the cumulative sum. *Cumulative sum* is a sequential analysis technique typically used for monitoring change detection. For example, to know the inventory on each day, we are not interested in the sales and purchases on each day, but in the sum of the sales and purchases from the beginning of the year to the current day: Those are the YTD values.

The formula for the YTD analysis is as follows:

Beginning inventory year values + YTD purchases – YTD sales = daily inventory

To describe the solution to calculate the cumulative sum, we will use the table Trans_DTL and the analytic view AN_TRANS, shown in Section 2.4. First, check the sales for each day by running the query shown in Listing 2.40.

```
SELECT DATE_SQL,SUM(SALES_NET) SALES_NET
FROM _SYS_BIC."test/AN_TRANS"
GROUP BY DATE_SQL;
```
Listing 2.40 Query to Aggregate the Sum

Next, use the window function shown in Listing 2.41.

```
SELECT DATE_SQL, SUM(SALES_NET) OVER (PARTITION BY YEAR ORDER BY DATE_
SQL ASC)
FROM (
SELECT DATE_SQL,YEAR,SUM(SALES_NET) SALES_NET
FROM _SYS_BIC."test/AN_TRANS"
GROUP BY DATE_SQL,YEAR
);
```
Listing 2.41 Query to Calculate Cumulative Sum

When the function SUM() combines with ORDER BY of the window definition, it returns the cumulative sum. When the order is ASC, it returns the sum from the current record to the record pointed by the lowest value of the order by column in the specified partition. When the order is DESC, it returns the sum from the current record to the record pointed by the greatest value of the ORDER BY column at the specified partition.

In this query, specify the column YEAR as the PARTITION BY column and column DATE_SQL as the ORDER BY column, and set the order as ASC. So for each day, it returns the sum from the first day of the year to the current day, which provides the YTD result.

The approach is straightforward, but it does have its limitations: If there are no records for a day on the transaction table, you will not be able to see the YTD result for that day on the result set.

To address this limitation, you need to create a new calendar table, CALENDAR_YTD, for join purposes. Listing 2.42 shows the code necessary to do so.

```
CREATE COLUMN TABLE CALENDAR_YTD(
DATE_SQL DATE,
DATE_SQL_S DATE);

INSERT INTO CALENDAR_YTD
SELECT A.DATE_SQL,B.DATE_SQL
FROM _SYS_BI.M_TIME_DIMENSION A,_SYS_BI.M_TIME_DIMENSION B
WHERE  A.YEAR=B.YEAR
AND A.DATE_SQL >=B.DATE_SQL;
```
Listing 2.42 Script to Generate a Table for a Cumulative Sum

Table 2.14 shows one record for the first day of each year, two records for the second day of each year, three records for the third day, and so on.

DATE_SQL	DATE_SQL_S
2004-01-01	2004-01-01
2004-01-02	2004-01-01
2004-01-02	2004-01-02
2004-01-03	2004-01-01
2004-01-03	2004-01-02
2004-01-03	2004-01-03

Table 2.14 Sample Records

You can then join this table to the output of the analytic view. This will allow you to make the record for each day link to all the records from the first day of the year up to the day that is referred to and then sum the records. You can get the YTD result with the query shown in Listing 2.43.

```
SELECT B.DATE_SQL,SUM(SALES_NET)
FROM _SYS_BIC."test/AN_TRANS" A, CALENDAR_YTD B
WHERE A.DATE_SQL=B.DATE_SQL_S
GROUP BY B.DATE_SQL;
```
Listing 2.43 Query to Calculate the Cumulative Sum Based on the Join Result

Also, you can create a graphical calculation view to make the join (see Figure 2.14).

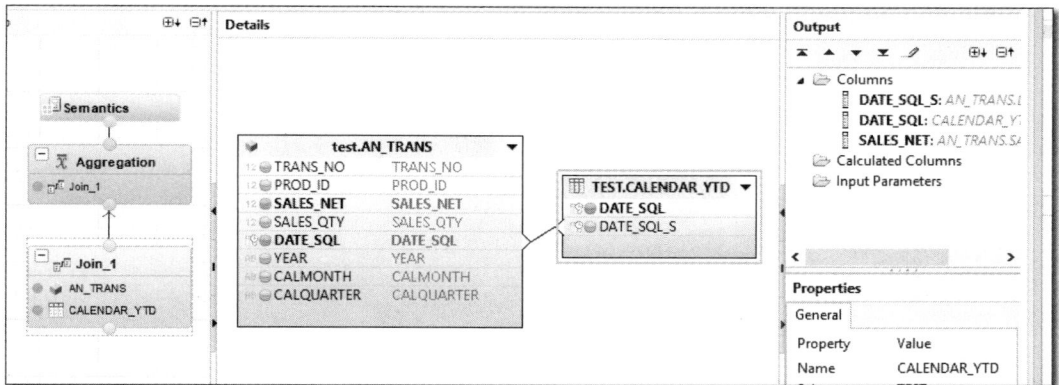

Figure 2.14 Calculation View for the Cumulative Sum

The query against the calculation view is shown in Listing 2.44.

```
SELECT DATE_SQL,SUM(SALES_NET)
FROM _SYS_BIC."test/CA_YTD"
GROUP BY DATE_SQL;
```
Listing 2.44 Query to Calculate the Cumulative Sum Against the Calculation View

The same approach can be applied to MTD (month-to-date), QTD (quarter-to-date), and so on. You must create a table that contains the day-to-day relationship for the cumulative total, make the join to distribute the records to each corresponding sum range, and then calculate the sum.

2.6 Filtering Data Based on Ranking

When you perform a data analysis, sometimes you may need to filter the data based on the ranking results. In this section, we will introduce four approaches to fulfill this requirement:

- Using a subquery
- Using a window function
- Manipulating a concatenated column
- Using a rank node in a calculation view

Let's explain the scenario with an example based on a medical health tracking table. Suppose you have the table HOSPITAL to save a patient's name, his temperature, and the date when his temperature was checked (see Listing 2.45).

```
CREATE COLUMN TABLE HOSPITAL(
PATIENT VARCHAR(20),
DTE DATE,
TEMP DECIMAL(5,1)
);
INSERT INTO HOSPITAL VALUES('David','2010-01-02',37.1);
INSERT INTO HOSPITAL VALUES('David','2010-02-02',37.2);
INSERT INTO HOSPITAL VALUES('David','2010-02-03',37.0);
INSERT INTO HOSPITAL VALUES('David','2010-04-02',36.1);
INSERT INTO HOSPITAL VALUES('David','2010-06-02',37.2);
```

Listing 2.45 Script to Create the Table HOSPITAL

When you create the report, you want to find the last time the patient's temperature was checked for each month and record the temperature values for each of those months. In the following sections, we will look at the different approaches to find this information.

2.6.1 Using a Subquery

One approach to find the sought-after information using subqueries. To get the last time the patient's temperature was checked each month, use the query shown in Listing 2.46.

```
SELECT PATIENT,B.CALMONTH,MAX(DTE)
FROM HOSPITAL A, _SYS_BI.M_TIME_DIMENSION B
```

```
WHERE A.DTE=B.DATE_SQL
GROUP BY PATIENT,B.CALMONTH;
```
Listing 2.46 Query to Get the Latest Record for Each Month

Then, to find the temperature values recorded during those times, and run the query in Listing 2.47.

```
SELECT T.PATIENT,T.CALMONTH,S.TEMP
FROM HOSPITAL S,
(
SELECT PATIENT,B.CALMONTH,MAX(DTE) DTE
FROM HOSPITAL A, _SYS_BI.M_TIME_DIMENSION B
WHERE A.DTE=B.DATE_SQL
GROUP BY PATIENT,B.CALMONTH) T
WHERE S.PATIENT=T.PATIENT
AND S.DTE=T.DTE;
```
Listing 2.47 Query to Get Results for the Latest Record in Each Month

This is the typical way to achieve this type of requirement, but this approach is not always efficient when it comes to larger tables, given that you have to join the intermediate result set back to the source table. In the next section, we will look at how we can remedy this drawback using window functions.

2.6.2   Using Window Functions

When a table is large enough, it can be time-consuming to join the intermediate result set back to the source table. In this section, we will look at how we can eliminate the join through the usage of window functions. Using a window function, you can split the result sets of a query by rows. Listing 2.48 shows the approach with a window function.

```
SELECT PATIENT,CALMONTH,TEMP
FROM
(
SELECT PATIENT,B.CALMONTH,TEMP,ROW_
NUMBER() OVER (PARTITION BY PATIENT,B.CALMONTH ORDER BY DTE DESC) R
FROM HOSPITAL A, _SYS_BI.M_TIME_DIMENSION B
WHERE A.DTE=B.DATE_SQL
)
WHERE R=1;
```
Listing 2.48 Query to Get the Result for the Latest Record in Each Month without Joining Back to the Source Table

In the query, set the window by `PATIENT` and `CALMONTH`. Use `ROW_NUMBER()` to return the result set sorted by date (`DTE` field), and then filter to return only the first record on each window.

2.6.3 Manipulating Concatenated Virtual Columns

Because window functions are not supported in analytic views, we need another approach to address this requirement. Say that you want to merge the `DTE` column with the `TEMP` column. Calculating the max `DTE||TEMP` will return the value that contains the largest `DTE`. To use this approach, run the query shown in Listing 2.49.

```
SELECT PATIENT,B.CALMONTH,TO_DECIMAL(SUBSTR_
AFTER(MAX(DTE||'@'||TEMP),'@')) TEMP
FROM HOSPITAL A, _SYS_BI.M_TIME_DIMENSION B
WHERE A.DTE=B.DATE_SQL
GROUP BY PATIENT,B.CALMONTH;
```

Listing 2.49 Query to Get the Result on the Latest Record in Each Month without Using a Window Function

The query then returns the desired result, and you can easily put the logic into the analytic view (see Figure 2.15).

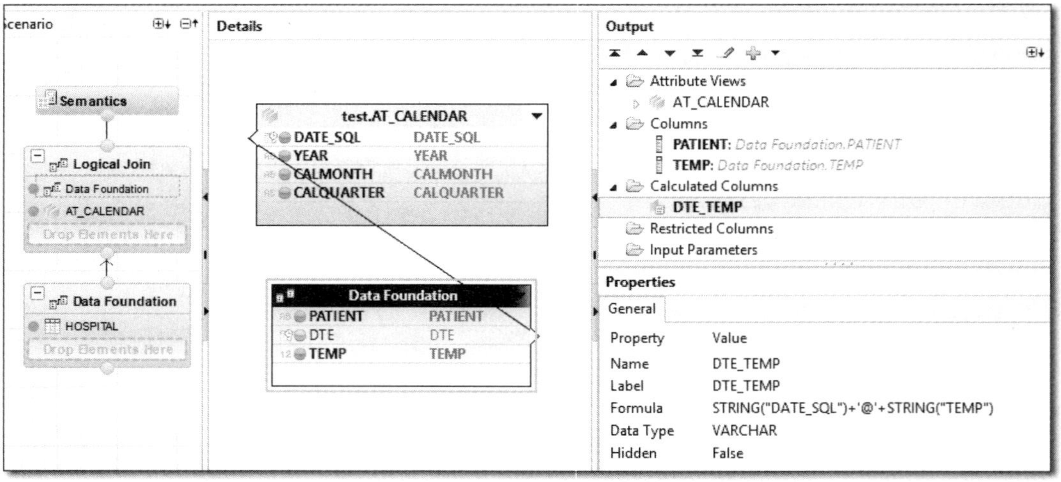

Figure 2.15 Calculated Column to Concatenate Two Columns

You then can run the query shown in Listing 2.50 against the analytic view.

```
SELECT PATIENT, CALMONTH, TO_DECIMAL(SUBSTR_AFTER(MAX(DTE_
TEMP),'@')) TEMP
FROM _SYS_BIC."test/AN_TEMPERATURE"
GROUP BY PATIENT,CALMONTH;
```
Listing 2.50 Query Against an Analytic View

In Table 2.15, the query returns four records from four months; for each month, only the last record is retrieved.

PATIENT	CALMONTH	TEMP
David	201001	37.1
David	201002	37
David	201004	36.1
David	201006	37.2

Table 2.15 Output of Filtering Based on the Aggregation of Different Columns

2.6.4 Using a Rank Node in a Calculation View

With a rank node in a calculation view, you can define filters based on the rank result. In Figure 2.16, you can see the definition of calculation view CA_RANK.

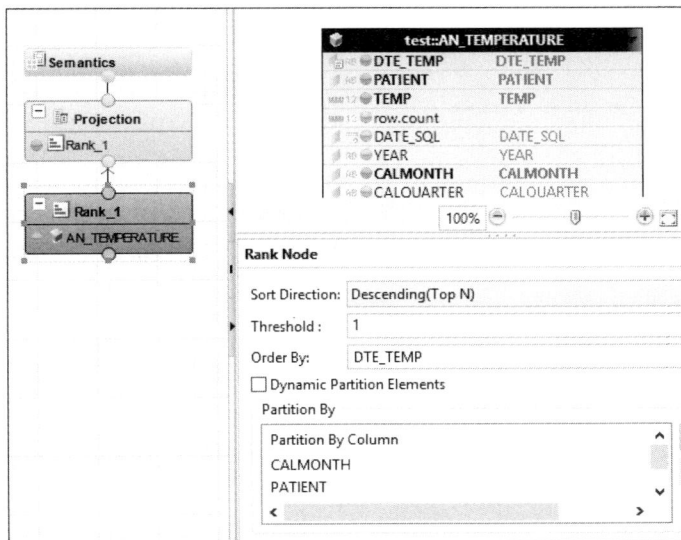

Figure 2.16 Rank Node in Calculation View

In the rank node, add the analytic view AN_TEMPERATURE, choose DESCENDING(TOP N) as the SORT DIRECTION, and set the THRESHOLD to 1. Set the ORDER BY column to DTE_TEMP. Choose columns CALMONTH and PATIENT for PARTITION BY COLUMN to retrieve the last record in every month for each patient.

After activating the calculation view, run the following query to get the desired result:

```
SELECT "PATIENT", "CALMONTH", "TEMP"
FROM "_SYS_BIC"."test/CA_RANK";
```

2.7   Controlling Join Paths via Filters

When creating joins on SAP HANA data models, you can choose an inner join, outer join, or referential join. The referential join acts as an inner join when the joined columns are part of the query; otherwise, SAP HANA does not perform the join process when running the query. Based on this feature, you can use SAP HANA models in a very flexible way.

Let's walk through this feature with an example. Suppose you have a table Trans_HDR (see Listing 2.51).

```
CREATE COLUMN TABLE Trans_HDR(
Trans_No BIGINT,
Dep_ID INT,
User_ID INT,
Sales_Amt DECIMAL(18,2));
```
Listing 2.51 Script to Create Table Trans_HDR

The transaction records shown in the query belong to two companies (A and B). They have separate user list tables, USERS_A and USERS_B, as shown in Listing 2.52.

```
CREATE COLUMN TABLE USERS_A(
User_ID INT,
User_name VARCHAR(20));

CREATE COLUMN TABLE USERS_B(
User_ID INT,
User_name VARCHAR(20));
```
Listing 2.52 Script to Create User Tables

Figure 2.17 shows the attribute views AT_USERS_A and AT_USERS_B for the two user list tables and an analytic view that we use with a referential join to link both attribute views.

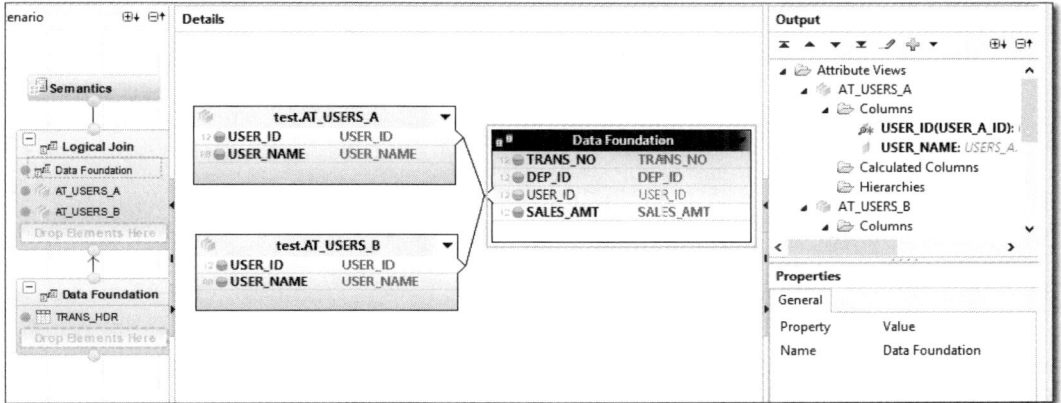

Figure 2.17 Referential Join to Link Attribute Views

In the analytic view, create the alias USER_A_ID for the COLUMN USER_ID of AT_ USER_A and the alias USER_B_ID for the COLUMN USER_ID of AT_USER_B. Then, when you want to perform a complete analysis, run the following query:

```
SELECT DEP_ID,SUM(SALES_AMT) FROM _SYS_BIC."test/AN_TRANS_
HDR" GROUP BY DEP_ID;
```

When the AT_USER_A and AT_USER_B columns do not exist in the query, the two referential joins are not executed, and the query returns the results for both companies, because the records that do not map to an attribute view are retained.

When you want to check the transactions for company A, run the following query:

```
SELECT DEP_ID,SUM(SALES_AMT) FROM _SYS_BIC."test/AN_TRANS_HDR"
WHERE USER_A_ID IS NOT NULL GROUP BY DEP_ID;
```

Because USER_A_ID exists in the query, the join between TRANS_HDR and AT_ USERS_A is performed, and the query returns the results for company A. In the same manner, you can run the following query to check the transactions for company B:

```
SELECT DEP_ID,SUM(SALES_AMT) FROM _SYS_BIC."test/AN_TRANS_HDR"
WHERE USER_B_ID IS NOT NULL GROUP BY DEP_ID;
```

If there are users that belong to both companies, and you want to check the transactions that belong to both, you can run Listing 2.53.

```
SELECT DEP_ID,SUM(SALES_AMT)
FROM _SYS_BIC."test/AN_TRANS_HDR"
WHERE USER_A_ID IS NOT NULL AND USER_B_ID IS NOT NULL
GROUP BY DEP_ID;
```
Listing 2.53 Query to Retrieve Records Belonging to Both Companies

In the query, the filter USER_A_ID IS NOT NULL forces the join to AT_USERS_A to be executed, and the filter USER_B_ID IS NOT NULL forces the join to AT_USERS_B to be executed. Then, the query returns the users that belong to both companies. By using filters, you can control the join path flexibly. If it is in a stored procedure and the user wants to control the join path with an input variable, then you can create the script shown in Listing 2.54.

```
SELECT DEP_ID,SUM(SALES_AMT) FROM _SYS_BIC."test/AN_TRANS_HDR"
WHERE (:INPUT_VAR='A' AND USER_A_ID IS NOT NULL)
OR (:INPUT_VAR='B' AND USER_B_ID IS NOT NULL)
GROUP BY DEP_ID;
```
Listing 2.54 Query to Control a Join Path with Input Variables in a Stored Procedure-1

In this query, when the value of the input variable is A, you can perform the join with AT_USERS_A; when the value of input variable is B, you perform the join with AT_USERS_B.

Alternatively, you can use the OR operator in the query. The OR operator can control the filter conditions. When one expression of the OR operation is true, the other expression will be neglected. Therefore, you can write the script as shown in Listing 2.55.

```
SELECT DEP_ID,SUM(SALES_AMT) FROM _SYS_BIC."test/AN_TRANS_HDR"
WHERE (:INPUT_VAR<>'A' OR USER_A_ID IS NOT NULL)
AND (:INPUT_VAR<>'B' OR USER_B_ID IS NOT NULL)
GROUP BY DEP_ID;
```
Listing 2.55 Query to Control a Join Path with Input Variables in a Stored Procedure-2

On the calculation view level, when required to enforce a join path, you can define the filter in a calculation view instead of a query. For example, you can create a dedicated calculation view for company A, and in the calculation view you can add a filter to trigger the transaction table join to AT_USERS_A (see Figure 2.18).

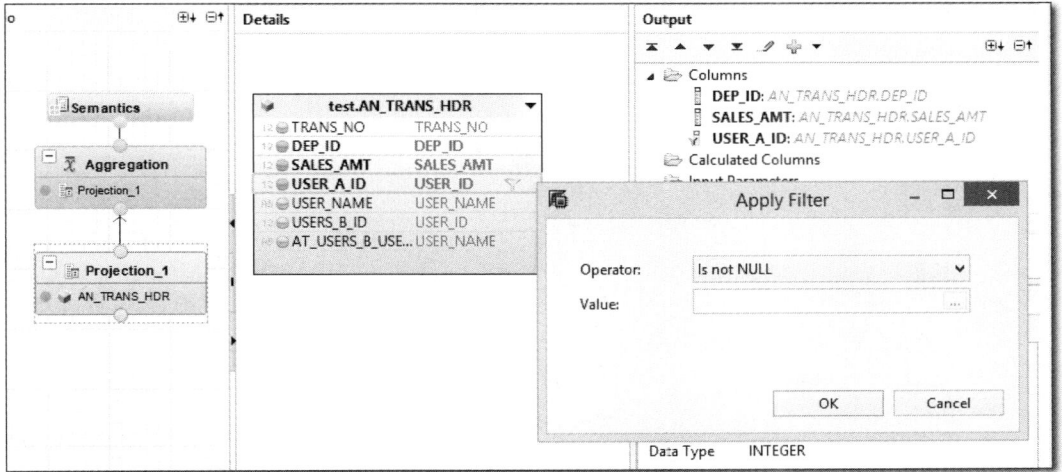

Figure 2.18 Calculation View to Set the Filter

To check the transaction records of company A, run the following query:

```
SELECT DEP_ID,SUM(SALES_AMT) FROM _SYS_BIC."test/CA_TRANS_HDR_A"
GROUP BY DEP_ID;
```

You can use a left outer join to achieve similar logic, providing even more flexibility. To see it in detail, let's create a new analytic view, AN_TRANS_HDR2, to change the referential join to a left outer join (see Figure 2.19).

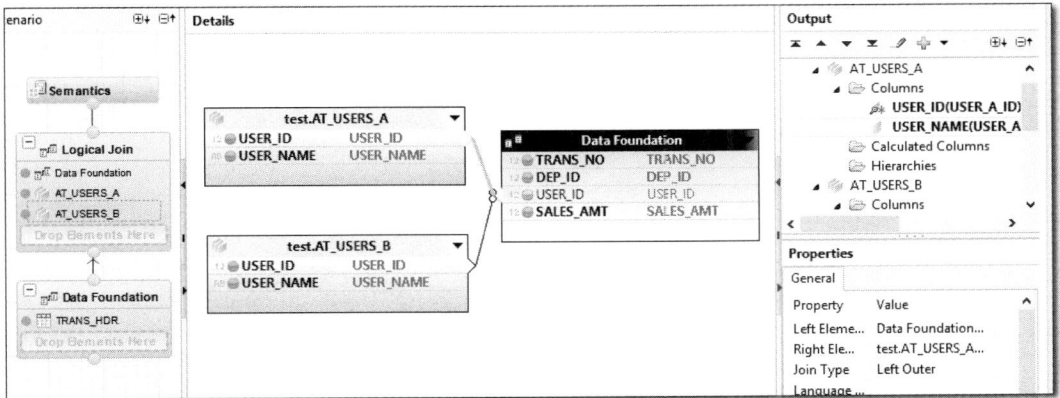

Figure 2.19 Left Outer Join in an Analytic View

You may assume that when you have a filter such as USER_A_ID IS NOT NULL, it should return the transactions for company A only. In fact, when using a left outer join, the joined column of the right table will be substituted with the joined column of the left table. Therefore, when you use the column USER_A_ID in a query, it actually points to USER_ID of TRANS_HDR. Hence, if you want to check the transactions of company A, you need to choose a different column on AT_USERS_ A. You can run the following query:

```
SELECT DEP_ID,SUM(SALES_AMT) FROM _SYS_BIC."test/AN_TRANS_HDR2"
WHERE USER_A_NAME IS NOT NULL GROUP BY DEP_ID;
```

If you want to check transactions that do not belong to company B, you can run the following query:

```
SELECT DEP_ID,SUM(SALES_AMT) FROM _SYS_BIC."test/AN_TRANS_HDR2"
WHERE USER_B_NAME IS NULL GROUP BY DEP_ID;
```

You can also have flexible combinations of filters. For example, if you want to check all transactions in company A except the records that belong to both companies, run the query shown in Listing 2.56.

```
SELECT DEP_ID,SUM(SALES_AMT)
FROM _SYS_BIC."test/AN_TRANS_HDR2"
WHERE USER_A_NAME IS NOT NULL AND USER_B_NAME IS NULL
GROUP BY DEP_ID;
```

Listing 2.56 Query to Retrieve Records Belonging to Company A Alone

If we want to check the transactions which belong to either company, we use the query shown in Listing 2.57.

```
SELECT DEP_ID,SUM(SALES_AMT) FROM _SYS_BIC."test/AN_TRANS_HDR2"
WHERE (USER_A_NAME IS NOT NULL AND USER_B_NAME IS NULL)
OR (USER_A_NAME IS NULL AND USER_B_NAME IS NOT NULL)
GROUP BY DEP_ID;
```

Listing 2.57 Query to Retrieve Records Belonging to Either Company

In this example, we used USER_A_NAME instead of USER_A_ID, but in some cases, the joined column of the right table is needed. To avoid confusion over the columns in the right and left tables, modify the attribute in the table to add the joined column to the output twice. You will see two attributes on the output pane; you can use one for the join and the other for referring to its own column after the join (see Figure 2.20).

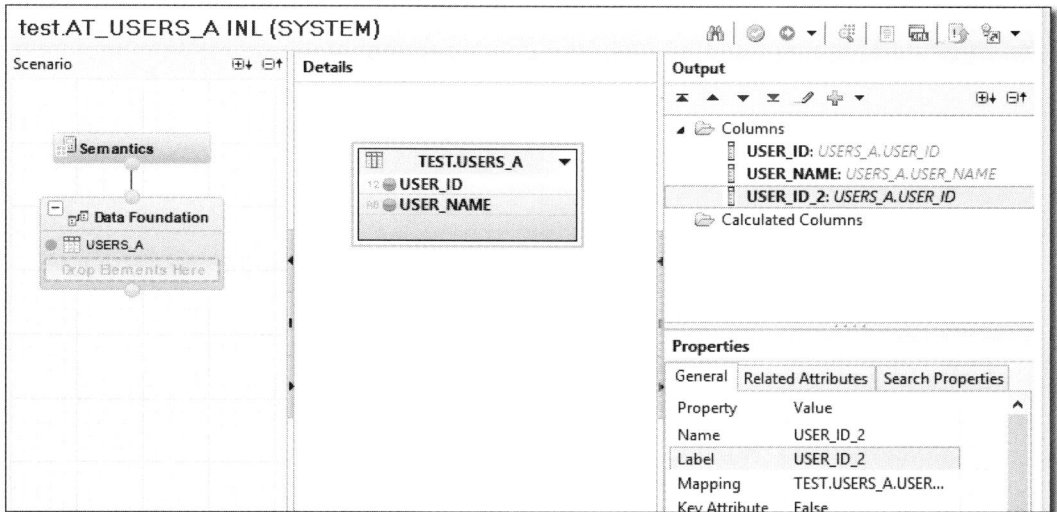

Figure 2.20 Attribute View to Create Additional Columns for Joined Columns

As shown in Figure 2.20, you can use the USER_ID column for the join and the USER_ID_2 column to refer to its own column. In this case, we can rewrite the previous query as follows:

```
SELECT DEP_ID,SUM(SALES_AMT) FROM _SYS_BIC."test/AN_TRANS_HDR2"
WHERE USER_ID_2 IS NOT NULL GROUP BY DEP_ID;
```

2.8   Full Outer Join in a Calculation View

Under normal circumstances, graphical calculation views do not support full outer joins. Usually, when there are such requirements, scripted calculation views are employed. In this section, we will discuss how to achieve full outer joins through graphical calculation views using complex logic.

As an example, suppose you are required to execute a full outer join between TRANS_HDR and TRANS_DTL. The query is shown in Listing 2.58.

```
SELECT A.TRANS_NO,A.DEP_ID,A.USER_ID,B.TRANS_DATE,B.PROD_ID,B.SALES_NET
FROM TRANS_HDR A
FULL OUTER JOIN TRANS_DTL B
ON A.TRANS_NO=B.TRANS_NO;
```
Listing 2.58 Query with Full Outer Join

The typical analysis based on the result set is sum() and count(), with the query shown in Listing 2.59.

```
SELECT TRANS_NO,DEP_ID,USER_ID,TRANS_DATE,PROD_ID,SUM(SALES_
NET),COUNT(*) C
FROM (
SELECT A.TRANS_NO,A.DEP_ID,A.USER_ID,B.TRANS_DATE,B.PROD_ID,B.SALES_NET
FROM TRANS_HDR A
FULL OUTER JOIN TRANS_DTL B
ON A.TRANS_NO=B.TRANS_NO)
GROUP BY TRANS_NO,DEP_ID,USER_ID,TRANS_DATE,PROD_ID;
```
Listing 2.59 Aggregation Against Result Set of a Full Outer Join

Without using a full outer join, you can leverage other operators (such as a left outer join, right outer join, inner join, or union) to simulate a full outer join. First, execute Listing 2.60 to union the result sets of the left outer join and right outer join.

```
SELECT A.TRANS_NO,A.DEP_ID,A.USER_ID,B.TRANS_DATE,B.PROD_ID,B.SALES_NET
FROM TRANS_HDR A
LEFT OUTER JOIN TRANS_DTL B
ON A.TRANS_NO=B.TRANS_NO
UNION ALL
SELECT A.TRANS_NO,A.DEP_ID,A.USER_ID,B.TRANS_DATE,B.PROD_ID,B.SALES_NET
FROM TRANS_HDR A
RIGHT OUTER JOIN TRANS_DTL B
ON A.TRANS_NO=B.TRANS_NO;
```
Listing 2.60 Query to Union a Left Outer Join and a Right Outer Join

The query returns the result set of a full outer join plus the result set of an inner join. The result is the same as the result of the query shown in Listing 2.61.

```
SELECT A.TRANS_NO,A.DEP_ID,A.USER_ID,B.TRANS_DATE,B.PROD_ID,B.SALES_NET
FROM TRANS_HDR A
FULL OUTER JOIN TRANS_DTL B
ON A.TRANS_NO=B.TRANS_NO
UNION ALL
SELECT A.TRANS_NO,A.DEP_ID,A.USER_ID,B.TRANS_DATE,B.PROD_ID,B.SALES_NET
FROM TRANS_HDR A
JOIN TRANS_DTL B
ON A.TRANS_NO=B.TRANS_NO;
```
Listing 2.61 Query to Union a Full Outer Join and an Inner Join

In the result set, each of the records for the inner join results appears twice. Based on these findings, the correct approach must first union the results of the left outer join and right outer join. Then, you need to remove the results of the inner join. You can achieve this with the query shown in Listing 2.62.

```
SELECT A.TRANS_NO,A.DEP_ID,A.USER_ID,B.TRANS_DATE,B.PROD_ID,B.SALES_NET
FROM TRANS_HDR A
LEFT OUTER JOIN TRANS_DTL B
ON A.TRANS_NO=B.TRANS_NO
UNION ALL
SELECT A.TRANS_NO,A.DEP_ID,A.USER_ID,B.TRANS_DATE,B.PROD_ID,B.SALES_NET
FROM TRANS_HDR A
RIGHT OUTER JOIN TRANS_DTL B
ON·A.TRANS_NO=B.TRANS_NO
MINUS
SELECT A.TRANS_NO,A.DEP_ID,A.USER_ID,B.TRANS_DATE,B.PROD_ID,B.SALES_NET
FROM TRANS_HDR A
JOIN TRANS_DTL B
ON A.TRANS_NO=B.TRANS_NO;
```
Listing 2.62 Query of a Left Outer Join Unioned to a Right Outer Join Minus the Inner Join

However, the MINUS operator removes all the records that match the inner join. Because there are two copies of the inner join results, both copies are removed, which is not what we want. Therefore, we need to approach the problem from a different angle.

What you need in your analysis is SUM(SALES_NET) and COUNT(*). Your objective is to provide accurate aggregation results on every level. Instead of making the query return exactly the same records on the detail level, you can make it return the same result on the aggregation level by running the query shown in Listing 2.63.

```
SELECT A.TRANS_NO,A.DEP_ID,A.USER_ID,B.TRANS_DATE,B.PROD_ID,B.SALES_
NET,1 C
FROM TRANS_HDR A
LEFT OUTER JOIN TRANS_DTL B
ON A.TRANS_NO=B.TRANS_NO
UNION ALL
SELECT A.TRANS_NO,A.DEP_ID,A.USER_ID,B.TRANS_DATE,B.PROD_ID,B.SALES_
NET,1 C
FROM TRANS_HDR A
RIGHT OUTER JOIN TRANS_DTL B
ON A.TRANS_NO=B.TRANS_NO
UNION ALL
SELECT A.TRANS_NO,A.DEP_ID,A.USER_ID,B.TRANS_DATE,B.PROD_ID,-B.SALES_
NET, -1 C
FROM TRANS_HDR A
```

```
JOIN TRANS_DTL B
ON A.TRANS_NO=B.TRANS_NO;
```
Listing 2.63 Union of a Left Outer Join, Right Outer Join, and Inner Join, with Negative Measure Values on an Inner Join

An additional column C in the query is used to represent the count, and you then use SUM(C) to substitute for COUNT(*). The value of C is 1 for the left outer join and right outer join and -1 for the inner join. When you aggregate at any level, the sum of the left and right outer join results will have the sum of the inner join results subtracted, which means that among the two copies of inner join results, one copy will be removed. The final result will be the same as for a full outer join.

For SALES_NET, use the formula of -SALES_NET on the inner join result. Here as well, when you aggregate the column, one of two copies of the inner join results will be removed.

As shown in Figure 2.21, in the calculation view you can create three join nodes: one each for the left outer join, right outer join, and inner join. You can also create a calculated column C on the left outer join node and the right outer join node and set the value to 1. On the inner join node, set the value of C to -1. You can also create a calculated column SALES_NET_N in the inner join node and set the formula as -SALES_NET.

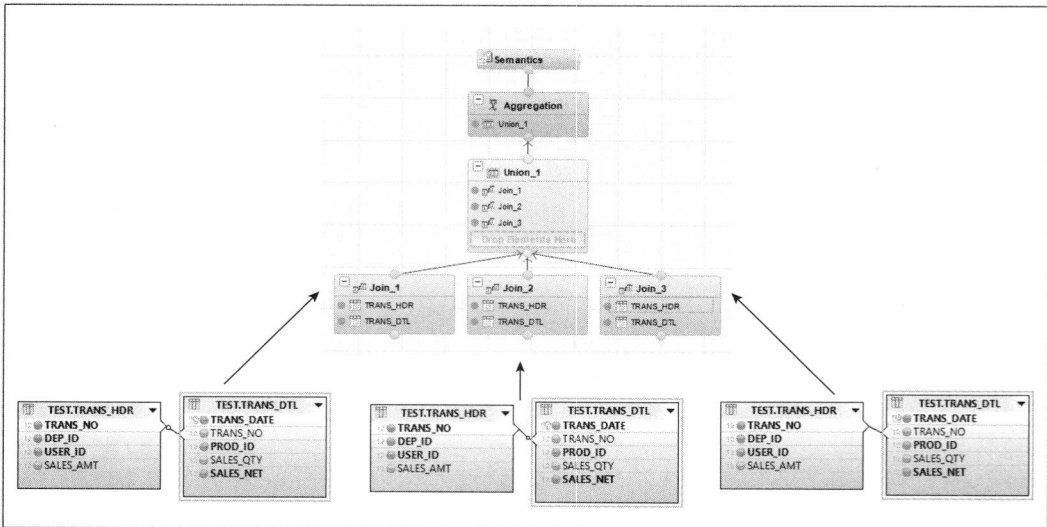

Figure 2.21 Calculation View to Make a Full Outer Join

At the union node, map column C from the three join nodes (see Figure 2.22). Then, map the SALES_NET_N column of the inner join node to the SALE_NET column of the left outer and right outer join nodes.

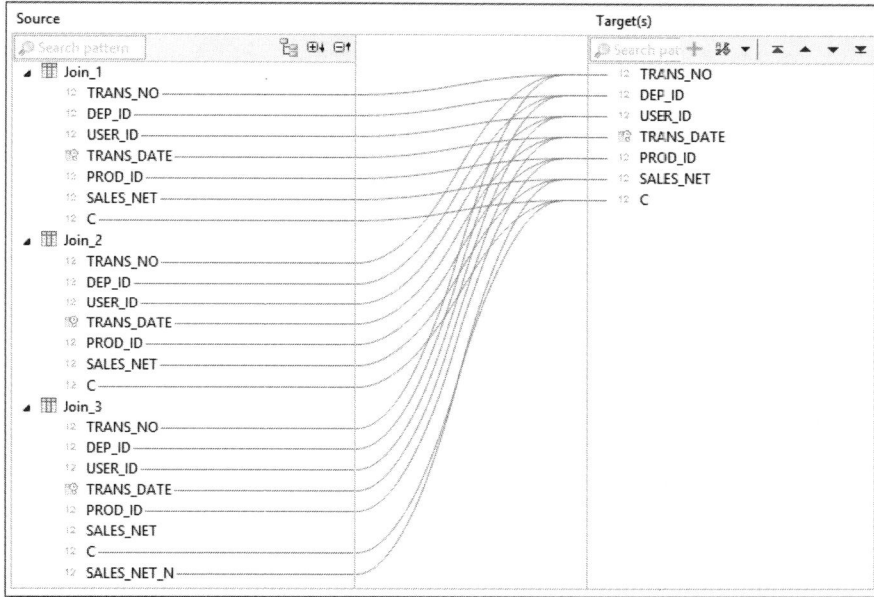

Figure 2.22 Union Node Definition

You can calculate the aggregation on any level, and it will return the correct result of the full outer join (see Listing 2.64).

```
SELECT DEP_ID,SUM(SALES_NET),SUM(C)
FROM _SYS_BIC."test/CA_FULL_OUTER"
GROUP BY DEP_ID;
```

Listing 2.64 Query Against the Calculation View for the Full Outer Join

In this query, SUM(C) replaces COUNT(*). If you need COUNT DISTINCT at a given column, no substitution is needed. See the following example:

```
SELECT DEP_ID,SUM(SALES_NET),SUM(C),COUNT(DISTINCT USER_ID)
FROM _SYS_BIC."test/CA_FULL_OUTER" GROUP BY DEP_ID;
```

2.9   Making Dynamic Queries in a Stored Procedure

We usually avoid adding dynamic queries in stored procedures for performance and security reasons. However, there are times when you may need to construct queries dynamically in a stored procedure based on input variables or intermediate results. In this section, we will explain some approaches for making a query dynamic without using dynamic SQL. The approaches we will look at include:

► Changing tables dynamically
► Changing filters dynamically
► Changing output columns dynamically

2.9.1   Changing Tables Dynamically

You can change tables dynamically by using input variables to assign tables or control the table selection. For the first example, suppose you want to use an input variable to control the stored procedure to select either table FACT_1 or table FACT_2. You can use an IF/THEN statement in the store procedure to switch the execution path (see Listing 2.65).

```
CREATE PROCEDURE DYNAMIC1(IN V VARCHAR(10))
LANGUAGE SQLSCRIPT
AS
BEGIN
IF :V='FACT_1' THEN
 SELECT DEP_ID,PROD_ID,SUM(SALES_NET) SALES
 FROM FACT_1
 GROUP BY DEP_ID,PROD_ID;
ELSE
 SELECT DEP_ID,PROD_ID,SUM(SALES_NET) SALES
 FROM FACT_2
 GROUP BY DEP_ID,PROD_ID;
END IF;
END;
```

Listing 2.65 Stored Procedure to Switch Tables Based on Input Variables

Pass the name of the table into the input variable when you run the stored procedure:

```
CALL DYNAMIC1('FACT_1');
```

The IF/THEN clause might be slower than a pure SQL query, but you can remove it and use UNION to link multiple execution paths (see Listing 2.66).

```
CREATE PROCEDURE DYNAMIC2(IN V VARCHAR(10))
LANGUAGE SQLSCRIPT
AS
BEGIN
SELECT DEP_ID,PROD_ID,SUM(SALES_NET) SALES
FROM FACT_1
WHERE :V='FACT_1'
GROUP BY DEP_ID,PROD_ID
UNION ALL
SELECT DEP_ID,PROD_ID,SUM(SALES_NET) SALES
FROM FACT_2
WHERE :V='FACT_2'
GROUP BY DEP_ID,PROD_ID;
END;
```
Listing 2.66 Stored Procedure to Switch Tables without IF/THEN Operator

In the stored procedure DYNAMIC2, you will use UNION ALL to link the two queries. In each query, use a filter to check the value of the input variable. If it points to the table, run the query; otherwise, skip the query.

You can also use a table variable and make the tables themselves dynamic in the stored procedure (see Listing 2.67).

```
CREATE PROCEDURE DYNAMIC3(
IN V TABLE(TRANS_DATE DATE,
  TRANS_NO BIGINT,
  DEP_ID INTEGER,
  PROD_TYPE INTEGER,
  USER_ID INTEGER,
  PROD_ID INTEGER,
  SALES_NET DECIMAL(18,2)) )
LANGUAGE SQLSCRIPT
AS
BEGIN
SELECT DEP_ID,PROD_ID,SUM(SALES_NET) SALES
FROM :V
GROUP BY DEP_ID,PROD_ID;
END;
```
Listing 2.67 Stored Procedure to Use Table Variables

When you call a stored procedure with the table name as the input variable, the table itself can be referred to within the script in the stored procedure. You can pass not only the table or view names but also the table variables if you call the procedure inside another procedure. Next, let's see how to make a filter dynamic.

2.9.2 Changing Filters Dynamically

In this section, we will look at the steps involved in changing filters dynamically within stored procedures.

You can create a sample stored procedure, DYNAMIC4, to filter on DEP_ID, PROD_ID, and USER_ID (see Listing 2.68).

```
CREATE PROCEDURE DYNAMIC4(IN V_DEP_ID INT, IN V_PROD_ID INT, IN V_USER_
ID INT)
LANGUAGE SQLSCRIPT
AS
BEGIN
SELECT PROD_TYPE,SUM(SALES_NET) SALE
FROM FACT_1
WHERE DEP_ID=:V_DEP_ID
AND PROD_ID=:V_PROD_ID
AND USER_ID=:V_USER_ID
GROUP BY PROD_TYPE;
END;
```

Listing 2.68 Stored Procedure to Use Input Variables as Filters

When you execute the stored procedure, you have to pass the values of all three columns. To make filters dynamic, you can enable a filter or disable a filter. In addition, you can use certain values (e.g., NULL) in the input variable to disable the filter on the corresponding column and use other values to enable the filter. To make it work, you can use the OR operator in the WHERE clause (see Listing 2.69).

```
CREATE PROCEDURE DYNAMIC5(IN V_DEP_ID INT, IN V_PROD_ID INT, IN V_USER_
ID INT)
LANGUAGE SQLSCRIPT
AS
BEGIN
SELECT PROD_TYPE,SUM(SALES_NET) SALE
FROM FACT_1
WHERE (:V_DEP_ID IS NULL OR DEP_ID=:V_DEP_ID)
AND (:V_PROD_ID IS NULL OR PROD_ID=:V_PROD_ID)
AND (:V_USER_ID IS NULL OR USER_ID=:V_USER_ID)
GROUP BY PROD_TYPE;
END;
```

Listing 2.69 Stored Procedure to Make a Filter Dynamic

If you do not want to filter on USER_ID, then you can pass the NULL value into the input variable V_USER_ID when executing the stored procedure. See the following example:

```
CALL DYNAMIC5(1,1,NULL);
```

In addition to using the OR operator, the input variable can be optional when calling a stored procedure. You can set an optional default value for the input variable. For this stored procedure, if you want the query to omit the filter when no value is passed to the input variable, you can write it as shown in Listing 2.70.

```
CREATE PROCEDURE DYNAMIC6(IN V_DEP_ID INT DEFAULT NULL, IN V_PROD_
ID INT DEFAULT NULL, IN V_USER_ID INT DEFAULT NULL)
LANGUAGE SQLSCRIPT
AS
BEGIN
SELECT PROD_TYPE,SUM(SALES_NET) SALE
FROM FACT_1
WHERE (:V_DEP_ID IS NULL OR DEP_ID=:V_DEP_ID)
AND (:V_PROD_ID IS NULL OR PROD_ID=:V_PROD_ID)
AND (:V_USER_ID IS NULL OR USER_ID=:V_USER_ID)
GROUP BY PROD_TYPE;
END;
```
Listing 2.70 Stored Procedure with Optional Input Variables

Then, you can call the stored procedure to pass the value with the token => to the columns that want filtered and skip the columns that you do not want filtered— for example:

```
CALL DYNAMIC6(V_DEP=>1,V_USER=>12);
```

In addition to using the OR operator, SAP HANA provides an APPLY_FILTER function to achieve a more flexible filter logic, as shown in Listing 2.71.

```
CREATE PROCEDURE DYNAMIC7(IN V_FILTER VARCHAR(100))
LANGUAGE SQLSCRIPT
AS
BEGIN
T=APPLY_FILTER(FACT_1,:V_FILTER);
SELECT PROD_TYPE,SUM(SALES_NET) SALE
FROM :T
GROUP BY PROD_TYPE;
END;
```
Listing 2.71 Stored Procedure to Use APPLY_FILTER Function

You can pass complex filters through the variable V_FILTER when you call the stored procedure—for example:

```
CALL DYNAMIC7('USER_ID BETWEEN 1 AND 40000 AND PROD_ID<20');
```

So far, you have learned how to change tables and filters dynamically. Next, let's look at how to change output columns dynamically.

2.9.3 Changing Output Columns Dynamically

Suppose you want to aggregate dynamically on the dimension levels specified by input variables. For the tables in the previous examples, you have three input variables: V_DEP_ID, V_PROD_ID, and V_USER_ID. You need to set the input variables to Y or N to control the output on whether to include the column (see Listing 2.72).

```
CREATE PROCEDURE DYNAMIC8(IN V_DEP_ID CHAR(1), IN V_PROD_
ID CHAR(1), IN V_USER_ID CHAR(1))
LANGUAGE SQLSCRIPT
AS
BEGIN
SELECT DEP_ID,PROD_ID,USER_ID,SUM(SALES) SALES
FROM
(
SELECT TOP 1000000000000
CASE WHEN :V_DEP_ID='Y' THEN DEP_ID ELSE NULL END DEP_ID,
CASE WHEN :V_PROD_ID='Y' THEN PROD_ID ELSE NULL END PROD_ID,
CASE WHEN :V_USER_ID='Y' THEN USER_ID ELSE NULL END USER_ID,
SALES
FROM (
SELECT  DEP_ID,PROD_ID,USER_ID,SUM(SALES_NET) SALES
FROM FACT_1
GROUP BY DEP_ID,PROD_ID,USER_ID
)
)
GROUP BY DEP_ID,PROD_ID,USER_ID;
END;
```
Listing 2.72 Stored Procedure to Make Output Columns Dynamic

In the stored procedure, for the first aggregate at the lowest level, and then based on the input variables, change the values of the dimensions that are not chosen to NULL; finally, aggregate on all the dimensions. When a dimension's value is NULL, the aggregation group by this dimension will be neglected, so the output will have actual values on the dimensions that are chosen and null values on the dimensions not chosen. TOP 1000000000000 at the inner query is for performance tuning; performance is poor without this trick. We will explain its usage in more detail in Chapter 3, Section 3.5.

2.10   Showing History Records Side By Side

When comparing data between current periods and periods of the previous years, it is not uncommon to want this data shown side by side in a report. In this section, we will describe the implementation for this specific logic. Again, we are using the table Trans_dtl, which you created with the script in Listing 2.34, and assuming you are going to generate the report shown in Table 2.16.

Month	Sales	Sales_Year-1	Sales_Year-2
01	213.23	234.23	244.3
02	313.23	224.23	248.3
03	453.23	444.23	334.3
04	243.23	254.23	274.3
05	213.23	274.23	144.3
06	223.23	234.23	224.3
07	273.23	264.23	274.32
08	213.23	234.23	244.3
09	213.23	211.23	244.32
10	213.23	222.23	244.31
11	23.23	56.23	244.33
12	23.23	674.23	244.38

Table 2.16 Output of History Comparison

It is not difficult to generate a report for any single year. For example, you can run the query specifically for the year 2014, as in Listing 2.73.

```
SELECT MONTH,SUM(SALES_NET) SALES
FROM _SYS_BIC."test/AN_TRANS"
WHERE YEAR=2014
GROUP BY MONTH;
```
Listing 2.73 Query to Show Result in Current Year

To combine the results from previous years, typically you have to run an analytic view three times and then union the results in a calculation view.

In the calculation view shown in Figure 2.23, there are three aggregation nodes. Each returns the aggregation result group by YEAR and MONTH. Aggregation_1 is for the current year, aggregation_2 is for the year before (create a YEAR1 calculated column with formula YEAR+1), and aggregation_3 is for two years before we created the YEAR2 calculated column with the formula YEAR+2. At the union node, we mapped YEAR1 and YEAR2 to the output column YEAR0 at aggregation_1 and created separate SALES_NET targets from the three aggregation nodes.

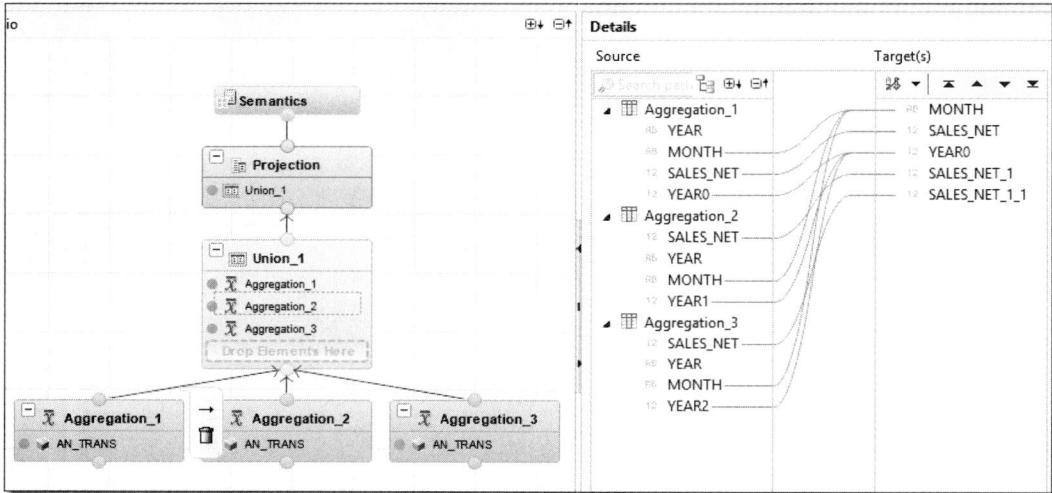

Figure 2.23 Calculation View to Union Result Sets

Run the query shown in Listing 2.74 to generate the report.

```
SELECT MONTH,SUM(SALES_NET),SUM(SALES_NET_1),SUM(SALES_NET_2)
FROM _SYS_BIC."test/CA_HISTORY1"
WHERE YEAR=2014
GROUP BY MONTH ;
```

Listing 2.74 Query to Show History Results Side by Side Against the Calculation View

In the query, specify the value of the year as 2014. On the node aggregation_1, the filter is YEAR=2014, which returns records in 2014. On the node for aggregation_2, the filter is YEAR+1=2014, which returns records in 2013. On the node for aggregation_3, the filter is YEAR+2=2014, which returns records in 2012. Therefore, you can see the records of 2014, 2013, and 2012 side by side in the output.

Instead of using a union, you also can construct the logic with a join (see Listing 2.75).

```
SELECT A.MONTH,A.SALES,B.SALES,C.SALES
FROM
(SELECT YEAR,MONTH,SUM(SALES_NET) SALES
FROM _SYS_BIC."test/AN_TRANS"
GROUP BY YEAR,MONTH) A
LEFT OUTER JOIN (SELECT YEAR,MONTH,SUM(SALES_NET) SALES
FROM _SYS_BIC."test/AN_TRANS"
GROUP BY YEAR,MONTH) B
ON A.YEAR=B.YEAR+1 AND A.MONTH=B.MONTH
LEFT OUTER JOIN (SELECT YEAR,MONTH,SUM(SALES_NET) SALES
FROM _SYS_BIC."test/AN_TRANS"
GROUP BY YEAR,MONTH) C
ON A.YEAR=C.YEAR+2
AND A.MONTH=C.MONTH
WHERE A.YEAR=2014;
```
Listing 2.75 SQL Query to Show History Results Side by Side

When you need the report on a daily basis, someone might try the query shown in Listing 2.76.

```
SELECT A.DATE_SQL,A.SALES,B.SALES,C.SALES
FROM
(SELECT DATE_SQL,SUM(SALES_NET) SALES
FROM _SYS_BIC."test/AN_TRANS"
GROUP BY DATE_SQL) A
LEFT OUTER JOIN (SELECT DATE_SQL,SUM(SALES_NET) SALES
FROM _SYS_BIC."test/AN_TRANS"
GROUP BY DATE_SQL) B
ON A.DATE_SQL=ADD_YEARS(B.DATE_SQL,1)
LEFT OUTER JOIN (SELECT DATE_SQL,SUM(SALES_NET) SALES
FROM _SYS_BIC."test/AN_TRANS"
GROUP BY DATE_SQL) C
ON A.DATE_SQL=ADD_YEARS(C.DATE_SQL,2)
WHERE A.DATE_SQL BETWEEN '2014-01-01' AND '2015-01-01';
```
Listing 2.76 Query to Show History Results Side by Side on a Daily Easis

Unfortunately, there is a bug in the preceding query. Because 2012 is a leap year, the expression ADD_YEARS('2012-02-29',2) and ADD_YEARS('2012-02-28',2) both point to 2014-02-28. As a result, when one record at 2014-02-28 on the first data set joins to two records on the third data set, the record is duplicated, and thus the query will produce the wrong result.

In addition to containing a bug in the join, the preceding query is not very efficient; you have to browse the analytic view three times to get the result from the three years. Therefore, let's try a different approach that allows us to run the analytic view only once. You can use calculated columns to define the measures for the current year and previous years (see Figure 2.24).

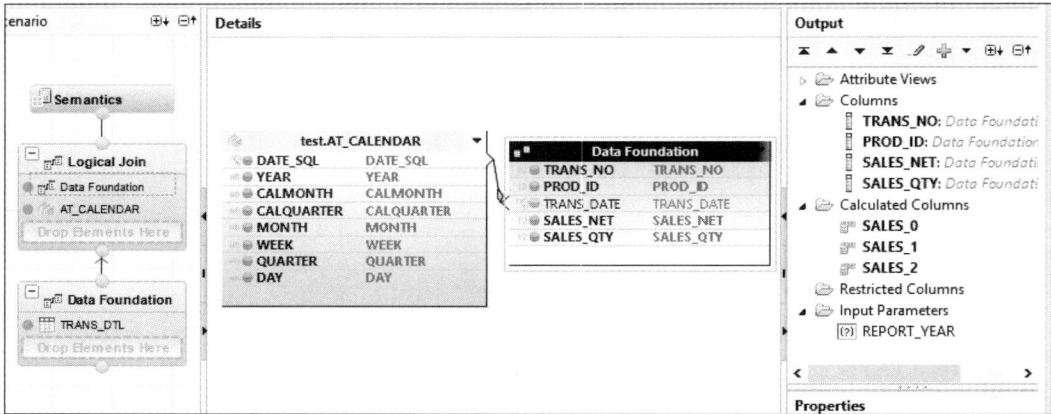

Figure 2.24 Analytic View with Calculated Columns for History Records

In an analytic view, you can create the input parameter REPORT_YEAR, which will set the value as a report year. You can then create two additional calculated measures to differentiate the measures from the report year: one year before, two years before (see Listing 2.77).

```
SALES_0→IF(INT("YEAR")=$$REPORT_YEAR$$,"SALES_NET",NULL)
SALES_1→IF(INT("YEAR")=$$REPORT_YEAR$$-1,"SALES_NET",NULL)
SALES_2→IF(INT("YEAR")=$$REPORT_YEAR$$-2,"SALES_NET",NULL)
```
Listing 2.77 Formulas for Calculated Columns for SALES_NET in Different Years

Then, run the following query for reporting on a monthly basis (see Listing 2.78).

```
SELECT MONTH,SUM(SALES_0),SUM(SALES_1),SUM(SALES_2)
FROM _SYS_BIC."test/AN_TRANS_HIST"
(PLACEHOLDER."$$REPORT_YEAR$$"=> '2014')
GROUP BY MONTH;
```
Listing 2.78 Query to Show History Results Side by Side Against an Analytic View

If you want the report on a daily basis, run the query shown in Listing 2.79. For this query, also add a filter on the date range to return the records within these three years for performance reasons.

```
SELECT MONTH,DAY,SUM(SALES_0),SUM(SALES_1),SUM(SALES_2)
FROM _SYS_BIC."test/AN_TRANS_HIST"
(PLACEHOLDER."$$REPORT_YEAR$$"=> '2014')
WHERE DATE_SQL BETWEEN '2012-01-01' AND '2014-12-31'
GROUP BY MONTH,DAY;
```
Listing 2.79 Query to Show History Results Side by Side on a Daily Basis

With calculated columns, you have a lot of flexibility to define formulas. For example, when using a fiscal calendar instead of a Gregorian calendar, one year will have 52 weeks, and the other year will have 53 weeks. To find the current year, first create a DAY1 calculated column that points to January 2 of the current year:

```
DAY1 → date(string(component(now(),1))+'-01-02')
```

Then, define the YEARBEGIN calculated column which is relies on the weekday of DAY1:

```
YEARBEGIN → if( weekday("DAY1")<4,adddays("DAY1",-weekday ("DAY1")
-1), adddays("DAY1",-weekday ("DAY1")+7-1))
```

To find the beginning of the year of previous year, first create a DAY1_1 calculated column that points to January 2 of the previous year:

```
DAY1_1 → date(string(component(now(),1)-1)+'-01-02')
```

Then, define the PREYEARBEGIN calculated column which is relies on the weekday of DAY1_1.

```
PREYEARBEGIN → if( weekday("DAY1_1")<4,
adddays ("DAY1_1",-weekday ("DAY1_1")-1),
adddays("DAY1_1",-weekday("DAY1_1")+7-1))
```
Listing 2.80 Formulas to Calculate Previous Fiscal Year Start

The number of days between a day of the current year and the corresponding day of the previous year is as follows:

```
PREYEARDAYS → daysbetween("PREYEARBEGIN","YEARBEGIN")
```

Different companies will have different fiscal years. As such, formulas will need to be adjusted to accommodate for these differences. As long as the logic can be put into a calculated column, you can make models work efficiently.

2.11   Sample Data

Sometimes, you need perform a rough analysis based on partial data, which requires retrieving some sample data. In this section, we will identify the different approaches that can be used to retrieve sample data. These include:

▶ Using the RAND() value
▶ Using $rowid$
▶ Using identity columns
▶ Using the LIMIT/OFFSET feature
▶ Using the TABLESAMPLE SYSTEM feature

2.11.1   Using RAND()

The first approach for retrieving sample data is to make a filter based on the function RAND()—for example:

```
SELECT * FROM FACT_1 WHERE RAND()<0.1;
```

When running the query, the value of RAND() will be generated at each record; the value's range is from 0 to 1, so it returns 10% of records based on the filter RAND()<0.1. Each time you run the query, it might return a different result set. However, because the formula is at the row level, the performance of this query is not good.

2.11.2   Using $rowid$

Each table in SAP HANA has a hidden $rowid$ column, on which you can add a filter to return a subset of the table—for example:

```
SELECT * FROM FACT_1 WHERE "$rowid$" <100000;
```

If you want to select a different subset, adjust the filter scope:

```
SELECT * FROM FACT_1 WHERE "$rowid$" BETWEEN 100000 AND 200000;
```

The value of the $rowid$ column is related to the partition ID. For a table without a partition, the value ranges from 1 to 18014398509481984. On a partitioned table, the value for partition 1 starts at 18014398509481985; partition 2 starts at 36028797018963969; partition 3 starts at 54043195528445953; and so on.

If you want to find out the partition ID of a record, use the formula TO_ INT(("$rowid$"-1) /18014398509481984). If you want to retrieve records on a particular partition—for example, partition 3—apply a filter on the $rowid$ as follows:

```
SELECT * FROM FACT_2 WHERE "$rowid$" between 18014398509481984*3+1
and 18014398509481984*4;
```

It is important to know that querying on the hidden $rowid$ column is not officially supported by SAP. Therefore, this option is to be used with caution and at your own risk. Also, due to triggering some internal processes, you will incur a performance penalty on queries that contain the hidden column. In general, it is better to choose features that SAP HANA officially supports.

2.11.3 Using Identity Columns

Next, let's try to use an identity column for data sampling. *Identity columns* are columns with autoincremented values (e.g., 1, 2, 3, 4). You can create an identity column on the table from which you want to retrieve sample records, as follows:

```
ALTER TABLE FACT_1 ADD(ID BIGINT GENERATED ALWAYS AS IDENTITY);
```

This generates a distinct number for each record, and you can perform data sampling with the following query:

```
SELECT * FROM FACT_1 WHERE ID<100000;
```

If you want to switch to a different subset, adjust the filter range:

```
SELECT * FROM FACT_1 WHERE ID BETWEEN 100001 AND 200000;
```

You can also make advanced configurations on the identity column; the syntax of its parameter is shown in Listing 2.81.

```
START WITH <start_value>
 | INCREMENT BY <increment_value>
 | MAXVALUE <max_value>
 | NO MAXVALUE
 | MINVALUE <min_value>
 | NO MINVALUE
 | CYCLE
 | NO CYCLE
 | CACHE <cache_size>
 | NO CACHE
```

Listing 2.81 Syntax for Identity Column

For example, if you want the identity number to be cycled for every 10 records, run the following statement:

```
ALTER TABLE FACT_
2 ADD(ID BIGINT GENERATED ALWAYS AS IDENTITY (START WITH 1 MAXVALUE 10
CYCLE));
```

Then, you can retrieve 10% of the records with the following query:

```
SELECT * FROM FACT_2 WHERE ID=1;
```

2.11.4 Using LIMIT/OFFSET

You can also perform data sampling with the LIMIT/OFFSET feature. The syntax is very simple:

```
SELECT * FROM FACT_1
LIMIT 100000 OFFSET 500000;
```

This query returns the 100,000 records from 500,001 to 600,000. If you create an identity column on the table, you do not guarantee that the query will return the values from 500,001 to 600,000, especially for a partitioned table. When you want to switch to a different subset, adjust the OFFSET value. One limitation of this approach is that you can only specify one record range in the query.

2.11.5 Using the TABLESAMPLE SYSTEM

As of SPS 9, SAP HANA has provided a feature called TABLESAMPLE SYSTEM (), which allows you to set a value from 1 to 100 to specify the percentage of records to be retrieved from a table. For example, to retrieve 10% of records, run the follow query:

```
SELECT COUNT(*) FROM FACT_1 TABLESAMPLE SYSTEM(10);
```

Instead of a row-by-row comparison using a mathematical calculation, the TABLE-SAMPLE SYSTEM() feature is handled by the SAP HANA engine directly, resulting in good sampling performance.

So far, we have described several approaches for data sampling in SAP HANA. There are some differences in the results; the RAND() and TABLESAMPLE SYSTEM() approaches are similar to each other in results, because both select random records. The $rowid$, identity column, and LIMIT/OFFSET approaches are also similar to one another, because they select fixed record sets. Based on your requirements, you must determine which approach is more appropriate for your needs.

2.12   Using a Vertical Union to Join Tables

When two tables have the same row count and a one-to-one relation between their records, you can use a vertical union to join them. In this section, we explain how to use a vertical union in detail.

Suppose you want to perform a join between the tables TRANS_DTL and TAX_DTL (see Listing 2.82).

```
SELECT A.TRANS_DATE,A.TRANS_NO,A.PROD_ID,A.SALES_NET,B.TAX
FROM TRANS_DTL A, TAX_DTL B
WHERE A.TRANS_DATE=B.TRANS_DATE
AND A.TRANS_NO=B.TRANS_NO
AND A.PROD_ID=B.PROD_ID;
```
Listing 2.82 Query to Join Two Tables

With a scripted calculation view and a stored procedure, you can use the calculation engine plan operators. One of the operators, CE_VERTICAL_UNION, unions not rows, but columns. Let's see its behavior with the example shown in Listing 2.83.

```
CREATE PROCEDURE VERTICAL(OUT O
TABLE(TRANS_DATE DATE,
TRANS_NO BIGINT,
SALES_NET DECIMAL(18,2),
TAX DECIMAL(18,2)
)
)
LANGUAGE SQLSCRIPT
AS
BEGIN
A=CE_COLUMN_TABLE(TRANS_DTL,[TRANS_DATE,TRANS_NO,PROD_ID,SALES_NET]);
B=CE_COLUMN_TABLE(TAX_DTL,[TRANS_DATE,TRANS_NO,PRCD_ID,TAX]);
O=CE_VERTICAL_UNION(:A,[TRANS_DATE,TRANS_NO,PROD_ID,SALES_NET],:B,[
TAX]);
END;
```
Listing 2.83 Script to Make a Vertical Union

In this stored procedure, we have merged the two tables and shown the SALES_NET and TAX columns side by side on each record. This returns the same result as the join query.

Prior to executing a vertical union, it is important that the records of the two datasets are in the same order. Therefore, before using a vertical union, you need to sort the tables (see Listing 2.84).

```
CREATE PROCEDURE VERTICAL2(OUT O
TABLE(TRANS_DATE DATE,
TRANS_NO BIGINT,
SALES_NET DECIMAL(18,2),
TAX DECIMAL(18,2)
)
)
LANGUAGE SQLSCRIPT
AS
BEGIN
A=SELECT TRANS_DATE,TRANS_NO,PROD_ID,SALES_NET FROM TRANS_
DTL ORDER BY TRANS_DATE,TRANS_NO,PROD_ID;
B=SELECT TRANS_DATE,TRANS_NO,PROD_ID,TAX FROM TAX_DTL ORDER BY TRANS_
DATE,TRANS_NO,PORD_ID;
O=CE_VERTICAL_UNION(:A,[TRANS_DATE,TRANS_NO,PROD_ID,SALES_NET],:B,[
TAX]);
END;
```
Listing 2.84 Script to Sort Tables Before Executing a Vertical Union

It is recommended not to mix SQL queries with calculation engine plan operators. Mixing calculation engine plan operators and SQL may lead to missed opportunities for applying optimizations, because calculation engine plan operators and SQL statements are optimized independently. This is not a strict rule, however. Sometimes, performance is even better when related steps are optimized independently. In this example, because there are no sorting functions among the calculation engine plan operators, you have to use SQL queries.

Despite its limitations, the performance of a vertical union is good—and it can also help you perform complex tasks with regular joins. In this particular example, suppose you have a transaction that contains two identical records. This is a common occurrence, as companies may sell two items of the same product within a transaction. Therefore, table TRANS_DTL has records as shown in Table 2.17.

TRANS_DATE	TRANS_NO	PROD_ID	SALES_NET
2014-01-01	234244	234	23.98
2014-01-01	234244	234	23.98

Table 2.17 Sample Records in Table TRANS_DTL

Also, table `TAX_DTL` has two identical records (see Table 2.18).

TRANS_DATE	TRANS_NO	PROD_ID	TAX
2014-01-01	234244	234	2.15
2014-01-01	234244	234	2.15

Table 2.18 Sample Records in Table TAX_DTL

When the two tables join on the `TRANS_DATE`, `TRANS_NO`, and `PROD_ID` columns, each record on the right table maps the two records in the left table. In addition, each record on the left table maps the two records in the right table. This is a many-to-many cardinality and will return four records for this transaction, which is not what you were looking for. On the contrary, when you use a vertical union to join these two tables, there are not many to many joins, and it returns the right row count.

2.13 Sorting Records

Sorting is a big topic for data analysis. In this section, we will discuss solutions for sorting in the following complex scenarios:

▶ Sorting IP addresses

▶ Sorting with exceptions

▶ Sorting based on user-defined rules

2.13.1 Sorting IP Addresses

First, let's examine the requirements for sorting IP addresses. Suppose you have a table `VISIT` that contains Internet connection details (see Listing 2.85).

```
CREATE COLUMN TABLE VISIT(
USER_NAME VARCHAR(20),
IP VARCHAR(20),
CONNCTION_DURATION INT
);
INSERT INTO VISIT VALUES('David Williams','12.234.12.32',345);
INSERT INTO VISIT VALUES('George Anderson','125.234.12.32',23);
INSERT INTO VISIT VALUES('Lucy Smith','48.124.102.16',456);
INSERT INTO VISIT VALUES('Betty Johns','234.77.132.66',35);
```

Listing 2.85 Script to Create Table VISIT

If you wanted to sort the records by IP address, you could run the following query:

```
SELECT * FROM VISIT
ORDER BY IP;
```

In Table 2.19, you can see that the record with IP address 48.124.102.16 is in the fourth position, because its first digit (4) is greater than the first digits 1, 1, and 3 of the other records. This behavior is due to the data type of the column (VARCHAR). However, you want the whole number prior to the dot to be compared, so that 48 would be compared to 12, 125, and 234; then, the current fourth record would be in the second position.

USER_NAME	IP	CONNECTION_DURATION
David Williams	12.234.12.32	345
George Anderson	125.234.12.32	23
Betty Johns	234.77.132.66	35
Lucy Smith	48.124.102.16	456

Table 2.19 Sorting Results

You need to parse the IP column into four integers and sort the records by those four integers. To perform parsing on the fly, create a user-defined function (see Listing 2.86).

```
CREATE FUNCTION PARSESTRING(SOURCE_
STR VARCHAR(500),DELIMITER CHAR(1),POSITION INT)
RETURNS RESULT VARCHAR(100)
AS
BEGIN
  DECLARE S nvarchar(500);
  DECLARE I integer;
  S := :SOURCE_STR;
  I := 1;
  WHILE :I <:POSITION DO
  S := SUBSTR_AFTER(:S,:DELIMITER);
  I:= :I + 1;
  END WHILE;
  IF LOCATE(:S,:DELIMITER) > 0 THEN
  S := SUBSTR_BEFORE(:S,:DELIMITER);
  END IF;
  RESULT:=:S;
END;
```

Listing 2.86 Function to Parse Strings

Given that a user-defined function can be shared by different queries, you should make it generic. Set three input variables: SOURCE_STR, DELIMITER, and POSITION. You can then use the function specifying a string, a delimiter, and a position, and it returns the substring, which is qualified with the appropriate criteria. Run the following query to check the parsing result:

```
SELECT PARSESTRING(IP,'.',1), PARSESTRING(IP,'.',2), PARSESTRING(IP,
'.',3),PARSESTRING(IP,'.',4) FROM VISIT;
```

In Table 2.20, the IP address of each record is parsed into four integers.

PAR..(IP,'.',1)	PAR..(IP,'.',2)	PAR..(IP,'.',3)	PAR..(IP,'.',4)
12	234	12	32
125	234	12	32
48	124	102	16
234	77	132	66

Table 2.20 Results of PARSESTRING() Function

Based on the function result, you can run the query in Listing 2.87, and it returns the expected result.

```
SELECT *
FROM VISIT
ORDER BY
TO_INT(PARSESTRING(IP,'.',1)),TO_INT(PARSESTRING(IP,'.',2)),TO_
INT(PARSESTRING(IP,'.',3)),TO_INT(PARSESTRING(IP,'.',4));
```
Listing 2.87 Query to Sort Record Order by IP Address

In Table 2.21, the records are sorted based on the integer of the first part of the IP address. If there is duplication in the first part, then the second part will be taken into consideration, and so on for the third and fourth parts.

USER_NAME	IP	CONNECTION_DURATION
David Williams	12.234.12.32	345
Lucy Smith	48.124.102.16	456
George Anderson	125.234.12.32	23
Betty Johns	234.77.132.66	35

Table 2.21 Sorting Results Based on Parsing Function

In the query, we used the TO_INT() function to change the string to an integer. When you sort records by name, sometimes you expect them to sort by last name. Similarly, you can use the same user-defined function to achieve this logic:

```
SELECT * FROM VISIT ORDER BY
PARSESTRING(USER_NAME,' ',2)||' '||PARSESTRING(USER_NAME,' ',1);
```

In Table 2.22, the records are sorted by last name and first name, so Anderson is in the first row, Johns is in the second, Smith is in the third, and Williams is in the fourth.

USER_NAME	IP	CONNECTION_DURATION
George Anderson	125.234.12.32	23
Betty Johns	234.77.132.66	35
Lucy Smith	48.124.102.16	456
David Williams	12.234.12.32	345

Table 2.22 Sorting Results Based on Last Name

2.13.2 Sorting with Exceptions

Sometimes, you will have additional conditions when sorting. For example, a company wants to report on the top three offices, with the added condition that if the headquarters is not within the top three, then you must report on the top two offices plus the headquarters. Let's reuse the content of the previous table and assume that "George Anderson" is the name of the headquarters (see Listing 2.88).

```
SELECT * FROM VISIT
WHERE USER_NAME='George Anderson'
UNION ALL
(SELECT TOP 2 * FROM VISIT
WHERE USER_NAME<>'George Anderson'
ORDER BY CONNCTION_DURATION DESC );
```

Listing 2.88 Query to Retrieve the User-Defined Top Three Records

It is not convenient to make the logic into a graphic calculation view or analytic view, but you can use a different approach based on the expression of the order by column (see Listing 2.89).

```
SELECT TOP 3 * FROM VISIT
ORDER BY CASE WHEN USER_NAME=
'George Anderson' THEN 999999 ELSE CONNCTION_DURATION END DESC;
```
Listing 2.89 Query to Retrieve the User-Defined Top Three Records with Sorting with Expressions

In this query, you set a value on a specific record that is greater than the value on the other records and make the top three always include that specific record. This conveniently achieves the required logic with a single query.

2.13.3 Sorting with User-Defined Rules

Sometimes, you may have to deal with user-defined sorting rules, which can be more complicated when they combine different languages. Let's examine a table that contains foreign characters. Suppose you define a special sorting rule to set the character sequence as γ, α, β, δ, ε, ζ, η, θ, λ, μ. To make the sorting work, you can encode the letters with characters that can be normally sorted. For example, you can use the A, B, C, D, E, F, G, H, I, and J characters to encode the special characters. In doing this, you create the function detailed in Listing 2.90.

```
CREATE FUNCTION TRANS_CHAR(SOURCE_CHAR VARCHAR(1))
RETURNS TARGET VARCHAR(1)
AS
BEGIN
DECLARE T NVARCHAR(1) ARRAY:=
ARRAY('A','B','C','D','E','F','G','H','I','J');
DECLARE S NVARCHAR(1) ARRAY:=
ARRAY('γ','α','β','δ','ε','ζ','η','θ','λ','μ');
DECLARE I INTEGER;
I:=1;
WHILE :SOURCE_CHAR <> :S[:I] DO
I:=:I+1;
END WHILE;
TARGET:=:T[:I];
END;
```
Listing 2.90 Function to Encode a Character

This function is for single-character encoding. To encode a string, you must create another function (see Listing 2.91).

```
CREATE FUNCTION TRANS_STRING(SOURCE_STR VARCHAR(500))
RETURNS RESULT VARCHAR(500)
AS
BEGIN
  DECLARE I integer;
```

```
DECLARE L INTEGER;
L := LENGTH(:SOURCE_STR);
I :=1;
RESULT:='';
WHILE :I <= :L DO
RESULT:= :RESULT||TRANS_CHAR(SUBSTRING(:SOURCE_STR,:I,1));
I:= :I + 1;
END WHILE;
END;
```

Listing 2.91 Function to Encode a String

When using the TRANS_STRING function, the query encodes the characters of the input string one by one with the previously created TRANS_CHAR function. When you execute TRANS_STRING('γαβ'), it returns ABC. Also, you can insert the function in the ORDER BY clause to achieve sorting with a user-defined rule.

You can use user-defined functions both within ORDER BY clauses to sort records and within GROUP BY clauses to set user-defined grouping rules, or with WHERE clauses to achieve complex filters.

2.14 Finding Missing Values

Developers often encounter requirements to list the missing dates from a transaction table; for example, to list the missing numbers in a sequence. In this section, we will discuss several approaches to find missing values, including the following:

- Using the NOT IN clause
- Using a self-join
- Using a vertical union
- Using a window function

To help describe the methods, let's create a table SEQ1 with some missing values (see Listing 2.92).

```
CREATE COLUMN TABLE SEQ1(ID INT);
INSERT INTO SEQ1 VALUES (1);
INSERT INTO SEQ1 VALUES (2);
INSERT INTO SEQ1 VALUES (5);
INSERT INTO SEQ1 VALUES (7);
INSERT INTO SEQ1 VALUES (8);
```

```
INSERT INTO SEQ1 VALUES (13);
INSERT INTO SEQ1 VALUES (14);
```
Listing 2.92 Script to Create Table SEQ1

In the sections that follow, we will look at the approaches listed previously to find the missing values.

2.14.1 Using the NOT IN Clause

First, let's try the NOT IN clause approach. To apply this approach, you need a table with the full sequence. However, instead of creating the table, you can create a scripted calculation view to return continuous numbers (see Figure 2.25).

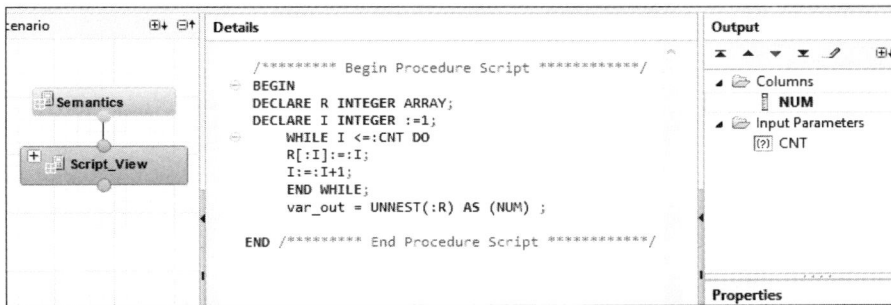

Figure 2.25 Calculation View to List Continuous Numbers

The script for this view is shown in Listing 2.93.

```
/********* Begin Procedure Script ************/
 BEGIN
 DECLARE R INTEGER ARRAY;
 DECLARE I INTEGER :=1;
   WHILE I <=:CNT DO
   R[:I]:=:I;
   I:=:I+1;
   END WHILE;
   var_out = UNNEST(:R) AS (NUM) ;
END /********* End Procedure Script ************/
```
Listing 2.93 Script of the Calculation View to Generate Continuous Numbers

The input parameter is to set the value with which you want the sequence to end. You can test the calculation view with the following query:

```
SELECT * FROM _SYS_BIC."test/CA_SEQ" (PLACEHOLDER."$$CNT$$"=> 5);
```

This query returns a list: 1, 2, 3, 4, 5. You can compare the source table with the full sequence to find out which value is not in the source table. Use the following query to perform this function:

```
SELECT NUM FROM _SYS_BIC."test/CA_SEQ" (PLACEHOLDER."$$CNT$$"=
> 14) WHERE NUM NOT IN (SELECT ID FROM SEQ1);
```

This will return seven records: 3, 4, 6, 9, 10, 11, and 12. Alternatively, you can use a NOT EXISTS clause in the query (see Listing 2.94).

```
SELECT NUM
FROM _SYS_BIC."test/CA_SEQ" (PLACEHOLDER."$$CNT$$"=> 14)
WHERE NOT EXISTS (SELECT * FROM SEQ1 WHERE ID=NUM);
```

Listing 2.94 Query to Find Missing Values with the NOT EXISTS Clause

When you check the execution plans of the preceding queries, they are actually using left outer joins in the background. To put the logic into an SQL query, see Listing 2.95.

```
SELECT NUM
FROM _SYS_BIC."test/CA_SEQ" (PLACEHOLDER."$$CNT$$"=> 14) A
LEFT OUTER JOIN SEQ1 B
ON A.NUM=B.ID
WHERE B.ID IS NULL;
```

Listing 2.95 Query to Find Missing Values with Left Outer Join

2.14.2 Using a Self-Join

Another solution to find the missing values is to compare the table to itself using a self-join (see Listing 2.96).

```
SELECT L.ID + 1 FROM_NUM, MIN(FR.ID) - 1 TO_NUM
FROM SEQ1   L
    LEFT OUTER JOIN SEQ1   R ON L.ID = R.ID - 1
    LEFT OUTER JOIN SEQ1   FR ON L.ID < FR.ID
WHERE R.ID IS NULL AND FR.ID IS NOT NULL
GROUP BY L.ID, R.ID;
```

Listing 2.96 Query to Find Missing Values with a Self-Join

There are two left outer joins in this query. The left outer join's join condition is L.ID=R.ID-1, and the filter is R.ID IS NULL. This is used to find the missing continuous number in the table and to make L.ID+1 the starting number of the range of missing numbers. The second left outer join's join condition is L.ID<FR.ID, and the filter is FR.ID IS NOT NULL. This retrieves the numbers existing in the table that are greater than the number that does not have continuous numbering. When the result set is grouped by L.ID, R.ID, MIN(FR.ID),-1 becomes the end number in the range of missing numbers. When you run the query, it returns three ranges: (3,4), (6,6), and (9,12).

2.14.3   Using a Vertical Union

The query of a self-join is a bit complex. As we previously introduced, you can substitute a vertical union for a join, and instead of comparing the values on the sequence, you can compare the values between adjacent records (see Listing 2.97).

```
CREATE PROCEDURE P_MISSING (OUT O TABLE(NUM_FROM INT,NUM_TO INT))
LANGUAGE SQLSCRIPT
AS
BEGIN
B=(SELECT ID "ID1" FROM SEQ1 ORDER BY ID) UNION ALL SELECT NULL "ID1"
FROM DUMMY;
A=SELECT NULL "ID" FROM DUMMY UNION ALL (SELECT "ID" FROM SEQ1
ORDER BY ID);
C=CE_VERTICAL_UNION(:A,["ID"],:B,["ID1"]);
D=CE_PROJECTION(:C,["ID","ID1",CE_CALC('"ID"+1',INT) AS NUM_FROM,CE_
CALC('"ID1"-1',INT) AS NUM_TO]);
O=CE_PROJECTION(:D,["NUM_FROM","NUM_TO"],'"NUM_FROM" <= "NUM_TO"');
END;
```
Listing 2.97 Query to Find Missing Values with a Vertical Join

To call the procedure, execute the following:

```
CALL P_MISSING(?);
```

As there is no join and no aggregation in the script, a vertical union approach can be more efficient than the self-join approach.

2.14.4   Using Window Functions

For this particular case, you can also try a window function. Simply run the query in Listing 2.98 to get the same result.

```
SELECT ID+1 FROM_NUM,ID2-1 TO_NUM
FROM (
SELECT ID,LEAD(ID) OVER (ORDER BY ID) ID2
```

```
FROM SEQ1)
WHERE ID+1<> ID2;
```
Listing 2.98 Query to Find Missing Values with a Window Function

The window function first sorts by ID and then compares the values between the adjacent records. If the gap is greater than 1, there are missing values, and the range is from the value ID+1 of the current record to the value ID-1 of the next record.

In addition to the examples shown here, window functions can solve many other complex problems via simple SQL queries instead of complex stored procedures. The next section discusses these solutions in further detail.

2.15 Using Window Functions for Complex Grouping

When you slice data by grouping on one dimension and at the same time make special groups by setting date ranges based on certain rules, graphical models are not enough to fulfill your needs. Instead, you have to use window functions in the query.

To better understand how window functions can be used in this scenario, let's look at a complex requirement: You need to group data based on the Product ID, Date, and Price_version, and you also need to check each row in a table to see if that particular product has a different range of values for Price_version when compared to the rows below. If yes, then you insert that date where a different range is encountered into the TO_Date column. If no change is detected, then you insert a future date of 2100-01-01. In the Total column, place the sum of Sales_count for the given From_Date/To_Date group. To create the test scenario, execute the statements shown in Listing 2.98.

```
CREATE TABLE TRANS_2(
Product_ID INT,
DT DATE,
Price_version INT,
Sales_count INT);
INSERT INTO TRANS_2 VALUES (22,'2010-04-05',5,100);
INSERT INTO TRANS_2 VALUES (22,'2010-04-06',5,80);
INSERT INTO TRANS_2 VALUES (22,'2010-04-07',4,50);
INSERT INTO TRANS_2 VALUES (22,'2010-04-08',5,60);
```

```
INSERT INTO TRANS_2 VALUES (22,'2010-04-09',5,40);
INSERT INTO TRANS_2 VALUES (22,'2010-04-10',5,70);
INSERT INTO TRANS_2 VALUES (22,'2010-04-11',20,300);
INSERT INTO TRANS_2 VALUES (22,'2010-04-12',5,55);
INSERT INTO TRANS_2 VALUES (22,'2010-04-14',5,75);
INSERT INTO TRANS_2 VALUES (22,'2010-04-15',10,150);
INSERT INTO TRANS_2 VALUES (22,'2010-04-16',5,30);
INSERT INTO TRANS_2 VALUES (22,'2010-04-17',5,95);
INSERT INTO TRANS_2 VALUES (22,'2010-04-19',5,60);
```

Listing 2.99 Script to Create Table TRANS_2

The table TRANS_2 has the records listed in Table 2.23.

Product_ID	DT	Price_version	Sales_count
22	Apr 5, 2010	5	100
22	Apr 6, 2010	5	80
22	Apr 7, 2010	4	50
22	Apr 8, 2010	5	60
22	Apr 9, 2010	5	40
22	Apr 10, 2010	5	70
22	Apr 11, 2010	20	300
22	Apr 12, 2010	5	55
22	Apr 14, 2010	5	75
22	Apr 15, 2010	10	150
22	Apr 16, 2010	5	30
22	Apr 17, 2010	5	95
22	Apr 19, 2010	5	60

Table 2.23 Records of the Source Table

This scenario requires you to group the price version along with the date sequence. For example, the records at 2010-04-05 and 2010-04-06 have the same value of PRICE_version and need to be grouped together, but the record at 2010-04-08 cannot be grouped with them even though it has the same value of PRICE_version, because it is blocked by the record on 2010-04-07, which has a different value of PRICE_version. The expected output is shown in Table 2.24.

Product_ID	Price_version	FROM_DATE	TO_DATE	TOTAL
22	5	Apr 5, 2010	Apr 6, 2010	180
22	4	Apr 7, 2010	Apr 7, 2010	50
22	5	Apr 8, 2010	Apr 10, 2010	170
22	20	Apr 11, 2010	Apr 11, 2010	300
22	5	Apr 12, 2010	Apr 14, 2010	130
22	10	Apr 15, 2010	Apr 15, 2010	150
22	5	Apr 16, 2010	Jan 1, 2100	185

Table 2.24 Expected Output

When dealing with such complex logic, approach the process on a step-by-step basis. With each step, you achieve a part of the requirement. For the first step, run a query that returns the value of Price_version side by side with the value of the next record. Use the window function LEAD() to retrieve the data from the subsequent record (see Listing 2.100).

```
SELECT Product_ID,DT,Price_version,
LEAD(Price_version) OVER (PARTITION BY Product_ID ORDER BY DT) P2,
SUM(Sales_count)  Sales_count
FROM TRANS_2
GROUP BY Product_ID,DT,Price_version;
```

Listing 2.100 Query to Retrieve the Value of Price_version from the Adjacent Record

You can see the result set in Table 2.25. For each value of Price_version, there is a value in the P2 column to show the subsequent price version. For the last record, there is no subsequent price version, so there is a null value in the P2 column.

Product_ID	DT	Price_version	P2	Sales_count
22	Apr 5, 2010	5	5	100
22	Apr 6, 2010	5	4	80
22	Apr 7, 2010	4	5	50
22	Apr 8, 2010	5	5	60
22	Apr 9, 2010	5	5	40
22	Apr 10, 2010	5	20	70

Table 2.25 Result to Show Price_version and the Value of the Adjacent Row

Product_ID	DT	Price_version	P2	Sales_count
22	Apr 11, 2010	20	5	300
22	Apr 12, 2010	5	5	55
22	Apr 14, 2010	5	10	75
22	Apr 15, 2010	10	5	150
22	Apr 16, 2010	5	5	30
22	Apr 17, 2010	5	5	95
22	Apr 19, 2010	5	?	60

Table 2.25 Result to Show Price_version and the Value of the Adjacent Row

You can determine the TO_DATE column by comparing the Price_version and P2 columns. If they are not equal, then the values of the DT column become the TO_DATE values. You can run a query based on the result set of the previous query (see Listing 2.101).

```
SELECT *, CASE WHEN Price_version<>P2 THEN DT WHEN P2 IS NULL
THEN '2100-01-01' ELSE NULL END TO_DATE
FROM
(
SELECT Product_ID,DT,Price_version,
LEAD(Price_version) OVER (PARTITION BY Product_ID ORDER BY DT)
P2, SUM(Sales_count)  Sales_count
FROM TRANS_2
GROUP BY Product_ID,DT,Price_version);
```

Listing 2.101 Query to Determine the Date Range for Each Price_version

In Table 2.26, the TO_DATE column shows the last day for the date range of each PRICE_version. When it is null, it means the record is not on the last day of its price version.

Product_ID	DT	Price_version	P2	Sales_count	TO_DATE
22	Apr 5, 2010	5	5	100	?
22	Apr 6, 2010	5	4	80	Apr 6, 2010
22	Apr 7, 2010	4	5	50	Apr 7, 2010
22	Apr 8, 2010	5	5	60	?
22	Apr 9, 2010	5	5	40	?

Table 2.26 Result of Query to Generate TO_DATE

Product_ID	DT	Price_version	P2	Sales_count	TO_DATE
22	Apr 10, 2010	5	20	70	Apr 10, 2010
22	Apr 11, 2010	20	5	300	Apr 11, 2010
22	Apr 12, 2010	5	5	55	?
22	Apr 14, 2010	5	10	75	Apr 14, 2010
22	Apr 15, 2010	10	5	150	Apr 15, 2010
22	Apr 16, 2010	5	5	30	?
22	Apr 17, 2010	5	5	95	?
22	Apr 19, 2010	5	?	60	Jan 1, 2100

Table 2.26 Result of Query to Generate TO_DATE (Cont.)

Because you need the sum of every Price_version range, you cannot use any filters; every intermediate result set should keep all the source records. To separate the records and calculate the sum, you can expand the value of TO_DATE to the adjacent records that have null values for the column. Run the query shown in Listing 2.102 using window function MIN().

```
SELECT *,MIN(TO_DATE) OVER(PARTITION BY Product_ID ORDER BY DT
DESC) TO_DATE2
FROM
(
SELECT * , CASE WHEN Price_version<>P2 THEN DT WHEN P2 IS NULL
THEN '2100-01-01' ELSE NULL END TO_DATE
FROM
(
SELECT Product_ID,DT,Price_version,
LEAD(Price_version) OVER (PARTITION BY Product_ID ORDER BY DT)
P2, SUM(Sales_count)  Sales_count
FROM TRANS_2
GROUP BY Product_ID,DT,Price_version));
```
Listing 2.102 Query to Generate TO_DATE2

Table 2.27 shows the result set. Here, the value of the TO_DATE column is assigned to the TO_DATE2 column for all records of the corresponding price version.

Product_ID	DT	Price_version	P2	Sales_count	TO_DATE	TO_DATE2
22	Apr 19, 2010	5	?	60	Jan 1, 2100	Jan 1, 2100
22	Apr 17, 2010	5	5	95	?	Jan 1, 2100
22	Apr 16, 2010	5	5	30	?	Jan 1, 2100
22	Apr 15, 2010	10	5	150	Apr 15, 2010	Apr 15, 2010
22	Apr 14, 2010	5	10	75	Apr 14, 2010	Apr 14, 2010
22	Apr 12, 2010	5	5	55	?	Apr 14, 2010
22	Apr 11, 2010	20	5	300	Apr 11, 2010	Apr 11, 2010
22	Apr 10, 2010	5	20	70	Apr 10, 2010	Apr 10, 2010
22	Apr 9, 2010	5	5	40	?	Apr 10, 2010
22	Apr 8, 2010	5	5	60	?	Apr 10, 2010
22	Apr 7, 2010	4	5	50	Apr 7, 2010	Apr 7, 2010
22	Apr 6, 2010	5	4	80	Apr 6, 2010	Apr 6, 2010
22	Apr 5, 2010	5	5	100	?	Apr 6, 2010

Table 2.27 Query Result to Generate Data for GROUP BY

For the last step, use TO_DATE2 as a GROUP BY column in the final query (see Listing 2.103).

```
SELECT Product_ID,Price_version,MIN(DT) FROM_DATE,TO_DATE2 TO_
DATE,SUM(Sales_count) TOTAL
FROM
(
SELECT *,MIN(TO_DATE) OVER(PARTITION BY Product_
ID ORDER BY DT DESC) TO_DATE2
FROM
(
SELECT * , CASE WHEN Price_
version<>P2 THEN DT WHEN P2 IS NULL THEN '2100-01-01' ELSE NULL END TO_
DATE
FROM
(
SELECT Product_ID,DT,Price_version,
LEAD(Price_version) OVER (PARTITION BY Product_ID ORDER BY DT) P2,
SUM(Sales_count)  Sales_count
FROM TRANS_2
GROUP BY Product_ID,DT,Price_version
ORDER BY Product_ID,DT
)))
```

```
GROUP BY Product_ID,Price_version,TO_DATE2
ORDER BY Product_ID, FROM_DATE;
```
Listing 2.103 Final Query

Table 2.28 shows the result set; the final query generates the expected report. Although the logic is complex, you can make it with a combination of window functions in a step-by-step approach.

Product_ID	Price_version	FROM_DATE	TO_DATE	TOTAL
22	5	Apr 5, 2010	Apr 6, 2010	180
22	4	Apr 7, 2010	Apr 7, 2010	50
22	5	Apr 8, 2010	Apr 10, 2010	170
22	20	Apr 11, 2010	Apr 11, 2010	300
22	5	Apr 12, 2010	Apr 14, 2010	130
22	10	Apr 15, 2010	Apr 15, 2010	150
22	5	Apr 16, 2010	Jan 1, 2100	185

Table 2.28 Result of the Final Query

We have shown the solution with pure SQL queries, but for real transaction tables with large data volumes, you need to create an analytic view and then put the script into a view or scripted calculation view to query against the output of the analytic view.

2.16 Joining Based on a Date Sequence

Inventory analysis may require you to consider the date sequence when making links. Because purchase and sales records are in different tables, an item sold on a specific day should be linked to a record in the purchase table according to a first-in, first-out (FIFO) rule. To do this, you use joins.

Let's begin with an example. Suppose you have a table that stores purchase information such as cost and quantity, and another table that stores information about sales details. You need to calculate the profit earned from each sale by calculating the difference between the purchase cost and the sales price. If an item is purchased more than once, it is assumed that the oldest stock will be sold first.

To set up the example, first create table T_PURCHASE (see Listing 2.104).

```
CREATE COLUMN TABLE T_PURCHASE(
P_DT DATE,
ID VARCHAR(10),
QTY INT,
COST DECIMAL(18,2));
INSERT INTO T_PURCHASE VALUES ('2010-01-01', 'A001', 10, 10.5);
INSERT INTO T_PURCHASE VALUES ('2010-02-01', 'A001', 10, 13.25);
INSERT INTO T_PURCHASE VALUES ('2010-03-01', 'A001', 10, 9.75);
INSERT INTO T_PURCHASE VALUES ('2010-01-01', 'A002', 55, 20.0 );
INSERT INTO T_PURCHASE VALUES ('2010-02-15', 'A002', 30, 19.75);
```

Listing 2.104 Script to Create Table T_PURCHASE

Next, create table T_SALES (see Listing 2.105).

```
CREATE COLUMN TABLE T_SALES(
S_DT DATE,
ID VARCHAR(10),
QTY INT,
PRICE DECIMAL(18,2));
INSERT INTO T_SALES VALUES ('2010-01-15', 'A001', 7, 15.00);
INSERT INTO T_SALES VALUES ('2010-02-15', 'A001', 5, 19.25);
INSERT INTO T_SALES VALUES ('2010-02-25', 'A001', 3, 18.75);
INSERT INTO T_SALES VALUES ('2010-03-03', 'A001', 7, 13.50);
INSERT INTO T_SALES VALUES ('2010-02-13', 'A002', 50, 23.75);
INSERT INTO T_SALES VALUES ('2010-02-25', 'A002', 25, 22.50);
```

Listing 2.105 Script to Create Table T_SALES

The purchase cost should be calculated using the FIFO method. For example, in the second sale of the A001 item, out of the five sold, three were purchased at $10.50 each, and the other two were purchased at $13.25 each. You need to see the sales total amount, the cost of what has been sold, the cost of what has not been sold, and the profit (see Table 2.29).

ID	COST_SOLD	SALES	PROFIT	COST_UNSOLD
A001	257	352	95	78
A002	1,495	1,750	255	197.5

Table 2.29 Expected Output to Calculate Profit

You can achieve the logic by splitting the records on an item-by-item basis and joining them at a one-to-one cardinality. Because each particular item has a fixed cost and price, you can find all the items sold and all the items not sold with the join and the sum based on the join result that will return the expected result. To do so, you need to split the records. Use the view CA_SEQ, which you created in Section 2.14.1. This view returns the sequential numbers with the row count as specified. Running the query in Listing 2.106 returns the split records.

```
SELECT P_DT,ID,COST,ROW_NUMBER() OVER (PARTITION BY ID ORDER BY P_
DT ASC) ROW_NUMBER
FROM T_PURCHASE A,_SYS_BIC."test/CA_SEQ" (PLACEHOLDER."$$CNT$$"=
> 100) B
WHERE QTY>=NUM;
```
Listing 2.106 Query to Split Table T_PURCHASE

The result set is shown in Table 2.30.

P_DT	ID	COST	ROW_NUMBER
Jan 1, 2010	A001	10.5	1
Jan 1, 2010	A001	10.5	2
Jan 1, 2010	A001	10.5	3
Jan 1, 2010	A001	10.5	4
Jan 1, 2010	A001	10.5	5
Jan 1, 2010	A001	10.5	6
Jan 1, 2010	A001	10.5	7
Jan 1, 2010	A001	10.5	8
Jan 1, 2010	A001	10.5	9
Jan 1, 2010	A001	10.5	10
Feb 1, 2010	A001	13.25	11
Feb 1, 2010	A001	13.25	12
..	..	..	..

Table 2.30 Split Rows of T_PURCHASE

For the first record in the purchase table, the quantity is 10, so split the record into 10 records; follow the same procedure for the other records.

Next, for each ID, use the formula ROW_NUMBER() OVER (PARTITION BY ID ORDER BY P_DT ASC) to generate the unique number for each item based on the date sequence.

For table T_SALES, repeat the same process (see Listing 2.107).

```
SELECT S_DT,ID,PRICE,ROW_NUMBER() OVER (PARTITION BY ID ORDER BY S_
DT ASC)
FROM T_SALES A,_SYS_BIC."test/CA_SEQ" (PLACEHOLDER."$$CNT$$"=> 100) B
WHERE QTY>=NUM;
```

Listing 2.107 Query to Split Table T_SALES

As shown in Table 2.31, you can also split the rows of the sales table and assign a dedicated record for each item.

S_DT	ID	PRICE	ROW_NUMBER
Jan 15, 2010	A001	15	1
Jan 15, 2010	A001	15	2
Jan 15, 2010	A001	15	3
Jan 15, 2010	A001	15	4
Jan 15, 2010	A001	15	5
Jan 15, 2010	A001	15	6
Jan 15, 2010	A001	15	7
Feb 15, 2010	A001	19.25	8
Feb 15, 2010	A001	19.25	9
Feb 15, 2010	A001	19.25	10
Feb 15, 2010	A001	19.25	11
Feb 15, 2010	A001	19.25	12
..	..	..	..

Table 2.31 Split Rows of Table T_SALES

You can then execute a left outer join between the two result sets (see Listing 2.108).

```
SELECT P.ID,SUM(CASE WHEN S.ID IS NULL THEN NULL ELSE P.COST END) COST_
SOLD,
SUM(S.PRICE) SALES,SUM(S.PRICE)-
SUM(CASE WHEN S.ID IS NULL THEN NULL ELSE P.COST END) PROFIT,
SUM(CASE WHEN S.ID IS NULL THEN P.COST ELSE NULL END) COST_UNSOLD
FROM
(SELECT P_DT,ID,COST,ROW_NUMBER() OVER (PARTITION EY ID ORDER BY
P_DT ASC) SEQ
```

```
FROM T_PURCHASE A,_SYS_BIC."test/CA_SEQ" (PLACEHOLDER."$$CNT$$"=>
  100) B
WHERE QTY>=NUM
) P LEFT OUTER JOIN
(SELECT S_DT,ID,PRICE,ROW_NUMBER() OVER (PARTITION BY ID ORDER BY S_
DT ASC) SEQ
FROM T_SALES A,_SYS_BIC."test/CA_SEQ" (PLACEHOLDER."$$CNT$$"=> 100) B
WHERE QTY>=NUM
) S
ON P.ID=S.ID AND P.SEQ=S.SEQ
GROUP BY P.ID;
```
Listing 2.108 Query to Join the Tables Item-by-Item

For each item in the purchase query with a mapping row in the sales query (meaning it was sold), use the formula SUM(CASE WHEN S.ID IS NULL THEN NULL ELSE P.COST END) to calculate the cost for the parts sold.

For each item in the purchase query without a mapping row in the sales query (meaning it was not sold), use the formula SUM(CASE WHEN S.ID IS NULL THEN P.COST ELSE NULL END) to calculate the cost for the unsold part. The output of the query is shown in Table 2.32.

ID	COST_SOLD	SALES	PROFIT	COST_UNSOLD
A001	257	352	95	78
A002	1,495	1,750	255	197.5

Table 2.32 Output of the Query

The split row approach on purchase and sales tables is straightforward, but it can be less efficient when the quantity is too large. For example, if a given item was purchased with a quantity of 10,000, it will be split into 10,000 rows.

Consider another, more efficient solution in such a case. Instead of comparing two tables at each item level, you can create a comparable range based on the date sequence of the two tables and map the records of the two tables based on the range comparison. For table T_PURCHASE, use the formula SUM(QTY) OVER(PARTITION BY ID ORDER BY P_DT) to generate the TO_QTY column to specify the range end value, and then use the formula LAG(TO_QTY) OVER (PARTITION BY ID ORDER BY TO_QTY) to generate the FROM_QTY column to specify the range start value. Then, run the query shown in Listing 2.109.

```
SELECT ID,COST,QTY,COALESCE(LAG(TO_
QTY) OVER (PARTITION BY ID ORDER BY TO_QTY),0) FRCM_QTY,TO_QTY
FROM (
SELECT ID,COST,QTY,SUM(QTY) OVER(PARTITION BY ID CRDER BY P_DT) TO_QTY
FROM T_PURCHASE );
```
Listing 2.109 Query to Generate Quantity Range of Purchase

In Table 2.33, the result dataset has two additional columns: the FROM_QTY column and the TO_QTY column, which show the range based on the sequence for each cost.

ID	COST	QTY	FROM_QTY	TO_QTY
A001	10.5	10	0	10
A001	13.25	10	10	20
A001	9.75	10	20	30
A002	20	55	0	55
A002	19.75	30	55	85

Table 2.33 Range of Quantity of Table T_PURCHASE

For table T_SALES, run the following query to generate the total quantity for each ID:

```
SELECT ID,SUM(QTY) QTY,SUM(PRICE*QTY) SALES
FROM T_SALES GROUP BY ID;
```

Table 2.34 shows the result set of the preceding query, which gives the total quantities and the total sales for each ID.

ID	QTY	SALES
A001	22	352
A002	75	1,750

Table 2.34 Total Quantity and Sales for Each ID

Next, join the result sets of these two queries on the ID column (see Listing 2.110).

```
SELECT P.ID,COST, FROM_QTY,TO_QTY,COALESCE(QTY,0) QTY,SALES
FROM
(
SELECT ID,COST,COALESCE(LAG(TO_QTY) OVER (PARTITICN BY ID ORDER BY TO_
QTY),0) FROM_QTY,TO_QTY
```

```
FROM (
SELECT ID,COST,SUM(QTY) OVER(PARTITION BY ID ORDER BY P_DT) TO_QTY
FROM T_PURCHASE )) P
LEFT OUTER JOIN
(SELECT ID,SUM(QTY) QTY,SUM(PRICE*QTY) SALES
FROM T_SALES
GROUP BY ID) S
ON P.ID=S.ID;
```
Listing 2.110 Query to Join Two Tables

Table 2.35 is the result set for the query in Listing 2.110. In the first row, the value of QTY is 22 and the value of TO_QTY is 10; because 22 is greater than 10, all of the items are sold in this range. The same is true for the second range. In the third range, the value of QTY is 22, the value of TO_QTY is 30, and the value of FROM_QTY is 20; because 20 is less than 22, which is less than 30, 22 minus 20 (i.e., 2) items are sold in this range, and 30 minus 22 (i.e., 8) items are not sold in this range.

ID	COST	FROM_QTY	TO_QTY	QTY	SALES
A001	10.5	0	10	22	352
A001	13.25	10	20	22	352
A001	9.75	20	30	22	352
A002	20	0	55	75	1,750
A002	19.75	55	85	75	1,750

Table 2.35 Join Results of the Two Queries

Based on the analysis, you can run Listing 2.111 to generate the report.

```
SELECT ID,SUM(CASE WHEN COST_SOLD<0 THEN 0 ELSE COST_SOLD END) COST_
SOLD,
MAX(SALES),
MAX(SALES)-SUM(CASE WHEN COST_SOLD<0 THEN 0 ELSE COST_SOLD END) PROFIT,
SUM(CASE WHEN COST_UNSOLD<0 THEN 0 ELSE COST_UNSOLD END) COST_UNSOLD
FROM(
SELECT ID,COST*(LEAST(QTY,TO_QTY)- FROM_QTY) COST_SOLD,
COST*(TO_QTY - GREATEST(QTY,FROM_QTY)) COST_UNSOLD, QTY,SALES
FROM
(SELECT P.ID,COST, FROM_QTY,TO_QTY,COALESCE(QTY,0) QTY,SALES
FROM
(SELECT ID,COST,COALESCE(LAG(TO_QTY) OVER (PARTITION BY ID ORDER BY
TO_QTY),0) FROM_QTY,TO_QTY
FROM (
```

```
SELECT ID,COST,SUM(QTY) OVER(PARTITION BY ID ORDER BY P_DT) TO_QTY
FROM T_PURCHASE )) P
LEFT OUTER JOIN
(SELECT ID,SUM(QTY) QTY,SUM(PRICE*QTY) SALES
FROM T_SALES
GROUP BY ID) S
ON P.ID=S.ID
))
GROUP BY ID;
```
Listing 2.111 Final Query

Table 2.36 shows the result set of the final query. It has the sales total, the cost for what has been sold, the cost for what has not been sold, and the profit.

ID	COST_SOLD	SALES	PROFIT	COST_UNSOLD
A001	257	352	95	78
A002	1,495	1,750	255	197.5

Table 2.36 Result from the Query

In the query, use the formula COST*(LEAST(QTY,TO_QTY)- FROM_QTY) to return the intermediate result, COST_SOLD. This allows you to compare the values of QTY and TO_QTY and take the column with the lesser value to consider only the sold items. Then, use the formula SUM(CASE WHEN COST_SOLD<0 THEN 0 ELSE COST_SOLD END) to calculate the final result of COST_SOLD in order to filter out the invalid negative values that might have been created in the previous step. For the SALES table, use the formula MAX(SALES) instead of SUM(SALES), because the value of the column is already aggregated beforehand.

In this section, we described different solutions for handling joins with consideration to date sequences. When there are no direct join columns, you can generate the join columns, and when there are no direct group by columns, you can generate those as well.

2.17   Using a Nested Calculation View

For a complex calculation view or stored procedure that contains duplicate parts, you can make a nested calculation view of a stored procedure to avoid duplication. When you tune the performance, you do not have to waste effort on duplicating parts, because when a nested view is cached, all views that contain the nested view can use the cache. The nested calculation view and stored procedure can be more generic and shared in other places.

In this section, we will show an example of a route analysis and describe the solution of a nested calculation view. For this example, suppose you have table ROUTE, which stores the city name, the ID of the flight line to which the city is connected, and the flight distance (see Listing 2.112).

```
CREATE COLUMN TABLE ROUTE(
CITY VARCHAR(20),
ROAD_ID VARCHAR(2),
LEN INT
);
INSERT INTO ROUTE VALUES ('A','AB',5);
INSERT INTO ROUTE VALUES ('A','AC',2);
INSERT INTO ROUTE VALUES ('A','AD',4);
INSERT INTO ROUTE VALUES ('A','AE',2);
INSERT INTO ROUTE VALUES ('B','AB',5);
INSERT INTO ROUTE VALUES ('B','BC',1);
INSERT INTO ROUTE VALUES ('B','BF',1);
INSERT INTO ROUTE VALUES ('C','BC',1);
INSERT INTO ROUTE VALUES ('C','CD',5);
INSERT INTO ROUTE VALUES ('C','AC',2);
INSERT INTO ROUTE VALUES ('D','AD',4);
INSERT INTO ROUTE VALUES ('D','CD',5);
INSERT INTO ROUTE VALUES ('F','BF',1);
INSERT INTO ROUTE VALUES ('E','AE',2);
INSERT INTO ROUTE VALUES ('E','EF',1);
INSERT INTO ROUTE VALUES ('F','EF',1);
```
Listing 2.112 Script to Create Table ROUTE

For the purposes of this example, you want to check the flights from city A to city B and see which routes are available and which route has the shortest distance. There might be a lot of combinations when you perform this comparison, but fortunately, you only have to consider the routes with limited stops.

Suppose the restriction on the count of stops is less than three. Then, routes such as A to E + E to F + F to B that contain two stops or fewer will be considered, and routes containing three or more stops will not be considered. It is difficult to set this up with a single query, but you can create calculation views one by one.

First, create a CA_R1 calculation view to find the city pairs connected with direct flights (see Figure 2.26).

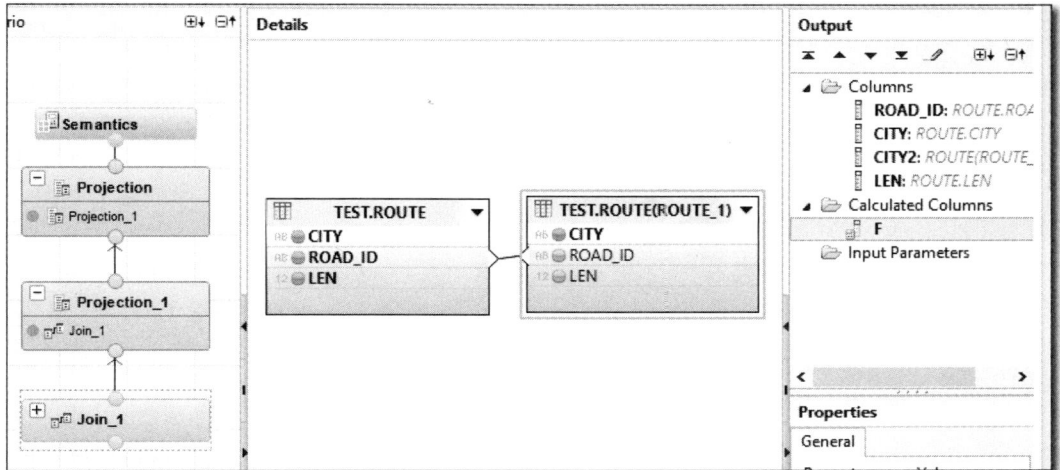

Figure 2.26 Calculation View to Find City Pairs Connected with Direct Flights

In this logic, if two cities are connected to the same line, then the cities are connected. Create a calculated column F= IF("CITY"="CITY2",0,1), and add a filter as F=1, which filters out records that are connected to themselves. This is a trick to define the join condition that contains the operator rather than an equality. You want to define the condition as CITY<>CITY2, and because you cannot define it as a join condition, define the calculated column F and then filter on it. When you run the following query, it returns all the city pairs with direct flight lines:

SELECT * FROM _SYS_BIC."test/CA_R1";

In Table 2.37, the CITY and CITY2 columns are the city pairs, the ROAD_ID column is the line ID, the LEN column is the distance between the city pairs.

CITY	CITY2	LEN	ROAD_ID
A	B	5	AB
A	C	2	AC
A	D	4	AD
A	E	2	AE
B	A	5	AB
B	C	1	BC

Table 2.37 City Pairs with Direct Lines

CITY	CITY2	LEN	ROAD_ID
B	F	1	BF
C	B	1	BC
..	..	..	..

Table 2.37 City Pairs with Direct Lines (Cont.)

Based on the first calculation view, you can create the second, CA_R2, which returns the city pairs connected with one-stop routes (see Figure 2.27).

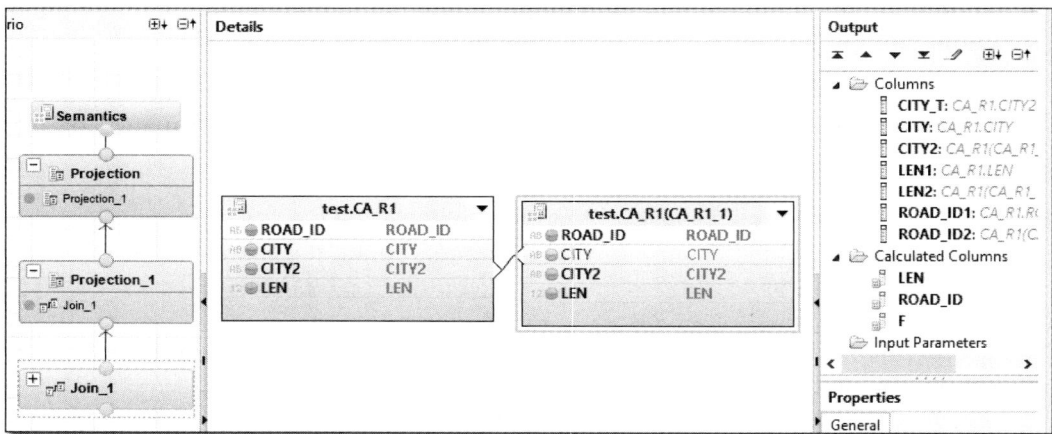

Figure 2.27 Calculation View to Find City Pairs Connected with One-Stop Routes

Also create the F= IF("CITY"="CITY2",0,1) calculated column, and add a filter as F=1, which will filter out the records for routes that fly back to the departure city. Add a LEN=LEN1+LEN2 calculated column, which retrieves the sum of the distances of the two lines, and a ROAD_ID=ROAD_ID1+'-'+ROAD_ID2 calculated column, which creates a tracking ID for the connected line. When you run the following query, it returns all the city pairs connected with one-stop routes:

```
SELECT * FROM _SYS_BIC."test/CA_R2";
```

In Table 2.38, the ROAD_ID column is the concatenation of the line IDs for the routes with one stop.

CITY	CITY2	LEN	ROAD_ID
C	B	7	AC–AB
D	B	9	AD–AB
E	B	7	AE–AB
B	C	7	AB–AC
D	C	6	AD–AC
..	..	..	..

Table 2.38 City Pairs with One-Stop Routes

In a similar manner, you can create the third calculation view, CA_R3, which returns the city pairs connected with two-stop routes, as shown in Figure 2.28.

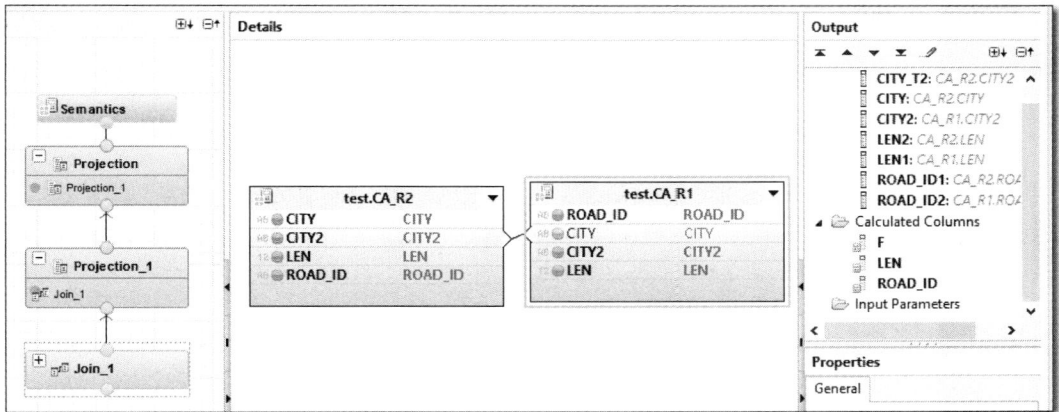

Figure 2.28 Calculation View to Find City Pairs Connected with Two-Stop Routes

Create the LEN and ROAD_ID calculated columns with the same formulas as in CA_R2, create a F=IF("CITY"="CITY2" OR instr("ROAD_ID1","ROAD_ID2")>0,0,1) calculated column, and also add a filter as F=1, which filters out records for routes that fly back to the first city and those that fly back to the second city. When you run the following query, it returns all the city pairs connected with two-stop routes:

```
SELECT * FROM _SYS_BIC."test/CA_R3";
```

In Table 2.39, the ROAD_ID column is the concatenated line ID for the routes with two stops.

CITY	CITY2	LEN	ROAD_ID
D	A	11	CD-BC-AB
E	A	7	EF-BF-AB
F	A	4	BF-BC-AC
B	A	10	BC-CD-AD
B	A	4	BF-EF-AE
D	B	12	CD-AC-AB
C	B	14	CD-AD-AB
F	B	8	EF-AE-AB
..	..	..	..

Table 2.39 City Pairs with Two-Stop Routes

Finally, create a CA_R4 calculation view to union all three views (see Figure 2.29).

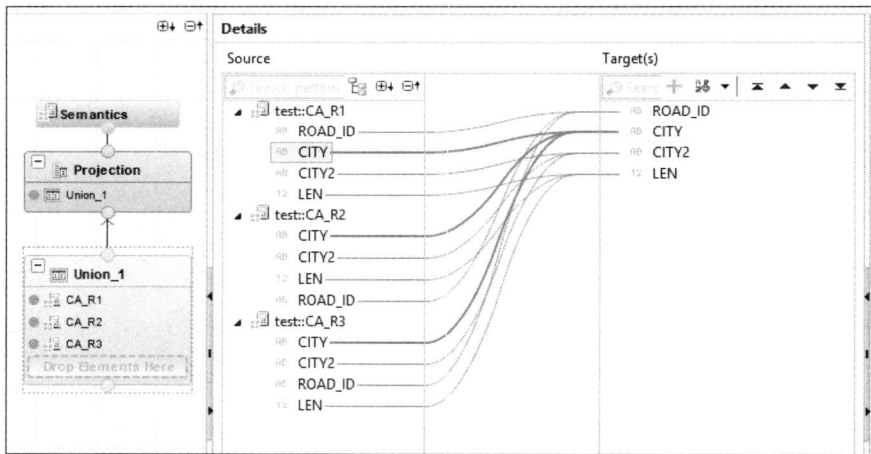

Figure 2.29 Calculation View to Union Three Views

Then, you can perform further analysis against this calculation view; for example, run the following to list all the routes between A and B and compare the distance of the routes:

```
SELECT * FROM _SYS_BIC."test/CA_R4"
WHERE CITY='A' AND CITY2='B' ORDER BY LEN;
```

Table 2.40 shows four routes, the shortest of which is AC-BC, with a distance of 3.

CITY	CITY2	LEN	ROAD_ID
A	B	5	AB
A	B	3	AC-BC
A	B	10	AD-CD-BC
A	B	4	AE-EF-BF

Table 2.40 Query Results of the Routes Between A and B

The logic for route analysis is complex, but with the step-by-step strategy, you can achieve it with a nested calculation view level by level, making the structure of each view much simpler, which greatly reduces the chance of making mistakes.

2.18 Summary

In this chapter, we examined the solutions provided by SAP HANA for tackling complex scenarios. The examples used in this chapter are simplified to focus on particular aspects; in the real world, situations can be much more challenging. However, it is important to remember that complex logic should be achieved using simple solutions.

SAP HANA provides many features that can be leveraged during modeling. In each revision, new features are added that provide newer solutions to different problems and help achieve specific requirements. There may be several ways to achieve your business requirements. Some approaches may have better performance, whereas other approaches may be more flexible. There is no absolute rule to judge which approach is better; to make a determination, you should compare overall statistics, including performance, resource consumption, maintenance, ease of use, and more.

In the next chapter, we will look at the modeling features available for scaling large datasets.

In this chapter, we will look at different techniques for scaling large datasets using SAP modeling features.

3   Scaling for Large Datasets

This chapter focuses on using SAP HANA features to scale for large datasets. To take advantage of SAP HANA features, developers translate query logic into models, but often this is not enough. SAP HANA provides features that benefit from the SAP HANA engines. For developers, it is time to rethink the way things are done with SQL queries; SAP HANA is more than just a simple replacement for SQL.

In this chapter, we will look at various techniques for scaling large datasets. Each section looks at a carefully chosen scaling topic for enhanced performance.

3.1   Partitioning

To deal with large datasets, the first solution that comes to mind is partitioning. Rows are limited to two billion for a nonpartitioned table. When the row count of a table exceeds this limit, you have to partition it (i.e., split the dataset into multiple slices and distribute them into multiple storage slots).

Partitioning a table has several advantages. When the data of a table is distributed to multiple nodes over the landscape, a query against the table will be processed on all these nodes, enabling parallel processing for queries on all nodes. A proper partition strategy is crucial to achieve good performance while dealing with large datasets. You can refer to some general recommendations, but there is no simple rule to follow. A particular partition strategy that works in one case may not work in another scenario.

In this section, we will look at some partitioning strategies. These strategies include the following:

- Round-robin
- Range
- Hash
- Two-level partitioning

3.1.1 Round-Robin Partitioning

To begin we'll look at round-robin partitioning. Suppose you have a transaction table that records the details of a sales order comprised of 50 billion rows (see Listing 3.1).

```
CREATE COLUMN TABLE Trans_DTL(
Trans_DATE DATE,
Trans_No INT,
Prod_ID BIGINT,
Sales_Qty BIGINT,
Sales_Net DECIMAL(18,2));
```
Listing 3.1 Definition of Table Trans_DTL

To evenly distribute the rows to 10 nodes, you might try a ROUNDROBIN partition:

```
ALTER TABLE Trans_DTL PARTITION BY ROUNDROBIN PARTITIONS 100;
```

Partitioning in this manner eliminates your ability to prune the table effectively. SAP HANA will always perform a full table scan on any query that does not provide optimal performance.

3.1.2 Range Partitioning

To leverage partition pruning, you can partition the table by range on the Trans_DATE column instead of ROUNDROBIN (see Listing 3.2).

```
ALTER TABLE Trans_DTL partition by range(Trans_DATE)(
PARTITION '2005-01-01'<= values <'2005-02-01',
PARTITION '2005-02-01'<= values <'2005-03-01',
PARTITION '2005-03-01'<= values <'2005-04-01',
PARTITION '2005-04-01'<= values <'2005-05-01',
......
......
PARTITION '2014-09-01'<= values <'2014-10-01',
PARTITION '2014-10-01'<= values <'2014-11-01',
PARTITION '2014-11-01'<= values <'2014-12-01',
```

```
PARTITION '2014-12-01'<= values <'2015-01-01',
PARTITION OTHERS);
```
Listing 3.2 Alter Statement to Set Partition by Range

Now, when there is a filter on a specific day or date range, SAP HANA will only scan the partition where the data of that day resides. This technique is called *partition pruning*. This database optimization feature scans only partitions that contain matching values instead of scanning all partitions, which enables the use of fewer resources while improving performance significantly.

This partition strategy will also benefit queries that calculate aggregates. Typically, these are performed on a daily, monthly, or yearly basis—for example:

```
SELECT SUM(SALES_NET) FROM Trans_DTL WHERE Trans_DATE BETWEEN
'2014-01-01' AND '2014-12-31';
```

Looking at the current partition strategy, you can see that all records within a particular month reside in a distinct partition, implying that each year's records are within 12 partitions. For the preceding query, SAP HANA would process the data on the different nodes where the partition resides, significantly reducing data transfer from one partition to another.

3.1.3 Hash Partitioning

Let's now see the effects of changing the partition strategy to a HASH partition for the same field (Trans_DATE):

```
ALTER TABLE Trans_DTL PARTITION BY HASH(Trans_DATE) PARTITIONS 100;
```

In general, it is not a good an idea to create a HASH partition by date column, because, again, you lose pruning capabilities whenever a date range is provided as a filter in a query. For example:

```
SELECT SUM(SALES_NET) FROM Trans_DTL WHERE Trans_DATE BETWEEN
'2014-10-01' AND '2014-10-15';
```

Also, when you combine multiple columns to create a HASH partition, you lose pruning unless you specify values for all the partition columns in the WHERE clause of a query. For example, in this table, the columns Trans_No and Prod_ID are most likely to be used frequently, so the table can be partitioned by HASH(Trans_No,Prod_ID) using the following syntax:

195

```
ALTER TABLE Trans_DTL PARTITION BY HASH(Trans_No, Prod_ID)
PARTITIONS 100;
```

This method provides an even distribution of data across partitions, as the combination of `Trans_No` and `Prod_ID` will have more distinct values. However, pruning will only happen when both columns are present in the `WHERE` clause with equal conditions. For example:

```
SELECT SUM(SALES_NET) FROM Trans_DTL WHERE Trans_No=11323 AND
Prod_ID=8762;
```

If both columns are not provided, a full table scan will be applied and pruning will be lost. The same goes for missing one column or having a range condition, as follows:

```
SELECT SUM(SALES_NET) FROM Trans_DTL WHERE Trans_No=11323 AND Prod_ID
> 8762;
```

Partitioning solutions will vary case by case. As a developer, you need to consider not only the even distribution of data, but also the join performance. Suppose you have a table to record the header of transactions `Trans_HDR(Trans_No, Dep_ID, User_ID, Sales_Amt)` with two billion rows (see Listing 3.3).

```
CREATE COLUMN TABLE Trans_HDR(
Trans_No BIGINT,
Dep_ID INT,
User_ID INT,
Sales_Amt DECIMAL(18,2));
```
Listing 3.3 Definition of Table Trans_HDR

The join condition of the header and detail tables is on the `Trans_No` column. You must avoid cross-node data transfer when performing the join, which can be achieved by applying the same `HASH` partition on the two tables, as shown:

```
ALTER TABLE Trans_DTL PARTITION BY HASH(Trans_No) PARTITIONS 10;
ALTER TABLE Trans_HDR PARTITION BY HASH(Trans_No) PARTITIONS 10;
```

With the hash partition strategy on the join column, the rows in the same hash value are distributed to the same physical node. As a result, when performing the join between the two tables, SAP HANA will not transfer data across nodes.

Defining Partitions after Table Creation

At this juncture, it is important to emphasize defining partitions correctly at the time of table creation. Once a table is created, a data user has to manually move the partitions to the destination physical nodes of the server when a repartition is performed.

The following statement shows the syntax to move partitions:

```
ALTER TABLE Trans_HDR MOVE PARTITION 1 TO 'hostname:32503' physical;
```

To avoid moving partitions, you may create partitions with the CREATE TABLE statement (see Listing 3.4).

```
CREATE COLUMN TABLE Trans_HDR(
Trans_No BIGINT,
Dep_ID INT,
User_ID INT,
Sales_Amt DECIMAL(18,2))
PARTITION BY HASH(Trans_No) PARTITIONS 10;
```

Listing 3.4 Definition of Table with Partition Specification

Because fact tables usually are partitioned and dimension tables usually are not, to improve the performance of a join between a fact table and a dimension table, you can create a replica of a dimension table on all nodes to avoid data moving among nodes when performing a join—for example:

```
ALTER TABLE Table_name ADD REPLICA AT ALL LOCATIONS;
```

3.1.4   Two-Level Partitioning

A common misconception among database designers is that more partitions provide better performance. The greater the amount of partitions, the more system resources will need to be consumed by the table. Moving data between partitions is also a resource-consuming activity. Based on our collective experience, a generic guideline to follow is to have about 200 million to 800 million rows per partition. In the running example, you can split the 50 billion rows of the table into 100 partitions with a two-level partition strategy (see Listing 3.5).

```
ALTER TABLE Trans_DTL PARTITION BY HASH(Trans_No) FARTITIONS 10,
range(Trans_DATE)(
PARTITION '2005-01-01'<= values <'2006-01-01',
PARTITION '2006-01-01'<= values <'2007-01-01',
PARTITION '2007-01-01'<= values <'2008-01-01',
PARTITION '2008-01-01'<= values <'2009-01-01',
......
......
PARTITION '2011-01-01'<= values <'2012-01-01',
PARTITION '2012-01-01'<= values <'2013-01-01',
PARTITION '2013-01-01'<= values <'2014-01-01',
PARTITION '2014-01-01'<= values <'2015-01-01',
PARTITION OTHERS);
```

Listing 3.5 Alter Statement to Set Partitions by Hash and Range

This strategy will set 500 million rows per partition for the table. The way this works is that the first-level partition on `HASH(Trans_No)` will distribute data to 10 nodes by creating a `HASH` value on the contents of column `Trans_No`. The second level on `range(Trans_DATE)` will then split the data inside each top-level partition into 10 partitions based on the range of date values in the `Trans_DATE` field.

Again, we emphasize here that no single partitioning strategy is the answer. Circumstances vary the effectiveness of each option, but in this section we presented common approaches to the problem. A little bit of experimentation is needed to find the most optimal combination that suffices for all of your requirements.

3.2   Using Input Parameters to Enforce Pruning

Input parameters process calculations input by users during the execution of a report. They define internal parameterization and are used as placeholders for unit of measure conversions, currency conversions, and formulas. There are different types of input parameters, such as direct, column, static lists, and those derived from tables.

For the purposes of scaling large datasets, we will use input parameters to enforce pruning. As an example, let's say that a developer needs to run a query against a 10 billion row table to return the results back in less than 10 seconds. The best option to consider in this situation is an analytic view. There are other options, such as using pure SQL queries or creating a calculation view, but performance comparisons have shown that using input parameters with analytic views is the best choice when underlying tables have large amounts of data.

In an analytic view, it is important to reduce the computational data volume at the lowest level, even before the join operation is performed. Let's look at an example to see how to reduce the data volume in an analytic view. Suppose you are going to perform the logic shown in Listing 3.6 with an analytic view.

```
SELECT T.CALMONTH,SUM(SALES_NET)
FROM Trans_DTL F, "_SYS_BI"."M_TIME_DIMENSION" T
WHERE F.Trans_DATE=T.DATE_SQL
AND T.YEAR BETWEEN 2010 AND 2011
GROUP BY T.CALMONTH;
```
Listing 3.6 Query with Aggregation on a Transaction Table

In Listing 3.6, table _SYS_BI.M_TIME_DIMENSION is an out-of-the-box SAP HANA calendar table. You can create the attribute view AT_CALENDAR against the calendar table, and then join the attribute view to the fact table in the analytic view AN_TRANS (see Figure 3.1).

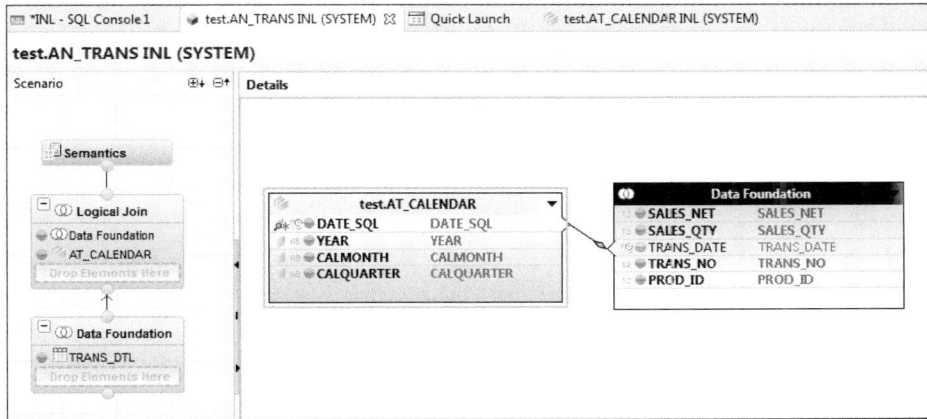

Figure 3.1 Analytic View AN_TRANS

After activating the analytic view, run the query shown in Listing 3.7.

```
SELECT CALMONTH,SUM(SALES_NET)
FROM _SYS_BIC."test/AN_TRANS"
WHERE YEAR BETWEEN 2010 AND 2011
GROUP BY CALMONTH;
```
Listing 3.7 Query Against Analytic View

This is a typical approach to execute the scenario we mentioned in Chapter 1, Section 1.3.2. That being said, for a larger dataset, it is better to fine-tune the model. In this analytic view, you have not yet reduced the data volume with a filter condition before the join, but are doing so after the join operation. Assuming the table is partitioned by the range in the Trans_DATE column, you will fail to leverage pruning to improve performance.

In order to leverage pruning, you can put a filter on column Trans_DATE. You can add the filter in the WHERE clause of the queries or add the filter at the data foundation of the analytic view. We recommend adding this filter at the data foundation (see Figure 3.2).

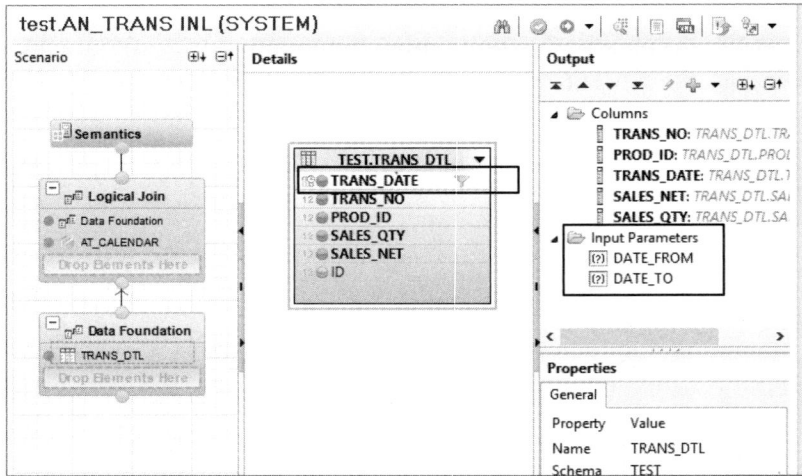

Figure 3.2 Input Parameters and Filter

To make the filter, first create two input parameters: DATE_FROM and DATE_TO. Then, create a filter at the TRANS_DATE column (see the filter definition in Figure 3.3).

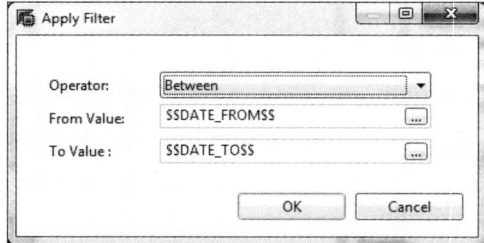

Figure 3.3 Filter Definition

When you use an analytic view, you need to specify the values for the input parameters DATE_FROM and DATE_TO (see Listing 3.8).

```
SELECT CALMONTH,SUM(SALES_NET)
FROM _SYS_BIC."test/AN_TRANS"
('PLACEHOLDER' = ('$$DATE_FROM$$','2010-01-01'),
 'PLACEHOLDER' = ('$$DATE_TO$$','2011-12-31'))
GROUP BY CALMONTH;
```

Listing 3.8 Query Against an Analytic View with a Filter on the Date Range

For all real-world applications, you will have a date range to analyze business data, so it is worth setting the filter with input parameters for all the queries against this analytic view.

3.3 Creating an Index

Working with columnar tables is unique, because each column behaves as an index; one naturally inherits the high-performance attributes of the column store. Usually, you do not need to consider creating an index on an SAP HANA database, because the execution process for queries is already optimal in most cases. However, for a large dataset, there is still a difference between a column and an index with regards to query performance.

Indexes can be resource-intensive. When creating an index, you need to compare the performance before the table is indexed and the performance after the table is indexed. In the unlikely scenario in which there is no performance gain after creating an index, dropping it would be wise.

Unique indexes or primary keys are more expensive for a large table. For a fact table, always avoid adding uniqueness constraints. Regardless, it is recommended to add a primary key on a dimension table.

To facilitate the filter on multiple columns, you can create a composite index. For example, on the table `Trans_DTL(Trans_DATE, Trans_No, Prod_ID, Sales_Qty, Sales_Net)`, you can create an index on the `Trans_No` and `Prod_ID` columns:

```
CREATE INDEX idx_trans ON Trans_DTL(Trans_No, Prod_ID);
```

The index will benefit the query when both columns are in the WHERE clause with equal conditions. For example:

```
SELECT SUM(SALES_NET) FROM Trans_DTL WHERE Trans_Nc=11323 AND
Prod_ID=8762;
```

The composite index can also benefit the join on multiple columns. For example, say that you have a table `Trans_log(First_name,Mid_name,Last_name,City, Trans_date, Trans_no,Net)`, as shown in Listing 3.9.

```
CREATE COLUMN TABLE Trans_log(
First_name VARCHAR(10),
Mid_name VARCHAR(10),
Last_name VARCHAR(10),
```

```
City VARCHAR(10),
Trans_date DATE,
Trans_no BIGINT,
Net DECIMAL(18,2));
```
Listing 3.9 Definition of Table Trans_log

You also have another table, Cust_inf(First_name, Mid_name, Last_name, City, Age, Phone, Company), as shown in Listing 3.10.

```
CREATE COLUMN TABLE Cust_inf(
First_name VARCHAR(10),
Mid_name VARCHAR(10),
Last_name VARCHAR(10),
City VARCHAR(10),
Age int,
Phone VARCHAR(10),
Company VARCHAR(10));
```
Listing 3.10 Definition of Table Cust_inf

Assuming the two tables need to be joined on the columns First_name, Mid_name, Last_name, and City, in an analytic view, make the join between the tables (see Figure 3.4).

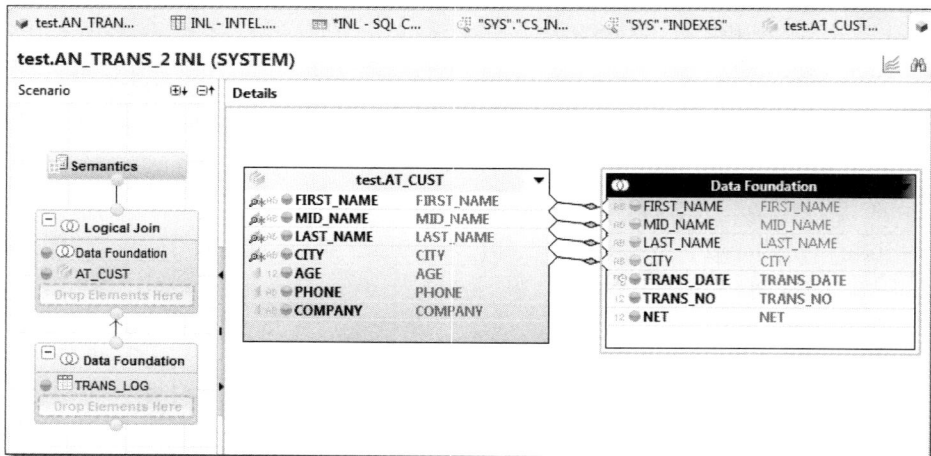

Figure 3.4 Join on Multiple Columns

To create the composite indexes, run the statements shown in Listing 3.11.

```
CREATE INDEX IDX_TRANS_LOG ON Trans_log(First_name, Mid_name,
Last_name,City);
CREATE INDEX IDX_Cust_idx ON Cust_inf(First_name, Mid_name,
Last_name,City);
```
Listing 3.11 Definition of a Composite Index

You can run a query against the view before the indexes are created and log the execution time. Run the same query after the indices are created, compare the execution time, and then decide whether to keep the indexes.

Composite indexing is used only when all the indexed columns exist in the query as a filter or a join condition. To also make the index usable for queries without all the indexed columns, you can create individual indexes for each column, as shown in Listing 3.12.

```
CREATE INDEX IDX_TRANS_LOG_F ON Trans_log(First_name);
CREATE INDEX IDX_TRANS_LOG_M ON Trans_log(Mid_name);
CREATE INDEX IDX_TRANS_LOG_L ON Trans_log(Last_name);
CREATE INDEX IDX_TRANS_LOG_C ON Trans_log(City);
CREATE INDEX IDX_Cust_inf_F ON Cust_inf(First_name);
CREATE INDEX IDX_Cust_inf_M ON Cust_inf(Mid_name);
CREATE INDEX IDX_Cust_inf_L ON Cust_inf(Last_name);
CREATE INDEX IDX_Cust_inf_C ON Cust_inf(City);
```
Listing 3.12 Definition of Separate Indexes for Each Column

With these indexes created on the tables, if a query has a filter or join on any indexed column, the index will be used. The actual performance gain depends on the table size, values distribution, and so on. You need to perform a test to determine whether to keep the indexes.

For this example, a better approach is to create a calculated column to concatenate the columns on each table, then join the two tables on the calculated column instead of on the four separate columns. The DDL of the calculated column is shown in Listing 3.13.

```
ALTER TABLE Trans_log ADD(FULLNAME VARCHAR(50) GENERATED ALWAYS AS
First_name||Mid_name||Last_name||City);
ALTER TABLE Cust_inf ADD(FULLNAME VARCHAR(50) GENERATED ALWAYS AS
First_name||Mid_name||Last_name||City);
```
Listing 3.13 Definition of Calculated Columns for Concatenated Strings

In an analytic view, you can select the Generate Concat Attributes checkbox under the View Properties tab to let the modeler tool automatically create the calculated column instead of doing it manually.

While joining the columns, the concatenated strings may have ambiguities. For example, "I sold." and "Is old." are different, but when they are concatenated as 'I'||'sold' and 'Is'||'old', they both become 'Isold'. To avoid ambiguity, you may add a special character, such as - , between the concatenated columns, as shown in Listing 3.14.

```
ALTER TABLE Trans_log ADD(FULLNAME VARCHAR(50) GENERATED ALWAYS
First_name||'-'||Mid_name||'-'||Last_name||'-'||City);
ALTER TABLE Cust_inf ADD(FULLNAME VARCHAR(50) GENERATED ALWAYS AS
First_name||'-'||Mid_name||'-'||Last_name||'-'||City);
```

Listing 3.14 Definition of Calculated Columns for Concatenated Strings with a Delimiter Character

Then, you can make the join on the concatenated single column instead of the four separate columns in the analytic view (see Figure 3.5). This results in significant performance improvement.

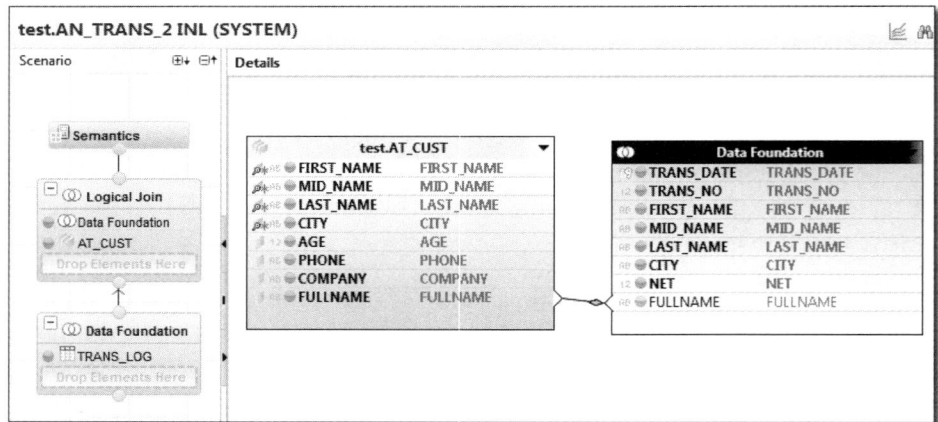

Figure 3.5 Join on One Column

In this section, we introduced how to create indexes. Again, indexes can be resource-intensive, so you should test the actual performance to decide whether to create them. For the joins on multiple columns, it is better to apply the join on a calculated column made of concatenated columns than to use an index.

3.4   Analyzing Query Performance with Tools

SAP HANA provides tools to help analyze query performance. The most commonly used tools are the explain plan, the visualize plan, and the performance trace.

3.4.1   Explain Plan

The explain plan tool in SAP HANA allows you to see the execution plan of a query and gives you step-by-step details of how the query will be executed in the database engine.

To see how this works, we will look at an example. Let's first see how to generate an execution plan with the explain plan tool (see Listing 3.15).

```
SELECT CALMONTH, SALES-(LAG(SALES) OVER (ORDER BY CALMONTH)) SALES_VAR
FROM
(
SELECT CALMONTH,SUM(SALES_NET) SALES
FROM TRANS_DTL T, "_SYS_BI"."M_TIME_DIMENSION" C
WHERE T.TRANS_DATE=C.DATE_SQL
GROUP BY CALMONTH
);
```
Listing 3.15 Query Example

To check the execution plan of the query, highlight the query in SAP HANA Studio and select EXPLAIN PLAN from the dropdown menu (see Figure 3.6).

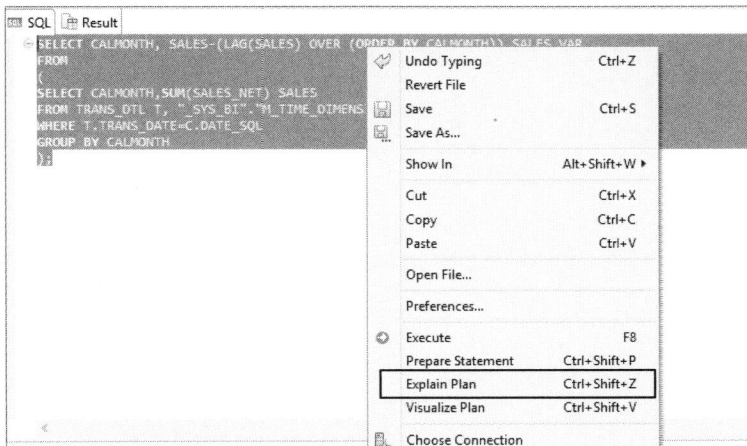

Figure 3.6 Explain Plan Menu

SAP HANA Studio will present the execution plan of the query plus the execution engine type, estimation of output size, cost, and so on (see Figure 3.7).

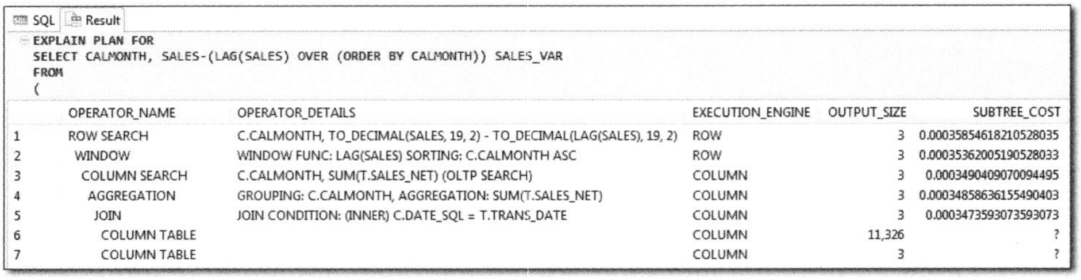
SQL Result

```
EXPLAIN PLAN FOR
SELECT CALMONTH, SALES-(LAG(SALES) OVER (ORDER BY CALMONTH)) SALES_VAR
FROM
(
```

	OPERATOR_NAME	OPERATOR_DETAILS	EXECUTION_ENGINE	OUTPUT_SIZE	SUBTREE_COST
1	ROW SEARCH	C.CALMONTH, TO_DECIMAL(SALES, 19, 2) - TO_DECIMAL(LAG(SALES), 19, 2)	ROW	3	0.00035854618210528035
2	WINDOW	WINDOW FUNC: LAG(SALES) SORTING: C.CALMONTH ASC	ROW	3	0.00035362005190528033
3	COLUMN SEARCH	C.CALMONTH, SUM(T.SALES_NET) (OLTP SEARCH)	COLUMN	3	0.0003490409070094495
4	AGGREGATION	GROUPING: C.CALMONTH, AGGREGATION: SUM(T.SALES_NET)	COLUMN	3	0.00034858636155490403
5	JOIN	JOIN CONDITION: (INNER) C.DATE_SQL = T.TRANS_DATE	COLUMN	3	0.0003473593073593073
6	COLUMN TABLE		COLUMN	11,326	?
7	COLUMN TABLE		COLUMN	3	?

Figure 3.7 Output of Explain Plan

When a query is sent to SAP HANA, it is parsed into several steps, and each step is sent to a related engine in a specified sequence. Figure 3.7 shows the following fields:

- `OPERATOR_NAME`
  The operator involved at each step.
- `OPERATOR_DETAILS`
  Provides the details that the engine follows.
- `EXECUTION_ENGINE`
  Describes which engine the query is executed on.
- `OUTPUT_SIZE`
  Provides the output row count for each step.
- `SUBTREE_COST`
  Provides the cost of each step.

You can write one query in multiple ways, then compare the execution plans of each to see which method is most efficient.

For a single query, some steps can be performed in the column engine, which is usually faster. Some steps have to be performed in the row engine, which is comparably slower. The size and cost are rough estimations that could differ from the actual run time.

A general thought on the query analysis is to find out which steps are in the row engine and which steps are in the column engine, then modify the query to change the steps from the row engine to the column engine.

3.4.2 Visualize Plan

SAP HANA also provides a way to perform query analysis on graphic views, via the visualize plan option. To use this option, highlight the query in SAP HANA Studio and select VISUALIZE PLAN from the dropdown menu (see Figure 3.8).

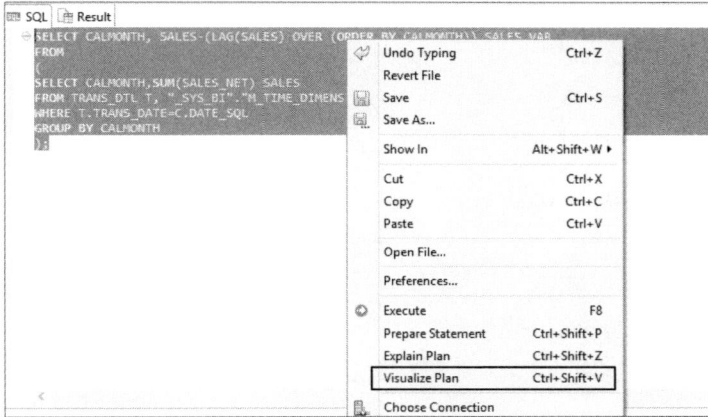

Figure 3.8 Visualize Plan Menu

The output is a graphic view of the execution plan. Each block shows one step. To check the details of each step, hover your mouse cursor over the relevant block; a popup box showing further details will appear (see Figure 3.9).

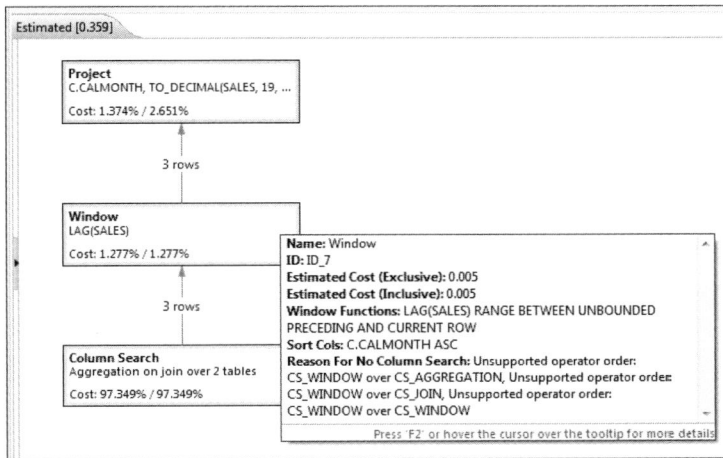

Figure 3.9 Output of Visualize Plan

3.4.3 Performance Trace

The explain plan and visualize plan functions provide estimated execution information on a query. However, to check how a query is actually processed, you need to use the performance trace function. You can find this function under the TRACE CONFIGURATION tab of the ADMINISTRATION panel in SAP HANA Studio (see Figure 3.10).

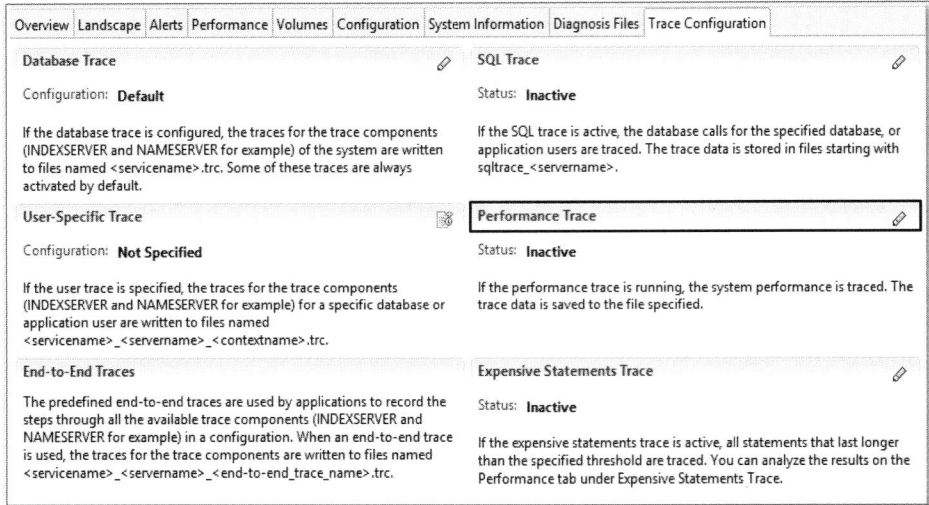

Figure 3.10 Administration Panel

You can edit the trace by clicking the EDIT button. You will see the popup window shown in Figure 3.11. Set the DURATION (MIN) field; make it long enough to cover the query you are going to run. Once the query completes its execution, you can wait for the trace to stop, or you can stop the trace manually from the TRACE CONFIGURATION window (see Figure 3.12).

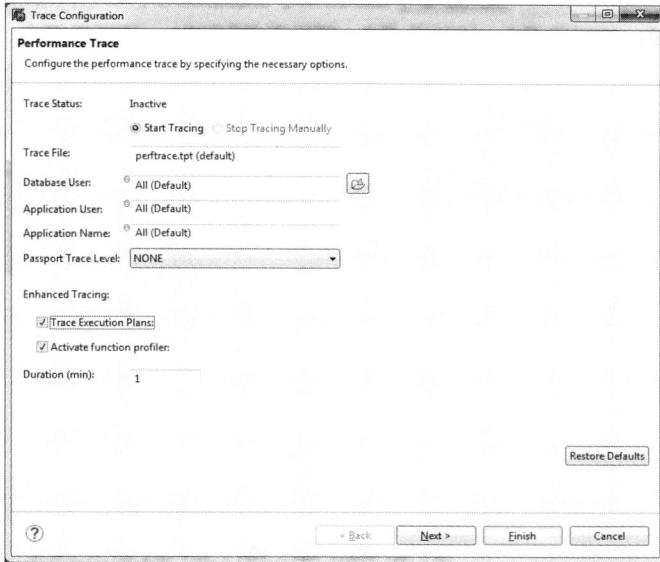

Figure 3.11 Trace Configuration Popup Window

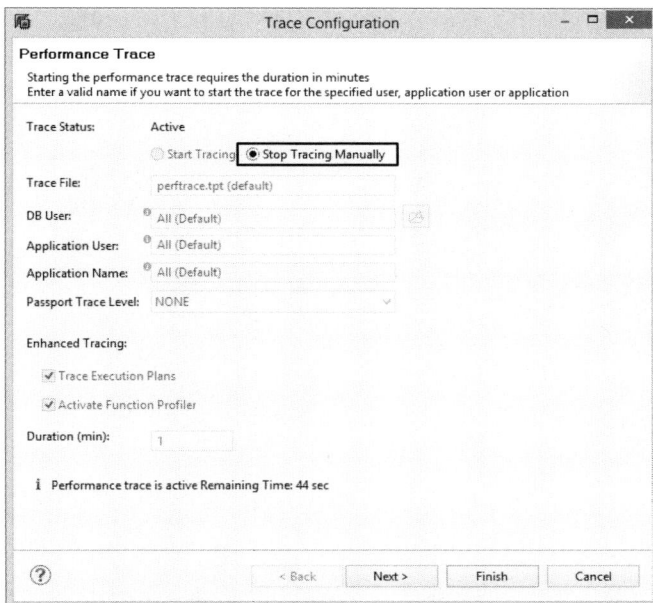

Figure 3.12 Stop a Performance Trace

To check the generated performance trace, you need to install X-Windows on a Microsoft Windows-based operating system. There are several varieties of X-Windows available. For the purposes of this chapter, we will use Cygwin, which is free to download. Figure 3.13 shows the software name and website address.

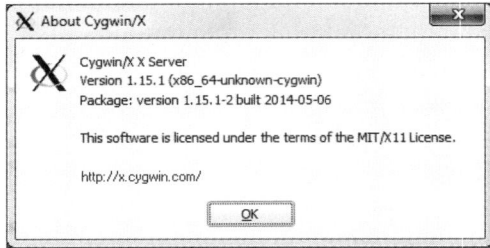

Figure 3.13 Cygwin/X Software

Launch the Cygwin Xwin Server application, as shown in Figure 3.14. Right-click the Xwin icon in the taskbar, and select Applications • xterm from the dropdown menu.

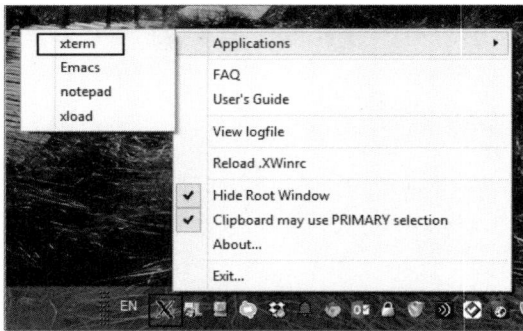

Figure 3.14 Starting xterm

From the xterm window, type the following command (see Figure 3.15):

```
ssh -Y user_name@host_name
```

Here, you choose the user name for the owner of the SAP HANA instance, such as xxxadm. The host name is the SAP HANA server host name. You will see the message Are you sure you want to continue connecting (yes/no)? Type "yes" and press ⌈Enter⌋. Now, you will see the Password field; type the user's password. Next, log on to the Linux server.

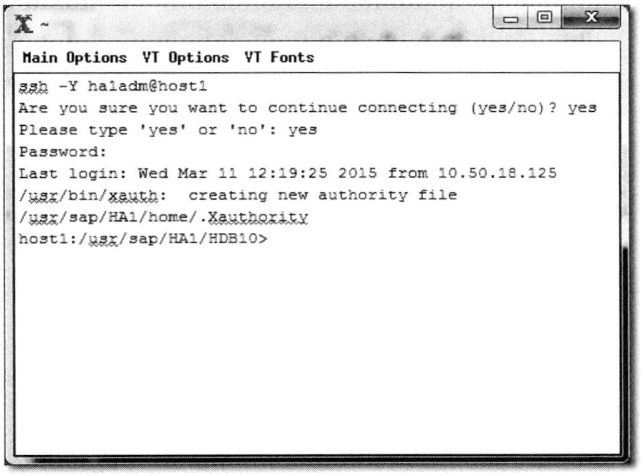

Figure 3.15 Logon to Linux Server

Enter the command "HDBAdmin.sh" in xterm, which will open the Xwin version of the SAP HANA Administration tool (see Figure 3.16).

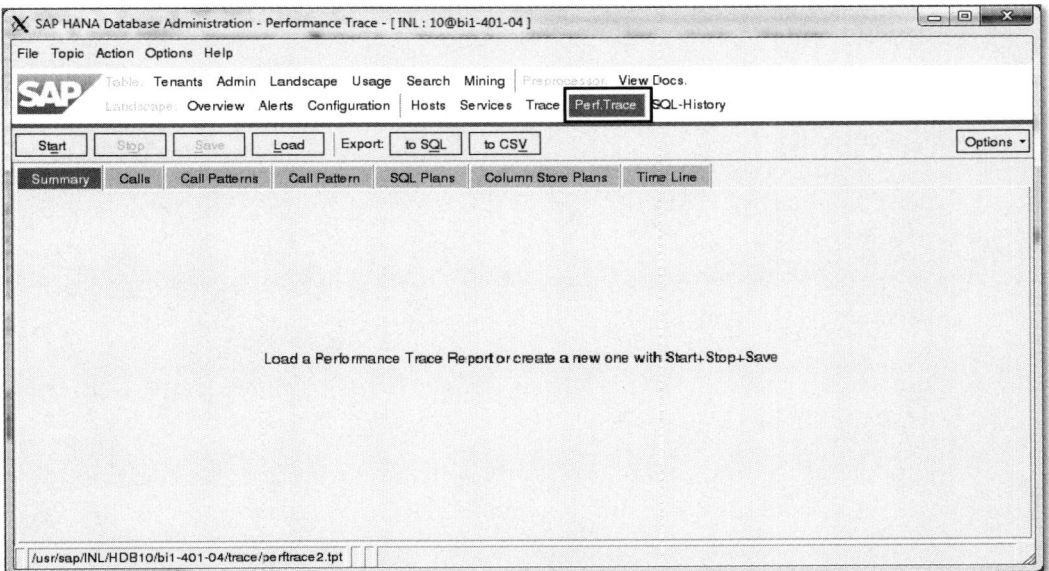

Figure 3.16 Xwin Verison of SAP HANA Administration Tool

From this tool, click the PERF. TRACE tab (see Figure 3.16). You can click on the START and STOP buttons to start and stop the performance trace. The functionality is the same as in SAP HANA Studio. To show the performance trace file, click the LOAD button. Find the trace file in the */usr/sap/SID/HDBnn/<hostname>/trace* folder, and load the file you have saved. The default file name is perftrace.tpt.

When the performance trace file is loaded, it opens to the SUMMARY tab, which displays information such as the host name, trace time, and so on (see Figure 3.17).

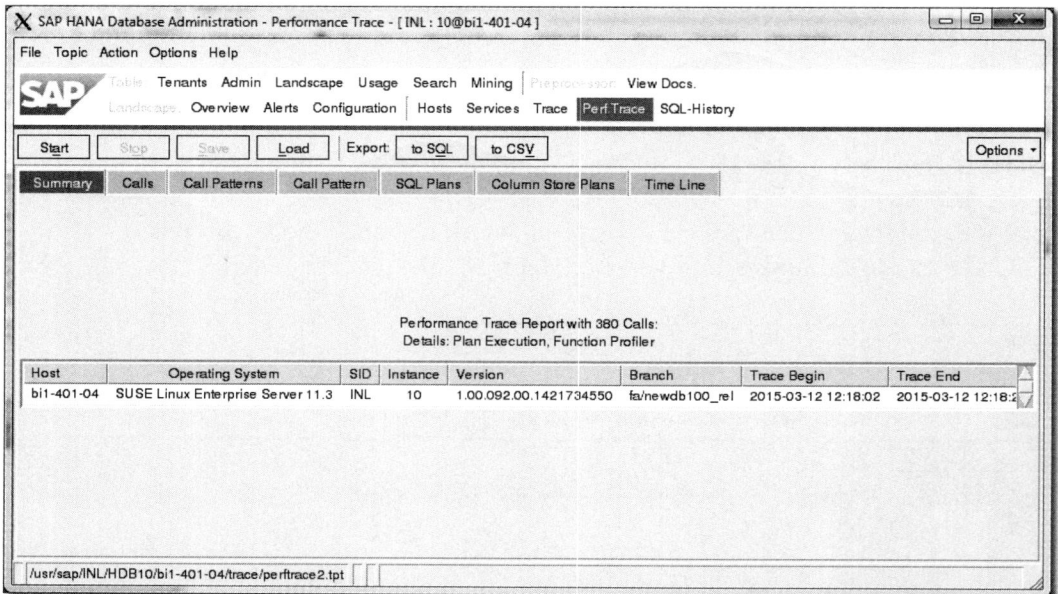

Figure 3.17 Load Performance Trace File

You can switch to the SQL PLANS tab, where you can see the queries captured in the trace file (see Figure 3.18).

Find the query you want to check, and double-click the line that contains it. You will see a detailed trace of the query under the CALL PATTERN tab (see Figure 3.19).

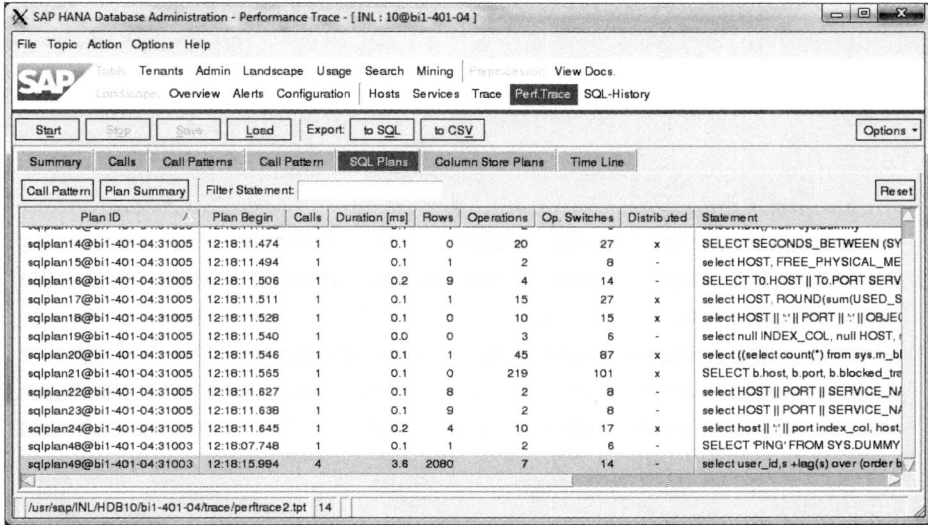

Figure 3.18 SQL Plans Tab

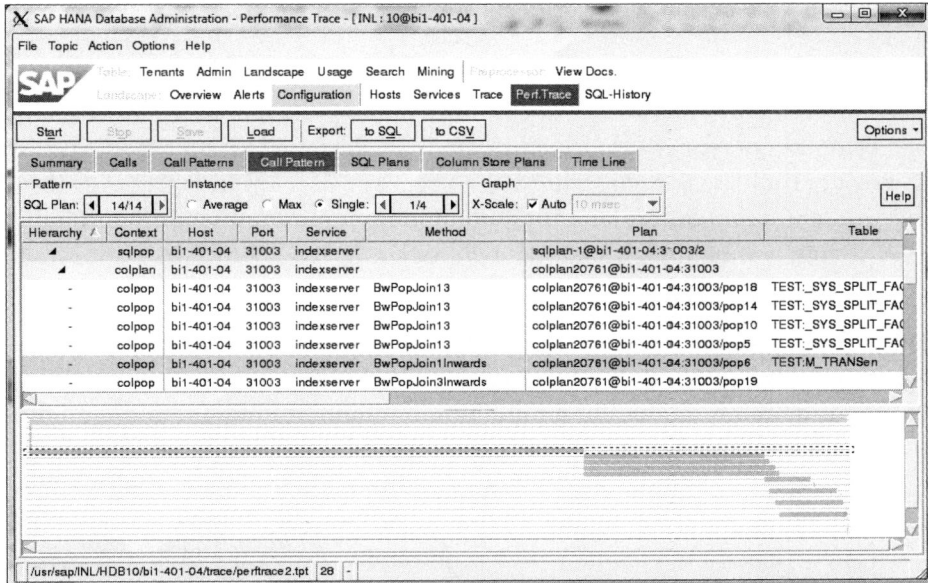

Figure 3.19 Call Pattern Tab

The CALL PATTERN tab contains two panels: The upper panel shows detailed steps, including METHOD, PLAN, ROW COUNT, DURATION, and so on. The lower panel provides a graphic view of the timespan. When you click on a step in the upper panel, the corresponding timeline in the lower panel will be highlighted, and vice versa.

As you can see, a query is parsed into several steps. Some steps can be processed in parallel, but some steps depend on other steps. If several steps are handled with multiple threads and processed within one period, that implies good parallelization. If a step is handled by a single thread that lasts a long time when all the other steps are delayed pending its completion, that implies a bottleneck in the query. Identifying bottlenecks can help when solving performance issues.

SAP HANA Engines

It is worth knowing the engines based on the prefixes of method names, such as `BwPop-AggregateParallel`. *Bw* means OLAP engine, *Sql* means SQL engine, and *CE* means calculation engine. Of these engines, the OLAP engine is the most powerful. By checking the method name, you can tell which steps are in faster engines and which are in slower engines.

3.5   Enforcing Execution Paths

For a complex query, performance may vary when the query is parsed into different execution plans. For example, when you have a query with joins for three tables, different join orders lead to different performance results (i.e., which two tables should join first, which table should join next).

Fortunately, with SAP HANA you do not have to collect a table's statistical information beforehand. Instead, you benefit from the column engine. In a column engine, it is easy for the SAP HANA optimizer to get statistical information, such as row count, distinct value count, maximum, minimum, and so on. As a result, the SAP HANA optimizer can make appropriate execution plans on the fly. The SAP HANA optimizer is powerful: When a complex query contains subqueries or views, the optimizer can break up the wrapping layers and drill up to the table level to reorganize the join path and aggregation path. Let's look at a simple example to see how the execution plan is made (see Listing 3.16).

```
SELECT A.*
FROM FACT_1 A,
```

```
(SELECT DEP_ID
FROM FACT_2 B, M_TRANS C
WHERE B.TRANS_NO=C.TRANS_NO
) D
WHERE A.DEP_ID=D.DEP_ID;
```
Listing 3.16 Query with Subquery

Here, you have a subquery in the query to wrap the join of the two tables. When you check the execution plan, you can see that the join at the subquery is brought up to the same level as the main query. Then, the SAP HANA optimizer will decide which join to proceed with based on the table's statistical information, regardless of the join order in your original SQL query (see Figure 3.20).

OPERATOR_NAME	OPERATOR_DETAILS
COLUMN SEARCH	A.TRANS_DATE, A.TRANS_NO, A.DEP_ID, A.PROD_TYPE, A.USER_ID, A.PROD_ID, A.SALES_NET (LATE MATERIALIZATION, OLTP SEARCH)
JOIN	JOIN CONDITION: (INNER) B.TRANS_NO = C.TRANS_NO, (INNER) A.DEP_ID = D.DEP_ID
COLUMN TABLE	
COLUMN TABLE	
COLUMN TABLE	

Figure 3.20 Execution Plan of a Reorganized Join Path

However, if the logic of a query is complex and contains multiple join or aggregation steps, different execution paths will be generated with different intermediate result sets, and the statistics of these intermediate result sets will not be available to the SAP HANA optimizer. All the SAP HANA optimizer can do is follow the general rules to make the execution plan based on the statistics of the underlying tables.

On the other hand, users who create queries usually have deep knowledge of a table's content and might understand the appropriate execution path. Such users usually wrap the logic with views or subqueries and expect the SAP HANA optimizer to follow the join and aggregation order when generating the execution plan. Unfortunately, the SAP HANA optimizer has to follow general rules when parsing the queries, and the actual execution plan can be quite different from what a user might expect.

Fortunately, there is a way to enforce the execution path and make it the same as shown in your SQL query or stored procedure. You can use the TOP/LIMIT clause to enforce the execution path. Let's look at an example SQL query (see Listing 3.17).

```
SELECT A.TRANS_DATE,B.TRANS_DESC
FROM FACT_1 A,M_TRANS B
```

```
WHERE A.TRANS_NO=B.TRANS_NO
AND A.TRANS_NO IN (
SELECT C.TRANS_NO
FROM FACT_2 C,M_TRANS D
WHERE C.TRANS_NO=D.TRANS_NO
AND C.DEP_ID=1);
```

Listing 3.17 Query without TOP/LIMIT Clause

You can see the execution plan in Figure 3.21. The join in the subquery is brought up to the main query level, which means that the SAP HANA optimizer does not comply with the join order wrapped in the query.

OPERATOR_NAME	OPERATOR_DETAILS	EXECUTION
COLUMN SEARCH	A.TRANS_DATE, B.TRANS_DESC (LATE MATERIALIZATION)	OLAP
DISTINCT	GROUPING: M_TRANS.ROWID, FACT_1.ROWID	OLAP
COLUMN SEARCH	[FACT] A.TRANS_DATE, FACT_1.ROWID, B.TRANS_DESC, M_TRANS.ROWID	COLUMN
JOIN	JOIN CONDITION: (INNER) C.TRANS_NO = D.TRANS_NO, (INNER) C.TRANS_NO = B.TRANS_NO, (INNER) A.TRANS_NO = B.TRANS_NO	COLUMN
COLUMN TABLE		COLUMN
COLUMN TABLE	FILTER CONDITION: C.DEP_ID = 1	COLUMN
COLUMN TABLE		COLUMN
COLUMN TABLE		COLUMN

Figure 3.21 Execution Plan When the Join Path Is Not Enforced

To resolve this, you can try to add a `TOP`/`LIMIT` clause to the wrapped logic for which you want to enforce the execution path. Examine the query using the `LIMIT` clause in Listing 3.18.

```
SELECT A.TRANS_DATE,B.TRANS_DESC
FROM FACT_1 A,M_TRANS B
WHERE A.TRANS_NO=B.TRANS_NO
AND A.TRANS_NO IN (
SELECT C.TRANS_NO
FROM FACT_2 C,M_TRANS D
WHERE C.TRANS_NO=D.TRANS_NO
AND C.DEP_ID=1
LIMIT 1000000000000);
```

Listing 3.18 Query with LIMIT Clause

Or, you can use the `TOP` clause in the query, as shown in Listing 3.19.

```
SELECT A.TRANS_DATE,B.TRANS_DESC
FROM FACT_1 A,M_TRANS B
WHERE A.TRANS_NO=B.TRANS_NO
AND A.TRANS_NO IN (
SELECT TOP 1000000000000 C.TRANS_NO
FROM FACT_2 C,M_TRANS D
```

```
WHERE C.TRANS_NO=D.TRANS_NO
AND C.DEP_ID=1);
```

Listing 3.19 Query with TOP Clause

The number 10000000000 is an arbitrary value that is supposed to be great enough to cover the intermediate result. Review the execution plan of the query in Figure 3.22.

OPERATOR_NAME	OPERATOR_DETAILS	EXECUTION_ENGINE
COLUMN SEARCH	A.TRANS_DATE, B.TRANS_DESC (LATE MATERIALIZATION, OLTP SEARCH)	COLUMN
JOIN	JOIN CONDITION: (INNER) C.TRANS_NO = B.TRANS_NO, (INNER) A.TRANS_NO = B.TRANS_NO	COLUMN
COLUMN TABLE		COLUMN
COLUMN TABLE		COLUMN
COLUMN SEARCH	C.TRANS_NO	OLAP
DISTINCT	GROUPING: C.TRANS_NO	OLAP
COLUMN SEARCH	[FACT] C.TRANS_NO	COLUMN
LIMIT	NUM RECORDS: 1000000000000	COLUMN
JOIN	JOIN CONDITION: (INNER) C.TRANS_NO = D.TRANS_NO	COLUMN
COLUMN TABLE	FILTER CONDITION: C.DEP_ID = 1	COLUMN
COLUMN TABLE		COLUMN

Figure 3.22 Execution Plan When the Join Path Is Enforced

You can see that the join in the subquery is processed first, and then the result set of the subquery participates in the join at the upper layer. The TOP/LIMIT clause also impacts the sequence of grouping steps and makes the grouping operation happen on the result set of the subquery instead of on the upper layer. You can find the differences by checking the timeline from the performance trace (see Figure 3.23).

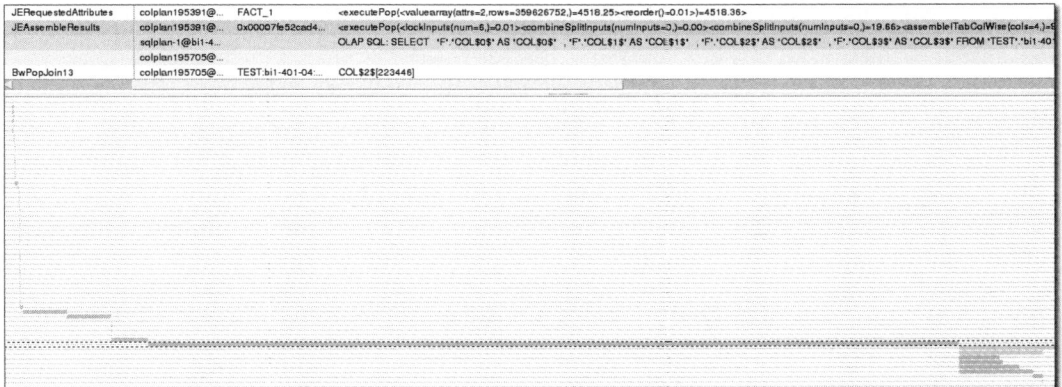

Figure 3.23 Performance Trace on a Query without an Enforced Execution Path

The performance trace without the enforced execution path has a very long time-line, which shows the operation on a large dataset. It takes more than two minutes to run this particular query. Next, let's look at the query with the enforced execution path (see Figure 3.24).

Figure 3.24 Performance Trace on Query with an Enforced Execution Path

From the performance trace on the query with the enforced execution path, you can see two comparably shorter timelines that show the operation on the two smaller datasets. It takes less than seven seconds to run this query. This example uses the TOP/LIMIT clause to split an expensive step into less expensive steps by enforcing the execution path.

To fine-tune a complex query or stored procedure, you can use the performance trace tool to get an idea of how the query is performed and to figure out the bottleneck. By testing different execution plans, you can determine whether the bottleneck is due to a bad execution path and also test whether a query with an enforced execution path can eliminate the bottleneck.

In the next section, we will discuss the less expensive method of using a union rather than a join.

3.6 Using a Union with Constant Values Instead of a Join

You can make a join in an attribute view, analytic view, calculation view, and so on. Whatever engine you choose, join operations between large tables are always expensive. If possible, you should consider other approaches rather than using a join. In this section, we will introduce using a union with constant values as an alternative.

Let's start with a simple example to see the kinds of joins that can be changed into unions. Suppose you have a large table `Trans_A(Trans_Date, Trans_No, Dep_id, Pro_id, Sales_net)`, as shown in Listing 3.20.

```
CREATE COLUMN TABLE Trans_A(
Trans_Date DATE,
Trans_No BIGINT,
Dep_id INT,
Pro_id INT,
Sales_net DECIMAL(18,2));
```
Listing 3.20 Definition of Table Trans_A

You also have another table `Credit_log(Trans_Date, Trans_No, Dep_id, Pro_id, Credit_point)`, as shown in Listing 3.21.

```
CREATE COLUMN TABLE Trans_B(
Trans_Date DATE,
Trans_No BIGINT,
Dep_id INT,
Pro_id INT,
Credit DECIMAL(18,2));
```
Listing 3.21 Definition of Table Trans_B

To perform an analysis based on the two tables, use the logic shown in Listing 3.22.

```
SELECT A.Dep_id,SUM(Sales_net),SUM(Credit)
FROM Trans_A A,Trans_B B
WHERE A.Trans_Date=B.Trans_Date
AND A.Trans_No=B.Trans_No
GROUP BY A.Dep_id;
```
Listing 3.22 Query to Join Two Tables

You can create this join in a calculation view on the TRANS_DATE and TRANS_NO columns (see Figure 3.25).

At this point, you can run a query based on the calculation view, as shown in Listing 3.23.

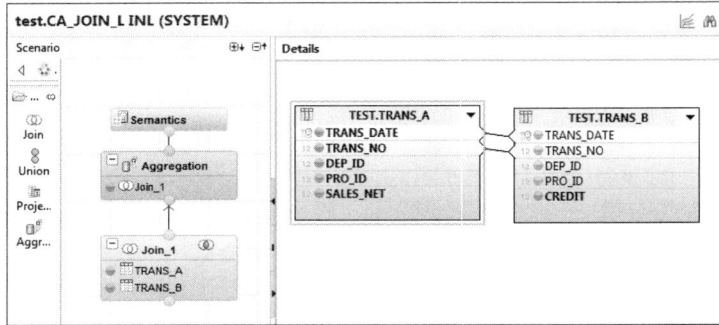

Figure 3.25 Join Two Tables in a Calculation View

```
SELECT Dep_id,SUM(Sales_net),SUM(Credit)
FROM _SYS_BIC."test/CA_JOIN_L"
GROUP BY Dep_id;
```
Listing 3.23 Query Against the Calculation View Using a Join

However, it would be time-consuming to run this query, because both tables are large. For this particular query, because the Dep_id column has redundancies across the two tables, you must create two aggregation nodes in the calculation view, group them by Dep_id, and then join the two result sets on the Dep_id column. However, by doing this you lose flexibility for analysis at other granularities.

A recommended approach in this sort of situation is to use a union with constant values instead of a join. The idea is to concatenate the two tables with the UNION ALL operator and specify a constant value or NULL for the missing columns on each table. The logic is shown in Listing 3.24.

```
SELECT Trans_Date, Trans_No, Dep_id, Pro_id, Sales_net, NULL as Credit
FROM Trans_A
UNION ALL
SELECT Trans_Date, Trans_No, Dep_id, Pro_id, NULL as Sales_net, Credit
FROM Trans_B;
```
Listing 3.24 Query to Union Two Tables

You can put the logic into a calculation view, as shown in Figure 3.26.

The union node shows that the Trans_Date, Trans_No, Dep_id, and Pro_id columns on Trans_A map their corresponding columns on Trans_B. The Sales_net and Credit columns do not have mapping columns (see Figure 3.27).

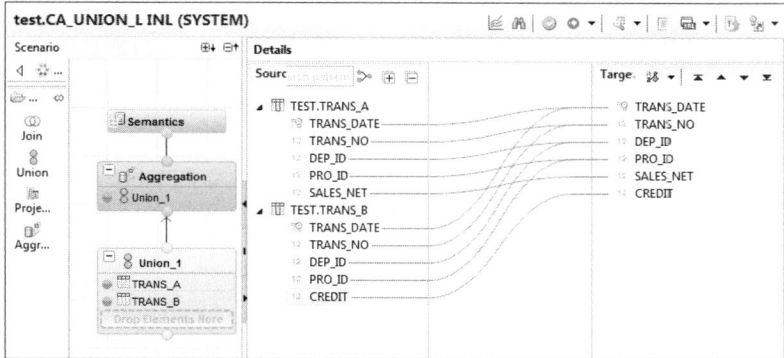

Figure 3.26 Union with Constant Values

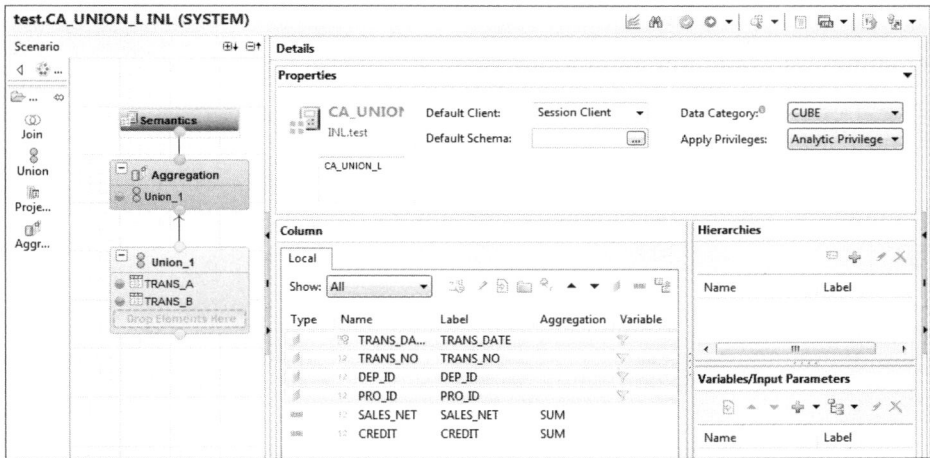

Figure 3.27 Aggregation after Union

After the union, you have an aggregation node with the group by columns Trans_Date, Trans_No, Dep_id, and Pro_id. As a result, the records of the two tables that were supposed to be joined will be united in the aggregation process. To analyze the granularity of Dep_id, you can execute the query shown in Listing 3.25.

```
SELECT Dep_id,SUM(Sales_net),SUM(Credit)
FROM _SYS_BIC."test/CA_UNION_L"
GROUP BY Dep_id;
```

Listing 3.25 Query Against the Calculation View Using a Union

A union with constant values can also handle different kinds of set operations, such as union, minus/except, intersect, and so on.

As an example, let's prepare two sets: Set_A with values A, B, C, and D, and Set_B with values C, D, E, and F. Prepare the tables with the statements shown in Listing 3.26.

```
INSERT INTO SET_A VALUES('A');
INSERT INTO SET_A VALUES('B');
INSERT INTO SET_A VALUES('C');
INSERT INTO SET_A VALUES('D');
INSERT INTO SET_B VALUES('C');
INSERT INTO SET_B VALUES('D');
INSERT INTO SET_B VALUES('E');
INSERT INTO SET_B VALUES('F');
```

Listing 3.26 INSERT Statements to Populate SET_A and SET_B

To identify each set, create a calculated column on each column:

```
ALTER TABLE Set_A ADD(SET_A_FLAG INT GENERATED ALWAYS AS 1);
ALTER TABLE Set_B ADD(SET_B_FLAG INT GENERATED ALWAYS AS 1);
```

In the calculation view, make the union with constant values. You can then map the column IDs between the two tables and set separate target columns for SET_A_FLAG and SET_B_FLAG (see Figure 3.28).

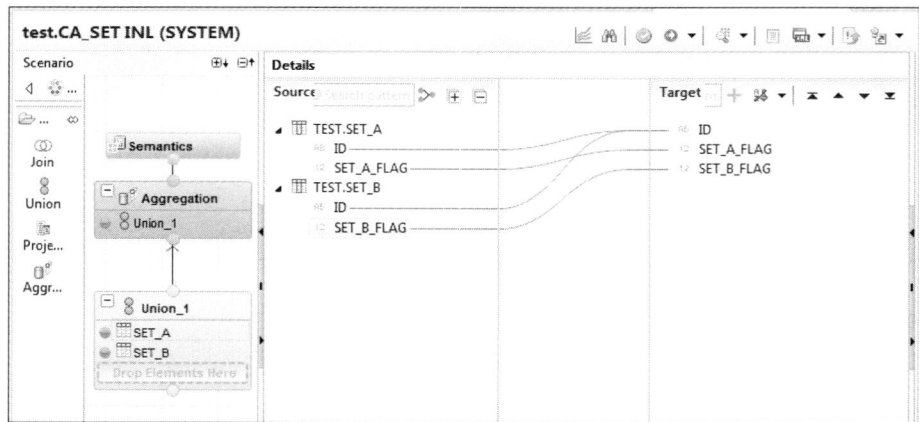

Figure 3.28 Determine Set with the Flag Column

The output of the calculation view is the aggregation of SET_A_FLAG and SET_B_FLAG grouped by column ID (see Figure 3.29).

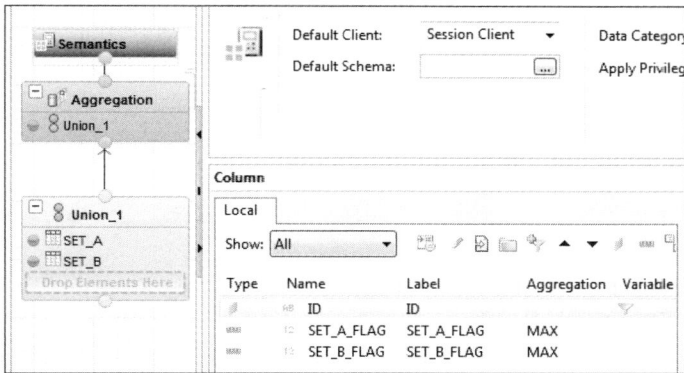

Figure 3.29 Set the Flag as an Aggregation Column

By filtering the aggregation columns of the calculation view, you can use the following set operations:

- **Union**
  No filter is needed.

  - SQL query logic:
    ```
    SELECT ID FROM SET_A UNION SELECT ID FROM SET_B;
    ```

  - Calculation view approach:
    ```
    SELECT ID FROM _SYS_BIC."test/CA_SET";
    ```

  The output is {A,B,C,D,E,F}.

- **Minus/except**
  Set the filter to choose records for SET_A_FLAG, but not SET_B_FLAG.

  - SQL query logic:
    ```
    SELECT ID FROM SET_A MINUS SELECT ID FROM SET_B;
    ```

  - Calculation view approach:
    ```
    SELECT ID FROM _SYS_BIC."test/CA_SET" WHERE SET_A_FLAG=1 AND
    SET_B_FLAG IS NULL;
    ```

  The output is {A,B}.

▶ **Intersect**
Set the filter to choose records with both SET_A_FLAG and SET_B_FLAG.

  ▹ SQL query logic:
```
SELECT ID FROM SET_A INTERSECT SELECT ID FROM SET_B;
```

  ▹ Calculation view approach:
```
SELECT ID FROM _SYS_BIC."test/CA_SET" WHERE SET_A_FLAG=1 AND
SET_B_FLAG=1;
```

  The output is {C,D}.

▶ **Special set operation to select all except intersection**
Set filter to include the records that have neither SET_A_FLAG or SET_B_FLAG.

  ▹ SQL query logic:
```
(SELECT ID FROM SET_A MINUS SELECT ID FROM SET_B)
UNION ALL
(SELECT ID FROM SET_B MINUS SELECT ID FROM SET_A);
```

  ▹ Calculation view approach:
```
SELECT ID FROM _SYS_BIC."test/CA_SET" WHERE SET_A_FLAG IS NULL OR
SET_B_FLAG IS NULL;
```

  The output is {A,B,E,F}.

In addition, the solution can be applied to set operations with more than two datasets and perform more complex set operations.

In this section, we introduced the use of a union with constant values. Note that not all types of joins are suitable for replacement with unions; you still need joins in many cases. In the next section, we will focus on techniques for joins in an analytic view.

3.7   Manipulating Joins in an Analytic View

In this section, we will look at the specific techniques that can be employed when manipulating joins in an analytic view. This includes breaking a union of dimension tables, leveraging the OLAP engine to create nonequi joins in an analytic view, and modifying tables for analytic views. Let's begin by looking at breaking unions of dimension tables.

3.7.1 Breaking a Union of Dimension Tables

Because the OLAP engine is the most powerful engine in SAP HANA and an analytic view can fully exploit it, you should try your best to put expensive joins in an analytic view—but there are some restrictions to note. For example, analytic views cannot perform union operations. If there is a join between a fact table and a union of dimension tables, you need a calculation view. However, there is a way around this that will allow you to harness the improved performance of the analytic view by eliminating unions from the process. The idea is to split the dimension table into multiple attribute views and then join to fact tables separately in the analytic view. This will allow you to efficiently leverage the OLAP engine.

Let's look at an example that shows how to eliminate the union from the dimension tables. Suppose you have the fact table `Trans_DTL(Trans_DATE, Trans_No, Prod_ID, Sales_Qty, Sales_Net)` and two dimension tables. One dimension table is `Prod_Category_A(Prod_ID, Prod_type, Prod_desc)`, and the other table is `Prod_Category_B(Prod_ID, Prod_type, Prod_desc)`. You want to perform the SQL query shown in Listing 3.27.

```
SELECT PROD_TYPE,SUM(SALES_NET)
FROM TRANS_DTL A
LEFT OUTER JOIN
(
SELECT PROD_ID,PROD_TYPE,PROD_DESC FROM PROD_CATEGORY_A
UNION
SELECT PROD_ID,PROD_TYPE,PROD_DESC FROM PROD_CATEGORY_B
) B
ON A.PROD_ID=B.PROD_ID
GROUP BY PROD_TYPE;
```
Listing 3.27 Query to Show the Logic of a Join after Union

For the purposes of comparison, create a calculation view. First, add a node to union the two tables `Prod_Category_A` and `Prod_Category_B`. Next, we add a node to join the union result set to the fact table `Trans_Dtl`. Finally, add an aggregation node to aggregate the join result set (see Figure 3.30).

For large datasets, the performance of a calculation view does not measure up to an analytic view. Therefore, for the best performance, you need to think about another approach using an analytic view. In this example, you can write the SQL query in a different way, one that eliminates the union to prepare the logic for an analytic view (see Listing 3.28).

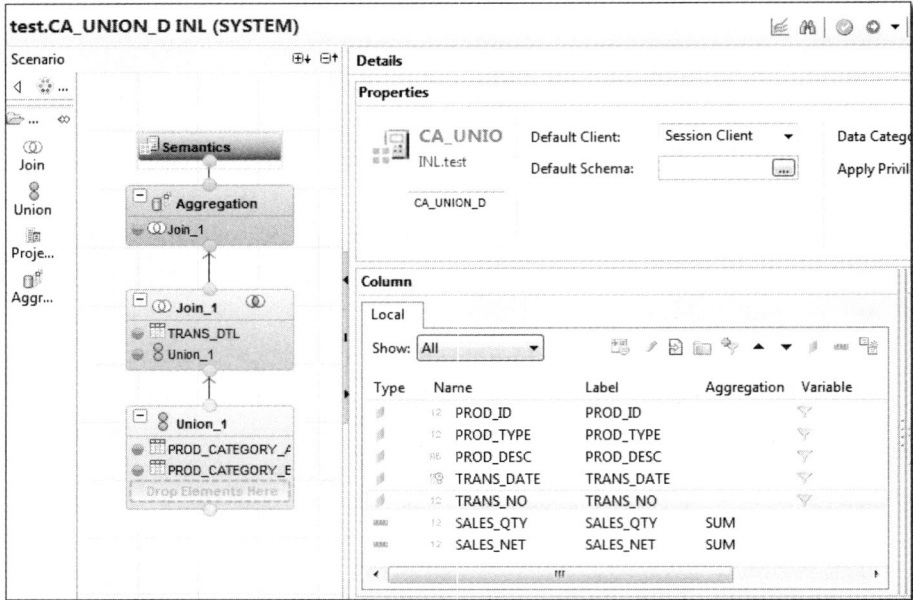

Figure 3.30 Calculation View with a Union and Join Nodes

```
SELECT COALESCE(A.PROD_TYPE,B.PROD_TYPE),SUM(SALES_NET)
FROM TRANS_DTL D
LEFT OUTER JOIN PROD_CATEGORY_A A
ON   D.PROD_ID=A.PROD_ID
LEFT OUTER JOIN PROD_CATEGORY_A B
ON   D.PROD_ID=B.PROD_ID
GROUP BY COALESCE(A.PROD_TYPE,B.PROD_TYPE);
```
Listing 3.28 Query to Show the Logic of Multiple Left Outer Joins

Because the union now has been eliminated, you can put the logic into an analytic view (see Figure 3.31).

For this process to succeed, you must first create separate attribute views for the dimension tables, then link them to the fact table in the analytic view with a left outer join. Next, create aliases for the PROD_TYPE column of the attribute views as PROD_TYPE_A and PROD_TYPE_B. Finally, define the PROD_TYPE calculated column as follows:

```
If(Isnull("PROD_TYPE_A"),"PROD_TYPE_B","PROD_TYPE_A")
```

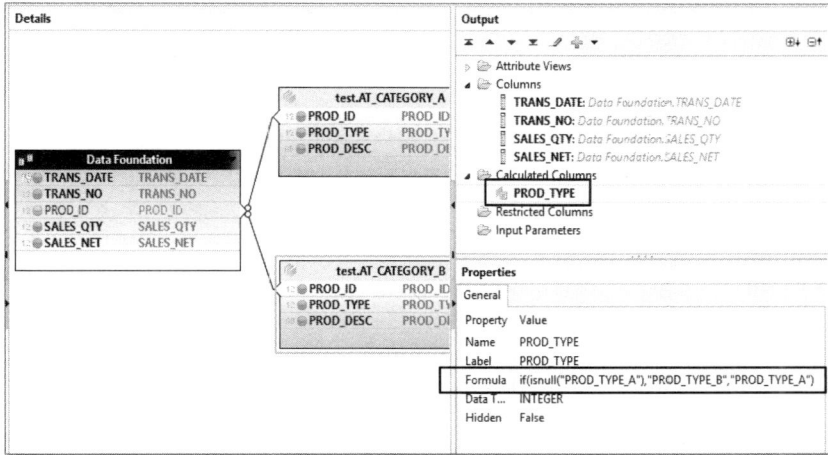

Figure 3.31 Analytic View to Break a Union of Dimension Tables

The query against the analytic view is shown in Listing 3.29.

```
SELECT PROD_TYPE,SUM(SALES_NET)
FROM _SYS_BIC."test/AN_UNION"
GROUP BY PROD_TYPE;
```

Listing 3.29 Query Against the Analytic View

Real-world scenarios can be more complex than the example we just showed. For example, assume you have a customer table that is updated three times each year. If there is a change in a customer record, you add a new record with a version ID each time. The version ID can have values of 1, 2, or 3, so each customer may have one, two, or three records in the table. Let's define the customer table as M_CUST(CUST_ID, CUST_TYPE, VERSION_ID), as shown in Listing 3.30.

```
CREATE COLUMN TABLE M_CUST(
CUST_ID INT,
CUST_TYPE INT,
VERSION_ID INT);
```

Listing 3.30 Definition of Table M_Cust

Now, define the fact table as F_TRANS(TRANS_NO, CUST_ID, SALES_NET), as shown in Listing 3.31.

```
CREATE COLUMN TABLE F_TRANS(
TRANS_NO BIGINT,
```

```
CUST_ID INT,
SALES_NET DECIMAL(18,2));
```
Listing 3.31 Definition of Table F_TRANS

For this example, to make a valid link between the fact table and dimension table, you have to determine the most current customer record, which should have the maximum VERSION_ID for each customer, and generate a dataset with has a distinct CUST_ID, then join the dataset to fact table. The SQL query can be defined as shown in Listing 3.32.

```
SELECT D.CUST_TYPE,SUM(SALES_NET)
FROM F_TRANS F
LEFT OUTER JOIN
(SELECT A.CUST_ID,A.CUST_TYPE
FROM M_CUST A,
(SELECT CUST_ID,MAX(VERSION_ID) VERSION_ID
FROM M_CUST
GROUP BY CUST_ID) B
WHERE A.CUST_ID=B.CUST_ID
AND A.VERSION_ID=B.VERSION_ID) D
ON F.CUST_ID=D.CUST_ID
GROUP BY D.CUST_TYPE;
```
Listing 3.32 Query to Show the Logic of a Join after Aggregation

This can be done easily with a calculation view, though in this case, try the approach of using an analytic view to improve performance.

First, create three attribute views, AT_CUST_1, AT_CUST_2, and AT_CUST_3, and make the filter on VERSION_ID with values of 1, 2, and 3 respectively (see Figure 3.32).

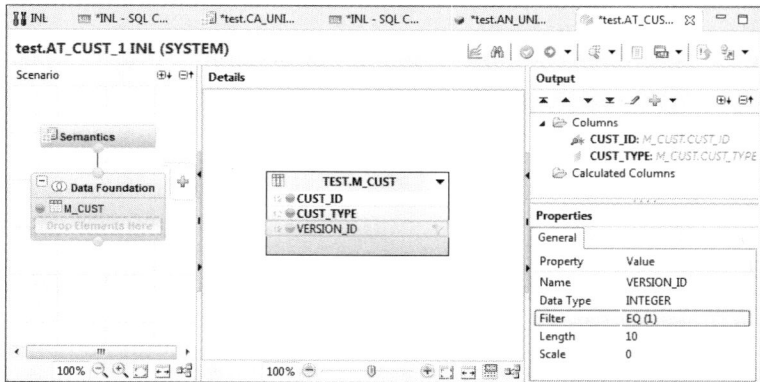

Figure 3.32 Attribute View with a Filter on VERSION_ID

Next, create an analytic view to link the three attribute views to the fact table (see Figure 3.33).

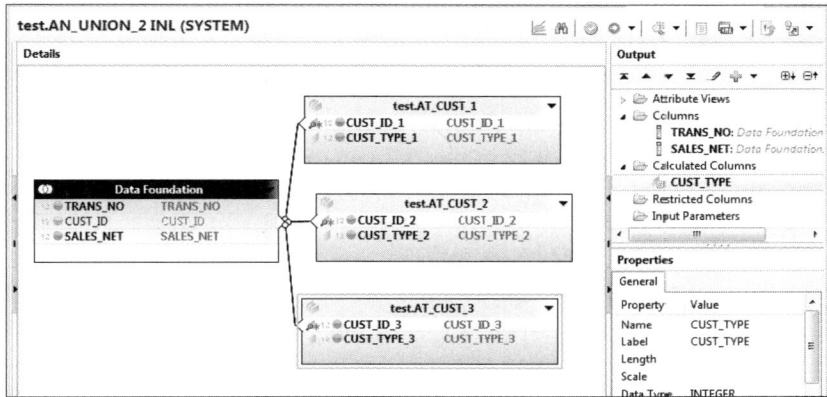

Figure 3.33 Analytic View to Link Three Attribute Views

In addition, you need to create a calculated column CUST_TYPE. The logic is to get the CUST_TYPE value from the record for VERSION_ID=3. If that record is not available, you can get the value from the record for VERSION_ID=2. Otherwise, you need to get the value from the record for VERSION_ID=1 (see the expression in Figure 3.34).

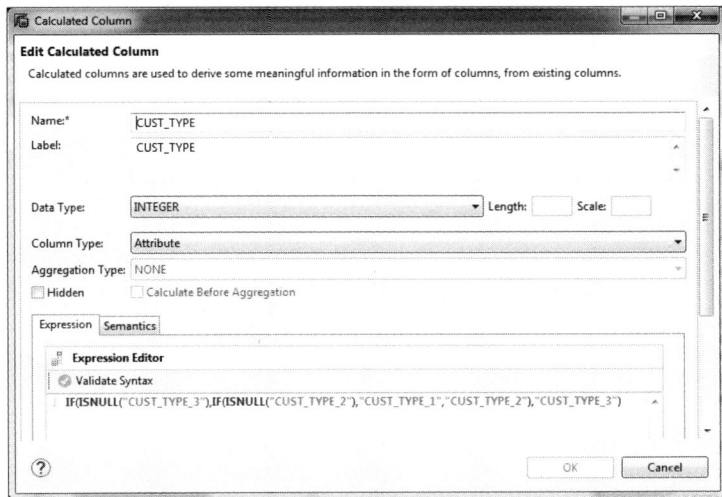

Figure 3.34 CUST_TYPE Calculated Column

The query against the analytic view is shown in Listing 3.33.

```
SELECT CUST_TYPE,SUM(SALES_NET)
FROM _SYS_BIC."test/AN_UNION_2"
GROUP BY CUST_TYPE;
```
Listing 3.33 Query Against the Analytic View

Again, the idea is to split the dimension table into multiple attribute views and join to the fact table separately in the analytic view in order to leverage the OLAP engine efficiently.

3.7.2 Making Nonequi Joins

You may encounter nonequi joins occasionally; nonequi joins are relatively more expensive than equi joins. In order to improve the join performance by leveraging OLAP, let's see how to create nonequi joins in an analytic view. Suppose you have a fact table TEST_RESULT, as shown in Listing 3.34.

```
CREATE COLUMN TABLE TEST_RESULT(
TEST_NO BIGINT,
TEST_DATE DATE,
FACTOR INT,
RESULT DECIMAL(18,2)
);
```
Listing 3.34 Definition of Table TEST_RESULT

To make the playground, create some sample records, as shown in Listing 3.35.

```
INSERT INTO TEST_RESULT VALUES(1,'2014-01-01',3,32.3);
INSERT INTO TEST_RESULT VALUES(2,'2014-01-01',300,324.5);
INSERT INTO TEST_RESULT VALUES(2,'2014-01-01',3000,3.23);
INSERT INTO TEST_RESULT VALUES(2,'2014-01-01',5000, 98099.12);
```
Listing 3.35 INSERT Statements of Table TEST_RESULT

You also need a dimension table M_BUCKET, like that in Listing 3.36.

```
CREATE COLUMN TABLE M_BUCKET(
BUCKET_ID INT,
BUCKET_FROM INT,
BUCKET_TO INT);
```
Listing 3.36 Definition of Table M_BUCKET

And, you also need to create some sample records, as shown in Listing 3.37.

```
INSERT INTO M_BUCKET VALUES(1,0,100);
INSERT INTO M_BUCKET VALUES(2,101,3500);
INSERT INTO M_BUCKET VALUES(3,3501,90000);
```
Listing 3.37 INSERT Statements of Table M_BUCKET Nonequi Join Operators

The nonequi join operators can be greater than, less than, or between. As an example, use a BETWEEN operator. Assume that you want to achieve the logic as shown in Listing 3.38.

```
SELECT BUCKET_ID,SUM(RESULT)
FROM TEST_RESULT A, M_BUCKET B
WHERE FACTOR BETWEEN BUCKET_FROM AND BUCKET_TO
GROUP BY BUCKET_ID;
```
Listing 3.38 Query of a Table Join with a Nonequi Condition

To make the join in the analytic view, first create a calculated column for each table:

```
ALTER TABLE TEST_RESULT ADD(F INT GENERATED ALWAYS AS 1);
ALTER TABLE M_BUCKET ADD(F INT GENERATED ALWAYS AS 1);
```

Then, join the two tables on this calculated column in the analytic view.

In Figure 3.35, in addition to the join column, we also set the TEMPORAL COLUMN as FACTOR on the fact table, set the FROM COLUMN as BUCKET_FROM, and set the TO COLUMN as BUCKET_TO on the dimension table. This works as a join condition as "Factor between BUCKET_FROM and BUCKET_TO."

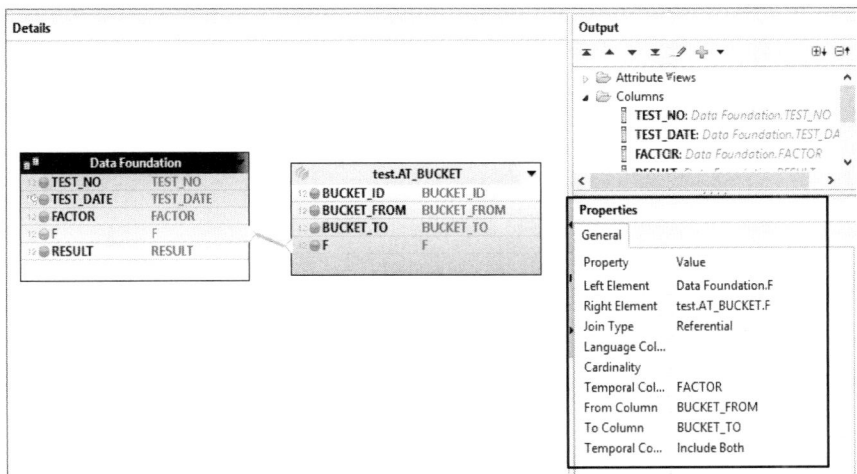

Figure 3.35 Nonequi Join in an Analytic View

The query against this analytic view is shown in Listing 3.39.

```
SELECT BUCKET_ID,SUM(RESULT)
FROM _SYS_BIC."test/AN_NON_EQUI"
GROUP BY BUCKET_ID;
```

Listing 3.39 Query Against an Analytic View That Has a Join with a Nonequi Condition

Figure 3.36 shows the output.

	BUCKET_ID	SUM(RESULT)
1	1	32.3
2	2	327.73
3	3	98,099.12

Figure 3.36 Output of the Nonequi Join Analytic View

This is an example for the BETWEEN operator; if you work with a GREATER THAN operator, you need to create a calculated column on the dimension table and set a constant value like 999999, which is large enough, then put the column into the join definition. Because the logic of A is greater than B is the same as A is between B and 999999, you can achieve the logic with the same approach.

The temporal column feature was originally designed for time-dependent dimension tables, but you can expand the capability whenever it is necessary.

3.7.3 Modifying Tables

On the SAP HANA platform, creating physical aggregated tables is not recommended. This allows you to stay close to the original source of information, which helps manage a single source of truth by retaining data at the most granular level. This does not mean that you cannot alter the table structure, however. You can encounter some situations that require you to modify the table structure, generate dimension data, and so on.

Let's start with a simple example to show how to modify a dimension table and make it usable in an analytic view. Suppose you have table Prod_cat(Prod_id, prod_cat, update_date) that contains time-dependent dimension data (see Listing 3.40).

```
CREATE COLUMN TABLE Prod_cat(
Prod_id int,
```

```
Prod_cat int,
Update_date date);
```
Listing 3.40 Definition of Table Prod_cat

To make the playground, insert some sample records:

```
INSERT INTO Prod_cat VALUES(1,1,'2013-01-01');
INSERT INTO Prod_cat VALUES(1,2,'2014-01-01');
```

In this example, the fact table is Trans_DTL(Trans_DATE, Trans_No, Prod_ID, Sales_Qty, Sales_Net). You expect to join the fact table to the time-dependent dimension table on the Prod_id column with the valid record. To check if a record on the dimension table is valid, see whether Update_date is less than or equal to Trans_DATE and whether Trans_DATE is less than the value of Update_date on the next record for the particular Prod_id in question. The value of the Update_date column in the record and the value of the Update_date column in the subsequent record is the range of validation. If the record is the last one of the particular Prod_id under review, then the range is from the Update_date column to a future date. You can put the logic into an SQL query, as in Listing 3.41.

```
SELECT Prod_cat,SUM(SALES_NET)
FROM TRANS_DTL F,
(SELECT Prod_id,Prod_cat,Update_date DATE_FROM,COALESCE(LEAD(Update_
date) over (PARTITION BY Prod_id ORDER BY Update_date),'2300-12-31')
DATE_TO
FROM Prod_cat) P
WHERE F.Prod_id=P.Prod_id
AND F.TRANS_DATE>=DATE_FROM
AND F.TRANS_DATE<DATE_TO
GROUP BY Prod_cat;
```
Listing 3.41 Query to Show the Join to Time-Dependent Dimension Table

In this query, you have a window function, which can be handled only on the row engine; therefore, you cannot put this logic into an analytic view. However, there is a simple solution to improve the performance. You can easily modify the structure of the dimension table by adding an additional column, Expire_date, and set the valid date range for each record with Update_date and Expire_date (see Listing 3.42).

```
ALTER TABLE Prod_cat ADD( Expire_date date);
UPDATE Prod_cat A
SET Expire_date =
(SELECT DATE_TO
FROM (
```

```
SELECT Prod_id,Prod_cat,Update_date,COALESCE(LEAD(Update_
date) over (PARTITION BY Prod_id ORDER BY Update_date),'2300-12-31')
DATE_TO
FROM Prod_cat) B
WHERE A.Prod_id=B.Prod_id AND A.Prod_cat=B.Prod_cat AND
A.Update_date=B.Update_date
);
```
Listing 3.42 Statements to Create Expire_date Column on Table Prod_cat

With the new column created on the dimension table, the query can be simplified to the query shown in Listing 3.43.

```
SELECT Prod_cat,SUM(SALES_NET)
FROM TRANS_DTL F, Prod_cat P
WHERE F.Prod_id=P.Prod_id
AND F.TRANS_DATE>=UPDATE_DATE
AND F.TRANS_DATE<EXPIRE_DATE
GROUP BY Prod_cat;
```
Listing 3.43 Query to Show the Join to the Time-Dependent Dimension Table

You also can make the join in an analytic view. When defining the join on PROD_ ID, set TEMPORAL COLUMN as TRANS_DATE, set TEMPORAL CONDITION as EXCLUDE TO INCLUDE FROM, set FROM COLUMN as UPDATE_DATE, and set TO COLUMN as EXPIRE_DATE (see Figure 3.37).

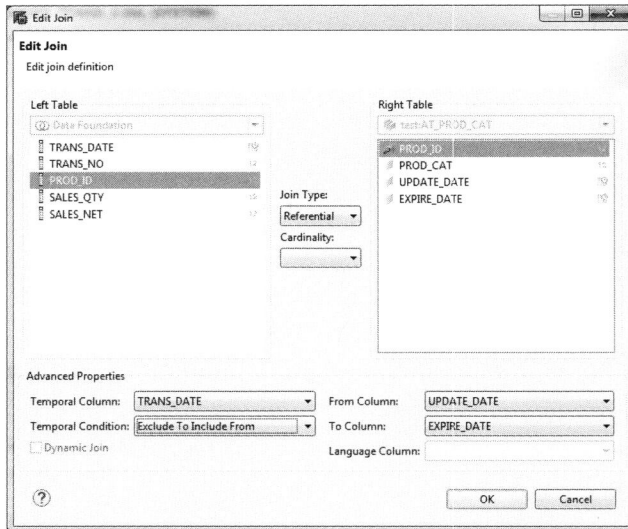

Figure 3.37 Join Definition with the Time-Dependent Dimension Table

The query against the analytic view is shown in Listing 3.44.

```
SELECT Prod_cat,SUM(SALES_NET)
FROM _SYS_BIC."test/AN_TRANS_3"
GROUP BY Prod_cat;
```

Listing 3.44 Query Against the Analytic View with a Join to the Time-Dependent Dimension Table

Next, let's see how to deal with the logic for long join paths. For example, suppose the fact table `Trans_DTL(Trans_DATE, Trans_No, Prod_ID, Sales_Qty, Sales_Net)` needs to join dimension table `Dim_1(Prod_ID,Attr_A)` on the `Prod_ID` column, and then the table `Dim_A` needs to join the dimension table `Dim_2(Attr_A,Attr_B)` on the `Attr_A` column, and then `Dim_2` needs to join table `Dim_3(Attr_B,Attr_C)` on the `Attr_B` column. The SQL query is shown in Listing 3.45.

```
SELECT ATTR_C,SUM(SALES_NET)
FROM TRANS_DTL F,DIM_1 A, DIM_2 B,DIM_3 C
WHERE F.PROD_ID=A.PROD_ID
AND A.ATTR_A=B.ATTR_A
AND B.ATTR_B=C.ATTR_B
GROUP BY ATTR_C;
```

Listing 3.45 Query with a Long Join Path

As shown in Figure 3.38, when you can make the join in an analytic view, the join path is long between the fact table and the dimension table `Dim_3`.

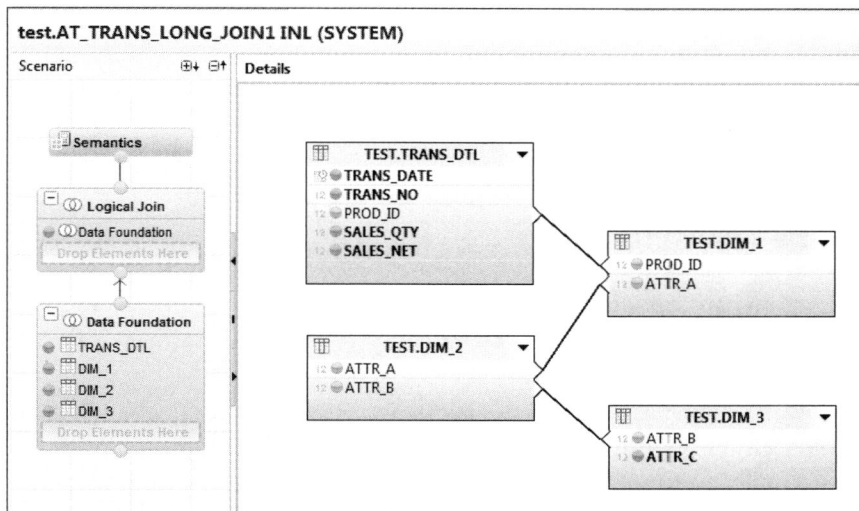

Figure 3.38 Long Join Path

To improve the performance, denormalize the dimension tables by merging them into one (see Listing 3.46).

```
ALTER TABLE Dim_1 add (Attr_B int, Attr_C int);
UPSERT Dim_1
SELECT A.PROD_ID,A.ATTR_A,B.ATTR_B,C.ATTR_C
FROM DIM_1 A, DIM_2 B,DIM_3 C
WHERE A.ATTR_A=B.ATTR_A
AND B.ATTR_B=C.ATTR_B;
```
Listing 3.46 Statement to Denormalize the Dimension Table

With the new denormalized dimension table, the fact table needs to join on a single table, and the performance can be improved. The SQL query is shown in Listing 3.47.

```
SELECT ATTR_C,SUM(SALES_NET)
FROM TRANS_DTL F,DIM_1 A
WHERE F.PROD_ID=A.PROD_ID
GROUP BY ATTR_C;
```
Listing 3.47 Query with a Join to Denormalize the Dimension Table

It is very expensive to denormalize a fact table. However, dimension tables are not volatile and do not change that often. Therefore, it is fine to denormalize dimension tables when necessary. In summary, you can see from the preceding examples that table modification can be an option when dealing with performance issues for long join paths. Although you usually will not make modifications on table structures or content, do not hesitate to do so if there is a need. In the next section, we will continue our discussion of tables with specific reference to history tables.

3.8   Time Traveling

When performing an analysis, sometimes you are checking not only current data, but also *historic data*, such as a customer's history balance, a warehouse's history storage, and so on. For *time travel*, you may have to capture the yearly, monthly, weekly, or even daily snapshots of the fact table. Let's see an example of a table that contains daily snapshots of inventory data, BOH(SNAPSHOT_DT, PROD_ID, STORE_ID, ON_HAND). The table contains the SNAPSHOT_DT column to represent the dates of snapshots, as shown in Listing 3.48.

```
CREATE COLUMN TABLE BOH(
SNAPSHOT_DT DATE,
PROD_ID INT,
STORE_ID INT,
ON_HAND INT);
```
Listing 3.48 Definition of Table BOH

It can be very resource-intensive to store daily snapshots in a table, because a table with one year of snapshots can be 365 times greater than the original table. In addition, such a table will contain a lot of redundant records. Each product that has not changed inventory during the year still consumes 365 records in a table. As a result, such a table can be quite large, and the performance of the query against the table can be poor as a result.

3.8.1   History Tables

SAP HANA provides the history table feature to achieve time travel. In this case, you can create a history table BOH_H, which does not include the SNAPSHOUT_DT column, as shown in Listing 3.49.

```
CREATE HISTORY COLUMN TABLE BOH_H(
PROD_ID INT,
STORE_ID INT,
ON_HAND INT,
PRIMARY KEY(PROD_ID,STORE_ID));
```
Listing 3.49 Definition of History Table BOH_H

There are three ways in which someone can utilize time travel queries and track historical values:

► Using a commit ID
► Using a UTC timestamp
► Setting a session to an earlier historic moment

In this section, we will explore these methods through an example.

The first step you need to take is to enable the history table. To make a history table work, you need to set the AUTO COMMIT option to OFF under SESSION in the SAP HANA Studio PROPERTIES tab (see Figure 3.39).

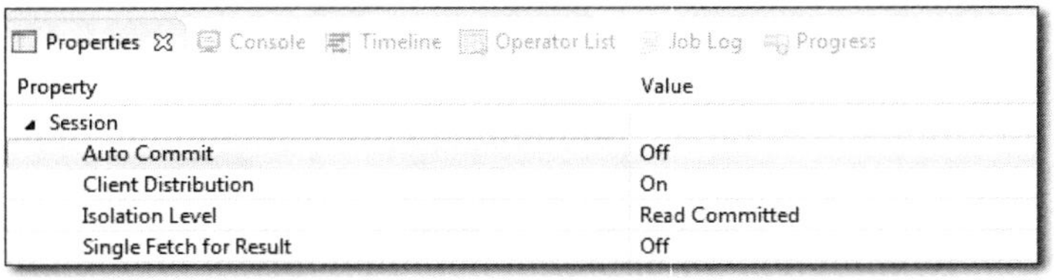

Figure 3.39 Session Properties

You can insert a record into this history table as follows:

```
INSERT INTO BOH_H VALUES (1,1,39);
COMMIT;
```

Then, change the content of the record using the following query:

```
UPSERT BOH_H VALUES (1,1,98);
COMMIT;
```

Because the AUTO COMMIT option is off, you need to perform a delta merge to complete the operation:

```
UPDATE BOH_H MERGE DELTA INDEX;
```

Behind the scenes, there are two hidden columns in the history table: $valid-from$ and $validto$. When a new record is inserted, it is given a value of the current commit ID on the $validfrom$ column and a null value on the $validto$ column. When the record is updated, a new record is inserted with the same primary key. A new commit ID is set on both the $validfrom$ column of the new record and the $validto$ column of the previous record. A null value is set on $validto$ of the new record. When the record is deleted, the null value on $validto$ of the last record will be replaced by a new commit ID. To check the values of the commit ID, you may run the following query:

```
SELECT *, "$validfrom$", "$validto$"

FROM BOH_H ('REQUEST_FLAGS'='ALLROWS');
```

As shown in Figure 3.40, you can check the valid range of each record from the output of the query.

SQL | Result

```
SELECT *, "$validfrom$", "$validto$"
FROM BOH_H ('REQUEST_FLAGS'='ALLROWS')
```

	PROD_ID	STORE_ID	ON_HAND	$validfrom$	$validto$
1	1	1	98	3,445,204	?
2	1	1	39	3,445,196	3,445,204

Figure 3.40 Content of the History Table

You can then time travel based on the commit ID:

```
SELECT * FROM BOH_H AS OF COMMIT ID 3445196;
```

This returns one record, in which `$validfrom$ =3445196`. To know the actual time when each record is valid, you need to check the timestamp of each commit ID. This information can be obtained from table `TRANSACTION_HISTORY`, as shown:

```
SELECT * FROM TRANSACTION_HISTORY ORDER BY COMMIT_ID;
```

This query returns the commit timestamp of each commit ID. Hence, you can get the transaction stamping information (called the *UTC timestamp*) of the commit ID with the following query:

```
SELECT COMMIT_TIME FROM TRANSACTION_HISTORY
WHERE COMMIT_ID=3445196;
```

Figure 3.41 shows the preceding query returning the timestamp of a specific commit ID.

```
SELECT COMMIT_TIME FROM TRANSACTION_HISTORY
WHERE COMMIT_ID=3445196
```

	COMMIT_TIME
1	Mar 22, 2015 6:32:08.128 PM

Figure 3.41 UTC Timestamp

Next, you can time travel based on the UTC timestamps:

```
SELECT * FROM BOH_H AS OF utctimestamp '2015-03-22 18:32:08.128';
```

Alternatively, you can time travel by setting the session to a history commit ID:

```
SET HISTORY SESSION TO COMMIT ID 3445196;
```

Or, set the session to a history UTC timestamp:

```
SET HISTORY SESSION TO utctimestamp '2015-03-22 18:32:08.128';
```

When a session is set to a moment in history, the query against the history table will return only those records that are valid for that specified moment. After setting the session to a moment in history, perform the following query to retrieve the records at that moment:

```
SELECT * FROM BOH_H;
```

To restore the session back to the current time, run the following statement:

```
SET HISTORY SESSION TO NOW;
```

You also can time travel by filtering on the columns $validfrom$ and $validto$ directly. For example, suppose we want to check the records of 2005-01-02. To do so, can run the query shown in Listing 3.50.

```
SELECT A.*
FROM BOH_H('REQUEST_FLAGS'='ALLROWS') A
JOIN TRANSACTION_HISTORY B
ON A."$validfrom$"=B.COMMIT_ID
LEFT OUTER JOIN TRANSACTION_HISTORY C
ON A."$validto$"=C.COMMIT_ID
WHERE B.COMMIT_TIME<= '2015-01-02'
AND ("$validto$" IS NULL OR C.COMMIT_TIME> '2015-01-02');
```

Listing 3.50 Time Travel Query

These three methods allow you to use time travel queries in a number of ways. In the next section, we will look at how to utilize simulated history tables to traverse some of the limitations of actual history tables.

3.8.2 Simulated History Tables

History tables can benefit time travel reporting, but they have some limitations: When you update a table, you always create new records, which makes it hard to modify the content of history records. Also, the time granularity of a history table is at the timestamp level, whereas analysis requirements can be on daily, weekly, monthly, or other intervals; a more detailed granularity can cause an unnecessary waste of resources.

For example, if your analysis requirement is on a monthly level, then only the last updated value in each month for a product is needed in the table. Therefore, based on that analysis requirement, you can create a regular table that simulates a history table rather than using a history table directly. You can achieve greater flexibility via this kind of table. Let's examine table BOH_S as an example (see Listing 3.51).

```
CREATE COLUMN TABLE BOH_S(
PROD_ID INT,
STORE_ID INT,
ON_HAND INT,
VALIDFROM DATE,
VALIDTO DATE,
PRIMARY KEY(PROD_ID,STORE_ID,VALIDFROM));
```

Listing 3.51 Definition of Table BOH_S to Simulate a History Table

There are two visible columns, VALIDFROM and VALIDTC, in the table. You can insert the values of a date range into these columns, which can be on a daily, weekly, and monthly basis according to your analysis requirements.

For the purposes of this example, assume you require a monthly basis. For each PROD_ID and STORE_ID, you have only one record for month 1. If that record is not changed on month 2, you do not need a new record for month 2; you just need to make the VALIDFROM and VALIDTO columns of the record include month 2. The idea is similar to using a history table. When you browse the current data, you can apply a filter on the VALIDTO column to return the recode where the column is null, as follows:

```
SELECT * FROM BOH_S WHERE VALIDTO IS NULL;
```

When you time travel and browse the data in a particular month, you can apply a filter and see if the first day of the month is between the VALIDFROM and VALIDTO columns (see Listing 3.52).

```
SELECT *
FROM BOH_S
WHERE VALIDFROM<= '2014-01-01'
AND (VALIDTO IS NULL OR VALIDTO> '2014-01-01');
```

Listing 3.52 Query to Simulate Time Travel

When you perform reporting with the data every month, you can join the table with a calendar table (see Listing 3.53).

```
SELECT PROD_ID,STORE_ID,CALMONTH,ON_HAND
FROM BOH_S A,"_SYS_BI"."M_TIME_DIMENSION" B
WHERE B.DAY=1
AND A.VALIDFROM<= B.DATE_SQL
AND (A.VALIDTO IS NULL OR VALIDTO> B.DATE_SQL);
```

Listing 3.53 Query to Generate a Monthly Report

Over time, the table becomes larger. If necessary, you can separate the dataset of the historical data on a yearly basis and partition the table by date range. This way, the records for different years will be distributed to different partitions, and you can leverage partition pruning to improve the performance of the query, as shown in Listing 3.54.

```
CREATE COLUMN TABLE BOH_S(
PROD_ID INT,
STORE_ID INT,
ON_HAND INT,
VALIDFROM DATE,
VALIDTO DATE,
PRIMARY KEY(PROD_ID,STORE_ID,VALIDFROM))
PARTITION BY RANGE(VALIDFROM)
(PARTITION '2010-01-01'<=VALUES<'2011-01-01',
PARTITION '2011-01-01'<=VALUES<'2012-01-01',
PARTITION '2012-01-01'<=VALUES<'2013-01-01',
PARTITION '2013-01-01'<=VALUES<'2014-01-01',
PARTITION '2014-01-01'<=VALUES<'2015-01-01',
PARTITION '2015-01-01'<=VALUES<'2016-01-01',
PARTITION OTHERS);
```

Listing 3.54 Definition of Table BOH_S with Partition

Listing 3.54 creates table BOH_S with a partition by year. When inserting a record into the table, if the range of a record crosses one year, it will be split into multiple records. For example, the record (1,1,23,'2014-10-01','2015-03-01') should be split into records (1,1,23,'2014-10-01','2015-01-01') and (1,1,23,'2015-01-01','2015-03-01').

Regarding the data provision of the table, the logic can be expressed in three steps. Suppose you have the history table BOH_H(PROD_ID, STORE_ID, ON_HAND) as the source table; perform the following three steps to transfer the records:

1. First, generate the data of the snapshot for each month.

2. Next, retrieve the ON_HAND value of the previous month for each record. If the value is equal to the value of the current month, filter out the record.

3. Finally, retrieve the value of DATE_SQL from the next record, show it side by side with the DATE_SQL value of current record, then insert the values into the target table in the VALIDFROM and VALIDTO columns.

These steps can be written into one SQL statement, as shown in Listing 3.55.

```
INSERT INTO BOH_S
SELECT PROD_ID,STORE_ID,ON_HAND,DATE_SQL,COALESCE(LEAD(DATE_
SQL) OVER(PARTITION BY PROD_ID,STORE_ID,YEAR ORDER BY DATE_SQL),
END_MONTH) D1
FROM
(
SELECT PROD_ID,STORE_ID,ON_HAND,DATE_SQL,YEAR,LAG(ON_
HAND) OVER(PARTITION BY PROD_ID,STORE_ID,YEAR ORDER BY DATE_SQL)
ON_HAND1,
ADD_MONTHS(MAX(DATE_SQL) OVER(PARTITION BY PROD_ID,STORE_ID),1)
END_MONTH
FROM
(
SELECT PROD_ID,STORE_ID,ON_HAND,DATE_SQL,YEAR
FROM
(SELECT PROD_ID,STORE_ID,ON_HAND,
B.COMMIT_TIME VALIDFROM,C.COMMIT_TIME VALIDTO
FROM BOH_H('REQUEST_FLAGS'='ALLROWS') A
JOIN TRANSACTION_HISTORY B
ON A."$validfrom$"=B.COMMIT_ID
LEFT OUTER JOIN TRANSACTION_HISTORY C
ON A."$validto$"=C.COMMIT_ID
) S,"_SYS_BI"."M_TIME_DIMENSION" CA
WHERE CA.DAY=1 AND CA.DATE_SQL<'2016-01-01'
AND S.VALIDFROM<= CA.DATE_SQL
AND (S.VALIDTO IS NULL OR VALIDTO> CA.DATE_SQL)
)
)
WHERE ON_HAND<>ON_HAND1 OR ON_HAND1 IS NULL;
```

Listing 3.55 Script to Generate Data for Table BOH_S

When you generate data from a table that contains snapshots, the logic is similar. This is a simple example compared to real-world cases, which are usually more complicated. From the example shown, you can see that data modeling is more than just dealing with join paths and engine selection; it also entails table design, application workflow design, and more.

3.9 Storing Temporary Data

In SAP HANA, you can create a temporary table to save intermediate result sets. There are two types of temporary tables in SAP HANA: *global temporary tables* and *local temporary tables*. As their names suggest, content in these tables is temporary and eliminated once the session expires. The key difference between the local and global types is as follows:

▶ **Local temporary tables**
The structure and content are deleted as soon as the user's session ends.

▶ **Global temporary tables**
The structure of the table persists. However, the content is deleted after the session ends. Because each connection has a different session, the contents of one session are not visible to others.

There is one key limitation of a temporary table: It cannot be added to an analytic view. For large datasets, if you want to use an analytic view to leverage the OLAP engine, then you may need a different approach.

The solution is to create a permanent table to store temporary data. To show how this works, let's see examine table Temp1 shown in Listing 3.56.

```
CREATE COLUMN TABLE Temp1(
USER_ID int,
USER_TYPE int,
CURRENT_CONN INT);
```
Listing 3.56 Definition of Table Temp1

To use this table as a temporary store, the workflow is as follows:

1. In a stored procedure, populate the table with the intermediate result set.

2. Next, use the table in an analytic view.

3. Eventually, delete the data when the task is complete.

In cases where multiple users might be using the table at the same time, you have to separate each user's result sets. The example shown in Listing 3.56 includes the CURRENT_CONN column. When you insert the table, you also update the column with the value of CURRENT_CONNECTION, which is the session ID. Different users should have different session IDs. When a user uses the table, a filter on this column is necessary to retrieve the rows that belong to a user's individual session.

Let's explain the detailed workflow with a simple example. Suppose you are analyzing the fact table F_TRANS and want to slice the data by user type. Here, the user types are generated based on users' statistics from the fact table. This analysis involves two steps:

1. The first step is to generate the intermediate result to show users' types.

2. The second step is to slice the data in the fact table by users' types.

You can make an analytic view to join the user type table with the fact table (see Figure 3.42). Add a filter on the CURRENT_CONN column to separate the result sets from different sessions.

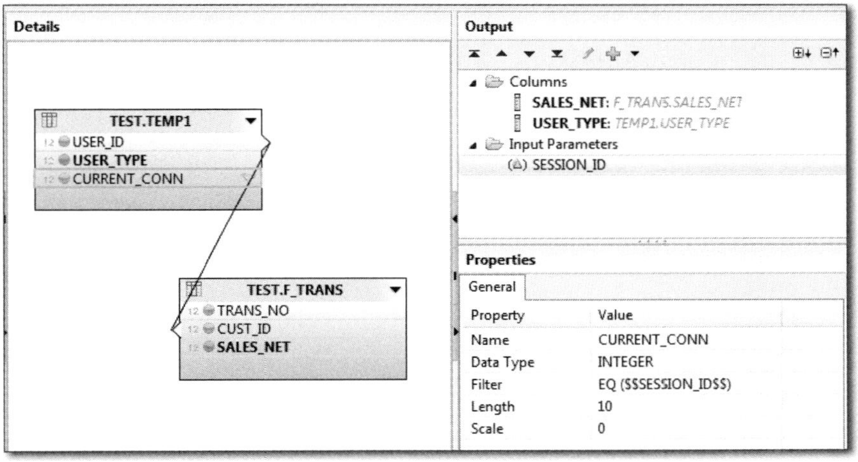

Figure 3.42 Analytic View with a Filter on the CURRENT_CONN Column

Next, put the logic into the stored procedure P_1 (see Listing 3.57).

```
CREATE PROCEDURE P_1() LANGUAGE SQLSCRIPT
AS
BEGIN
INSERT INTO TEMP1
SELECT CUST_ID,NTILE(10000) OVER( ORDER BY C), CURRENT_CONNECTION
FROM (
SELECT CUST_ID,COUNT(*) C
FROM "F_TRANS"
GROUP BY CUST_ID);
SELECT USER_TYPE,SUM(SALES_NET) SALES_NET
FROM _SYS_BIC."test/AN_TEMP1"
("PLACEHOLDER"."$$SESSION_ID$$"=> CURRENT_CONNECTION)
GROUP BY USER_TYPE;
DELETE FROM TEMP1 WHERE CURRENT_CONN=CURRENT_CONNECTION;
END;
```

Listing 3.57 Script of the Stored Procedure with a Temporary Table that Is Not Shared

In this stored procedure, table TEMP1 behaves like a global temporary table, but it can be utilized by an analytic view.

There are both advantages and disadvantages to this stored procedure. Because it is not read-only, you may have more performance penalties than a read-only procedure. However, you will have better performance with an analytic view compared to other kinds of modeled views. In essence, you have to compare the overall performance before settling on an optimal approach.

When you use a permanent table to store temporary data, the content does not have to be invisible to different sessions; the intermediate result set can sometimes be useful for multiple analysis. If you want to save system resources, you can share the content of the table with other sessions.

Let's walk through the solution to share intermediate datasets with multiple users in an example. Again, suppose you want to perform an analysis based on user type, and the type information is based on user statistics from the fact table. It can be time-consuming to calculate the type information. Therefore, to improve the performance, you can save the type information into a permanent table first when performing the analysis, and then other people can use the content of the table directly in their analyses.

Suppose the content of the table needs to be renewed on a daily basis. In this case, add the UPDATE_DATE column to the table to show on which date the records were updated (see Listing 3.58).

```
CREATE COLUMN TABLE TEMP2(
USER_ID int,
USER_TYPE int,
UPDATE_DATE DATE
);
```

Listing 3.58 Definition of Table TEMP2

In the procedure, check if there are any datasets that have already been inserted. If there are, then use the data directly to generate the report; otherwise, populate the table with the intermediate result set and then generate the report (see Listing 3.59).

```
CREATE PROCEDURE P_2() LANGUAGE SQLSCRIPT
AS
V INT ;
BEGIN
```

```
SELECT COUNT(*) INTO V FROM TEMP2 WHERE UPDATE_DATE=TO_DATE(CURRENT_
TIMESTAMP);
IF :V=0 THEN
DELETE FROM TEMP2;
INSERT INTO TEMP2
SELECT CUST_ID,NTILE(10000) OVER( ORDER BY C), TO_DATE(CURRENT_
TIMESTAMP)
FROM (
SELECT CUST_ID,COUNT(*) C
FROM "TEST"."F_TRANS"
GROUP BY CUST_ID);
END IF;
SELECT USER_TYPE,SUM(SALES_NET) SALES_NET
FROM _SYS_BIC."test/AN_TEMP2"
GROUP BY USER_TYPE;
END;
```

Listing 3.59 Script of SP with Intermediate Data that Can Be Shared

With this approach, it might take some time for the first user to perform the analysis. When the stored procedure finishes, other users can rely on the intermediate results on the permanent table, saving a lot of system resources.

There are other ways to reduce resource consumption. In this particular example, you can make an extraction, transformation, and loading (ETL) job to populate the physical table of the intermediate result set. Again, there is no simple rule to follow when deciding on an approach; you have to compare overall performance.

> **Query Results Cache**
>
> As of SAP HANA SPS 09, you can leverage a feature called the *query results cache*. You can enable this feature from the VIEW PROPERTIES tab and set the CACHE INVALIDATION PERIOD to daily or hourly. This option is suitable for a view that can be used repeatedly.

3.10   Calculating Count Distinct

It can be time-consuming to calculate count distinct for a large dataset. However, you can fine-tune a model and make the calculation as efficient as possible. Best practices include the following:

▸ Avoid concatenating count columns

▸ Split large count distinct aggregations into smaller ones

Let's start with an example. Suppose you want to run the following query:

```
SELECT COUNT(DISTINCT TRANS_NO||DEP_ID)
FROM FACT_2;
```

It is important to note that calculating at the row level is never a good idea here. Instead, you should remove the concatenation from the query, and change it into the query shown in Listing 3.60.

```
SELECT COUNT(*)
FROM (
SELECT DISTINCT TRANS_NO,DEP_ID
FROM FACT_2);
```

Listing 3.60 Query without Concatenation of Strings

Figure 3.43 defines a counter on an analytic view and adds TRANS_NO and DEP_ IN row columns in the EDIT COUNTER window.

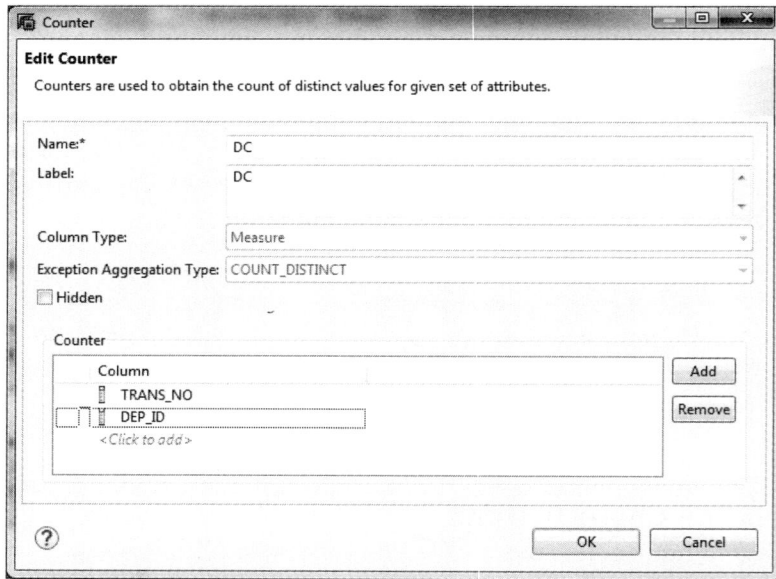

Figure 3.43 Counter with Two Columns

Then run the following query:

```
SELECT SUM(DC) FROM _SYS_BIC."test/AN_FACT_1";
```

If you just stopped here, the performance of the query would not be optimal. Instead, a better approach is to separate the columns totally, leaving only one column as the counter and putting the other column into a GROUP BY clause (see Figure 3.44).

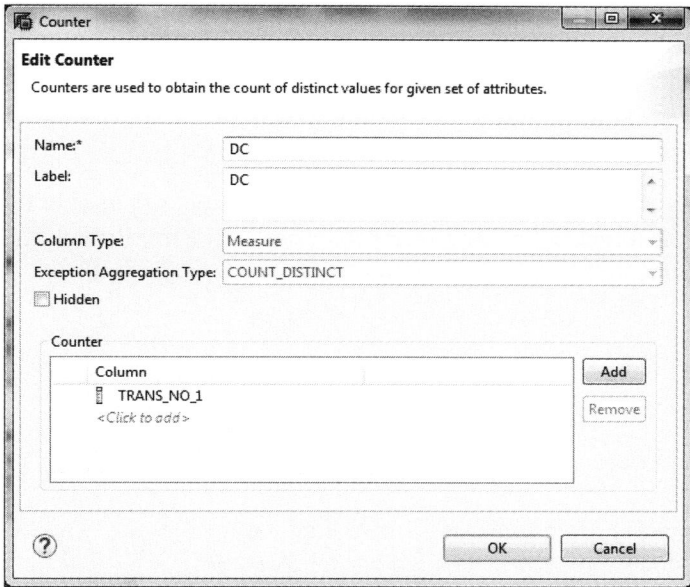

Figure 3.44 Counter with a Single Column

To calculate count distinct, you need two levels of SELECT statements, as shown in Listing 3.61.

```
SELECT SUM(DC)
FROM (
SELECT SUM(DC) DC
FROM _SYS_BIC."test/AN_FACT_1"
GROUP BY DEP_ID);
```

Listing 3.61 Query to Calculate Count Distinct with Two-Level Aggregation

If there are more than two combined columns, perform the same process; leave one column as a counter, and put the other columns into the GROUP BY clause.

To address poor performance for count distinct values on a single column against a large dataset, you need to try a different approach. First, examine the following query:

```
SELECT COUNT(DISTINCT TRANS_NO)
FROM FACT_2;
```

Assuming the table is partitioned by Hash (USER_ID), you can check if there are multiple distinct values of USER_ID for each TRAN_NO with the following query:

```
SELECT TRANS_NO
FROM FACT_2 GROUP BY TRANS_NO HAVING COUNT(DISTINCT USER_ID)>1;
```

If the query returns no rows, you can separate the count distinct calculation on each individual partition to get the subtotal, and then use SUM() to calculate the total. To achieve this logic, perform the query in Listing 3.62.

```
SELECT SUM(C)
FROM (
SELECT COUNT(DISTINCT TRANS_NO) C
FROM FACT_2
GROUP BY USER_ID);
```
Listing 3.62 Query to Calculate Count Distinct Group by USER_ID

To calculate the query with an analytic view, run Listing 3.63.

```
SELECT SUM(C)
FROM (
SELECT SUM(DC) C
FROM _SYS_BIC."test/AN_FACT_1"
GROUP BY USER_ID);
```
Listing 3.63 Query Against an Analytic View to Calculate the Count Distinct Group by USER_ID

With less data being transferred between the partitions, the performance has been greatly improved.

3.11   Using Cached Views

SAP HANA provides a feature to cache the result sets of views in memory. This feature benefits users dealing with time-consuming views. With the cache feature enabled on the view, if the view is frequently used, it accesses underlying tables once and stores the result set into the cache. The subsequent queries against the same view will browse the cached result set instead of accessing underlying tables, and the execution time can be reduced.

In this section, we will look at two types of cache: a result cache and a view cache.

3.11.1 Defining a Result Cache

Before you use the cache feature, make sure to check the cache setting of *Indexserver.ini* under the CONFIGURATION tab of SAP HANA Studio, as shown in Figure 3.45.

Overview	Landscape	Alerts	Performance	Volumes	Configuration	System Information	Diagnosis Files	Trace Configuratio

Filter: ✖

Name	Default	System
◢ [ ] cache		
cs_statisticscache_clear_reconfig	no	
cs_statisticscache_enabled	no	
resultcache_clear_reconfig	no	
resultcache_enabled	no	● yes
resultcache_maximum_value_size_in_bytes	1048576	
resultcache_minimum_query_execution_time_in_milliseconds	100	
resultcache_request_timeout_in_milliseconds	0	

Figure 3.45 Parameters for Cache in Indexserver.ini

There are a few parameters in the *Indexserver.ini* file for the cache feature, including the following:

▶ RESULTCACHE_ENABLED
To enable the cache feature, set the value of this parameter to YES. The default value is NO, which means no cache is made.

▶ RESULTCACHE_CLEAR_RECONFIG
To clear the cache upon configuration update, set this parameter to YES. The default value is NO.

▶ RESULTCACHE_REQUEST_TIMEOUT_IN_MILLISECONDS
This parameter defines how long the result cache should wait for requests in a distributed environment. The default is 0 ms, which means to ignore result caches on other nodes.

▶ RESULTCACHE_MAXIMUM_VALUE_SIZE_IN_BYTES
This parameter specifies the maximum size of a result set to be cached. Results with larger data sizes will not be cached. The default value is 1 million bytes.

▶ RESULTCACHE_MINIMUM_QUERY_EXECUTION_TIME_IN_MILLISECONDS
This parameter specifies the minimum query execution time to cache a result. Queries with a lower execution time will not be cached. The default value is 100 ms.

Not all views are suitable for caching; consider the following criteria to determine whether to cache a view:

▶ Is the view expensive? If it takes long to run or consumes a lot of system resources, such as CPU, memory, or network, to run a query against the view, you may consider caching the view.

▶ Is the query against the view executed repeatedly?

▶ Is the result set of the view small? Large caches consume a lot of memory. On the other hand, if the cache size is not significantly smaller than the underlying tables, there will be no benefit to use a cache.

▶ Is stale data acceptable? The data read from the cache might be one hour or one day older than the current data, so it might not be suitable to use a cache if real-time data is required.

You can control the behavior of a cache individually with parameters in queries at run time. The following are a few options for controlling the behavior of a cache:

▶ To make the query not cache the result, run the following:
```
SELECT ... FROM _SYS_BIC."test/AN_TRAN" WITH PARAMETERS
('CACHE'=('OFF'));
```

▶ A result cache can be in real-time mode, which makes the query read data from the underlying view or table instead of caching when the underlying tables or views are updated. To make the cache in real-time mode, run the following:
```
SELECT ... FROM _SYS_BIC."test/AN_TRAN" WITH PARAMETERS ('CACHE'=
('REALTIME'));
```

▶ Different than a real-time cache, you can define the cache as time-controlled. The cache will last a specified period of time before it expires. To define the cache as time controlled at run time, run the following:
```
SELECT ... FROM _SYS_BIC."test/AN_TRAN" WITH PARAMETERS ('CACHE'=
('TIME_CONTROLLED', '60'));
```

To check how much memory is consumed in a cache, run the following:

```
SELECT HOST,PORT,CACHE_ID,USED_SIZE FROM M_CACHES;
```

Table 3.1 shows the results of the preceding query, which returns the statistics of the cache. The record for which CACHE_ID is CS_QueryResultCache[Realtime] shows the size of the cached results in real-time mode, and the record for which CACHE_ID is CS_QueryResultCache[TimeControlled] shows the size of the cached results in time-controlled mode.

HOST	PORT	CACHE_ID	USED_SIZE
bi1-401	31,003	CS_QueryResultCache[Realtime]	6,206,507
bi1-401	31,003	CS_QueryResultCache[TimeControllec]	23,047

Table 3.1 Content of M_CACHES

In addition to defining the caches at run time, you can define them at design time when creating the modeled views. To turn on a cache for a modeled view, edit the CACHE INVALIDATION PERIOD option under the VIEW PROPERTIES tab of the view and set it to HOURLY or DAILY (see Figure 3.46).

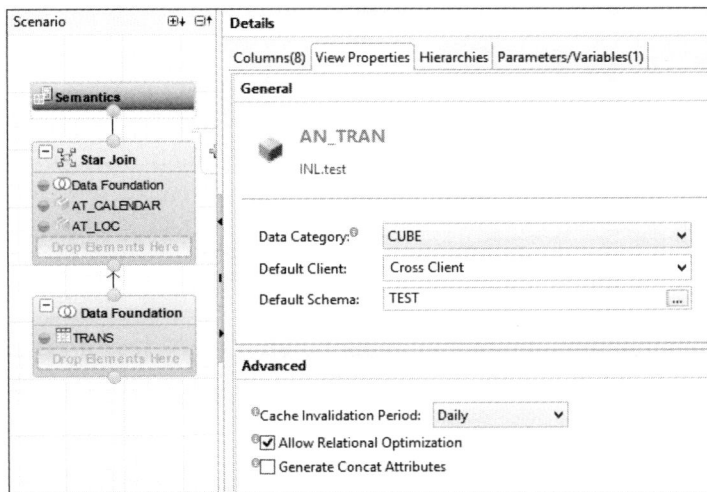

Figure 3.46 Cache Flag of the Modeled View

When the model is activated, the corresponding column view is created with the parameter CACHE_INVALIDATION_PERIOD set to HOURLY or DAILY (see Listing 3.64).

```
CREATE COLUMN VIEW _SYS_BIC."test/AN_TRANS" ... WITH PARAMETERS
('CACHE_INVALIDATION_PERIOD' = 'HOURLY');
CREATE COLUMN VIEW _SYS_BIC."test/AN_TRANS" ... WITH PARAMETERS
('CACHE_INVALIDATION_PERIOD' = 'DAILY');
```
Listing 3.64 DDL to Set the Cache on the Column View

The views with the cache flag enabled will generate a time-controlled cache. The cache will last one hour or one day, based on the CACHE_INVALIDATION_PERIOD setting. When using the cache, you should be aware that the query result might not be based on the most current data in the underlying tables. If you want current data, you can add the parameter ('CACHE'=('OFF')) in the query.

3.11.2   Defining a View Cache

A *view cache* is another type of cache that can be created on SQL views and calculation views. You can enable the view cache feature by using the ALTER VIEW statement:

```
ALTER VIEW _sys_bic."test/CA_SALES_PURCHASES" ADD CACHE RETENTION 60;
```

This statement makes the calculation view or SQL view cacheable. By defining the RETENTION parameter in a query, you set the maximum staleness threshold that a user can see for a cached result. The RETENTION parameter is measured in minutes.

In this case, the cached result set expires in 60 minutes based on the RETENTION parameter. When you run a query after the cache has expired, the query accesses the underlying tables again to retrieve the new result set and then caches it. The RETENTION parameter can be adjusted to satisfy your individual business requirements.

When the source tables are updated daily with the ETL jobs running every night and there is no change during the day, you can set the RETENTION parameter to 1,440 minutes. After the first query caches the result set, the cache can be used by subsequent queries for the whole day.

If the source tables are updated every second, the result set in the cache will not be quite up-to-date if you set RETENTION to 60 minutes. This cached result set may miss some records in the underlying tables that were updated in the last 60 minutes. Therefore, you need to check if your specific business requirements allow some degree of staleness before you enable a cache on the view.

Disabling the Cache Feature on a View

To disable the cache feature on the view, run the following:

```
ALTER VIEW _sys_bic."test/CA_SALES_PURCHASES" DROP CACHE;
```

Defining a Cache with Limited Columns

In many cases, not all columns need to be cached in a view. To define a cache with limited columns, you can specify the column to be listed with the following statement:

```
ALTER VIEW _sys_bic."test/CA_SALES_
PURCHASES" ADD CACHE RETENTION 60 OF DATE_SQL,CITY,SALES_NET;
```

In this statement, the columns DATE_SQL, CITY, and SALES_NET are set as cacheable. When you run a query that contains only these three columns, the result would be cached, as shown:

```
SELECT DATE_SQL,CITY,SUM(SALES_NET) from _sys_bic."test/CA_SALES_
PURCHASES" GROUP BY DATE_SQL,CITY;
```

If the query is SELECT * or it contains other columns, the result will not be cached.

Separating Cache Results by Filter Values

A cache can be defined with a specified filter, as shown in the following statement:

```
ALTER VIEW _sys_bic."test/CA_SALES_PURCHASES" ADD CACHE RETENTION
60 OF DATE_SQL,CITY,SALES_NET FILTER PROD_ID=1;
```

In the preceding statement, only the result set of the query with filter PROD=1 will be cached. From one view, we may have different result sets based on different filters. To cache different result sets for different filter values, we use the question mark (?) in the cache definition statement, as shown in the following query:

```
ALTER VIEW _sys_bic."test/CA_SALES_PURCHASES" ADD CACHE RETENTION
60 OF DATE_SQL,CITY,SALES_NET FILTER PROD_ID=?;
```

You can run multiple queries with different filter values on the PROD_ID column, which will enable each result set to be cached separately. To check the cache details, run the following query:

```
SELECT * FROM M_VIEW_CACHE;
```

In Figure 3.47, you can see the result of the query, which shows multiple cached result sets for the same view. In the DETAILS column, you can see different filter values.

CACHE_ID	DETAILS
6	VIEW_NAME:"_SYS_BIC"."test/CA_SALES_PURCHASES", USER_NAME:, PLACEHOLDERS:[$$language$$=>E], INCREMENTAL CACHE KEY:[?1: 111], VIEW_AP_NAM...
5	VIEW_NAME:"_SYS_BIC"."test/CA_SALES_PURCHASES", USER_NAME:, PLACEHOLDERS:[$$language$$=>E], INCREMENTAL CACHE KEY:[?1: 1], VIEW_AP_NAME:[...

Figure 3.47 Details of a View Cache in Table M_VIEW_CACHE

Refreshing a Cached Result Set

In addition to filtering capabilities, you can also use refresh parameters to refresh your cache. Rather than waiting for the expiration of a cached result set, you can manually refresh the cache to save current results by running the following statement:

```
ALTER VIEW _sys_bic."test/CA_SALES_PURCHASES" REFRESH CACHE;
```

Suppose the underlying tables are updated in ETL jobs every night, and it takes a lot of time to run queries against the view. You can set the retention time of the view to 1,440 minutes and run the statement after ETL jobs have finished. Then, all queries against the view the next day can read data from the cache with high performance, instead of accessing the underlying tables.

You can also refresh a specific cache by specifying the cache ID in the statement, as shown in the following query:

```
ALTER SYSTEM REFRESH VIEW CACHE ENTRY 5;
```

Deleting All or Single Caches

To delete all cached results, run the following statement:

```
ALTER SYSTEM CLEAR VIEW CACHE;
```

To delete a single cache by specifying the cache ID, run the following statement:

```
ALTER SYSTEM REMOVE VIEW CACHE ENTRY 5;
```

Using Hints

For a view that is cache-enabled, you have the option to use or to ignore the cache in each query by using a *hint*. As shown in Listing 3.65, you can add

`HINT(IGNORE_VIEW_CACHE)` to make the query read data from the underlying table instead of using the cache.

```
SELECT DATE_SQL,CITY,SUM(SALES_NET) FROM _sys_bic.'test/CA_SALES_
PURCHASES" WHERE PROD_ID=1 GROUP BY DATE_SQL,CITY WITH HINT(IGNORE_
VIEW_CACHE);
```
Listing 3.65 Query with Hint to Ignore a Cache

The default behavior of a cache-enabled view is to use the cache in each query when the hint is not added in the query.

Using a Cache for Time Travel

In Section 3.8, we discussed the methods involved in using both real and simulated history tables for time travel. Cached views can also be used to perform time traveling in SAP HANA.

Because cached result sets are retrieved from underlying tables during the day and the cached result is not changed within the retention period, you can take advantage of the cache feature to achieve time travel by caching multiple result sets.

For example, suppose you want to analyze the history status of the view CA_SALES_PURCHASES on an hourly basis. To do this, you can cache the result sets of the view every hour. To separate the cached result sets, add a dummy input parameter "TS" to the view. This parameter is used to differentiate the cached result sets; it does not have a connection to any column in the view. Each hour, run a query with a value from the timestamp assigned to the input parameter. For example, for 10:00, run the following:

```
SELECT * FROM _sys_bic."test/CA_SALES_PURCHASES" (PLACEHOLDER."TS" =>
'2015-06-01 10:00:00');
```

And for 11:00, run the following:

```
SELECT * FROM _sys_bic."test/CA_SALES_PURCHASES" (PLACEHOLDER."TS" =>
'2015-06-01 11:00:00');
```

The results sets of the queries with different input parameter values will be cached separately. By checking the table for M_VIEW_CACHE, you can find multiple entries for the view CA_SALES_PURCHASES. After the result sets are cached, you can access each cached result set by specifying the timestamp values of the input parameters in the query to achieve time travel.

For example, to check the history data at 10:00, you can run the following query to use the cached result captured at 10:00:

```
SELECT * FROM _sys_bic."test/CA_SALES_PURCHASES" (PLACEHOLDER."TS" =>
'2015-06-01 10:00:00');
```

In this section, we introduced how to use the cache feature to deal with time-consuming views. There are pros and cons for this feature; the pros include improved performance, whereas the cons include data staleness and additional cache maintenance for database users.

3.12   Summary

In this chapter, we explained several ways in which you can improve performance when dealing with larger datasets. You can follow some general recommendations, such as partitioning tables, leveraging data pruning, leveraging the OLAP engine, pushing filters down, and so on. However, because the root causes of performance issues can differ, it is a good idea to use SAP HANA tools such as the explain plan, visualize plan, or performance trace to figure out the actual bottleneck before modifying queries or models. In addition, you can also redesign the database on the server side or redefine an analysis strategy on the client side.

In the next chapter, we will move on to predictive modeling for forecasting, finding anomalies, discovering data relationships, and more.

In this chapter, we will look at data mining processes and the predictive analytics lifecycle in SAP HANA and discuss the tools and frameworks in SAP HANA that enable you to build predictive models.

4   Basic Predictive Modeling

Predictive models can help solve a number of business scenarios by forecasting the outcome of multiple strategies prior to implementation, finding anomalies in data, discovering data correlations and relationships, exploring influences on data, and locating trends based on data history. Through such actions, companies can make informed investments and as a result more accurately allocate resources.

Within SAP HANA, SAP Predictive Analytics 2.x works as a frontend tool, providing both an expert and business user mode. By integrating R with SAP HANA's in-memory analytics, SAP HANA has the ability to support a wide range of predictive analytic scenarios. SAP HANA's data mining algorithms are embedded into the database through the Predictive Analysis Library (PAL). In addition, SAP HANA Studio has the ability to perform data mining processing with SAP GUI.

Through SAP Predictive Analytics for visualizations, R's data mining and statistical capabilities, and PAL, SAP HANA has the ability to create advanced predictive data models for countless scenarios. In this chapter, we will look into basic predictive modeling tasks and data mining processes. We will discuss specific tools and design considerations for predictive models and perform data mining tasks in SAP HANA. Let's begin by looking at the predictive analytics lifecycle in SAP HANA.

4.1   Predictive Analytics Lifecycle in SAP HANA

In the predictive analytics lifecycle, there are a number of processes that enable the creation of advanced predictive models. Figure 4.1 illustrates the different phases that are usually encountered in the predictive analysis and data mining processes in SAP HANA.

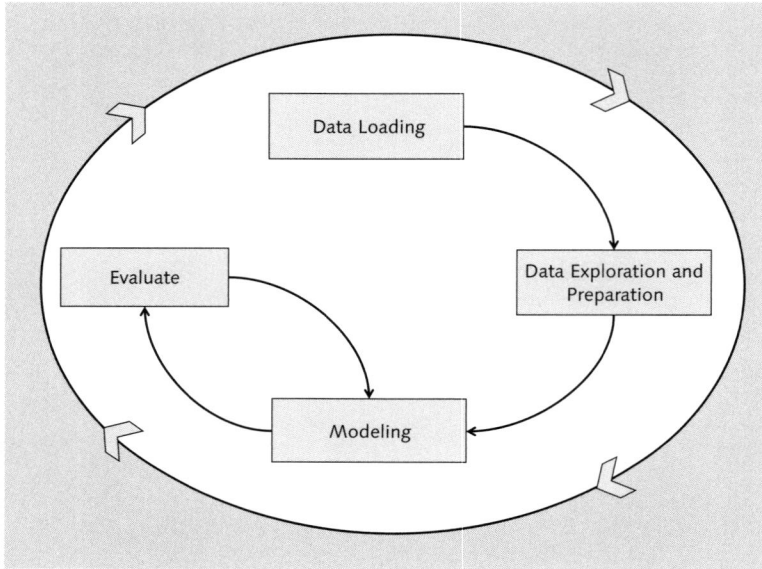

Figure 4.1 SAP HANA Model Process

The phases shown in Figure 4.1 can be described as follows:

▶ **Data loading**
In this phase, data comes into SAP HANA. The sources of the data can be applications running within the SAP HANA platform, SAP Business Suite applications, data loaded through SAP ETL tools, or data management tools.

Data Loading Process	
Data loading is beyond the scope of this book. Assume that data is loaded into SAP HANA through applications, SAP SLT or SAP Data Services, either in real time or through ETL processes.	

▶ **Data exploration and preparation**
Based on the business problem that needs to be solved, in the data exploration phase you will look for various attributes, associativity, or correlations with target variables or predictive tasks, using SAP tools such as SAP Predictive Analytics or SAP HANA Studio to explore data.

In the data preparation phase, you will prepare data for algorithms. In SAP HANA, logical models such as attribute views, analytic views, or calculation views prepare data with newly derived columns and/or perform minor transformation tasks. If you need to perform complex transformations, we recommend using SQL statements and creating materialized views or tables. In SAP HANA, you have the flexibility to leverage any of these techniques.

▶ **Modeling**
In this phase, you will create predictive models using various algorithms in SAP HANA. SAP HANA provides a rich set of techniques to create models by using native PAL, R algorithms, or SAP InfiniteInsight algorithms.

▶ **Evaluate**
Once the predictive models are created, they are evaluated on a regular basis for improvement and accuracy. These evaluated models are used regularly for scoring in production systems.

Now that we've looked at the various phases involved in predictive analytics and data mining, let's turn our attention to some of the more commonly used models in the next section. Then, we will discuss predictive algorithms and the Application Function Library (AFL). Finally, this section will conclude with an example.

4.1.1 Commonly Used Models

Cross Industry Standard Process for Data Mining (CRISP-DM) and *Sample, Explore, Modify, Model and Assess (SEMMA)* are two well-known data mining process models used in solving data mining problems. The third most followed model after CRISP-DM and SEMMA is a custom or specific process model. In the sections that follow, we will look at the two main model types—CRISP-DM and SEMMA—and their processes.

CRISP-DM

Figure 4.2 depicts data mining process for the CRISP-DM model. CRISP-DM is a six-stage model that begins by understanding the business requirements for deploying models. The model's six phases are as follows:

1. **Business understanding**
In this phase, the business requirement is understood and translated into the data mining problem definition, and the plan for the project is prepared.

2. **Data understanding**
   This phase starts with data selection: loading and understanding the data and generating hypotheses.

3. **Data preparation**
   In this phase, the raw data is transformed into the usual form for data mining.

4. **Modeling**
   Here, modeling techniques are applied and calibrated with model parameters.

5. **Evaluation**
   In this phase, the model output is reviewed from the process to create models and achieve solutions to business problems.

6. **Deployment**
   In the final phase, models are deployed in production to enable consumption by the application.

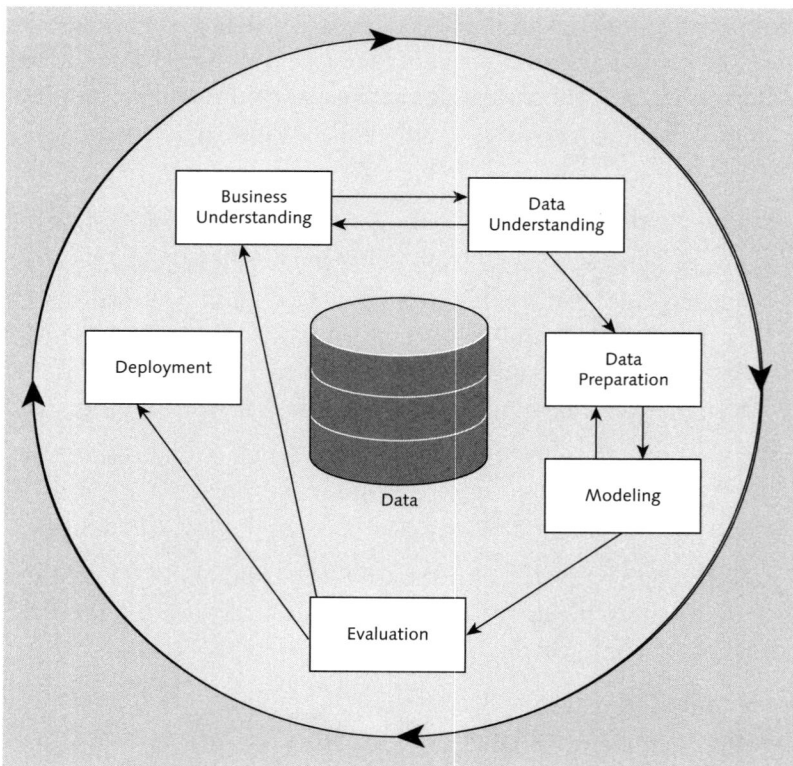

Figure 4.2 CRISP-DM Model

The model enhancement cycle starts from the business understanding stage to the deployment stage. The data loading phase of SAP HANA is equivalent to the business data understanding phases of CRISP-DM. The business understanding phase of CRISP-DM also covers identifying correlations and factors as part of the data exploration phase in SAP HANA. The rest of the phases are similar to SAP HANA's predictive analytics lifecycle phases.

CRISP-DM also deploys models in production as an additional phase. In the case of SAP HANA, storing and executing models both happen in the SAP HANA database.

SEMMA

SEMMA is enhanced by SAP HANA's integration with SAS Analytics using the SAS Predictive Modeling Workbench for SAP HANA. SEMMA has five phases for modeling:

1. **Sample**
   Acquire a representative sample of a large dataset to create models more easily.

2. **Explore**
   Understand patterns in the data.

3. **Modify**
   Perform data manipulations and transformations for model execution.

4. **Model**
   Apply models to the dataset.

5. **Assess**
   Evaluate the models for reliability and achieving expected results.

Note that these phases are more technical and more aligned to the various SAS Analytics tools that enable you to perform these activities. In SAP HANA sampling, exploration and modeling is performed in the data understanding and preparing phase due to the native availability of technical capabilities with the database itself.

4.1.2   Predictive Algorithms in SAP HANA

SAP HANA contains algorithms natively in the database, with additional tools to consume and manage predictive modeling. The algorithms in the SAP HANA database provide performance enhancements, reduced data movement, and improved overall efficiency. SAP HANA also enables R algorithms as operators so that SAP HANA's calculation power can be combined with open packages of R.

There are a number of predictive tools and algorithms available through SAP HANA, and Figure 4.3 provides an illustration of some of these elements.

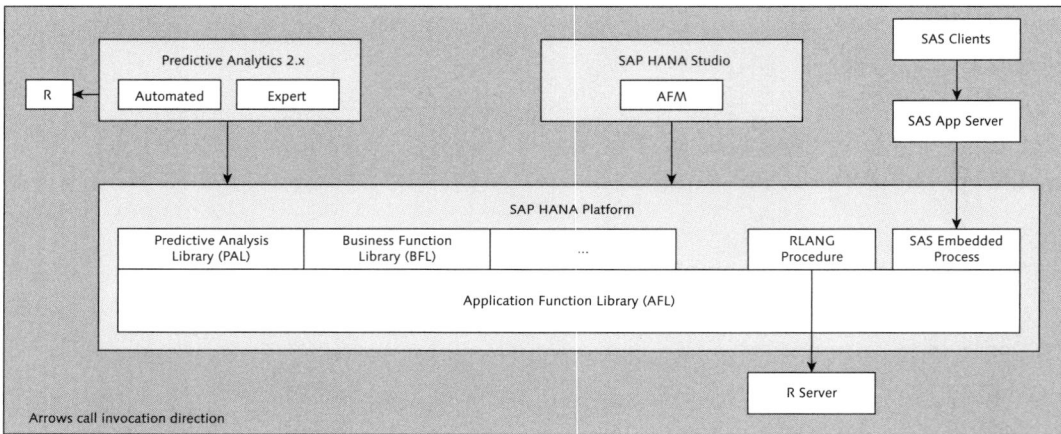

Figure 4.3 Predicitve Analysis in SAP HANA

Let's take a closer look at the elements of Figure 4.3:

▶ **Application Function Library framework**
  This is the core framework library that enables on-demand loading. The functional libraries such as the PAL and the Business Function Library (BFL) are enabled on an AFL framework controlled and enabled through wrapper procedures. SAP HANA role-based security uses the AFL to control the execution of AFL procedures.

▶ **Predictive Analysis Library**

This library provides functions for predictions, machine learning, statistical algorithms to serve data preparation, classification, regression, association, link prediction, and more.

▶ **Business Function Library**

This library contains functions needed for applications, especially in the financial area.

▶ **RLANG procedures**

SAP allows you to write R code in SAP HANA. As an R client, SAP HANA manages the communications and data transformations from the columnar structure to the R data types and vice versa.

▶ **SAP Predictive Analytics**

SAP Predictive Analytics is an application that can be installed on a desktop or server. This application supports automated algorithms through which business users can choose to work on predictive tasks like classification/regression, social network analysis, and more, without deep algorithm knowledge. This tool also supports expert mode to perform all the data mining processes, utilizing PAL, SAP HANA, and R integration. A data scientist can customize the parameters of algorithms for their data mining processes. This tool also enables consumption of local R in a desktop environment.

▶ **SAP HANA Studio**

SAP HANA Studio has different perspectives to perform tasks ranging from administration to various developments on the SAP HANA platform. Using SAP HANA Studio as an SAP HANA modeler, you can develop procedures, views, and more. You can create wrapper procedures on the AFL and consume them in views and procedures. A graphical editor in SAP HANA Studio called the *Application Function Modeler (AFM)* enables the easy creation of wrapper procedures on the AFL and BFL in SAP HANA.

With these tools, you can develop the phases discussed at the beginning of this section. Figure 4.4 shows the tools that can be used in each of the phases.

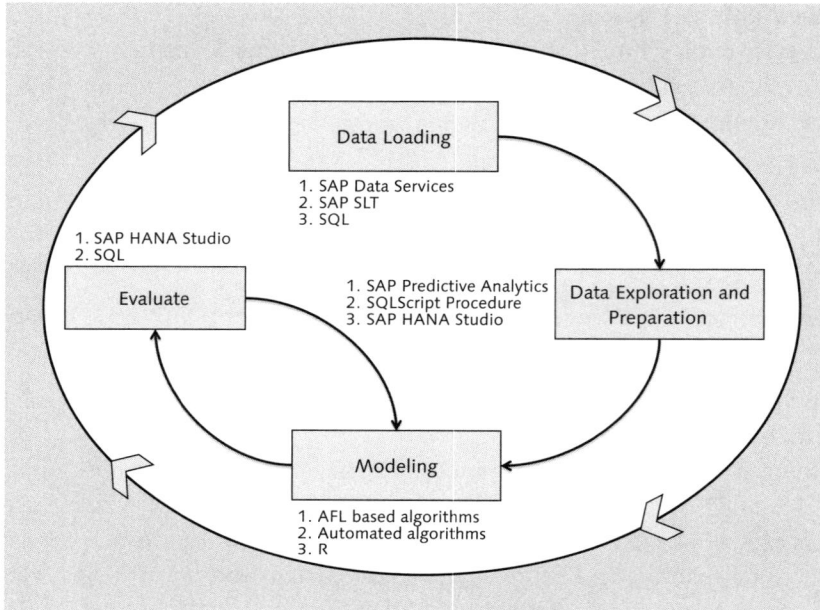

Figure 4.4 SAP HANA Modeling with Tools

In the subsequent sections, we will look into how to perform each of the phases in SAP HANA with the help of the aforementioned tools. First, however, the next section will look at the AFL and its use in predictive modeling.

4.1.3 Application Function Library

The AFL framework provides a consistent way to consume the algorithms provided by function libraries such as the PAL and BFL while adhering to SAP HANA security standards. Figure 4.5 shows the architecture overview of the AFL framework.

As shown in Figure 4.5, PAL is consumed through the AFL framework with wrapper functions. For every function in PAL or BFL, a wrapper function needs to be generated for application consumption. The execution of this wrapper procedure is controlled by access rights set through roles in SAP HANA.

Every algorithm will have a parameter table. The typical structure of this table includes a parameter name and values (in one of three types: integer, double, or string). Based on the type of value for the parameter, the respective column will be populated, and the remaining two columns of the other types will have a null value. Every function requires different parameters to work, and these act as inputs for algorithms along with the data. The consumption of these wrapper functions happens through SQLScript or through script based on a calculation view. For more information, the PAL reference guide is available at *http://help.sap.com/hana/sap_hana_predictive_analysis_library_pal_en.pdf*. Every wrapper procedure's input and output parameters are documented in the reference guide. Before generating a wrapper procedure, you need to understand the input data and output tables of the algorithms. Input table types are designed for particular predictive tasks. If you want two different input data types to be processed by an algorithm in two different invocations, there should be two wrapper procedures. Each wrapper procedure will have its own input types.

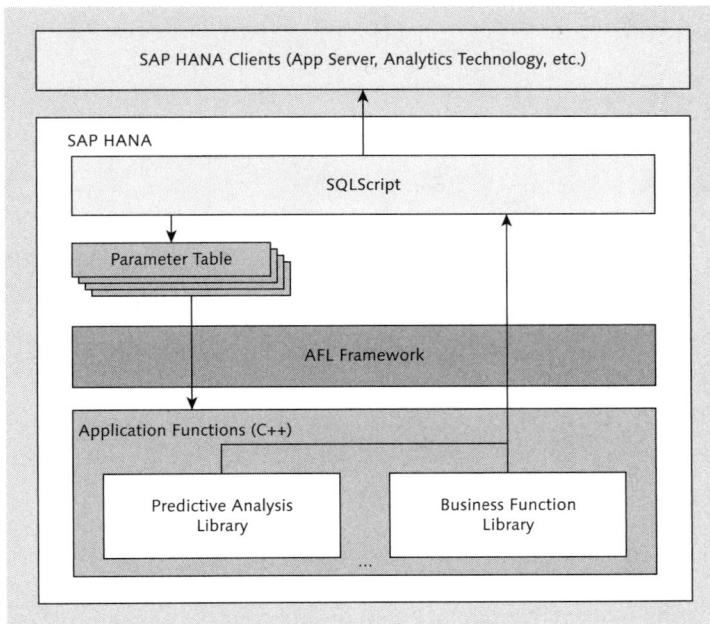

Figure 4.5 AFL Framework

An algorithm is controlled by its set of parameters. Most algorithms require at least one parameter. In SAP HANA, most algorithm parameters default to generic values, including the structure of the control table. You can set a few values at runtime in a SQLScript procedure before invoking the wrapper procedure. Figure 4.6 shows the PAL lifecycle in SAP HANA.

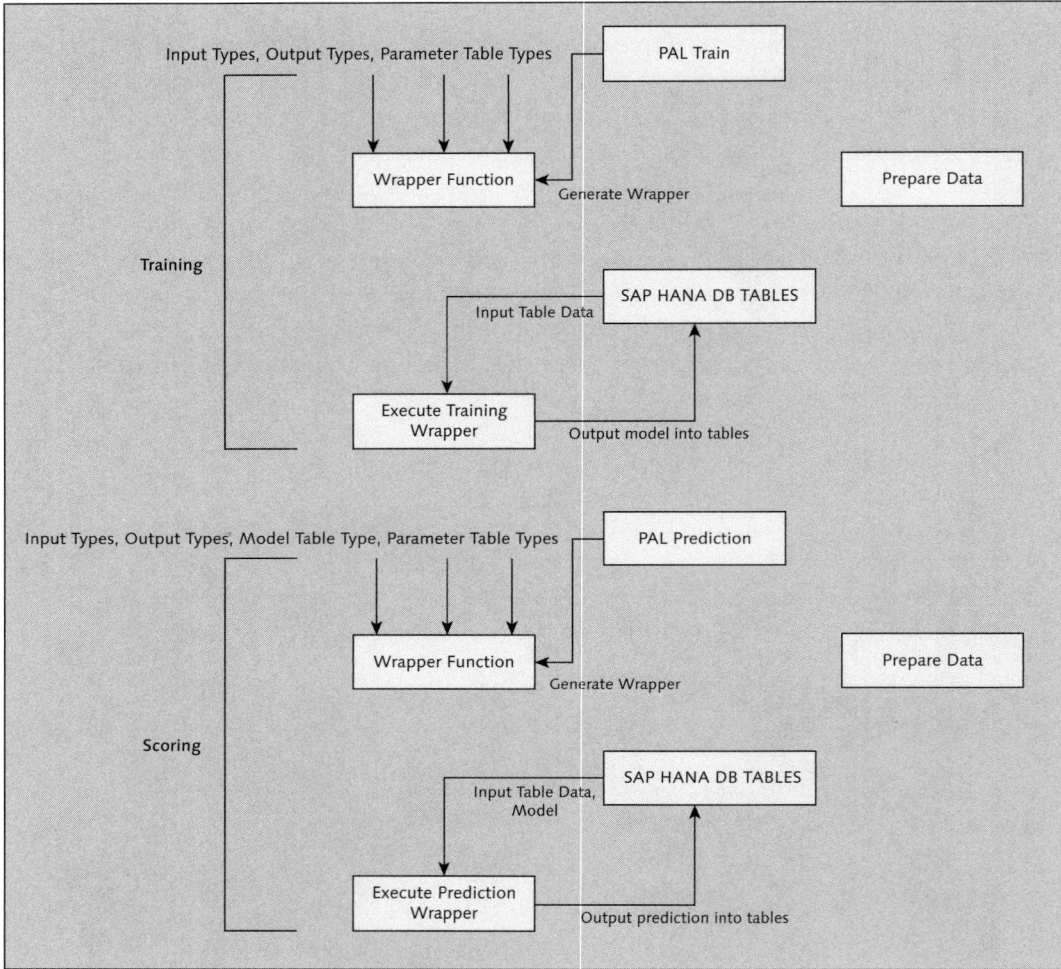

Figure 4.6 PAL Lifecycle

Although the training function requires input data, with parameter tables as an input and providing models as outputs, the predicting function takes the model and prediction dataset as an input, along with the algorithm parameters, and produces future values as output. The models can then be placed in a table and used as an input for predictions.

However, not all algorithms use training and scoring. Some algorithms involve unsupervised learning, like k-means, which do not produce a model as an output but instead create insight results. In such cases, a scoring process is not required.

Now, let's discuss an example, which we will use in rest of the chapter to explain how to perform the predictive modeling phases in SAP HANA.

4.1.4 Business Example

This example will look at forecasting the sales of two products: Product A and Product B. These two products will have unique product IDs (numbers), but we will refer to them as A and B throughout this chapter.

The initial step for this task is to have a good understanding of the business problem itself. Some questions that may impact your modeling include the following: What is the frequency of the forecast, such as a daily forecast, a weekly forecast, or a sometime-in-the-future forecast? You have to understand what variables the daily or weekly sales are dependent on, such as seasonality, weather, day of the week, promotions, effect of competitiveness, and so on. The next step is to get the dataset for the products—data loading from sales, master data-like promotions, weather calendars, and so on—into SAP HANA.

After loading data into SAP HANA, the next step is to analyze the data. For this particular example, you want to understand the historic sales time series. A *time series* is a sequence of data observations (measures) over successive intervals of time and can be used to predict future values, which are used extensively for business, social, and general public needs. You can perform a correlation with variables and identify the variables, white noise, and more.

White Noise in Data

White noise or noise in a time series represents uninterpretable or random shocks in the data. It can include a sudden high increase or decrease of values outside of the mean, moving average, or standard deviation. If there is no correlation between the different lags of data, this is referred to as white noise.

This step will also identify which algorithms suit forecasting, such as cause-and-effect-based regression models, boosting-based algorithms, seasonal-based algorithms, or autoregressive models.

Once you have identified these factors, you can prepare the data for the training model. This can be a logical model along with sales and variables or can be materialized based on the complexity of identified variables. Finally, once you train a model for forecast, you can evaluate its accuracy and improvise the models in the evaluate phase.

4.2 Data Exploration

In this section, we will continue to use the forecasting problem introduced in Section 4.1.4 and cover the data exploration phase of predictive modeling.

Data exploration involves the following set of activities:

▶ Understanding the behavior of target data (in this case, sales of a product).

▶ Understanding the correlations and autocorrelations of time series behavior.

▶ Understanding the casual attributes for the behavior.

▶ Determining the model types for training best suited for the task (forecasting) based on data patterns.

4.2.1 Understanding Sales Data

Let's consider a simple time series data for product sales in a table. Because this is a time series, you can create a column table with the SERIES storage class, as defined in Listing 4.1.

```
DROP TABLE SALES_SERIES_DATA;
CREATE COLUMN TABLE SALES_SERIES_DATA (
YEAR_WEEK          INTEGER not null,
STORE_ID     INTEGER not null ,
PROD_ID      VARCHAR(10)_ not null ,
SALESQTY         double, primary key(STORE_ID,PROD_ID,YEAR_WEEK)
) SERIES (
SERIES KEY(STORE_ID, PROD_ID)
EQUIDISTANT INCREMENT BY 1 MISSING ELEMENTS NOT ALLOWED PERIOD
FOR SERIES (YEAR_WEEK,NULL)
);
```
Listing 4.1 Series Data Table Creation

Note that the SERIES class definition enables the creation of the time series data. This gives you the flexibility to use time series functions such as correlation or Pearson correlation on the data.

Based on Listing 4.1, the table definition looks as shown in Figure 4.7.

	Name	SQL Data Type	Di...	Column Store Data Type
1	YEAR_WEEK	INTEGER		INT
2	STORE_ID	INTEGER		INT
3	PROD_ID	INTEGER		INT
4	SALESQTY	SMALLINT		INT

Figure 4.7 Series Table Structure

We have inserted two years of sales quantities for products into the series table shown in Figure 4.7. The sample sales data should look like Figure 4.8.

YEAR_WEEK	STORE_ID	PROD_ID	SALESQTY
201,001	1	A	103
201,002	1	A	141
201,003	1	A	100
201,004	1	A	122
201,005	1	A	89
201,006	1	A	113
201,007	1	A	148
201,008	1	A	104
201,009	1	A	123
201,010	1	A	98
201,011	1	A	108
201,012	1	A	92
201,013	1	A	110
201,014	1	A	83
201,015	1	A	88
201,016	1	A	87
201,017	1	A	82
201,018	1	A	101
201,019	1	A	104
201,020	1	A	75
201,021	1	A	66
201,022	1	A	85
201,023	1	A	76
201,024	1	A	65
201,025	1	A	89
201,026	1	A	62
201,027	1	A	90
201,028	1	A	109
201,029	1	A	77
201,030	1	A	44
201,031	1	A	90
201,032	1	A	113
201,033	1	A	93
201,034	1	A	63
201,035	1	A	68
201,036	1	A	57

Figure 4.8 Series Sample Data

In SAP HANA Studio, you can observe the time series via TABLE DATA PREVIEW under the DATA ANALYSIS tab. In Figure 4.9, note that overall SALESQTY across historic time for all products is aggregated. Drag the appropriate columns to the label access, measure the axes, and choose the proper chart type (see Figure 4.9). This will let you see whether there are any trends or broader level seasonality/outliers seen in the data.

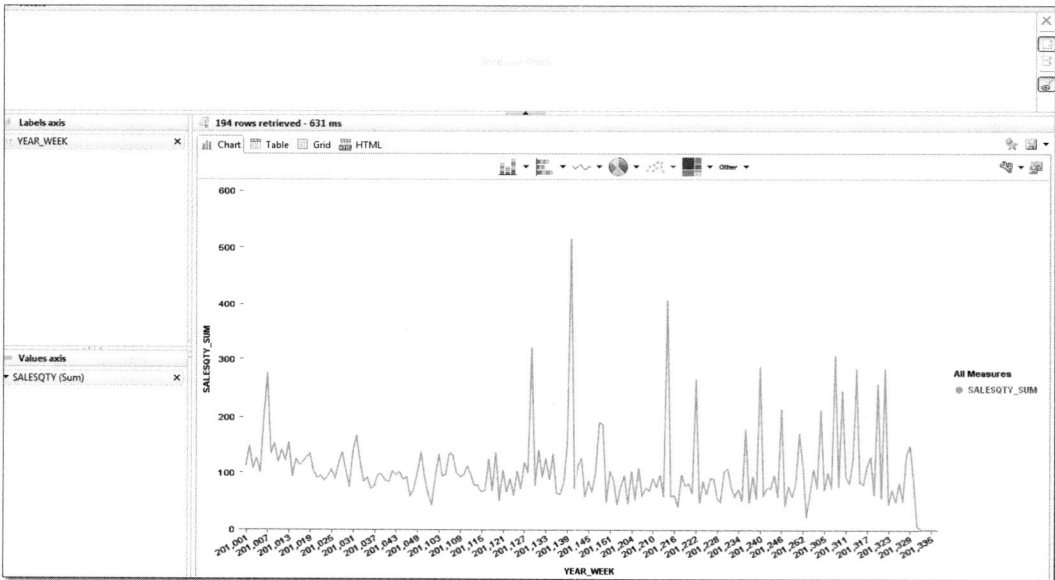

Figure 4.9 All Products Time Series

Now, you can focus on individual product sales patterns by choosing a particular product in the filters. The Product A sales series is shown in Figure 4.10.

The behavior of Product A looks more or less similar to the initial overall sales pattern in Figure 4.9. This might be due to the fact that the quantity sold of this product is the most significant percentage in aggregation; the numbers on the y-axes in Figure 4.9 and Figure 4.10 are close to each other. You can see the trend of Product B in Figure 4.11.

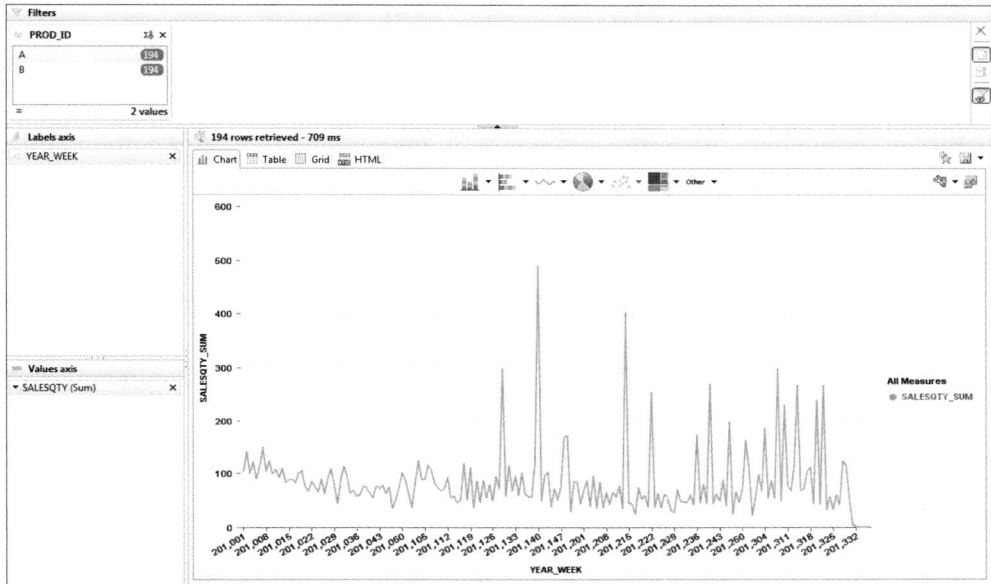

Figure 4.10 Product A Sales Series

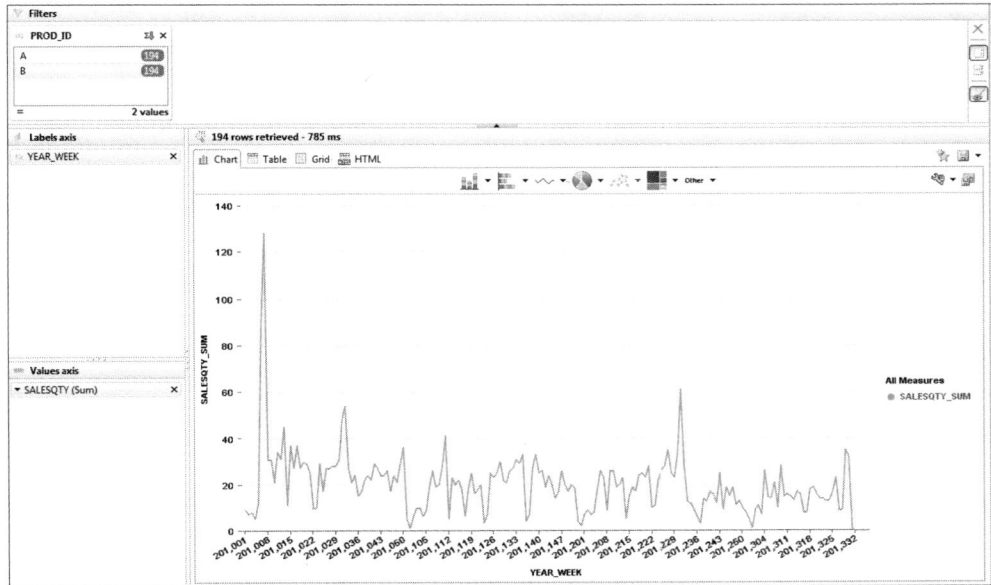

Figure 4.11 Product B Trend

Let's now look at the statistical behaviors of these two products. To do so, generate a wrapper procedure for the `UNIVARSTAT` function from PAL as `PAL_UNIVARIA-TESTAT_PROC`. Listing 4.2 is sample code for the *univariant statistical analysis* of both products. The univariant analysis of distribution function `UNIVARSTAT` in SAP HANA provides the following statistical calculations:

▶ **Mean, median, and mode**
The mean, median, and mode provide the average value of distribution, the middle values of distribution, and the most frequently occurring values of distribution, respectively. The output of the univariant analysis provides the mean and median.

▶ **Lower quartile and upper quartile**
The median of the lower half and higher half are referred to as the lower quartile and upper quartile. The median of the entire distribution is considered for dividing the distribution into two halves. These values will help you understand the value differences in the distribution.

▶ **Variance and standard deviation**
The variance for a population is the calculated average of the squared difference of each element in the distribution, with a mean of the distribution and the standard deviation as the square root of the variance. The formula for variance is $\sigma^2 = (\Sigma\, (n_i - \mu)^2)/n$, where the standard definition (σ) is the square root of the variance. These values help you understand the spread of distribution in SAP HANA and also support sample dataset variance and standard deviation with the `DATASET_TYPE` parameter.

▶ **Skewness**
This calculation measures the symmetric level of a distribution. *Symmetric distribution* will have a mean, median, and mode at the same point with values that occur at regular frequencies. A higher value of greater than 1 is referred to as *asymmetric*.

▶ **Kurtosis**
This calculation measures the flatness or peakedness of the data. A *Gaussian distribution* has 0 kurtosis. A negative kurtosis indicates that data is flat, and a positive kurtosis indicates high peaks in the data.

Listing 4.2 shows the univariant analysis at work.

```
DROP PROCEDURE CALL_UNIVAR;
CREATE PROCEDURE CALL_UNIVAR() LANGUAGE SQLScript AS
BEGIN

input1 = SELECT "SALESQTY"

  FROM "ANIL_FORECAST"."SALE_SERIES_WITH_ATTRIBUTES"
  WHERE PROD_ID = 'A'
  ORDER BY YEAR_WEEK ASC;

control_1 = SELECT * FROM PAL_CONTROL_TBL_U;

CALL "ANIL_FORECAST"."PAL_UNIVARIATESTAT_PROC" (:input1, :control_1,
v_result1);

input2 = SELECT "SALESQTY"

  FROM "ANIL_FORECAST"."SALE_SERIES_WITH_ATTRIBUTES"
  WHERE PROD_ID = 'B'
  ORDER BY YEAR_WEEK ASC;

CALL "ANIL_FORECAST"."PAL_UNIVARIATESTAT_PROC" (:input2, :control_1,
v_result2);

select * from :v_result1;
select * from :v_result2;
END;
```

Listing 4.2 Univariant Statistical Analysis Code for Both Products

Note that in the procedure shown in Listing 4.2, the PAL function is called for both Product A and Product B separately. The other possible approach is to call PAL once for both Products A and B distributed as two individual columns. You need to ensure that the sales quantities of each product are available for all the weeks for each product.

The results of the preceding procedure for each product are shown in Figure 4.12 (Product A) and Figure 4.13 (Product B).

	STATISTICSNAME	SALESQTY
1	mean	84.0876288659794
2	median	71
3	lower quartile	50
4	upper quartile	95
5	variance	4,043.9871000480734
6	standard deviati...	63.59235095550465
7	skewness	2.9721586149608097
8	kurtosis	12.275360475944723

Figure 4.12 Product A Univariant Statistical Analysis

	STATISTICSNAME	SALESQTY
1	mean	19.793814432989702
2	median	19
3	lower quartile	10
4	upper quartile	26
5	variance	192.71374392393574
6	standard deviati...	13.882137584822294
7	skewness	3.169408956020122
8	kurtosis	20.22937923223032

Figure 4.13 Product B Univariant Statistical Analysis

Both products have a high kurtosis and skewness, which confirms that their peaks are quite significant. You can also see that these two products show distinct behaviors, with cyclic effects shown in Product B and no cycles shown in Product A.

Cyclic Effects in Data	
Cyclic effects in data occur when trends or patterns repeat themselves in a particular season or time period.	

To confirm the hypothesis that these two products are exhibiting different behaviors, execute the correlation of these two products. In this example, assume that SALEQTY is in the same unit and that there is no need to normalize the data. In order to perform this correlation, self-join the table on the YEAR_WEEK column to get both products' results for the correct time period. Listing 4.3 shows the self-join query.

```
SELECT SE.YEAR_WEEK, SE.SALESQTY A, HW.SALESQTY B
FROM "ANIL_FORECAST"."SALE_SERIES_WITH_ATTRIBUTES" SE
JOIN "ANIL_FORECAST"."SALE_SERIES_WITH_ATTRIBUTES" HW ON HW.YEAR_WEEK =
  SE.YEAR_WEEK
AND SE.PROD_ID = 'A' and HW.PROD_ID = 'B';
```

Listing 4.3 Self-Join Table with Distinct Products

The output of the query in Listing 4.3 is shown in Figure 4.14.

	YEAR_WEEK	A	B
1	201,001	103	9
2	201,002	141	7
3	201,003	100	8
4	201,004	122	5
5	201,005	89	12
6	201,006	113	88
7	201,007	148	128
8	201,008	104	31
9	201,009	123	31
10	201,010	98	21
11	201,011	108	34
12	201,012	92	31
13	201,013	110	45
14	201,014	83	11
15	201,015	88	37
16	201,016	87	27
17	201,017	82	37
18	201,018	101	27
19	201,019	104	30
20	201,020	75	29
21	201,021	66	25
22	201,022	85	10
23	201,023	76	10
24	201,024	65	29
25	201,025	89	17
26	201,026	62	27
27	201,027	90	27

Figure 4.14 Self-Join Output

Now, perform the correlation for the sales patterns of these two products with the SQL statements shown in Listing 4.4. In SAP HANA, two types of correlations functions are supported as SQL functions:

▶ **Pearson correlation**

Pearson correlation measures the linear dependency between two products. Its value is between -1 and 1, with both boundary values inclusive. A positive correlation indicates the movement of the products in the same direction. Negative values indicate movement in opposite directions. Values towards the boundaries indicate a strong correlation, and values around zero indicate no correlation between products. Pearson correlation is calculated via the following formula:

$$\rho A, B = Cov(A,B)/(\sigma A \sigma B)$$

Where:

▷ $Cov(A,B)$ is the covariance of products A and B

▷ σA indicates the standard deviation of Product A

▸ **Spearman correlation**

Spearman correlation measures the strength of association between two ranked or ordinal variables. It can be used when the non-normality of values or one of the variables is ordinal. Spearman correlation does not measure a linear relationship like Pearson correlation. Its measure defines the strength of associativity.

The usual values of these coefficients is between -1 and 1. The closer to the boundaries you are, the stronger the correlation (see Listing 4.4).

```
SELECT CORR(SE.SALESQTY, HW.SALESQTY) PEARSONCORR, CORR_
SPEARMAN(SE.SALESQTY, HW.SALESQTY) SPEARMANCORR
FROM "ANIL_FORECAST"."SALE_SERIES_WITH_ATTRIBUTES" SE
JOIN "ANIL_FORECAST"."SALE_SERIES_WITH_ATTRIBUTES"
HW ON HW.YEAR_WEEK = SE.YEAR_WEEK
AND SE.PROD_ID = 'A' and HW.PROD_ID = 'B';
```

Listing 4.4 Correlation Query

The output for Listing 4.4 is shown in Figure 4.15.

	PEARSONCORR	SPEARMANCORR
1	0.06234	0.107905

Figure 4.15 Correlation Output

Note that both of the correlation coefficients are close to zero, confirming the hypothesis that these products exhibit different behaviors.

Ranked Variables

Until now, we have not used any ordinal variables (ranked variables); Spearman correlation is not relevant in such cases.

In our example, we used time series forecasting to explore product behavior. When you have a different problem to solve, such as determining the probability of a bank losing a valuable customer (churn analysis) or any association, the tools you leverage are similar. In such cases, use SAP HANA Studio, SQL-based queries, and statistical algorithms in PAL. Frontend tools support different types of charts, allowing you to leverage PAL for statistical analysis. We can also use SAP Predictive Analytics GUI tools to analyze the data further.

In this section, we looked at the behavior of each product's sales data using SQL queries and the SAP HANA Studio Analysis tab as part of the data exploration phase. In the next section, we will look for factors that influence the behaviors we have found between Product A and Product B.

4.2.2 Correlation and Autocorrelation

In this section, we will continue the example from previous sections to further understand the factors that may have affected Product A and B sales behaviors. Product A has exhibited no cycles or upward trends, and Product B is exhibiting cyclic sales without any seasonal dependency and no upward or downward trend. However, there are still sales patterns that need to be interpreted.

You can look at additional data associated with products A and B that may have impacted sales. General factors could include data such as weather, local events, holidays, and days of the week (if using daily forecasts). With such data, you can perform a correlation analysis. You can also perform a factor analysis with specific business factors, such as the price of the product or promotions to push more sales, or look at indirect factors, such as the impact of competitive product sales and availability. Identifying these factors involves a certain amount of business knowledge to some extent and the availability of data. For instance, intraday and interday weather data needs to be corroborated with national weather institutions. Similarly, the granularity of information should be the same as the historic sales data granularity—for example, weekly information and/or daily information.

We will present a couple of examples to investigate the hypotheses that Product B has seasonal-based sales and that Product A has noise within its data that can be understood by applying factor analysis.

Generate calendar data using SAP HANA Studio, which will populate the data into table M_TIME_DIMENSION(_XXXX) under schema _SYS_BI. Figure 4.16 shows the navigation to the calendar object generation.

Open Quick View from the SAP HANA Studio menu, and select Generate Time Data. Choose the SAP HANA instance on which you want to generate this information. Figure 4.16 shows the options for generating time data. Because we are focusing on the weekly forecast, select Week for Granularity, and input the year range. If the information is rolled up from the daily level, the week start date will affect the number to be considered for the sales aggregation.

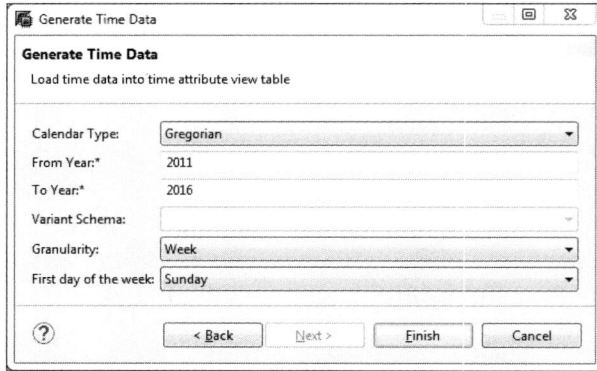

Figure 4.16 Generate Time Data

Once you click the FINISH button, table `M_TIME_DIMENSION_WEEK` is populated with information based on the chosen weekly granularity. Now, enhance this table in the attribute view to join both the year and week. You can use the month column from `M_TIME_DIMENSION` to aggregate the information and perform a correlation. Listing 4.5 shows two queries that provide a look at the sales correlation between the sales and month for Product A.

```
SELECT CORR(M, A), CORR_SPEARMAN(M,A) FROM (
SELECT HW."YEAR_INT", HW.MONTH_INT M, SUM(SE.SALESQTY) A
FROM "ANIL_FORECAST"."SALE_SERIES_WITH_ATTRIBUTES" SE
JOIN "_SYS_BI"."M_TIME_DIMENSION_WEEK" HW ON HW.YEAR_WEEK = SE.YEAR_
WEEK
AND SE.PROD_ID = 'A'
GROUP BY HW.YEAR_INT, HW.MONTH_INT);

SELECT CORR(M, A), CORR_SPEARMAN(M,A) FROM (
SELECT HW."YEAR_INT", HW.MONTH_INT M, SUM(SE.SALESQTY) A
FROM "ANIL_FORECAST"."SALE_SERIES_WITH_ATTRIBUTES" SE
JOIN "_SYS_BI"."M_TIME_DIMENSION_WEEK" HW ON HW.YEAR_WEEK = SE.YEAR_
WEEK
AND SE.PROD_ID = 'A'
GROUP BY HW.YEAR_INT, HW.MONTH_INT);
```

Listing 4.5 Product A Queries for Weekly and Monthly Correlation

Figure 4.17 and Figure 4.18 show the monthly and weekly correlation coefficients for Product A.

	CORR(M,A)	CORR_SPEARMAN(M,A)
1	-0.154573	-0.158284

Figure 4.17 Product A Sales Correlation: Month

	CORR(M,A)	CORR_SPEARMAN(M,A)
1	-0.014857	-0.087527

Figure 4.18 Product A Sales Correlation: Week

Both of these values confirm that the sales of Product A do not correlate to any particular season.

Let's perform the same actions for Product B. Listing 4.6 shows both queries for correlation (month and week).

```
SELECT CORR(M, A), CORR_SPEARMAN(M,A) FROM (
SELECT HW.YEAR_INT, HW.MONTH_INT M, SUM(SE.SALESQTY) A
FROM "ANIL_FORECAST"."SALE_SERIES_WITH_ATTRIBUTES" SE
JOIN "_SYS_BI"."M_TIME_DIMENSION_WEEK" HW ON HW.YEAR_WEEK = SE.YEAR_
WEEK
AND SE.PROD_ID = 'B'
GROUP BY HW.YEAR_INT, HW.MONTH_INT);

SELECT CORR(M, A), CORR_SPEARMAN(M,A) FROM (
SELECT HW.YEAR_INT, HW.WEEK_INT M, SUM(SE.SALESQTY) A
FROM "ANIL_FORECAST"."SALE_SERIES_WITH_ATTRIBUTES" SE
JOIN "_SYS_BI"."M_TIME_DIMENSION_WEEK" HW ON HW.YEAR_WEEK = SE.YEAR_
WEEK
AND SE.PROD_ID = 'B'
GROUP BY HW.YEAR_INT, HW.WEEK_INT);
```

Listing 4.6 Product B Correlations: Month and Week

The output for each query is shown in Figure 4.19 and Figure 4.20.

	CORR(M,A)	CORR_SPEARMAN(M,A)
1	-0.139866	-0.164543

Figure 4.19 Product B Sales Correlation: Month

	CORR(M,A)	CORR_SPEARMAN(M,A)
1	0.011319	0.03082

Figure 4.20 Product B Sales Correlation: Week

Although you can note cycles in the data, Product B sales are not correlated based on the month or week, telling you that this product is not seasonal.

Another data exploration method that can better help you understand whether trend factors and seasonality influence your product data is autocorrelation for time. In Listing 4.5 and Listing 4.6, you saw the correlation between the two products and factor analysis via monthly factors. Based on one- and two-period lags and correlation value trends, you can determine the trends of a product and also its seasonality. Listing 4.7 shows the autocorrelation and Spearman autocorrelation with a one-period (one-week) lag to a six period lag. Autocorrelation and Spearman autocorrelation can be defined as follows:

- **Autocorrelation**

  A cross-correlation of a signal with itself at different points in time is called *autocorrelation*. It will find the similarity of observations with itself with different time lags. For detecting appropriate time series models, such as seasonally based or moving average based, autocorrelation is performed with many lags. Autocorrelation also helps to detect randomness in the data when performed with the first lag.

- **Spearman autocorrelation**

  Spearman autocorrelation is a measure of associativity with rank order data. It helps to identify trends within the same variable.

```
SELECT CORR(SALESQTY, LAG1), CORR_SPEARMAN(SALESQTY, LAG1) FROM (
select YEAR_WEEK, PROD_
ID, SALESQTY, LAG(SALESQTY) over (partition by prod_id order by year_
week asc) as LAG1
FROM "ANIL_FORECAST"."SALE_SERIES_WITH_ATTRIBUTES"
WHERE PROD_ID = 'B')
WHERE LAG1 IS NOT NULL
UNION ALL
SELECT CORR(SALESQTY, LAG1), CORR_SPEARMAN(SALESQTY, LAG1) FROM (
select YEAR_WEEK, PROD_
ID, SALESQTY, LAG(SALESQTY,2) over (partition by prod_id order by year_
week asc) as LAG1
FROM "ANIL_FORECAST"."SALE_SERIES_WITH_ATTRIBUTES"
WHERE PROD_ID = 'B')
WHERE LAG1 IS NOT NULL
UNION ALL
SELECT CORR(SALESQTY, LAG1), CORR_SPEARMAN(SALESQTY, LAG1) FROM (
select YEAR_WEEK, PROD_
ID, SALESQTY, LAG(SALESQTY,3) over (partition by prod_id order by year_
week asc) as LAG1
FROM "ANIL_FORECAST"."SALE_SERIES_WITH_ATTRIBUTES"
```

```
WHERE PROD_ID = 'B')
WHERE LAG1 IS NOT NULL
UNION ALL
SELECT CORR(SALESQTY, LAG1), CORR_SPEARMAN(SALESQTY, LAG1) FROM (
select YEAR_WEEK, PROD_
ID, SALESQTY, LAG(SALESQTY,4) over (partition by prod_id order by year_
week asc) as LAG1
FROM "ANIL_FORECAST"."SALE_SERIES_WITH_ATTRIBUTES"
WHERE PROD_ID = 'B')
WHERE LAG1 IS NOT NULL
UNION ALL
SELECT CORR(SALESQTY, LAG1), CORR_SPEARMAN(SALESQTY, LAG1) FROM (
select YEAR_WEEK, PROD_
ID, SALESQTY, LAG(SALESQTY,5) over (partition by prod_id order by year_
week asc) as LAG1
FROM "ANIL_FORECAST"."SALE_SERIES_WITH_ATTRIBUTES"
WHERE PROD_ID = 'B')
WHERE LAG1 IS NOT NULL
UNION ALL
SELECT CORR(SALESQTY, LAG1), CORR_SPEARMAN(SALESQTY, LAG1) FROM (
select YEAR_WEEK, PROD_
ID, SALESQTY, LAG(SALESQTY,6) over (partition by prod_id order by year_
week asc) as LAG1
FROM "ANIL_FORECAST"."SALE_SERIES_WITH_ATTRIBUTES"
WHERE PROD_ID = 'B')
WHERE LAG1 IS NOT NULL;.
```

Listing 4.7 Autocorrelation and Spearman Autocorrelation

If you change the query from Product B to Product A in Listing 4.7, you will notice an autocorrelation and Spearman autocorrelation for that product.

Figure 4.21 shows the autocorrelation and Spearman autocorrelation for Product A, with increasing lags of 1 to 6. Clearly, there is no consistent trend found in either of the autocorrelations, indicating no overall trend for this product. You can clearly confirm that the peaks are noise, and that you need to interpret other specific relevant business factors such as sales, etc.

	CORR(SALESQTY,LAG1)	CORR_SPEARMAN(SALESQTY,LAG1)
1	-0.076097	0.018476
2	0.137764	0.362931
3	-0.091728	-0.018596
4	0.117793	0.388385
5	-0.076713	-0.007763
6	0.178573	0.368442

Figure 4.21 Product A Autocorrelation and Spearman Autocorrelation with Increasing Lags from 1 to 6

Figure 4.22 shows the autocorrelation and Spearman autocorrelation for Product B. Although the autocorrelation shows some trends in longer intervals, the Spearman autocorrelation definitely shows a decreasing trend in the data. To a greater extent, the hypothesis of cycles and trends in Product B is confirmed.

	CORR(SALESQTY,LAG1)	CORR_SPEARMAN(SALESQTY,LAG1)
1	0.508988	0.537685
2	0.174626	0.313695
3	0.098797	0.273317
4	0.105995	0.206984
5	0.051947	0.11337
6	0.08217	0.07055

Figure 4.22 Product B Autocorrelation and Spearman Autocorrelation with Increasing Lags from 1 to 6

PAL supports time series testing functions to estimate trends, white noise, and seasonality aspects. These test functions include the following:

► **Trend test**
This function tests whether there are any upward or downward trends that exist in the time series. The two techniques that are supported by this function are as follows:

  ► *Difference-sign test*: This is based on the number of times there is a difference between the consecutive values in a time series. For a large number of values in a time series, if the absolute value of difference of the mean is greater, than the standard deviation of the differences indicates that a trend exists.

  ► *Rank test*: This is based on the Mann-Kendall (MK) test for design trends. The null hypothesis of the test is that there is no trend, and for any given tolerance probability the tests will conclude the hypothesis of the trend with an estimation between -1 and 1, where -1 indicates a negative trend, 1 indicates a positive trend, and 0 indicates no trend. The minimum length of the time series has to be 3.

► **Seasonality test**
This test identifies the seasonality of the time series by decomposing the time series. The two different models for decomposing are as follows:

  ► *Additive*
  $xt = mt + st + yt$

  ► *Multiplicative*
  $xt = mt \times st \times yt$

Where m, s, and t are trend, seasonality, and random components, respectively. These formulas will satisfy the following property, where d is the length of the seasonal periods:

$$E(y_t) = 0, s_{t+d} = s_t, \sum_{j=1}^{d} s_j = 0$$

▶ **White noise test**
This function will classify the time series as white noise or not using the Ljung-Box test for autocorrelation with different lags. The Ljung-Box formula for statistical tests is as follows:

$$Q = n(n+2) \sum_{h=1}^{m} \frac{\hat{\rho}_h^2}{n-h}$$

Where $\hat{\rho}_h$ is a sample autocorrelation at lag h, m is the number of lags being tested, and n is the sample size. Q follows a chi-square distribution.

Because you have created hypotheses for both products, we will continue without executing these techniques, but you should note that they are important functions to remember.

In this section, we used nonparametric autocorrelations to identify trends and seasonality aspects within data and parametric correlations with generic parameters, such as month and week. The concepts of correlation are commonly used in most data analysis and factor analysis. In the next section, we will do more with the deterministic variable analysis of products A and B.

4.2.3 Deterministic Variables

Deterministic variables are nonrandom variables in the context of other variables. This means that the value of variables such as sales quantity can be determined and dependent on other variables, and thus there is no randomness involved in determining the value of the sales quantity. In other words, a sales quantity can be calculated using a function in which the variables and outcome of the sales quantity contain the same set of variable values.

We have populated the time series input table used in Section 4.2.1 with variables such as price offers and flagged promotions. We will perform an exploration analysis in SAP HANA Studio to determine whether some of the noise in the data can be attributed to these variables. Use SAP HANA Studio to plot a time series using the offer price changes in correlation with the sales quantities for Product A (see Figure 4.23).

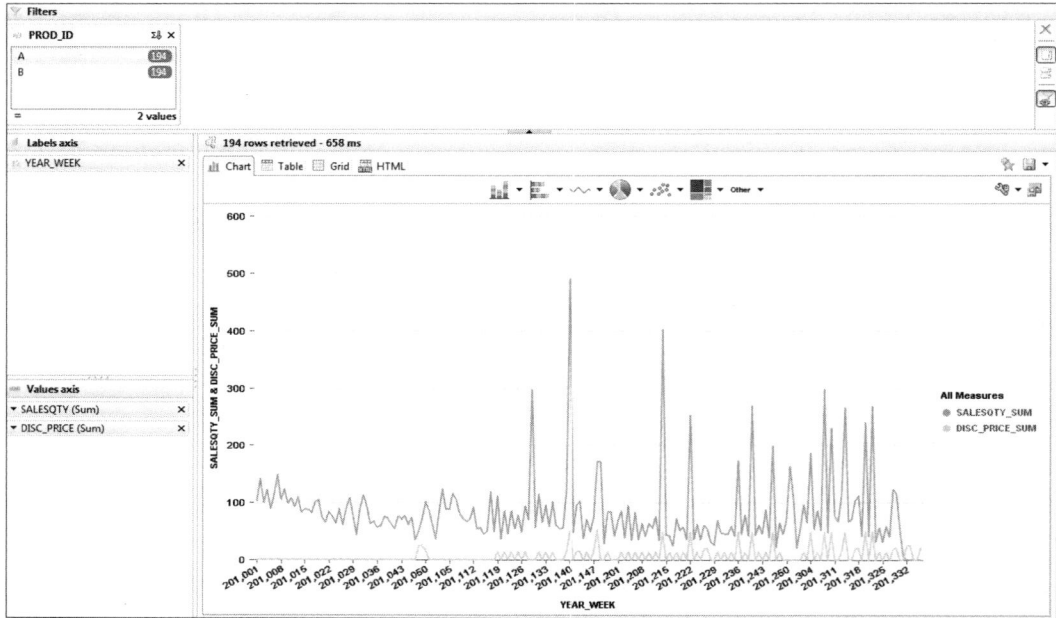

Figure 4.23 Product A Correlation with Price

Figure 4.23 clearly shows that most of the high sales quantities happen when the price is reduced and are dependent on the quantum of the price reduced. You also can see that some low quantum price reductions have no, little, or inconsistent effect. This may be due to other business factors that need new data to be loaded. Let's now observe Product B's pattern, shown in Figure 4.24.

In Figure 4.24, you can see that there is an impact on sales based on the price reduction for only a few occasions. However, there are instances in which you cannot attribute this as a factor because of high sales (peaks) without any price reduction. Considering all the possible factors, you can execute a multivariant correlation coefficient and determine the relevant variables for the sales quantity.

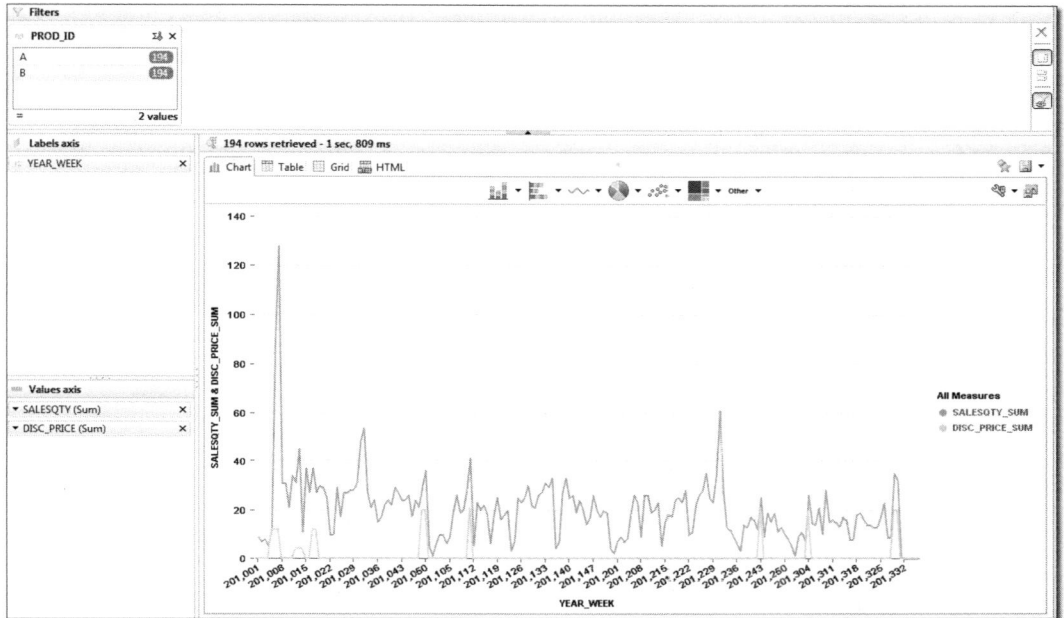

Figure 4.24 Product B Sales with Price

Multivariant analysis in PAL supports the basic statistics of multiple variables, such as the covariance matrix. There are two options for covariant analysis calculations:

▸ **Covariance matrix**

The covariance between two variables x and y is calculated using the following formula:

$$\text{cov}(x, y) = \frac{1}{n-1} \sum_{i=1}^{n} (x_i - \bar{x}) * (y_i - \bar{y})$$

The covariance of each input variable with all other variables is the covariance matrix.

▸ **Pearson correlation coefficient matrix**

The Pearson correlation coefficient between two variables is calculated using the following formula:

$$\text{cor}(x, y) = \frac{\text{cov}(X, Y)}{s_x * s_y}$$

The correlation coefficient of each of the input variables with all other variables is referred to as the correlation coefficient matrix.

With this function, you can see which two variables are strongly correlated and also the variables with which the target variable has a strong correlation.

Use the PAL reference guide at *help.sap.com/hana/sap_hana_predictive_analysis_library_pal_en.pdf* to build a wrapper procedure for the PAL function MULTI-VARSTAT; call this wrapper SALES_VARIABLES.

Similar to the code for univariant statistical analysis, Listing 4.8 shows the code for multivariant analysis.

```
DROP PROCEDURE CALL_MULTIVAR;
CREATE PROCEDURE CALL_MULTIVAR() LANGUAGE SQLScript AS
BEGIN

input1 = SELECT "SALESQTY" ,
  "OFFER_PRICE",
  "OUTOFSTOCK_COUNT"   ,
  "OFFER_FLAG"   ,
  "SHOW_TYPE"   ,
  "PROMOTE_TYPE"
  FROM "ANIL_FORECAST"."SALE_SERIES_WITH_ATTRIBUTES"
  WHERE PROD_ID = 'A'
  ORDER BY YEAR_WEEK ASC;

control_1 = SELECT * FROM PAL_CONTROL_TBL;

CALL "ANIL_FORECAST"."SALES_VARIABLES" (:input1, :control_1,
v_result1);

input2 = SELECT "SALESQTY" ,
  "OFFER_PRICE",
  "OUTOFSTOCK_COUNT"   ,
  "OFFER_FLAG"   ,
  "SHOW_TYPE"   ,
  "PROMOTE_TYPE"
  FROM "ANIL_FORECAST"."SALE_SERIES_WITH_ATTRIBUTES"
  WHERE PROD_ID = 'B'
  ORDER BY YEAR_WEEK ASC;



CALL "ANIL_FORECAST"."SALES_VARIABLES" (:input2, :control_1,
v_result2);

select * from :v_result1;
```

```
select * from :v_result2;
END;
```

Listing 4.8 Multivariant Analysis Invocations

With the sales quantity and five other variables, the Pearson correlation matrix for Product A is shown in Figure 4.25.

	ID	SALESQTY	OFFER_PRICE	OUTOFSTOCK_COUNT	OFFER_FLAG	SHOW_TYPE	PROMOTE_TYPE
1	SALESQTY	1	0.6681490787750827	0.13929033427070275	0.007461012076002653	0.06074850301025544	0.08207143753108298
2	OFFER_PRICE	0.6681490787750827	1	0.11299250669618933	0.0735938421510267	0.37915271266166417	0.4108452081744983
3	OUTOFSTOCK_COUNT	0.13929033427070...	0.11299250669618...	1	0.22839988984822546	0.07291337172851388	0.1283201664366424
4	OFFER_FLAG	0.00746101207600...	0.07359384215102...	0.22839988984822546	1	0.07549663300078151	0.02085537631872491
5	SHOW_TYPE	0.06074850301025...	0.37915271266166...	0.07291337172851388	0.07549663300078151	1	0.8695835220906335
6	PROMOTE_TYPE	0.08207143753108...	0.4108452081744983	0.1283201664366424	0.02085537631872491	0.8695835220906335	1

Figure 4.25 Product A Multivariant Correlation

You can see that the sales quantity (SALESQTY) has a high correlation with the OFFER_PRICE factor and that the OFFER_PRICE correlates with the SHOW_TYPE and PROMOTE_TYPE. Figure 4.23 seemed to indicate that the sales quantity for Product A is affected by reduced price offers. Based on that data and the data here, you can confirm this idea statistically.

Similarly, look at Product B's variable correlation. In Figure 4.26, you can see that the sales quantity correlates with the offer price, but not as strongly as for Product A. This again confirms the information suggested by Figure 4.24.

	ID	SALESQTY	OFFER_PRICE	OUTOFSTOCK_COUNT	OFFER_FLAG	SHOW_TYPE	PROMOTE_TYPE
1	SALESQTY	1	0.36936195631623736	-0.02306906119925194	-0.1679830295025022	0.16457027868904345	0.1285291635241717
2	OFFER_PRICE	0.36936195631623736	1	0.08089901706053641	-0.04673120764827273	0.7793068200970095	0.600519724228165
3	OUTOFSTOCK_COUNT	-0.02306906119925...	0.08089901706053641	1	0.2546546425454444	-0.03743315508021...	-0.04012515639213...
4	OFFER_FLAG	-0.1679830295025022	-0.04673120764827...	0.2546546425454444	1	-0.08961713901425...	-0.1575669541739...
5	SHOW_TYPE	0.16457027868904345	0.7793068200970095	-0.03743315508021385	-0.08961713901425031	1	0.7939048800443215
6	PROMOTE_TYPE	0.1285291635241717	0.600519724228165	-0.04012515639213217	-0.15756695417391298	0.7939048800443215	1

Figure 4.26 Product B Multivariant Pearson Correlation

You can also perform multivariant analysis with Principle Component Analysis (PCA) to identify good features representation and to reduce high dimensional space. Let's look at PCA for both the Product A time series. In PAL, when you execute PCA you get three outputs, referred to as the loading matrix, relevance table, and scoring table.

The *loading matrix* provides the correlation matrix with variable proportions and is useful for identifying which components move together (see Figure 4.27)

	PCID	X1_WEIGHT	X2_WEIGHT	X3_WEIGHT	X4_WEIGHT	X5_WEIGHT	X6_WEIGHT
1	Comp1	-0.33436812764044327	-0.5107613340705522	-0.1778794170145556	-0.09974177087490198	-0.534827750151528	-0.5474400283591332
2	Comp2	0.6523386612417811	0.3808619421833456	0.21901398454700938	0.11869621002546482	-0.4413931979712426	-0.41534874639122643
3	Comp3	-0.230739514512193	-0.19711029219883...	0.6229517243157161	0.7208889412695556	0.003255540532842...	-0.0121034761593802
4	Comp4	-0.020957144495530...	-0.14134530113284...	0.7241082276628744	-0.6697086609131983	-0.04078112086928...	0.0712515842047444
5	Comp5	0.6380535728828478	-0.7282441599103705	-0.06384336286647...	0.0607579332061037...	0.2171923803763268	0.08722413751226026
6	Comp6	0.0431270093585018...	-0.06997515793617...	-0.06256385854717...	0.06388040602533489	-0.6857733546847112	0.7176095746781836

Figure 4.27 Product A PCA Correlations

The *relevance table* contains the reduced order of variability in the components. The relevance component matrix for the Product A time series is shown in Figure 4.28.

	PCID	X1_WEIGHT	X2_WEIGHT	X3_WEIGHT	X4_WEIGHT	X5_WEIGHT	X6_WEIGHT
1	Comp1	0.2475648749895941	0.5501036306477763	-0.024209015993717588	-0.13301144796577247	0.5761406024920062	0.534678887402836
2	Comp2	-0.1960675361183323	0.15504620351060408	0.6808929825094044	0.6812530334431564	0.0943602221989311	0.02988971926851566
3	Comp3	0.8542526807344876	0.12956877679455575	0.3361918113166737	-0.07574100806676759	-0.2251667561509294	-0.28983199816965...
4	Comp4	-0.27161667494895...	-0.09384197742495...	0.6432519643723852	-0.7002655962178852	-0.03123793016201...	0.11089302026880899
5	Comp5	0.288900910918065...	-0.6460510523856298	0.0665539188121152	0.14788377311337977	-0.10151337626192...	0.6801105067217689
6	Comp6	-0.11524824063820...	0.47996908586849596	-0.06761081370830442	0.0149680738553107...	-0.7727724844417556	0.39290576677473105

Figure 4.28 Product A Variable Proportions

The *scorings table* contains the variability for the component, as shown for Product A in Figure 4.29.

	ID	Comp1	Comp2	Comp3	Comp4	Comp5	Comp6
1	201,001	0.848994945098716	0.24385077338430391	-0.7571914410074249	0.45410196614031806	0.40230373519523493	0.0073043840680053227
2	201,002	0.6491912162001385	0.6336597481229854	-0.8950712554775385	0.4415788956945125	0.7835765676230387	0.033075193465707864
3	201,003	0.8647689236959721	0.2130763806417764	-0.7463061924966264	0.4550906295965658	0.3722032484246188	0.00526984648402784
4	201,004	0.7490930806494273	0.4387552607536447	-0.8261313482424817	0.4478404309174152	0.5929401514091368	0.020189788766880545
5	201,005	0.9226068452192445	0.10023694058584229	-0.7063936146236989	0.4587157289361411	0.26183479693235984	-0.0021901246557398...
6	201,006	0.7964150164411956	0.34643208252606217	-0.7934756027100864	0.4508064212861587	0.5026386910972885	0.01408617601448 0441
7	201,007	0.6123852661398743	0.705466664522216	-0.9204701686694015	0.4392720142966009	0.8538110367544762	0.03782244782843369
8	201,008	0.843736952232964	0.2541089042 98 47965	-0.760819857177691	0.4537724116549021	0.41233723078544027	0.0079828563262728337
9	201,009	0.7438350877836752	0.4490133916678205	-0.8297597644127479	0.44751087643199927	0.6029736469993422	0.020867967961555656
10	201,010	0.8752849094274762	0.19256011881342475	-0.7390493601560941	0.4557497385673977	0.3521362572442081	0.00391348809467762
11	201,011	0.8227049807699558	0.29514142795518306	-0.7753335218587556	0.45245419371323836	0.4524712131462617	0.010695280041428834
12	201,012	0.9068328666219885	0.1310111333332836976	-0.7172788631344973	0.4577270654798933	0.2919352837032979	-0.000155587073373...
13	201,013	0.812188995038451 8	0.3156576897835347	-0.7825903541992879	0.4517950847424065	0.472538204 3266725	0.01205163843 0779055
14	201,014	0.9541548024137567	0.0386881551007873	-0.6846231176021019	0.46069305584863673	0.20163382339112762	-0.006259199825449...
15	201,015	0.9278648380849965	0.0899788096716 6647	-0.7027651984534327	0.45904528342155704	0.25180130134215445	-0.00286830385 2073...
16	201,016	0.9331228309507487	0.07972067875749062	-0.6991367822831666	0.459374837906973	0.2417678057519491	-0.003546483046748...
17	201,017	0.9594127952795088	0.028430024186611...	-0.6809947014318358	0.4610226103340527	0.19160032780092226	-0.006937379020124...
18	201,018	0.8595109308302201	0.2233345115559 5221	-0.7499346086668925	0.4547610751111499	0.38223674401482416	0.005948025678703006
19	201,019	0.843736952232964	0.2541089042984 7965	-0.760819857177691	0.4537724116549021	0.41233723078544027	0.0079828563262728337
20	201,020	0.9962187453397731	-0.04337689221261...	-0.6555957882399728	0.46332949173196425	0.12136585866948471	-0.01168463338 2850...
21	201,021	1.0435406811315415	-0.13570007044020...	-0.6229400427075774	0.46629548210070765	0.0310643983576 3647	-0.0177882461349263
22	201,022	0.943638816682252 7	0.05920441692913897	-0.6918799499426342	0.46003394687780486	0.2217008145715383 4	-0.004902841436098...
23	201,023	0.990960752474021	-0.03311876129844...	-0.6592242044102389	0.4629999372465483	0.1313993542596 9007	-0.011006454188175...
24	201,024	1.0487986739972934	-0.14595820135437...	-0.6193116265373113	0.4666625036586 1236	0.0210309027674 3108	-0.01846642532960141
25	201,025	0.9226068452192445	0.10023694058584229	-0.7063936146236989	0.4587157289361411	0.26183479693235984	-0.0021901246557398...
26	201,026	1.0645726525945496	-0.1767325940969051	-0.6084263780265129	0.4676137000423714	-0.00906958400318...	-0.020500962913626...

Figure 4.29 Product A PCA Scorings Table

In this section, we looked at using SAP HANA Studio to understand whether certain variables have an impact on product sales and how to statistically execute the multivariant analysis of a Pearson correlation with multiple variables in a single call and PCA. In Section 4.2.2, we looked at correlations (Pearson and Spearman) and autocorrelations (Pearson and Spearman) using SQL functions, which execute correlations between two variables.

You have learned how to perform correlations, autocorrelations, casual analyses, and statistical techniques (univariant and multivariant), which combined with visualization tools can help interpret data behavior and dependent variable behavior. We also looked at various data needs and data types, such as time series data. Refer to the PAL reference guide for more information on the other statistical algorithms supported in SAP HANA. You must choose an appropriate algorithm for your task and type of data.

In the next section, we will look at what algorithms work best for forecasting and at the design aspects of performing modeling.

4.3 Data Preparation

With data exploration, you have seen the types of patterns that can be found in a time series. In this section, we will move into predictive data type definitions and data preparation, followed by a discussion of various algorithms.

4.3.1 Predictive Data Types

While observing data, column data is classified into one of the following types:

- **Nominal or classificatory scale**
  Numbers or other symbols are used simply to classify an object or characteristic—for example, the designation of postal zones.

- **Ordinal or ranking scale**
  If a greater than relationship holds for all pairs of classes of a nominal scale, you have an ordinal scale—for example, military service ranks.

- **Interval scale**
  An ordinal scale in which the differences (or distances) between any two num-

bers on the scale have comparative meaning—for example, the measurement of temperature.

▶ **Ratio scale**
An interval scale in which the zero point cannot be arbitrarily chosen—for example, the measurement of mass (as contrasted with temperature, for which the assignment of zero to different temperatures on alternative scales, such as Celcius and Fahrenheit, is permissible).

▶ **Random variable**
A variable whose occurrence is governed by a probability density function.

▶ **Categorical type variable**
A variable whose measurement is in the nominal or classificatory scale.

These types or scales are commonly used when describing the type of column or data expected by algorithms.

4.3.2 Cleaning and Preparing Data

This step is essential; it ensures that cleaned and transformed data is given as an input in the algorithms to process. Identifying missing values, outliers' detection and addressing outliers, normalization of data, and transforming data per algorithm requirements are just a few steps to ensure accurate data in algorithms.

In SAP HANA's PAL, the following algorithms can be used for data preparation activities:

▶ **Scale range to normalize data**
Normalization transforms data into consistent units of scale. Algorithms like k-means, neural networks, and others perform best when data is on a consistent scale. In SAP HANA, there are three types of normalizations: min-max normalization, z-score normalization, and normalization by decimal scaling. There is no explicit data preparation required for some of these algorithms, because they offer normalization as part of their parameters.

▶ **Substitute missing values**
Missing values are often due to technical problems that lead to the actual values being unavailable. Substituting missing values in SAP HANA is done with mean, median, and mode values. Some algorithms use moving averages or trends to substitute for missing values. Some of these options are available as algorithm parameters.

▶ **Convert category type to binary type**

This transforms category variables into true or false (1 or 0) value variables using conditional expressions on category values.

▶ **Anomaly detection**

This technique is used to identify records that are different from other records. There are various techniques for identifying these records, including the k-means-based anomaly detection technique.

We will now apply filters on the time series data for our two products. In Figure 4.10 and Figure 4.11, you will see that the sales quantities in the initial time frame are distinctly different than recent patterns. Therefore, only consider the last two and half years of sales histories. Note that other scenarios might require a longer sales history.

In this example, there are a few instances that do not follow typical trends or are exhibiting different behavior for similar offer prices. You can use anomaly detection to identify such records in the time series.

The PAL includes an anomaly detection function; you can generate a wrapper producer for that function and execute the anomaly detection for both products (see Listing 4.9). You want to find the top 10 anomalies for each product as one of the input parameters.

```
CREATE PROCEDURE CALL_AND() LANGUAGE SQLScript AS
BEGIN

input1 = SELECT
  "YEAR_WEEK",
  "SALESQTY" ,
  "OFFER_PRICE"
  FROM "ANIL_FORECAST"."SALE_SERIES_WITH_ATTRIBUTES"
  WHERE PROD_ID = 'A' and YEAR_WEEK > 201100 and YEAR_WEEK < 201300
  ORDER BY YEAR_WEEK ASC;

control_1 = SELECT * FROM AD_PAL_CONTROL_TBL;

CALL "ANIL_FORECAST"."PAL_ANOMALY_DETECTION_PROC" (:input1,
:control_1, v_result11, v_result12, v_result13);

input2 = SELECT
  "YEAR_WEEK",
  "SALESQTY" ,
  "OFFER_PRICE"
  FROM "ANIL_FORECAST"."SALE_SERIES_WITH_ATTRIBUTES"
```

```
WHERE PROD_ID = 'B' AND YEAR_WEEK > 201100 and YEAR_WEEK < 201300
ORDER BY YEAR_WEEK ASC;


CALL "ANIL_FORECAST"."PAL_ANOMALY_DETECTION_PROC" (:input2, :control_
1, v_result21, v_result22, v_result23);

insert into ANA_OUT
select 'A', * from :v_result11
union all
select 'B', * from :v_result21;
END;
```

Listing 4.9 Anomaly Detection

Figure 4.30 shows the anomalies found for Product A, and Figure 4.31 the same for Product B.

	YEAR_WEEK	SALESQTY	OFFER_PRICE
1	201,140	491	52
2	201,214	403	50
3	201,129	299	0
4	201,253	22	0
5	201,247	23	0
6	201,217	25	0
7	201,229	26	0
8	201,150	29	0
9	201,228	31	0
10	201,240	270	50

Figure 4.30 Product A Anomalies

	YEAR_WEEK	SALESQTY	OFFER_PRICE
1	201,231	61	0
2	201,111	41	21
3	201,243	25	21
4	201,253	1	0
5	201,153	2	0
6	201,227	35	0
7	201,237	3	0
8	201,123	3	0
9	201,230	34	0
10	201,136	4	0

Figure 4.31 Product B Anomalies

In order to evaluate the anomalies, put the anomaly results for Product A and Product B into a table and join the outputs in an attribute view. This will allow you to visualize the anomalies along with the time series. Figure 4.32 shows a simple attribute view between the time series table and output table with a left outer join.

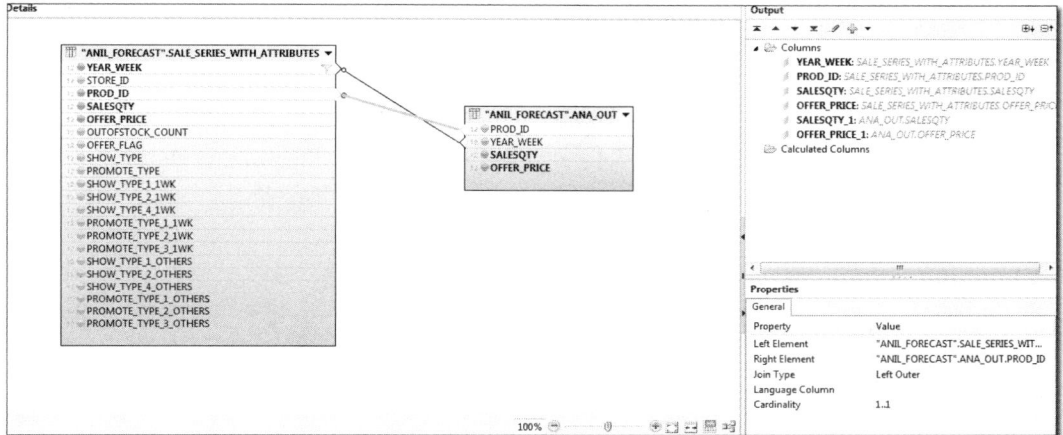

Figure 4.32 Anomaly Output Analysis Model

If you perform a data preview on the model in Figure 4.32 model and select the ANALYSIS tab, you will produce various visualizations. Figure 4.33 shows the anomalies detected along with the time series and offer price for Product A.

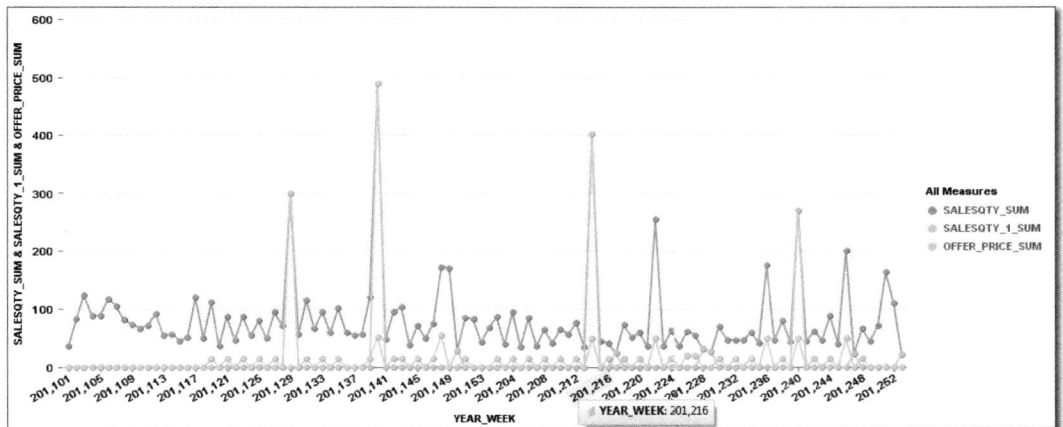

Figure 4.33 Anomalies of Product A in the Time Series

You can see via anomaly detection that high sales frequently occur when a price reduction offer is being promoted and lower sales when no price reduction is being promoted. You can attribute the high sales with the same offer price (anomalies) to some other business activity and introduce an additional variable (OUTLIER). This gives you the ability to forecast with and without that flag to prepare unprecedented sales. The other approach to adding a new variable is to identify the new data that is required and follow the modeling process again.

Figure 4.34 shows the anomaly records of Product B in the time series.

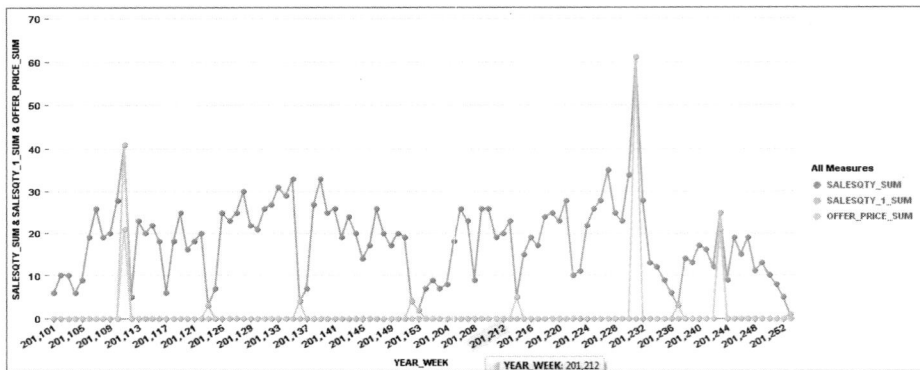

Figure 4.34 Anomalies of Product B Plotted in the Time Series

In the case of Product B, note that price reductions do not affect the sales of this product in peak or low sales. There must be missing data with respect to the offer price. Therefore, you need to go back and check the initial data load and the business application system in which the offer prices were created.

Introducing an anomaly flag as a variable and providing both forecasts with and without anomalies help in the short term until the process of identifying the problems in the transaction system, like the offer price setting, or determining the relevant additional data that explains the behavior is concluded.

Listing 4.9 shows the same code for applying the filters and using anomaly detection to identify the outliers that you have seen in this section.

In this section, we walked through the data preparation phase in SAP HANA using an example. You used PAL functions and UI tools during this phase. In the next section, we will discuss the modeling phase and will continue using Product A and B sales for the forecasting problem.

4.4   Modeling

PAL contains functions that allow you to perform various types of predictive tasks, such as clustering, classification, regression, association, time series, social network analysis, statistical functions, and preprocessing algorithms. Most often, preprocessing and statistical functions are used to test distributions, perform initial exploratory analysis, and execute data preparation.

Predictive models are created by algorithms on data that contain patterns and statistical information about the data, enabling that information to be applied to new data to produce predictions or inferences.

4.4.1   Predictive Modeling Tasks

In this section, we will look at the predictive modeling tasks commonly used along with the algorithms for each respective task. We will be referring to algorithms that are supported in SAP HANA PAL, but please refer to the PAL documentation for a complete list of algorithms supported.

Clustering

Clustering is the task of grouping data into multiple sets, with similar data put into each group. The identification of similar data is performed by using techniques such as identifying centroids or exemplars and determining the distance between them and data, divisive-based hierarchy creations, or density-based scanning techniques.

The most renowned technique is *k-means*, wherein a user has to specify a number of groups. *Affinity propagation* is a new technique based on exemplars, and does not require users to provide number inputs for groups to be identified, similar to agglomerate hierarchical clustering.

Classification

Classification involves assigning a class to a data record based on the similarity of the data to other, like-data classes. Classification relies on the probability of an object belonging to or resembling a class or a propensity to act. An example of this is classifying a transaction as a fraud transaction based on the similarity of this transaction to other fraud transactions. Another example is finding the probability of a bank losing its high-value customers (propensity to churn).

Typical classification techniques include rule-based models (e.g., decision trees) and artificial intelligence/mathematical models (e.g., neural networks, support vector machine, or nonparametric models, such as k-nearest neighbor).

Regression

Regression is a statistical model that estimates the relationship between a dependent variable and an independent variable. This type of model is dependent on the type of relationship. If the relationship is linear between the dependent and independent variable, then the model is a mathematical linear equation, referred to as *linear regression*.

Most regression models have a continuous dependent variable, excluding the logistical (logit) regression, which takes a binary categorical variable as its dependent variable but still produces a mathematical model. Usually, when the target (dependent) variable is categorical, you use classification models, as discussed earlier. *Logistic regression* is another alterative that can be used to classify a binary outcome.

Association

Association analysis helps determine which items should go together based on the correlations and patterns among them. This is also called *basket analysis*. It uses transaction baskets as inputs and identifies patterns or common associations in those transactions. Algorithms that fall under association analysis include apriori, FP-growth, and K-Optimal Rule Discovery (KORD).

Time Series

As previously stated, a time series is a sequence of data observations (measures) over successive intervals of time used to do such things as predict future values. The complexity of predicting a future value depends on the type of behavior exhibited in the past—ranging from simple seasonal behavior that is repeatedly consistent to something that cannot be accurately predicted, based on unknown factors and inconsistent behavior.

Algorithms for this task include seasonally based smoothing algorithms, autoregressive moving average techniques, linear regression with smoothing and trends, and supported vector machine regression.

Social Network Analysis

Social network analysis describes links among nodes and enables you to predict missing or possible links. In the design phase, you identify the input parameters for algorithms. Then, execute the algorithms until you get satisfactory results. The changes between algorithm executions during modeling can lead to adding more variables or changing the algorithm-specific parameters. This cycle of executing and adding new variables continues until you get satisfactory results.

4.4.2 Setting Control Parameters

Modeling in real time may require you to set algorithm parameters on the fly before calling PAL functions. In most cases, once these parameters are set, they do not need to be changed until the model is enhanced.

THREAD_NUMBER is a generic parameter that enables you to make algorithms execute faster in multiple threads. Similarly, there are algorithm-specific numbers such as NUM_ITERATIONS for k-means that should be considered for performance.

4.4.3 Creating and Maintaining Models

Models that are created using wrapper procedures work via SAP HANA tables. All models are stored as CLOB data types with a name. Multiple versions of the same model can be maintained with different names or in an enhanced table with version details and other details. The invocation of a wrapper procedure needs to be followed by a procedure that enhances the output with additional details or by inserting new models with version names.

4.4.4 Validating Models

Every model developed needs to be validated. The general practice is to divide the available data into three partitions for training, validating, and scoring. The PAL stratified partition function can be used to create partitions for this purpose.

The stratified partition will ensure that proportional distribution of the data prevails even after partitioning the data.

4.4.5 Scoring Models

In SAP HANA, there are different functions for prediction, and a wrapper procedure needs to be generated. The predict function takes the model table type as an input along with the other data inputs. Choose a model by name. If you have enhanced the model into a new table, you need to retrieve model scoring based on the logic and call the respective prediction function with the model data as one of the inputs.

4.4.6 Business Example

For products A and B, let's look at examples of forecasting. You have seen that the sales forecast is dependent on the offer price. There were also a few outliers in the data preparation. You enhanced the table with the outlier indicator column, and for each product marked three outlier records identified through anomaly detection in Section 4.3.2. In this section, we will create forecasting models, perform predictions, and evaluate the models. As you have already seen what factors are included on the sales quantities for both Product A and Product B, you know there is more inconsistency involved for Product A.

The PAL includes the following time series functions:

- **ARIMA (Autoregressive Integrated Moving Average)**
  This algorithm is an improvisation of ARMA. It has three parts: AR (autoregressive), for differencing the models to adjust nonstationary time series; moving average (MA), for which a nonseasonal model is denoted as $ARIMA\ (p,\ d,\ q)$, where p stands for the autoregressive order, d is the degree of differencing, and q is the order of the moving average model; and a seasonal model denoted $ARIMA(p,d,q)(P,D,Q)_m$, in which the capital letters represent the seasonal parts of autoregressive, differencing, and moving average.

  There are three ARIMA variants overall in PAL:

  - *ARIMA*: Standard ARIMA without seasonal and external factors
  - *ARIMAX*: Supports external regression factors and nonseasonal factors
  - *SARIMA*: Seasonal ARIMA

  Neither the ARIMA nor SARIMA variant supports external factors.

- ▶ **Smoothing**

  Smoothing techniques enable you to see patterns and trends in the time series. Smoothing seasonality allows you to see a trend, and smoothing models identifies irregularities and smooths the time series. Moving average is the most commonly used method in smoothing. PAL supports the following smoothing algorithms:

  - ▷ *Single exponential smoothing*: Uses the smoothing constant parameter as an input and applies smoothing equations to start calculating from the second observation in the series. Does not adjust to trends.

  - ▷ *Double exponential smoothing*: An enhanced version of single exponential smoothing with additional trend constants as a second parameter.

  - ▷ *Triple exponential*: Along with the smoothing trend constants of double exponential smoothing, this algorithm also supports a third seasonal parameter to adjust the series for seasonality. The estimation of these three parameters is manual in all functionality.

  - ▷ *Forecast smoothing*: All three parameters of triple exponential smoothing are optional, and the algorithm automatically uses parameter space techniques and global and local search techniques. The only mandatory input is the model type chosen: single, double, or triple exponential smoothing.

  - ▷ *Brown exponential smoothing*: Used when there is a trend, but no seasonality.

  - ▷ *Croston's smoothing*: If there is intermittent smoothing, Croston's smoothing technique estimates the average demand size and the average period between intermittent demand and also estimates demand.

- ▶ **Linear regression with damped trend and seasonality**

  This technique provides damping parameters to avoid overcasting due to an indefinite increase or decrease in the time series.

You can also perform forecasting using non-time-series algorithms, such as the following:

- ▶ **Linear regression**

  A linear mathematical equation is created based on the correlation of coefficients with independent variables. The difference between time series models and linear regression is that each observation is created as an individual observation; no sequential analysis of trend or moving average is automatic. This can be achieved manually with additional variables for such values.

▶ **Support vector machine**
This algorithm can be used for both classification and regression analysis. It recognizes patterns from the data using hyperplanes.

Based on hypotheses for Product A and Product B and related factors, select ARIMA and forecast smoothing for prediction purposes. Specifically, choose ARIMAX (Autoregressive Integrated Moving Average), which supports external factors, because we have identified price reduction and outliers as external factors. Listing 4.10 creates ARIMAX models.

```
DROP PROCEDURE CALL_ARIMAX;
CREATE PROCEDURE CALL_ARIMAX() LANGUAGE SQLScript AS
BEGIN

input1 = SELECT
  "YEAR_WEEK",
  "SALESQTY" ,
  "OFFER_PRICE",
  "OUTLIER"
  FROM "ANIL_FORECAST"."SALE_SERIES_WITH_ATTRIBUTES"
  WHERE PROD_ID = 'A' and YEAR_WEEK > 201100 and YEAR_WEEK < 201300
  ORDER BY YEAR_WEEK ASC;

control_1 = SELECT * FROM ARIMAX_PAL_CONTROL_TBL;

CALL "ANIL_FORECAST"."PAL_ARIMAXTRAIN_PROC" (:input1, :control_1,
v_result11);

input2 = SELECT
  "YEAR_WEEK",
  "SALESQTY" ,
  "OFFER_PRICE",
  "OUTLIER"
  FROM "ANIL_FORECAST"."SALE_SERIES_WITH_ATTRIBUTES"
  WHERE PROD_ID = 'B' AND YEAR_WEEK > 201100 and YEAR_WEEK < 201300
  ORDER BY YEAR_WEEK ASC;


CALL "ANIL_FORECAST"."PAL_ARIMAXTRAIN_PROC" (:input2, :control_1,
v_result21);

insert into PAL_ARIMAX_MODEL_TBL
select 1, 'A', * from :v_result11
union all
select 1, 'B', * from :v_result21;
END;
```
Listing 4.10 ARIMAX Model Creation

Create a wrapper procedure, `PAL_ARIMAXTRAIN_PROC`, for the PAL `ARIMAXTRAIN` function. Then, filter the pre-2011 outlier records and use two years of information for training the model. Define `PAL_ARIMAX_MODEL_T3L` for storing the model and enhance the standard table with two additional columns. Figure 4.35 shows a list of columns in the model storage table.

Name	SQL Data Type	Di...	Column Store Data Type
VERSION	INTEGER		INT
MODEL_ID	VARCHAR	100	STRING
NAME	VARCHAR	100	STRING
VALUE	CLOB		LOB

Figure 4.35 Model Storage Structure

The last part of Listing 4.10 inserts the model with an initial version of 1 and the product ID as the model ID. The overall model table is shown in Figure 4.36.

	VERSION	MODEL_ID	NAME	VALUE
1	1	A	ARParameters	0.958017;
2	1	A	MAParameters	-0.894122;
3	1	A	d	0
4	1	A	Intercept	53.7919
5	1	A	Sigma2	2426.07
6	1	A	logLikelihood	-563.601
7	1	A	SeriesData	
8	1	A	DeltaSeriesData	22;
9	1	A	Eps	-31.482;
10	1	A	OFFER_PRICE	3.8513
11	1	A	OUTLIER	0
12	1	B	ARParameters	0.225539;
13	1	B	MAParameters	0.429775;
14	1	B	d	0
15	1	B	Intercept	17.7382
16	1	B	Sigma2	60.6726
17	1	B	logLikelihood	-368.219
18	1	B	SeriesData	
19	1	B	DeltaSeriesData	1;
20	1	B	Eps	-10.2641;
21	1	B	OFFER_PRICE	1.00962
22	1	B	OUTLIER	0

Figure 4.36 ARIMAX Model for Both Products

The model is a representation of patterns or mathematical parameter values that can be used for forecasting. These parameters differ from algorithm to algorithm.

Listing 4.11 provides sample code for using the model and forecasting the next three periods of sales, and also measures the forecast accuracy using PAL forecast accuracy measures to validate the model.

```
DROP PROCEDURE CALL_ARIMAX_FORECAST;
CREATE PROCEDURE CALL_ARIMAX_FORECAST() LANGUAGE SQLScript AS
BEGIN

input1 = SELECT
  "YEAR_WEEK",
  "OFFER_PRICE",
  "OUTLIER"
   FROM "ANIL_FORECAST"."SALE_SERIES_WITH_ATTRIBUTES"
  WHERE PROD_ID = 'A' and YEAR_WEEK > 201300 and YEAR_WEEK < 201304
  ORDER BY YEAR_WEEK ASC;

model_1 = SELECT "NAME", "VALUE" FROM PAL_ARIMAX_MODEL_TBL WHERE
MODEL_ID = 'A';

control_1 = SELECT * FROM PAL_ARIMAX_FORECAST_CONTROL_TBL;

CALL "ANIL_FORECAST"."PAL_ARIMAXFORECAST_PROC" (:input1, :model_
1, :control_1, v_result11);

input2 = SELECT
  "YEAR_WEEK",
  "OFFER_PRICE",
  "OUTLIER"
  FROM "ANIL_FORECAST"."SALE_SERIES_WITH_ATTRIBUTES"
  WHERE PROD_ID = 'B' AND YEAR_WEEK > 201300 and YEAR_WEEK < 201304
  ORDER BY YEAR_WEEK ASC;

model_2 = SELECT "NAME", "VALUE" FROM PAL_ARIMAX_MODEL_TBL WHERE
MODEL_ID = 'B';

CALL "ANIL_FORECAST"."PAL_ARIMAXFORECAST_PROC" (:input2, :model_
2, :control_1, v_result21);

result1 = select 1, 'A' PROD_ID, "TIMESTAMP" + 201301 AS YEAR_
WEEK, "MEAN" FORECASTCOL from :v_result11
union all
select 1, 'B' PROD_ID, "TIMESTAMP" + 201301 YEAR_
WEEK, MEAN FORECASTCOL from :v_result21;

join1 = select a.PROD_ID, a.YEAR_
WEEK, "SALESQTY" ACTUALCOL, "FORECASTCOL" FORECASTCOL FROM
"ANIL_FORECAST"."SALE_SERIES_WITH_
ATTRIBUTES" a JOIN :result1 b ON a.YEAR_WEEK = b.YEAR_WEEK and
a.PROD_ID = B.PROD_ID;

select * from :result1;
select * from :join1;

input_3 = SELECT ACTUALCOL, "FORECASTCOL" FROM :join1 WHERE
```

```
PROD_ID = 'A';
input_4 = SELECT ACTUALCOL, "FORECASTCOL" FROM :join1 WHERE
PROD_ID = 'B';

control_3 = SELECT * FROM FA_PAL_CONTROL_TBL;

CALL PAL_FORECASTACCURACYMEASURES_PROC(:input_3, :control_3,
v_fa_result1);
CALL PAL_FORECASTACCURACYMEASURES_PROC(:input_4, :control_3,
v_fa_result2);

select 'A', * from :v_fa_result1
union all
select 'B', * from  :v_fa_result2;

END;
```
Listing 4.11 ARIMAX Forecast and Validation

The regression variable's future data is supplied as an input along with the number of periods to forecast in the algorithm wrapper procedure PAL_ARIMAXFORE-CAST_PROC for the ARIMAXFORECAST PAL function. The outlier factors for the future data values are *not* set to 1, and you can forecast with 1 to see a potential exception value for case(Peaks). The ARIMAX result contains the future expected sales value along with 80–95% low and high intervals. We are more interested in the expected value and the forecast output for the next periods of both products using ARIMA (see Figure 4.37). Note that the future time period value (the YEAR_WEEK value) is adjusted in the procedure in a simpler way and in a real scenario requires a join on table M_TIME_DIME_SION_WEEK CALENDAR.

	STORE_ID	PROD_ID	YEAR_WEEK	FORECASTCOL
1	1	A	201,301	51.4834681417
2	1	A	201,302	109.34988303640702
3	1	A	201,303	51.67322915308954
4	1	B	201,301	9.5518295327
5	1	B	201,302	15.891854191175625
6	1	B	201,303	17.32177701262356

Figure 4.37 ARIMAX Forecast Output

Next, validate this result and the accuracy of the sales quantities forecasted. First, assign the future times to the forecast output and then look at the side-by-side results of the actuals and the forecast, as shown in Figure 4.38.

	PROD_ID	YEAR_WEEK	ACTUALCOL	FORECASTCOL
1	A	201,301	54	51.4834681417
2	B	201,301	9	9.5518295327
3	A	201,302	97	109.34988303...
4	B	201,302	11	15.891854191...
5	A	201,303	66	51.673229153...
6	B	201,303	7	17.321777012...

Figure 4.38 ARIMAX Forecast Compared with Actuals

Based on these results, you can clearly see the closeness of the actual sales value to that of the forecasted values for both products A and B. The usual benchmark for validating the accuracy of a time series model is through standard accuracy measurements such as *Mean Absolute Percentage Error* (MAPE) or *Mean Absolute Squared Error* (MASE).

The forecast accuracy measures PAL function provides most of the standard error calculation techniques for forecasting. When you execute this function in Listing 4.11, you can see the accuracy of the models for each of the products, as shown Figure 4.39.

	PROD_ID	NAME	VALUE
1	A	ET	4.4934196688034405
2	A	MAD	9.731061913872495
3	A	MAPE	0.13033103639941...
4	A	MASE	0.26300167334790...
5	A	MPE	0.04545211518699...
6	A	MSE	121.36963550221878
7	A	RMSE	11.0167888017434
8	A	SMAPE	0.13697121796097...
9	A	WMAPE	0.134530809869205
10	B	ET	-15.765460736499...
11	B	MAD	5.2551535788330614
12	B	MAPE	0.6601893277112538
13	B	MASE	1.7517178596110206
14	B	MPE	-0.6601893277112...
15	B	MSE	43.59127798640219
16	B	RMSE	6.6023691192179035
17	B	SMAPE	0.42402523617072...
18	B	WMAPE	0.5839059532036734

Figure 4.39 Forecast Accuracy Measures for Each Product

Mean Absolute Deviation (MAD) is the average difference between the actual and forecast values. This example shows deviations of 9.73 and 5.25. These numbers are measured in absolute units of the quantities. For Product A, with sales of about 100 units, an average deviation of 9.75 units is not large. Given the lower sales of Product B, 5.25 seems a little high for a deviation. Another commonly used accuracy measure is MASE, for which you want the values to be less than 1.

The results of Product A seem to be good based on the previous accuracy measurement.

Because there are no new variables, let's try a different model for Product B. A simple forecast smoothing algorithm with a single exponential smoothing model name parameter has produced the forecast shown in Figure 4.40.

	PROD_ID	ACTUALCOL	FORECASTCOL
1	B	9	8.256132833075158
2	B	11	6.420515580412817
3	B	7	7.336676087115684

Figure 4.40 Forecast Smoothing Output

Similar to the ARIMA model, we will execute the forecast accuracy function for understanding the model performance. Figure 4.41 shows the accuracy measurement for Product B for the smoothing algorithm. Note that the MAD is 1.88, and 60% below the ARIMA 5.25 result. Also note that MASE is now 1 at 0.62. This is a much better forecast than determined earlier with ARIMA.

	PROD_ID	NAME	VALUE
1	B	ET	4.98667549939634
2	B	MAD	1.8866758912092363
3	B	MAPE	0.1823550855755931
4	B	MASE	0.6288919637364121
5	B	MPE	0.15029069632648032
6	B	MSE	7.212788899635357
7	B	RMSE	2.685663586459659
8	B	SMA...	0.2196465146069545
9	B	WM...	0.20963065457880403

Figure 4.41 Forecast Smoothing Accuracy of Product B

The input parameters of the smoothing algorithm are depicted in Figure 4.42. The input parameters consist of FORECAST_MODEL_NAME and CYCLE. We have chosen a triple exponential smoothing. Because there are weekly sales, we have configured 52 periods for the cycles.

	NAME	INTARGS	DOUBLEARGS	STRINGARGS
1	THREAD_NUMBER	8	?	?
2	FORECAST_AUTOMATIC	1	?	?
3	MAX_ITERATION	300	?	?
4	FORECAST_NUM	3	?	?
5	FORECAST_MODEL_NAME	?	?	TESM
6	CYCLE	52	?	?

Figure 4.42 Smoothing Algorithm Input Parameters for Product B

In this section, we looked at the modeling phase for predictive analysis in SAP HANA and covered how to validate and maintain models for the products A and B forecast problem.

We have looked at the predictive analytics lifecycle using both PAL and SQLScript procedures, but there are additional tools in SAP HANA Studio (e.g., the Application Function Modeler and SAP Predictive Analytics 2.2) that can provide alternative models through R and SAP InfiniteInsight. We will see how to execute these two models in the next section.

4.5   Creating Models Using SAP Applications on SAP HANA

In this section, we will use two different tools: the Application Function Modeler (AFM) in SAP HANA Studio and SAP Predictive Analytics, which can be utilized by data scientists on the SAP HANA platform for models. As discussed in Section 4.1.2, we have looked at various tools and applications available in SAP HANA that allow us to create various types of data models, and in the next two sections, we will look at two additional models.

4.5.1   Application Function Modeler

AFM is a graphical model in SAP HANA Studio that facilitates the creation of flow graphs with SQL and predictive functions together. Flow graphs are created as SAP HANA repository objects, which can be used to execute the flow graph. In this section, we will look at an example of AFM in action.

As an example, consider again the forecast for Product A. The following operations should be fulfilled when selecting your sales tables for products A and B as input: filter the records for Product A, execute a forecast smoothing algorithm with a single exponential smoothing model name, and store the result as output into another table.

Figure 4.43 shows a flow graph creation area panel that lists the possible flow functions categorized by general operations, such as filter, join, and more, as well as functions from the AFL, such as the PAL and BFL. The graphical editor enables you to create the flow with a set of operations for this example in a single info graph. Each operation is a node, and each node has properties to configure for required functionality. One node's connection to another indicates a data flow between the nodes, which requires mapping the first node's output to the input of the next node. The properties of both nodes and their connections can be set in the PROPERTIES panel below the editor. Figure 4.43 illustrates a flow graph for forecast smoothing algorithms.

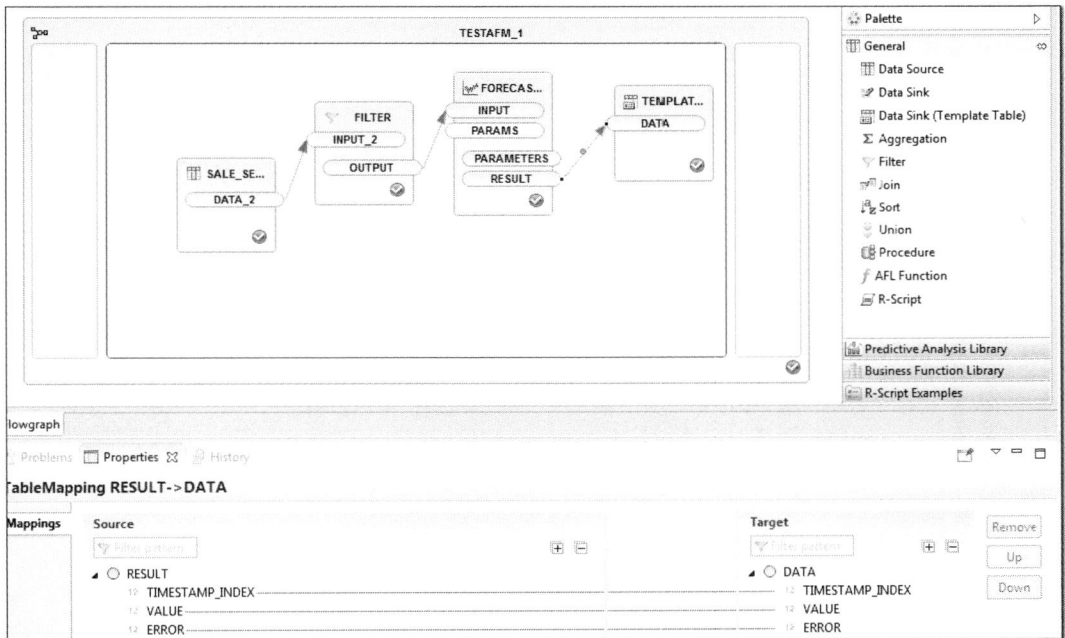

Figure 4.43 Flow Graph for Forecast Smoothing

In Figure 4.43, the flow graph model has an input node that reads the product time series data table, a preprocessing node with a filter operation to reduce the number of columns required by the algorithm input and a required product, and a node to configure the forecast smoothing algorithm and store the results into a new table.

The parameters panel of the algorithm node shown in Figure 4.44 facilitates the controlled input of data with mapping from input nodes. Parameters and output requirements of algorithms and annotations are available in other tabs.

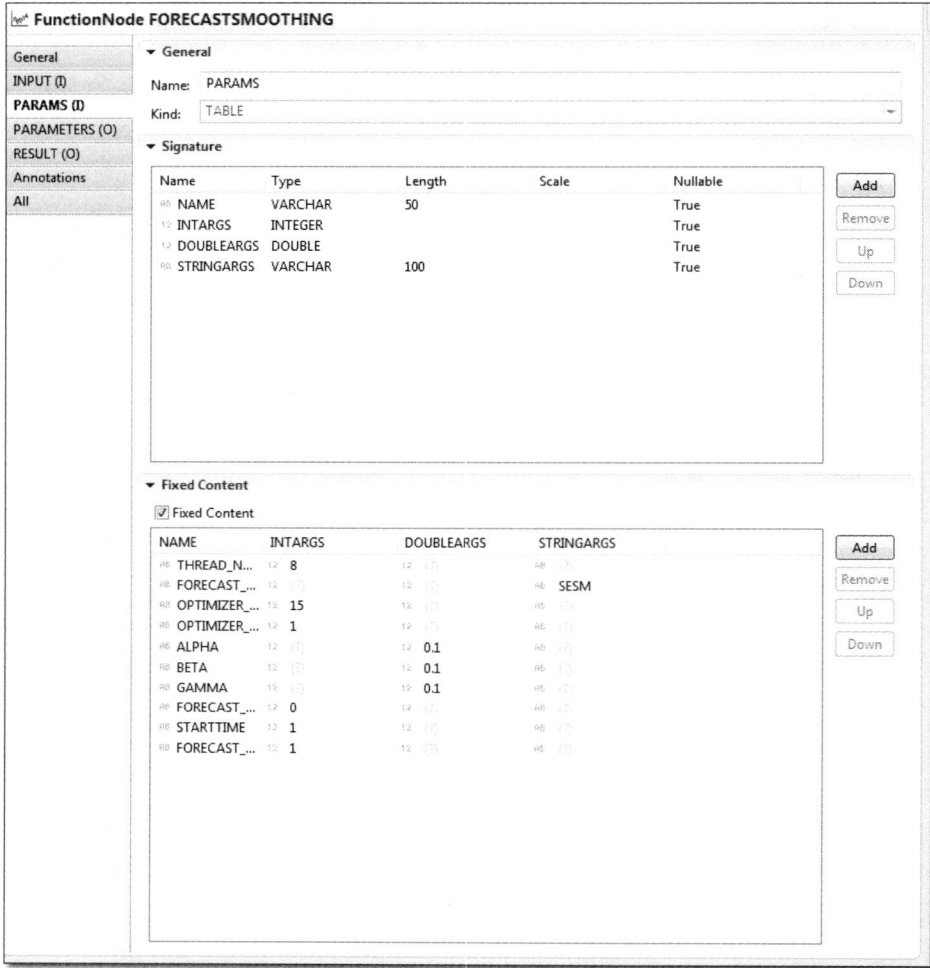

Figure 4.44 Algorithm Properties Panel

During the activation of the flow graph object, the flow graph generates a stored procedure that processes the complete logic starting from table reading to the algorithm output and creates all the table types and wrapper procedures required for processing.

Some advantages of the AFM tool include generating data mining flows with table types and tables in a GUI and hiding the complexity of each function's input and output data structures manually. Because this tool manages the input and output of algorithm executions, the modeling, storage, and persistence does not differ from what we discussed in Section 4.4.

Because this tool does not support logical filtering with complex logic and nonalgorithm, SQL-oriented transformations, it can be used when the inputs from tables are joined and multiple algorithms are executed in simpler scenarios.

4.5.2 SAP Predictive Analytics

SAP Predictive Analytics is an application that supports *automated analytics* and *expert analytics*. Prior to SAP Predictive Analytics 2.x, there were two tools in its place called SAP InfiniteInsight and SAP Predictive Analysis, respectively. The SAP Predictive Analytics combined application enables algorithms from SAP InfiniteInsight, SAP HANA, and R to create models from these algorithms.

The next two sections look at both automated analytics and expert analytics in greater detail.

Automated Analytics

Automatic analytics provides the following set of algorithms:

- **Modeler**
  Includes classification/regression, clustering, time series, and association rules algorithms. Unlike the PAL algorithms, you do not need to be aware of the inner parameters and technical details of the algorithms. These are automatic algorithms with minimal user input about how they should behave. The task of regression or classification is automatic based on whether the target variable is continuous or categorical.

- **Social network**
  A *network* has nodes and connections; if these nodes are people, then the network is considered a *social network*. There are various types of analytics that are possible in social networks, such as identifying cliques (subgroups), identifying probable nodes that perform similar actions as their connections, and more. In automatic analytics, this set contains social network analysis, colocation analysis, and frequent path analysis.

- **Recommendation**
  This feature utilizes social network analysis to recommend products to customers based on their connections. Using both social network analysis and recommendations can enable use cases such as recommending a next best action based on node properties.

Each of these sets supports storing and loading models for further analysis.

Let's perform a time series of one of the products in a stepwise fashion using automated analytics. Once you have finished loading the data from your table, the analyze phase enables automatic classification of measurement scales for each column of the input table. Figure 4.45 shows the automatic classification. This automatic classification step is important, because the behavior of automatic analytics algorithms depends on this classification. You should review the analysis and update the metadata as needed.

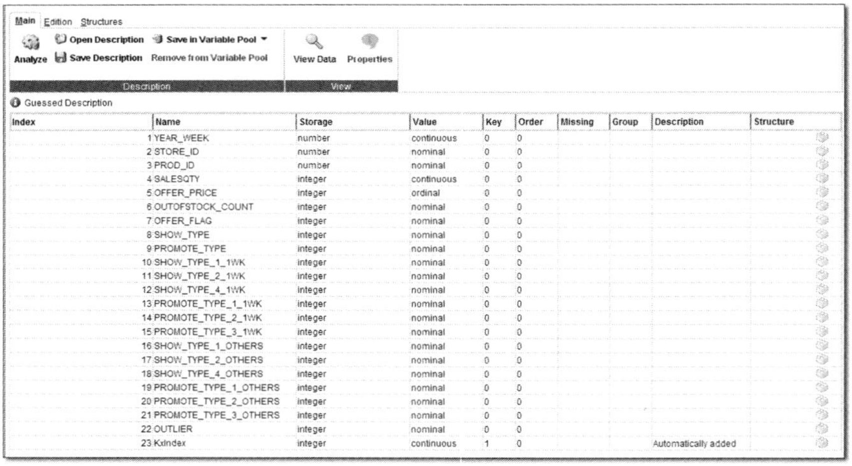

Index	Name	Storage	Value	Key	Order	Missing	Group	Description	Structure
1	YEAR_WEEK	number	continuous	0	0				
2	STORE_ID	number	nominal	0	0				
3	PROD_ID	number	nominal	0	0				
4	SALESQTY	integer	continuous	0	0				
5	OFFER_PRICE	integer	ordinal	0	0				
6	OUTOFSTOCK_COUNT	integer	nominal	0	0				
7	OFFER_FLAG	integer	nominal	0	0				
8	SHOW_TYPE	integer	nominal	0	0				
9	PROMOTE_TYPE	integer	nominal	0	0				
10	SHOW_TYPE_1_1WK	integer	nominal	0	0				
11	SHOW_TYPE_2_1WK	integer	nominal	0	0				
12	SHOW_TYPE_4_1WK	integer	nominal	0	0				
13	PROMOTE_TYPE_1_1WK	integer	nominal	0	0				
14	PROMOTE_TYPE_2_1WK	integer	nominal	0	0				
15	PROMOTE_TYPE_3_1WK	integer	nominal	0	0				
16	SHOW_TYPE_1_OTHERS	integer	nominal	0	0				
17	SHOW_TYPE_2_OTHERS	integer	nominal	0	0				
18	SHOW_TYPE_4_OTHERS	integer	nominal	0	0				
19	PROMOTE_TYPE_1_OTHERS	integer	nominal	0	0				
20	PROMOTE_TYPE_2_OTHERS	integer	nominal	0	0				
21	PROMOTE_TYPE_3_OTHERS	integer	nominal	0	0				
22	OUTLIER	integer	nominal	0	0				
23	KxIndex	integer	continuous	1	0			Automatically added	

Figure 4.45 Analyze the Input Measurement Scales

For this example, keep the default identification, and click the NEXT button.

The next step is to select the variables. On the screen shown in Figure 4.46, set the target variables and exclude any variables that are not needed. Note that some of the automatic algorithms consider only necessary variables and ignore the rest. These algorithms will also enhance the variables set by creating additional variables, using techniques such as binning continuous variables into categorical variables to generate optimal models.

Selecting Variables

Predictable Variables Kept **3**

YEAR_WEEK
OFFER_PRICE
OUTLIER

Time **1**

KxIndex

Target **1**

SALESQTY

Plot Data...

Weight **0**

Excluded Variables **18**

STORE_ID
PROD_ID
OUTOFSTOCK_COUNT
OFFER_FLAG
SHOW_TYPE
PROMOTE_TYPE
SHOW_TYPE_1_1WK
SHOW_TYPE_2_1WK
SHOW_TYPE_4_1WK
PROMOTE_TYPE_1_1WK
PROMOTE_TYPE_2_1WK
PROMOTE_TYPE_3_1WK
SHOW_TYPE_1_OTHERS
SHOW_TYPE_2_OTHERS
SHOW_TYPE_4_OTHERS
PROMOTE_TYPE_1_OTHERS
PROMOTE_TYPE_2_OTHERS
PROMOTE_TYPE_3_OTHERS

☐ Alphabetic Sort

Last Training Date 52   line: 52

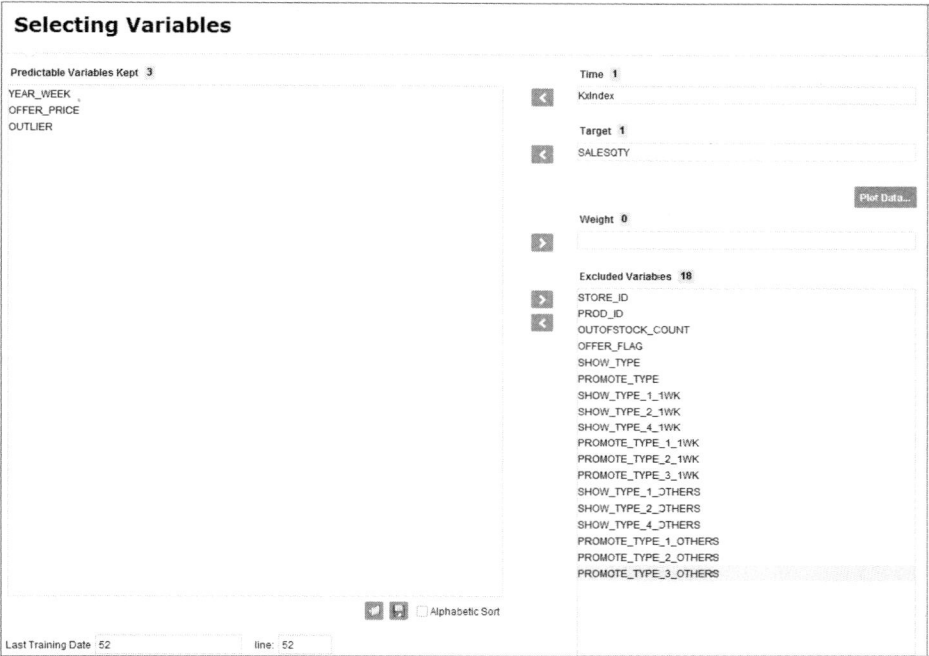

Figure 4.46 Variable Selection

For a time series, you need to choose the training period (see Figure 4.47).

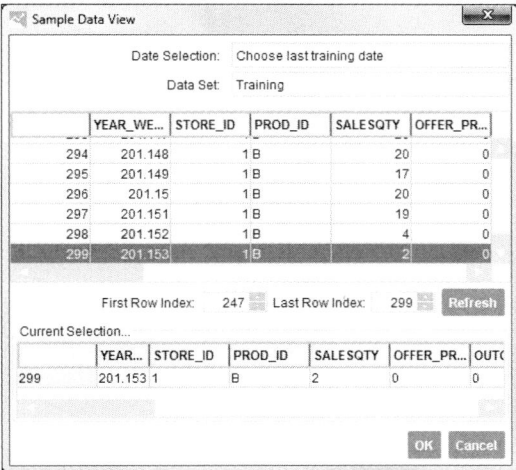

Sample Data View

Date Selection: Choose last training date

Data Set: Training

	YEAR_WE...	STORE_ID	PROD_ID	SALESQTY	OFFER_PR...
294	201.148	1 B		20	0
295	201.149	1 B		17	0
296	201.15	1 B		20	0
297	201.151	1 B		19	0
298	201.152	1 B		4	0
299	201.153	1 B		2	0

First Row Index: 247   Last Row Index: 299   **Refresh**

Current Selection...

	YEAR...	STORE_ID	PROD_ID	SALESQTY	OFFER_PR...	OUTC
299	201.153 1		B	2	0	0

OK **Cancel**

Figure 4.47 Date Selection for the Time Series

After choosing the right inputs and generating the model, the model summary is shown (see Figure 4.48). This model can be autosaved or exported as a script.

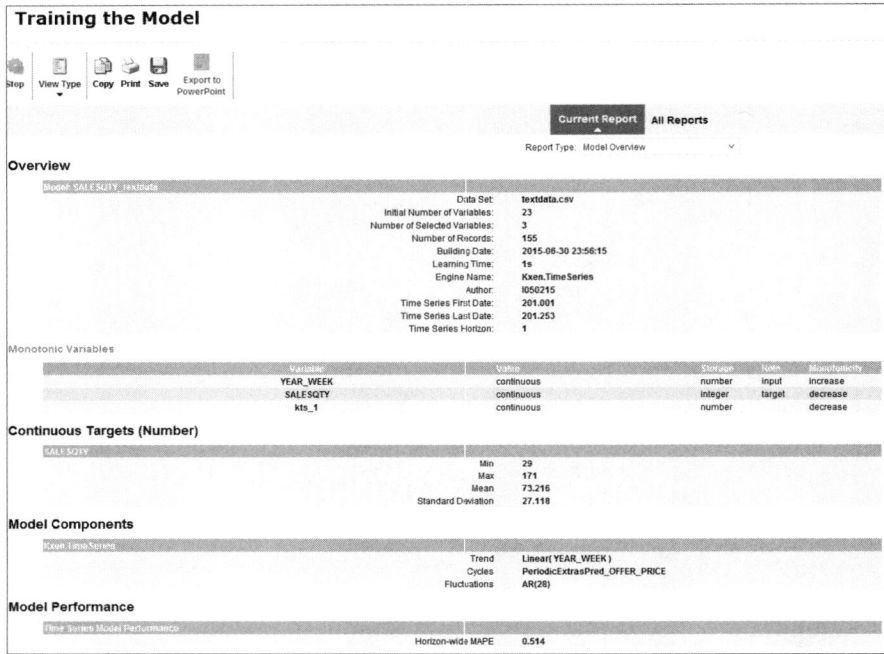

Figure 4.48 Training Model Overview

The model details contain the autoregression trends and cycles identified and also provides accuracy for the models using the MAPE error calculation formula. The MAPE 0.5 result is slightly higher for Product A than the ARIMA MAPE of 0.13 in Figure 4.39. You can save this model as a file in disk or as a SQLScript, and execute the model on the new data for prediction purposes.

The application supports model validation by forecasting and divides the data into training and validation. With the application, you can validate the models with these forecasts. Figure 4.49 is the forecast versus the signal provided by the tool for validating the accuracy of the model.

Automatic analysis provides algorithm execution without needing to have any deeper knowledge of how to do so by providing various statistics to decide on a model. Almost the entire predictive analytics lifecycle can be managed by SAP Predictive Analytics in the automated mode.

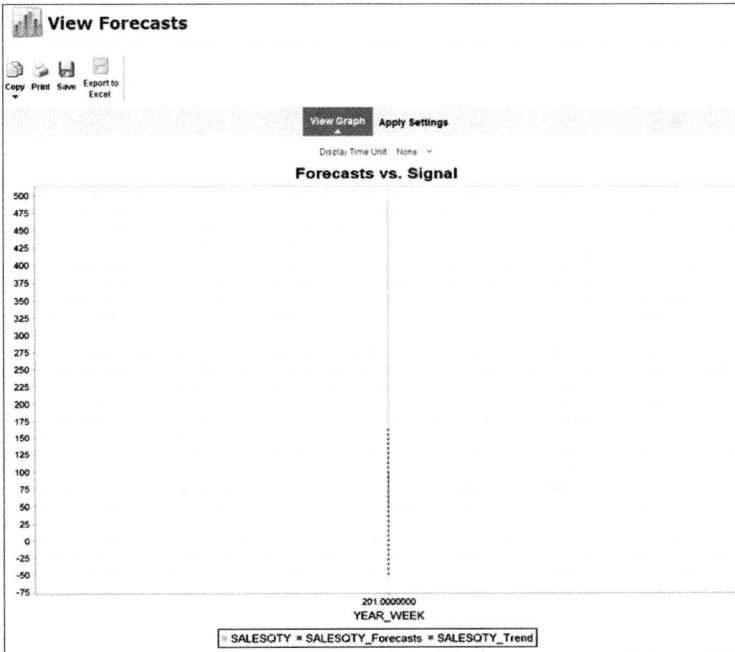

View Forecasts

Copy Print Save Export to
                   Excel

View Graph Apply Settings

Display Time Unit None ∨

Forecasts vs. Signal

201.0000000
YEAR_WEEK

SALESQTY ▪ SALESQTY_Forecasts ▪ SALESQTY_Trend

Figure 4.49 Forecast vs. Signal

Expert Analytics

Expert analytics allows users to perform exploratory data analysis and prepare the data before they perform modeling. The initial phase of this tool connects to SAP HANA online, which allows you to execute PAL functions and R procedures through SAP HANA and R locally on the desktop. Expert analytics shares the SAP Lumira platform to utilize common visualizations and data preparation techniques and contains additional predictive-related processes and visualizations.

This tool has five phases: prepare, visualize, predict, compose, and share. The first three phases involve business understanding, preparing data, and executing algorithms, and the last two phases are about building storyboards and sharing them publicly.

Once you connect to the data source, you can initiate the prepare view by clicking on the PREPARE tab. In the prepare view, you filter, create new columns, and change the semantics of the columns. In Figure 4.50, we have applied the filters that we need for our product example.

Figure 4.50 Preparation of Data in Expert Analytics

Once you prepare the data, you can perform an exploratory analysis to under-stand the product behavior. You can utilize more predictive-specific and exploratory analysis-oriented visualizations in expert analytics than in SAP HANA Studio. For example, you can see the impact of the offer price on the sales quantity in a parallel coordinates chart, as shown in Figure 4.51.

You can clearly see that a higher price reduction leads to higher sales and a lower price reduction leads to lower sales. Also, you can identify outliers, such as high sales with lower price reductions and vice versa. With this understanding, you can create a predictive flow and execute. Take note that there is a lag of algorithm availability in this tool from PAL, meaning there may not be any newly added PAL algorithms.

We have used single exponential smoothing, because forecast smoothing is not available yet. The configuration of parameters is more expert-oriented. Figure 4.52 shows a chain that has nodes for the data source, filtering, and algorithm.

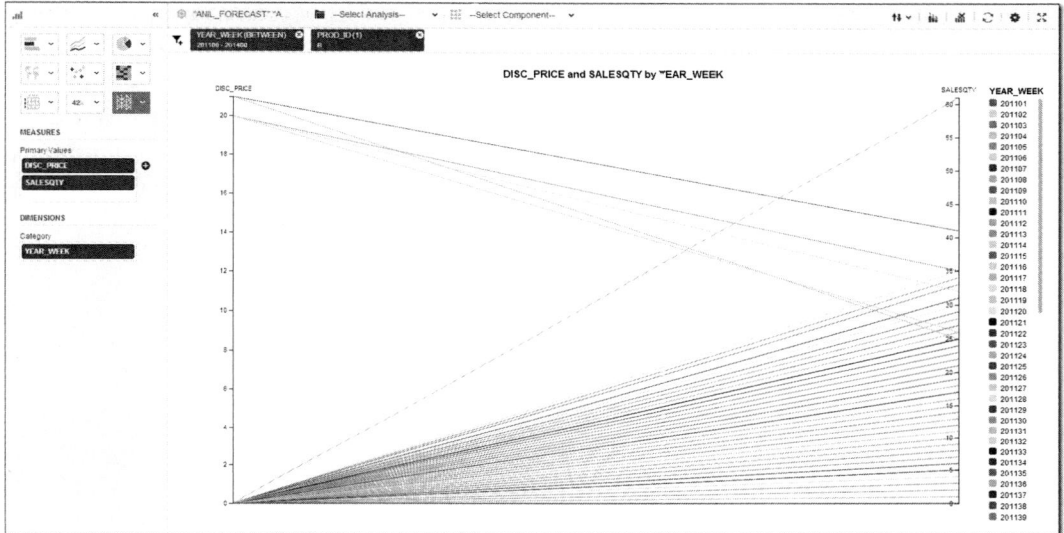

Figure 4.51 Parallel Coordinates

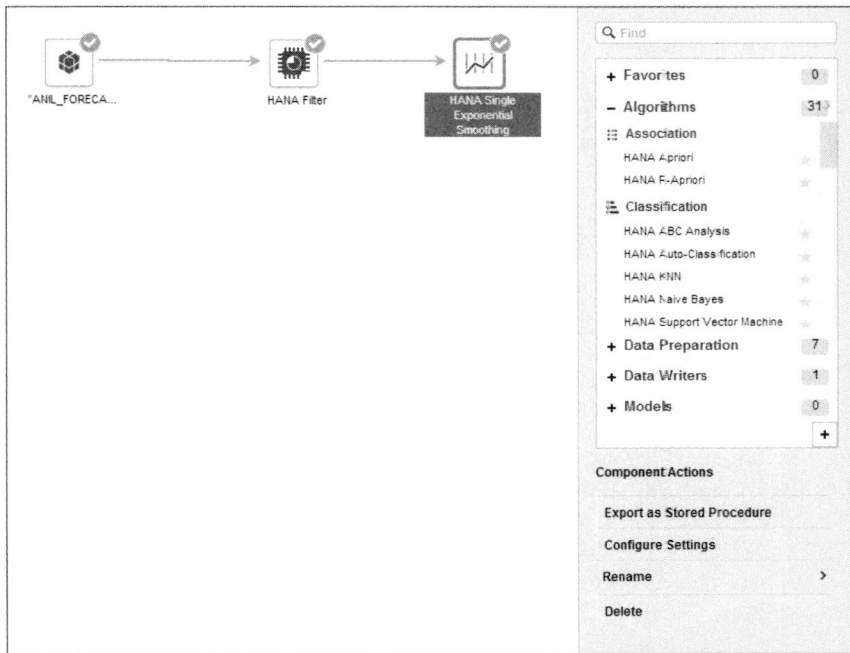

Figure 4.52 Expert Analytics Flow

The parameters for specific algorithms are shown as function descriptions. Advanced properties will allow you to change the detail parameters of the algorithms. You can execute the chain up to any node in the chain. Once you run the flow, you can see the algorithm-specific visualization to better understand the results of the algorithm. Chain designing can be found in the designer view. Once the chain is executed, the results can be analyzed in the results mode. Each node in the chain can have a specific visualization. For exponential smoothing, look at the specific line chart, as shown in Figure 4.53.

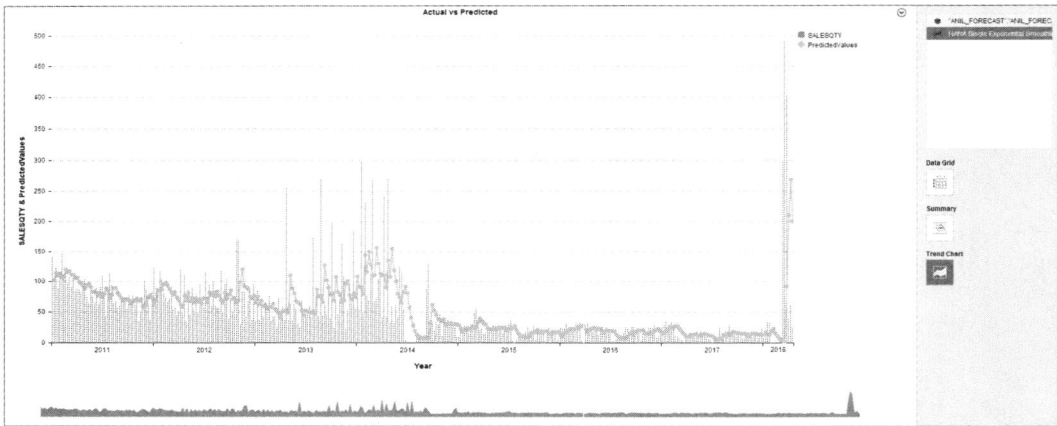

Figure 4.53 Single Exponential Smoothing Output

Each model can be saved and used for scoring new data in another chain as a node. All chains are stored in the database.

4.6 Summary

In this chapter, we looked at the SAP HANA predictive analytics lifecycle. You saw how to execute each phase of the process in SAP HANA, along with the tools and algorithms to perform analysis on our two example products.

Now that you have explored the basic predictive modeling techniques, in the next chapter we will move on to more advanced modeling using R and PAL.

In this chapter, we will discuss advanced modeling concepts in SAP HANA, including using R and SAP HANA together.

5   Advanced Predictive Modeling

In this chapter, we will address predictive modeling requirements using SAP HANA's multiple algorithm providers and the interoperating data between them. We will use examples to explain how to model the processes for complex scenarios in SAP HANA. Subsequent sections in this chapter will cover enabling Predictive Analysis Library (PAL) functions for real-time consumption and how to use PAL together with RLANG. Finally, we will look at scaling these procedures for batch jobs with large datasets.

5.1   R Script Modeling and Design

R is a language and environment for statistical computers and graphics. It is GNU licensed and provides data mining methods for machine learning, math, statistics, and predictive analysis algorithms and computations as R packages and distributions. Most people in the machine learning world leverage R for data science-oriented jobs.

In this section, we will look at SAP HANA/R interactions, data volumes, and type compatibilities and an example implementation of stored procedures in RLANG.

5.1.1   SAP HANA and R Integration

SAP HANA is an in-memory database, with most commonly used machine learning and statistical algorithms available as native functions within the database. With a vast amount of algorithms available through R packages, if users want to leverage other SAP HANA functionality, the SAP HANA and R integration helps them to do so.

Figure 5.1 illustrates the overall components involved in using the R environment with SAP HANA.

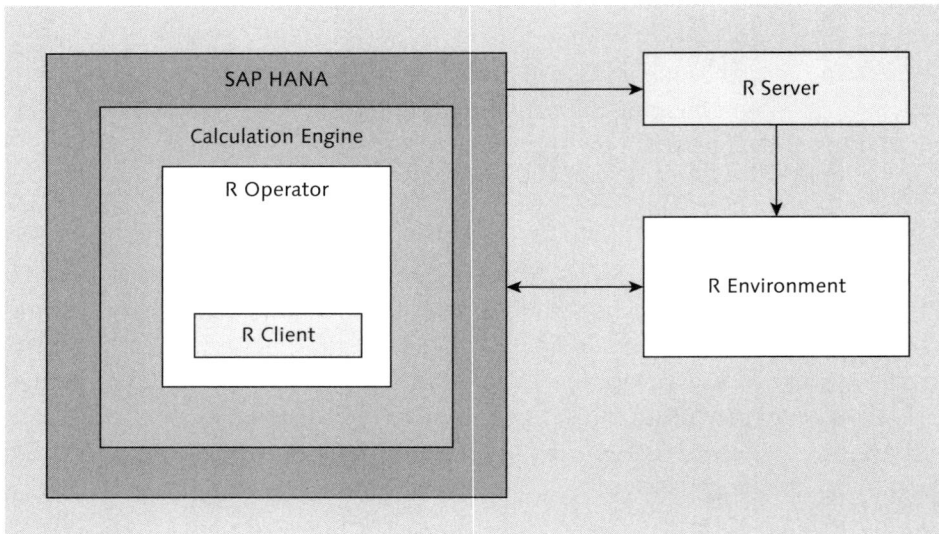

Figure 5.1 SAP HANA/R Intergration

The calculation engine within SAP HANA establishes a communication channel to the R environment whenever it encounters an R operator. An R operator can be used as part of any SQLScript procedure, calculation view, or CALL statement. An R client in the calculation engine enables you to connect to and communicate with the R server environment. Communication involves executing R commands in an R environment, transferring data to the R server, and receiving a response from the R server. SAP HANA supports the R server and environment running on different machines, but R cannot coexist in the same machine on which SAP HANA is running.

On the R server, whenever an R client request indicates a new R session, it forks the process, and the R client communicates with the child process to execute R commands from that R operator.

Please refer to the SAP HANA R Integration Guide for details about the configuration and setup between SAP HANA and R at *help.sap.com/hana/sap_hana_r_ integration_guide_en.pdf.*

5.1.2 Data Considerations

As shown in Figure 5.1, both SAP HANA and the R server run on two different machines, and it is important to understand the data transfer between these two entities. The general rule for executing algorithms is that they run in the database closer to the data to avoid data movement and to reduce overhead. Following the same principle by leveraging the native algorithms available in PAL avoids needing to transfer data between the servers.

However, not all algorithms and statistical techniques are natively available in SAP HANA. Therefore, it is imperative to keep in mind the cost of transferring this data between the servers before deciding to execute a process in R. Unsupervised learning techniques are the most common techniques used that call for large data transfer between the servers.

We should consider some data preprocessing techniques, such as sampling with random replacement, sampling without random replacement, and stratification sampling, to reduce the amount of data to transfer in these circumstances. In this section, we will focus primarily on data transfer. Of the sampling techniques, stratification sampling poses the least amount of sampling errors, because it maintains the proportions of data distribution and ensures that each subgroup is represented in the sampled data. Let's look into stratification sampling further in the next section.

Stratified Random Sampling

Stratification is the process of identifying and dividing populations into subgroups based on values chosen categorically. Each of these subgroups are referred to as *strata* or *stratum*. Within each stratum, systematic or random samplings are performed to randomly select portions of the data population.

In SAP HANA, there are two methods for stratification in PAL. The first is through a sampling function, and the second is through a partition function that divides the dataset into training, testing, and validation datasets. For reducing the dataset, consider the sampling function. To start, generate a wrapper function SAMPLING_TEST_PROC with the PAL SAMPLING function using the Application Function Library (AFL) framework.

Table 5.1 shows the required parameters for stratification. The PERCENTAGE parameter provides the sampling size. The value of 0.5 as an input is expected to provide half of the population as the sampling output. STRATA_NUM is the number of subgroups to be considered by the algorithm, and COLUMN_CHOOSE is the categorical column to be used for subgrouping.

	NAME	INTARGS	DOUBLEARGS	STRINGARGS
1	SAMPLING_METHOD	7	?	?
2	SAMPLING_SIZE	8	?	?
3	PERCENTAGE	?	0.5	?
4	STRATA_NUM	2	?	?
5	COLUMN_CHOOSE	6	?	?

Table 5.1 Stratification Sampling Control Parameters

Table 5.2 shows the distribution of the distinct values for the chosen column for stratification. There are two distinct values and the population size of each value in the X6 column (arbitrary data column).

	COUNT (*)	X6
1	368	1
2	1,188	0

Table 5.2 Input Distribution for the Example Column

Table 5.3 shows the distribution of the X6 column after stratification sampling has been performed. Because we have chosen to sample 50% of values, stratification ensures that the proportions of the population are the same; the output in Table 5.3 shows half the original population for each value of X6.

	COUNT (*)	X6
1	184	1
2	594	0

Table 5.3 Output Distribution for Stratified Sampling

Random Sampling with Replacement

In this technique, the sampling algorithm with replacement will replace the item selected, and hence the probability of selection for each item remains the same for every item selected for the sampling.

In order to run this technique, use the same wrapper you generated previously and the same inputs expected for SAMPLING_METHOD. Let's set this value to 4 and rerun the algorithm. Table 5.4 shows the selected sample distribution.

Count(*)	X6
176	1
602	0

Table 5.4 Random Sampling with Replacement

Random Sampling without Replacement

In this technique, each sampling selection algorithm will not replace the item selected, and hence the probability of each item selected is reduced by an order of 1. Update the SAMPLING_METHOD to 5 and run the algorithm. Table 5.5 depicts the distribution of X6 after sampling without replacement.

Count(*)	X6
606	0
172	1

Table 5.5 Random Sample without Replacement

Systemic Sampling

In this technique, the algorithm selects all elements randomly. The SAMPLING_METHOD is 6 and below.

Count(*)	X6
595	0
183	1

Table 5.6 Systemic Sampling

With nearly 1,600 rows, each technique has a similar output, with deviation around 10%. However, stratification sampling is able to precisely sample, keeping the distribution of the stratification column. In addition to these sampling techniques, SAP HANA also supports sampling based on row offsets (First N, Last N, Middle N, and Every Nth), and each of these aforementioned techniques works on a row offset.

Each of the techniques discussed thus far enables you to reduce the transfer of datasets by maintaining the homogeneity of the data. The recommended approach is to run these techniques in SAP HANA using logical models such as attribute views, analytic views, calculation views, and/or predictive analytics preprocessing algorithms. Apart from the preprocessing algorithms, your design should also consider the data types in the data structures that are being transferred between the two systems. In the next section, we will cover how to define these data types.

5.1.3 Data Types and RLANG Script

Put simply, *data types* indicate data value characteristics. SAP HANA supports writing R code in a stored procedure. With the CREATE PROCEDURE statement, you can specify the language as RLANG as follows:

```
CREATE PROCEDURE GET_TS_CHARACTERISTICS (IN metrics
CLUSTER_TS_CBC_INPUT, OUT cbc CLUSTER_TS_CBC) LANGUAGE RLANG AS BEGIN
```

RLANG script represents the logic in a stored procedure. The input and output of these stored procedures must be in the form of *table types*, which are used to define the procedure parameters that signify tabular results. The table type is transformed by SAP HANA into a table-like structure called a *data frame* in the R language. Similarly, the output in the RLANG script is also transformed into a data frame. Upon response from the RLANG server, SAP HANA transforms the data frame into the relevant table type columns in the memory.

Primitive Types	
Primitive types are not supported as data transfer types.	

When defining the table types for a stored procedure, we recommend using shorter data types like numeric types to reduce the amount of data transferred between the systems.

Extending the code shown at the beginning of this section, Listing 5.1 shows the sample table types and RLANG procedure.

```
DROP TYPE CLUSTER_TS_CBC_INPUT;
CREATE TYPE CLUSTER_TS_CBC_INPUT AS TABLE ("METRIC_
ID" VARCHAR(100), "METRIC_VALUE" DOUBLE);

DROP TYPE CLUSTER_TS_CBC;
CREATE TYPE CLUSTER_TS_CBC AS TABLE ("METRIC_
ID" VARCHAR(100), "CORRELATION" DOUBLE, "HURST" DOUBLE, "SKEWNESS" DOUB
LE, "KURTOSIS" DOUBLE);

CREATE PROCEDURE GET_TS_CHARACTERISTICS (IN metrics CLUSTER_TS_CBC_
INPUT, OUT cbc CLUSTER_TS_CBC) LANGUAGE RLANG AS BEGIN

library(foreach)
library(doParallel)
library(e1071)
library(pracma)

inputMetrics <- metrics
colnames(inputMetrics) <- c("id", "value")
inputMetrics$id <- as.character(inputMetrics$id)


# Find all metric IDs and number of metrics in the input table
lMetrics <- levels(as.factor(inputMetrics$id))
nMetrics <- length(lMetrics)

# Select desired metrics
wantMetrics <- 1:nMetrics

findACF <- function(x) {
  acfout <- acf(x, lag.max = 100, plot=F)
  return(acfout)
}

performCBC <- function(x, METRIC_ID) {
  acfOut <- findACF(x)
  CORRELATION <- as.numeric(sum(acfOut$acf[1:2]))
  HURST <- as.numeric(round(hurst(x),2))
  SKEWNESS = as.numeric(skewness(x))
  KURTOSIS = as.numeric(kurtosis(x), na.rm = FALSE, type = 2)

  res <- data.frame(METRIC_ID, CORRELATION, HURST, SKEWNESS, KURTOSIS)
  return (res)
}
for (i in wantMetrics) {
```

```
finput <- inputMetrics[inputMetrics$id ==lMetrics[i],]
tmp <- performCBC(finput$value, lMetrics[i] )
if (i == 1) {
  result <- tmp
} else
  result <- rbind(result, tmp)

}
cbc <- result
END;
```
Listing 5.1 RLANG Procedure for Analyzing the Statistical Behavior of Multiple Time Series

In Listing 5.1, the input is a time series of multiple products passed to R from SAP HANA. This procedure measures the statistical behavior of each time series by calculating the kurtosis, skewness, correlation factors, and Hurst. We have defined all of these measures, with the exception of Hurst, in Chapter 4, Section 4.2.1.

A *Hurst* exponent classifies a time series as random walk, antipersistent, or persistent. *Random walk* describes whether there is no correlation among the time series with various lags. The usual Hurst exponent is around 0.5 for a random walk. An *antipersistent* time series will increase and decrease one after another. This option returns the mean value of the time series due to the increase and decrease of movements. The usual Hurst exponent value of an antipersistent time series is between 0 and 0.5. A *persistent* time series is one in which increase is followed by another increase and similarly for decreases in the short term. The Hurst exponent of the persistent time series is between 0.5 and 1. The result of Listing 5.1 is a data frame with these three characteristics for each time series.

In this section, we have explained the architecture between SAP HANA and R and their various design aspects and also looked at an example. In the next section, we will discuss how to consume predictive analysis models, keeping in mind the various model types and possible outputs from the algorithms.

5.2   PAL Model Consumption

In Chapter 4, Section 4.4, we saw how to create predictive models. In this section, we will look at how to consume those models. The consumption of models often depends on the type of predictive algorithms and the following tasks:

▶ **Supervised learning**

In supervised learning, an algorithm will take inputs as target variables and additional variables as independent variables or causal factors on which the target variable outcome is dependent. Target variables are also called *dependent variables*. Understanding dependent variable behavior is often linked to the quality of the independent variables. The outcome of this task is usually created as a model that can be applied to new data. Classifications and regressions are good examples of supervised learning.

▶ **Unsupervised learning**

Unsupervised learning techniques are deep learning techniques in which each observation is interpreted independently and more complex patterns or hierarchical depth is created. Unlike supervised learning, where the outcome of the target variable is locked, in this technique there is no target variable and all input information is processed to identify the patterns. Neural networks, k-means (unsupervised clustering), and self-organizing maps are a few examples of unsupervised learning. An unsupervised learning technique can be followed by a supervised learning technique to make a model. For example, k-means can be followed by a decision tree, with the cluster number as the target variable.

In SAP HANA, every wrapper procedure that is generated contains algorithm results. The following three types of results are possible, and they are dependent on supervised and unsupervised learning:

▶ **Algorithm-specific results**

These are algorithm outputs. An example of this result type is k-means, which provides the results with the input data's ID column and cluster number.

▶ **Summary results**

Summary results provide additional information on the data processed by an algorithm. For k-means, you can classify information such as distance between the data point and center, center coordinates, statistical values such as a sum of squares or the density of a cluster, cluster quality, and so on. Unless a data science-oriented application is consuming the results, this type of information is useful for optimizing and enhancing the output of models.

▶ **Model**

The representation of an algorithm output that can be used on new set of data is called a *model*. Every supervised learning technique will have a model. Unsupervised learning techniques can also have models, such as apriori (basket analysis), in which the model can be applied to retrieve items associated with a given item. The model is stored in a generic CLOB data structure in SAP HANA. *Predictive Model Markup Language* (PMML), a standard way to represent models across an industry, gives an XML representation of a model, and each algorithm model has an XML schema. This can be used to consume models created by various software. PMML has limitations with respect to generalizing the parameters of models, due to several variants of algorithms.

Based on your application needs, models must be applied appropriately. For example, models can be consumed by applying them to new datasets in real time to make real-time decisions or by applying them in batch mode for large dataset combinations. Models can be consumed in a SQLScript procedure and included as part of calculation views, result views, or can be in a stored procedure.

In order to use a model in a calculation view, you first need to create a SQL scripted calculation view, as shown in Figure 5.2.

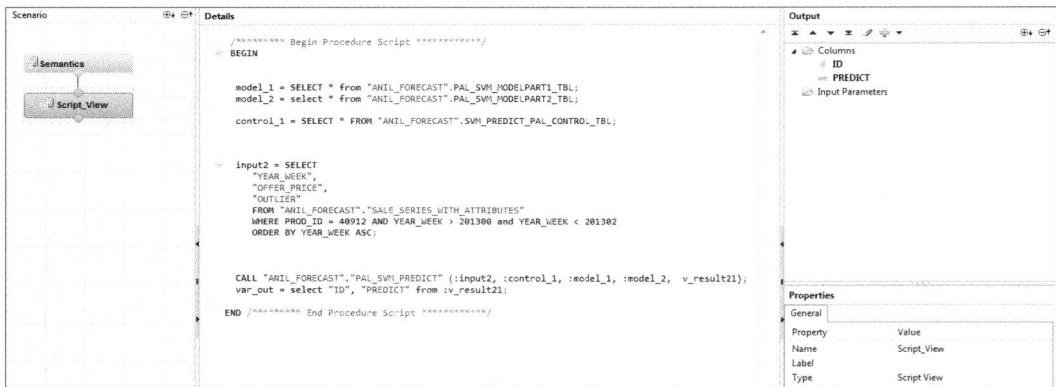

Figure 5.2 Calculation View for Model Scoring

All the values for a wrapper procedure call should be added as output columns in the calculation view. Once this calculation view is activated, it can be added and joined/projected with other nodes in the calculation. You can add input parameters to this calculation-like product or store. Prediction values can be joined to the time to add projections and aggregations for reporting purposes.

You now have seen how PAL models can be consumed for reporting. In the next section, we will look into model consumption in real time versus batch models.

5.3   Real-Time Model Consumption vs. Batch Predictive Modeling

In this section, we will look at designing predictive analysis models for real-time use and in batch scenarios. Please refer to the PAL reference guide for creating wrapper functions and the Application Function Modeler reference guide for using PAL.

The availability of commonly used predictive analysis algorithms for the in-memory SAP HANA database has enabled users to provide models for various compelling problems. As an example, you can execute unsupervised learning more frequently, and if required execute it in real time for massive data volumes to make business decisions quickly. Similarly, the ability to create forecast models for product and location combinations—which can run into millions of combinations for retail chain outlets—in a few minutes allows a user to create autoregressive models on a daily basis for better replenishment purposes.

In the next two subsections, we will look into how to address such scenarios in SAP HANA for real-time and batch modeling.

5.3.1   Real-Time Model Execution

Because algorithms run in an SAP HANA database, not moving data between the database and a separate algorithm environment makes algorithm performance dramatically faster. For example, you can use unsupervised learning, such as clustering, followed by classification or association within each cluster, to offer promotions in real time with very large transaction datasets with *multithread processing*.

In SAP HANA, there is no significant difference in technique for how you achieve real-time aspects for models due to the real-time nature of the database platform itself. Keep the following points in mind when working with real-time data:

▶ Consider the execution time of the algorithms and responsiveness to the UI. Algorithms like k-means can group a massive number of records (in the millions) in a second on SAP HANA.

▶ The aggregation of data based on algorithm outputs should be straightforward. However, aggregating against hierarchies requires joining the output in logical models.

In most real-time scenarios, the scoring or execution of multiple algorithms in a single interaction with a user is not required. The output persistence for the next execution *is* required, and it can be time-consuming. Because of this, in SAP HANA, global or local temporary tables should be used.

If multiple algorithms need to be executed in a single user interaction, an ideal approach is to model using a calculation view and join the hierarchies.

5.3.2 Batch Predictive Model Execution

Batch execution allows you to create, score, and execute many models in the quickest possible time. Using batch executions, you can perform parallel executions for microlevel jobs.

Let's consider a scenario in which you have to forecast next week's demand for all products for multiple retail chain locations. Figure 5.3 depicts the forecasting flow for one product at a time. Analyzing each product involves steps for the SQL query, training model, and forecast predictions. Some scenarios might involve calling millions of SQLs executions and training model creation calls—which is quite an expensive process.

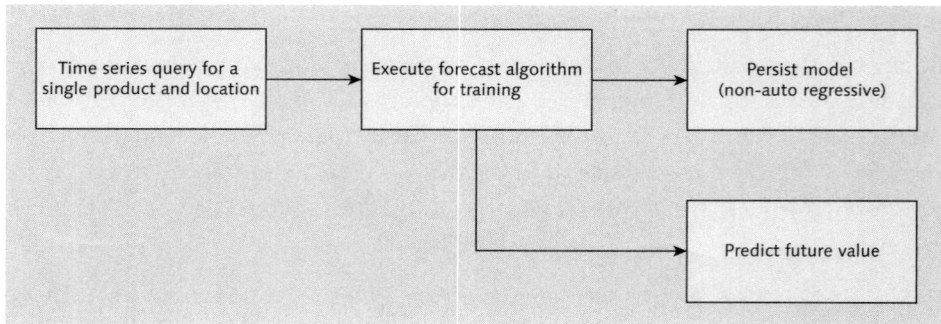

Figure 5.3 Single Product Model

In Figure 5.3, there are two areas in which you can optimize the processing for better performance: You need to determine how the number of queries in a database can be reduced while still allowing the prediction of product demand at multiple locations, and you need to reduce the number of calls to train and predict. In the two sections that follow, we look at both of these areas.

Query Reductions

The number of queries at the product level can be reduced if you select all the product time series with single SQL statements and loop each product in the result set to predict the future value loop. Here, the focus is to get the predicted value of each product at the lowest granularity of each location, a technique referred to as *bottom-up forecasting*.

There are three possible approaches to reduce the number of queries and perform parallel processing for each product while improving performance:

- Create a loop in the SQL procedure on the virtual table, and execute multiple procedures at the same time.
- Create a loop in an RLANG procedure in `_doparallel` for each product, and execute multiple procedures at the same time.
- Create a loop in an LLANG procedure with a partition parallel block on the virtual table, and execute multiple procedures at the same time.

Improved performance is possible in SAP HANA with multiple executions of procedures in parallel and predicting the future product demand values. Although this is not an option for R procedures with single R services, these procedures can be optimized if multiple R servers are installed. For an example of `_doparallel` in R, please refer to Listing 5.1; for an example of parallel processing in LLANG, refer to Chapter 6.

Training Reductions

Training reductions depend on the type of modeling task. In the previous section, the focus was to get the predicted value of each product at the lowest granularity of each location.

Another possible approach is to perform *top-down forecasting*. In this technique, a product with multiple locations is considered with a time series. Once forecasted, the product is proportioned to each location based on the historic sales proportion for each location. This works well when the time series frequency is sufficiently long (weekly, monthly), resulting in a consistent pattern. If there is too much deviation in the time series, top-down forecasting will not work.

The top-down approach for forecasting involves the following steps:

1. Execute the SQL for a product for all locations as an aggregation (execute multiple products at the same time).
2. For each product and all locations together, create a forecast model and perform a prediction.
3. Identify the proportion of sales contributed by each location to overall sales (each product).
4. Distribute the predicted value as per the proportion of each location.

You can clearly see that this large-scale modeling can result in improved performance. However, accuracy depends completely on the consistency of the proportions and the period of historic data considered for calculating the proportions.

In this section, we presented model considerations for batch and real-time models. The additional factor that needs to be considered for predictive models is the partitions of large tables in multiple nodes in an SAP HANA deployment. In the next section, we will look at the impact of data partitions on the predictive modeling process.

5.4   Impact of Data Partitions in Predictive Modeling

The amount of data generated every day is quite large. The data in a database table is distributed across multiple nodes to cater to growing data volumes using partitions. Hash, round-robin, and range partitions are single-level partitioning strategies, and hash-range, round-robin-range, hash-hash, and range-range are multilevel partitioning strategies. Notable advantages of partitions include parallelization, load balancing, and overcoming size limitations.

During normal SQL query processing, the sequel processing is parallelized on multiple nodes combined together based on distributed data. However, for predictive tasks, the data from each node should be combined before invoking algorithms and executing partitioning on the combined data.

In order to identify patterns in the data, algorithms require relevant data. A common question to ask is, "Do we need all the data for the algorithms to create models or detect patterns?" If you do need all the data from all the nodes for the algorithms, then you need to first combine all the data in a single node (such as a master node) and invoke PAL or R. Alternately, invoking PAL could automatically distribute the algorithm execution to the multiple nodes, and the algorithm could have additional processing to interpret the results from each node and produce a combined pattern or model. The latter option is cumbersome, however, because the algorithm outcome itself could be compromised without proper handling.

Most classification or regression algorithms work with sample data. Creating models on sample data is also the most commonly used technique. The quality of the sample data determines the fit of the model for the entire dataset. Some unsupervised learning techniques, such as basket analysis or k-means, might require an entire data population in order to identify patterns.

Based on your partition strategy and the type of predictive task, executing algorithms on each node and combining the results makes sense. This is especially true when a dataset is partitioned on business columns representing a store, region, and so on.

5.5   Using Multiple R Servers and Data Partitions

In this section, we will look into PAL and RLANG procedure performance artifacts in an SAP HANA multiple node deployment.

5.5.1   Predictive Analysis Library

Normally, PAL is used in SQLScript stored procedures. The input data for algorithms is calculated or fetched from tables, views, or logical views in SAP HANA. The complex process involved in fetching data from these multiple nodes is hidden from the normal developer when writing a stored procedure and consuming any of these sources. Because data is aggregated from multiple nodes in distributed environments by the SAP HANA index server before invoking the PAL function, PAL is executed most often in the master node in SAP HANA deployment scenarios. Figure 5.4 shows this normal behavior of SAP HANA when executing PAL.

Within each node, PAL functions can be scaled with the NUM_THREAD control parameter. In most scenarios, this scaling is sufficient. For classification problems, you can perform a sampling stratification or stratification partition to create datasets for model training, testing, and validation from the overall population (see Section 5.1.2). However, there will be some scenarios in which a large set of products is distributed into individual nodes based on geographies, and certain algorithms will need to be executed in each dataset.

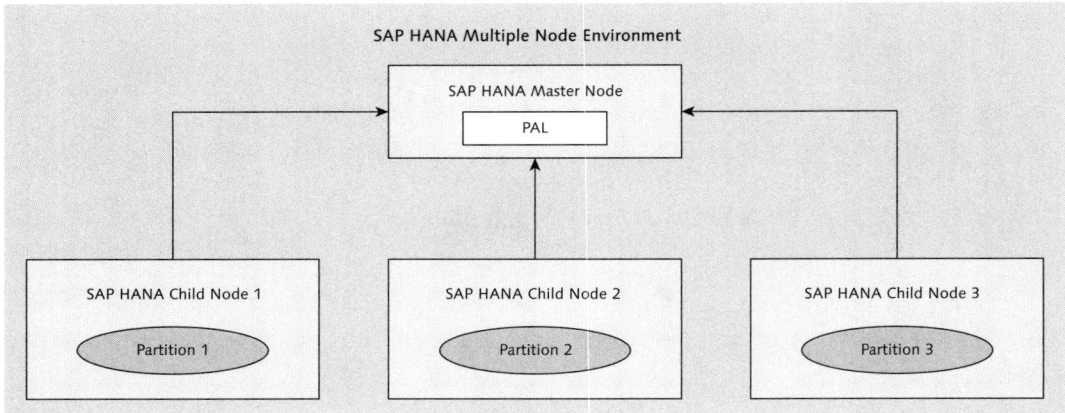

Figure 5.4 PAL Current Execution Architecture

Like the scenario we discussed in Section 5.3.2, in which the time series were distributed into multiple nodes per location as part of the partition strategy, you will not be able to utilize all of the resources for executing PAL from a single node; instead, you need to utilize PAL from as many resources as possible. In such a scenario, you can execute PAL from various instances, with each instance having a script server. At this point in time, SAP HANA cannot automatically execute PAL in each node in which data is available; this execution needs to be handled manually due to the previously mentioned logic about mashing the results.

Suppose that you are working with a table in which daily consolidated sales are populated with a partition strategy based on location, such as state, region, and so on. In this scenario, you want to execute forecasting of each product in those nodes and in all available nodes to which the data is distributed. Figure 5.5 proposes an alternate approach for executing PAL in each of the nodes.

In this approach, you execute the PAL algorithms in each partition node in which the data is present with a dedicated connection. The procedures in each node should be parallelized. The advantage of this is that the data is moved to a single master node, and you can manually scale across the node.

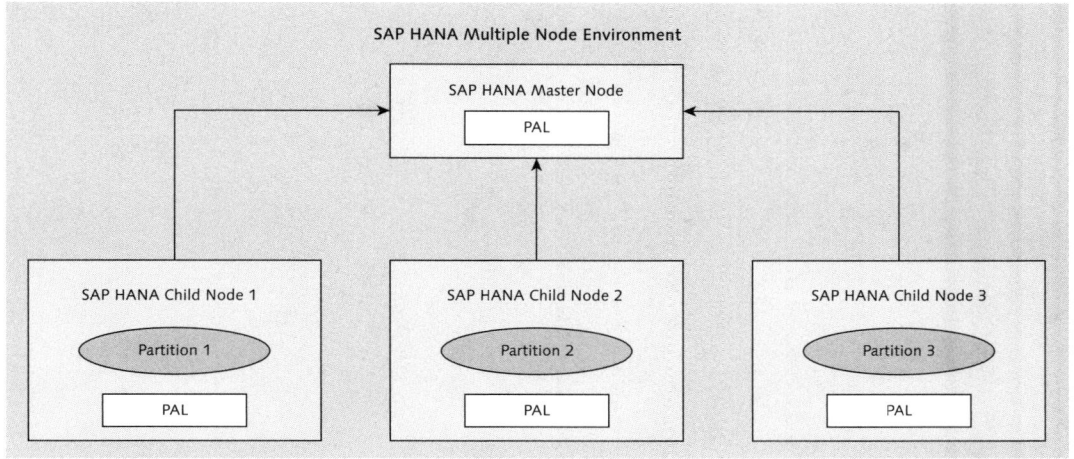

Figure 5.5 Alternative Approach for Executing PAL

This technique cannot be applied when data is distributed. An algorithm is required for all data from other nodes. In most cases, this scenario does not arise when preprocessing techniques are good enough. This technique is applicable only when the data on each node is sufficient for the algorithm to run, especially in multiple or million time series predictions. For unsupervised learning, in which the data is being taken from multiple nodes, sampling is a better approach.

We have looked at PAL scaling in multiple nodes. Next, we will look at multiple R servers and scaling within a single R server.

5.5.2 Using Multiple R Servers

R server information is configured in SAP HANA Studio, as shown in Figure 5.6. In parameter `cer_rserve_addresses`, you can list the addresses for high availability. If SAP HANA cannot reach one address, it will try another one.

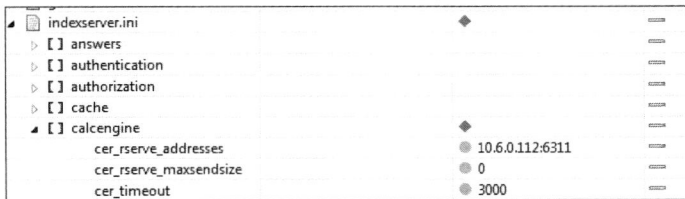

Figure 5.6 R Server Configuration

When executing a procedure or view, if there is a call to the RLANG procedure (R operator), the calculation engine in SAP HANA will invoke the R server.

Within an R procedure, you can scale the R script execution by using packages such as doParallel or any other CRAN R package to utilize the resources of the R server, as shown in Listing 5.2.

```
registerDoParallel()

result <- foreach ( i = wantMetrics, .combine=rbind) %dopar%
{
 tmp <- performCBC(inputMetrics[inputMetrics$id ==lMetrics[
i],]$value, lMetrics[i] )

}
```
Listing 5.2 Sample Scale Up in R

In Listing 5.2, each execution of the loop is performed in parallel to ensure that all of the cores in the R server are fully utilized. In Figure 5.7, R servers 2 and 3 are shown as high-availability servers when server 1 cannot be reached by the calculation engine in SAP HANA.

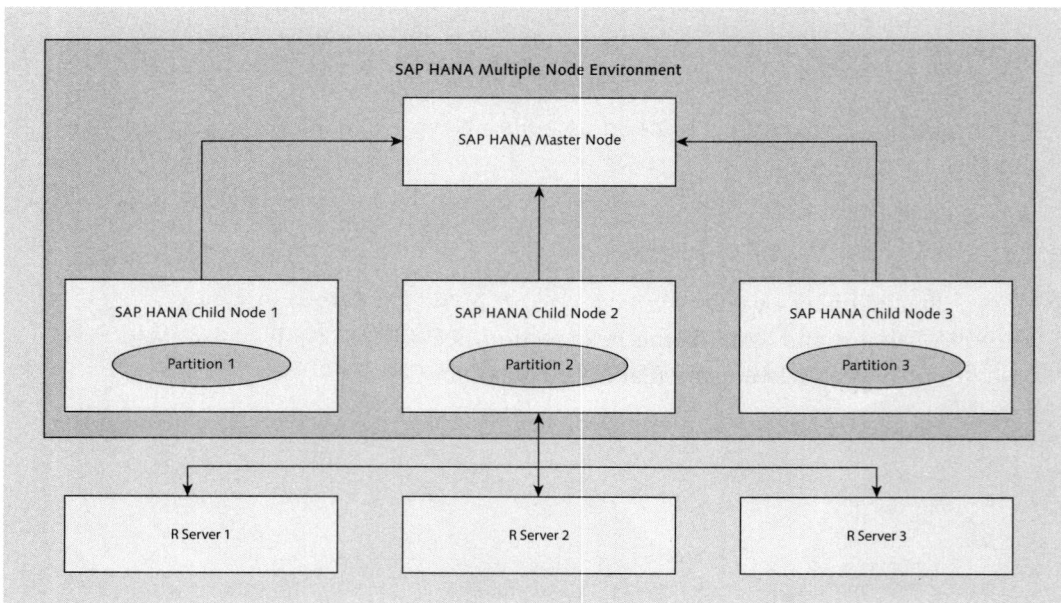

Figure 5.7 SAP HANA/R Deployment

This configuration is sufficient in most scenarios, but if you want to leverage multiple R servers, you can configure different R servers in each of the SAP HANA nodes and execute the procedure in those nodes as shown in Figure 5.8. This technique can be useful for partition tables in which data is distributed in each node. This technique also assumes that running the algorithm independently on each node with the consolidation of data from other SAP HANA nodes is a requirement.

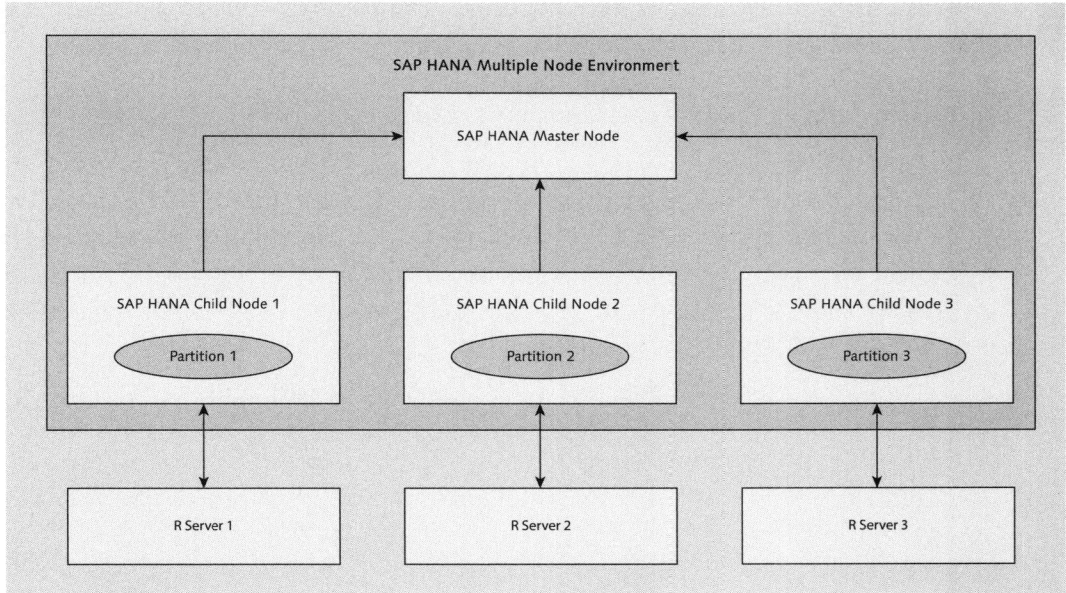

Figure 5.8 Alternative Approach for Partition Tables

We have seen complex algorithm execution scenarios and how to scale them in SAP HANA using R and PAL. In the next section, we will look into what cases should be considered when using R and PAL together.

5.6   Modeling Using R and PAL Simultaneously

In the previous chapter, we looked at the sales time series for the products of a retail store. In some cases, you may have millions of products and store combinations and their respective time series; you will need to understand these time series and the group-related products that are similar in their time series proper-ties. This is also called *clustering* for time series. From large sets of products, you can identify groups that exhibit similar statistical behavior. There are many ways to work within this scenario via techniques such as dynamic time warping, SAP-based algorithms for time neutrality, and character-based analysis. For the example in this section, we will focus on character-based clustering time series.

To perform this operation, you need to characterize each time series with statisti-cal attributes such as kurtosis, skew, Hurst, and correlation. These attributes can have additional characteristics, such as quartile deviations with normalized data. After determining these statistical quartiles, you can group (cluster) these time series using k-means by calculating the number of clusters.

In SAP HANA, you can get the time series for millions of products by using an RLANG procedure to get all characteristics of each time series. Listing 5.3 shows an example of retrieving time series characteristics. Note that it uses the parallel option for each time series. An alternative to this is to use the LLANG partition parallel in LLANG within SAP HANA, but you might miss a few statistical charac-teristics, such as Hurst.

```
CREATE PROCEDURE GET_TS_CHARACTERISTICS (IN metrics CLUSTER_TS_CBC_
INPUT, OUT cbc CLUSTER_TS_CBC) LANGUAGE RLANG AS BEGIN

library(foreach)
library(doParallel)
library(e1071)
library(pracma)

inputMetrics <- metrics
colnames(inputMetrics) <- c("id", "value")
inputMetrics$id <- as.character(inputMetrics$id)


# Find all metric IDs and number of metrics in the input table
lMetrics <- levels(as.factor(inputMetrics$id))
nMetrics <- length(lMetrics)

# Select desired metrics
wantMetrics <- 1:nMetrics

findACF <- function(x) {
  acfout <- acf(x, lag.max = 100, plot=F)
  return(acfout)
}
```

```
performCBC <- function(x, METRIC_ID) {
  acfOut <- findACF(x)
  CORRELATION <- as.numeric(sum(acfOut$acf[1:2]))
  HURST <- as.numeric(round(hurst(x),2))
  SKEWNESS = as.numeric(skewness(x))
  KURTOSIS = as.numeric(kurtosis(x), na.rm = FALSE, type = 2)

  res <- data.frame(METRIC_ID, CORRELATION, HURST, SKEWNESS, KURTOSIS)
  return (res)
}



registerDoParallel()

result <- foreach ( i = wantMetrics, .combine=rbind) %dopar%
{
 tmp <- performCBC(inputMetrics[inputMetrics$id ==lMetrics[
i],]$value, lMetrics[i] )

}


cbc <- result

END;
```

Listing 5.3 Characteristics of a Time Series

The next step in the exercise is to get the number of clusters needed for the time series characteristics. Listing 5.4 shows how to calculate the number of possible clusters in R.

```
CREATE PROCEDURE GET_TS_NCLUSTERS(IN num_clusters CLUSTER_TS_NUM_
CLUSTERS, OUT nclusters CLUSTER_TS_NUM) LANGUAGE RLANG AS BEGIN

library(foreach)
library(doParallel)
library(e1071)
library(pracma)
library(fpc)

inputKmeans <- num_clusters

numericKM <- data.matrix(inputKmeans, rownames.force = NA)
#identify number of clusters

pamk.best <- pamk(numericKM)
```

```
KNUM <- pamk.best$nc;
nclusters <- data.frame(KNUM)

END;
```

Listing 5.4 Calculate the Number of Clusters Required for Characteristics of a Time Series

Once you calculate the number of clusters, you can use k-means in SAP HANA to segment the millions of time series within milliseconds. Generate an AFL wrapper procedure for KMEANS "GROUP_TIME_SERIES". Listing 5.5 shows a procedure to call the cluster calculation, followed by calling PAL KMEANS.

```
CREATE PROCEDURE EXECUTE_TS(IN cbc CLUSTER_TS_CBC, OUT out2 "_SYS_
AFL"."T_KMEANS_RESULT_ASSIGN", OUT out3 "_SYS_AFL"."T_KMEANS_
CENTERS") LANGUAGE SQLSCRIPT AS BEGIN

numofClustersInput =
 select "CORRELATION", "HURST", "SKEWNESS", "KURTOSIS" FROM :cbc;

CALL GET_TS_NCLUSTERS(:numofClustersInput, v_kumn);

kNum = select * from :v_kumn;

UPDATE CTS_KMEANS_CONTROL_TAB SET "intArgs" =
 (SELECT TOP 1 KNUM FROM :v_kumn) WHERE "NAME" = 'GROUP_NUMBER';

CALL "GROUP_TIME_SERIES"(:cbc, :out2, :out3);

END;
```

Listing 5.5 Calling KMEANS

You can perform overall orchestration in a single procedure that calls characteristics and grouping. In this example, we have shown you how to use both R and PAL for a single use case.

5.7 Summary

In this chapter, we discussed SAP HANA's integration with R, design and deployment options for both batch models and real-time consumption models, using multiple R servers during data partitioning, and using both PAL and R in a single use case.

In the next chapter, we will move on to performing more complex operations, including Monte Carlo simulations and portfolio optimizations.

In this chapter, we will discuss how to design and model optimizations and simulations on an SAP HANA platform.

6   Simulations and Optimizations

This chapter explains how to use SAP HANA to design simulation and optimization models through an in-depth case study. While considering an equally distributed portfolio with *n* symbols/stock securities, we will simulate value-at-risk with a Monte Carlo simulation using the Geometric Brownian Motion (GBM) model. This chapter also covers complex operations such as matrix inversion, matrix algebra, and the creation of mean-covariance matrices with stock securities on an SAP HANA platform for optimizing an investment portfolio.

Let's begin by reviewing the parameters of the case study that will serve as a running example throughout this chapter.

6.1   Case Study

Many countries have stock markets, such as NASDAQ, S&P, and so on. Companies listed in these markets allow the public to invest in their stocks. These stocks are traded every working day of the stock market, and investment management companies create portfolios to manage the investments in these stocks in order to produce better returns on clients' investments. The following terms and definitions will be found throughout this chapter and case study:

▶ **Security**
The financial instrument of a listed company in a stock market. The terms *symbol* and *stock* are used similarly in this case study.

▶ **Portfolio**
A range of securities in which an organization or individual has invested.

▶ **Security return**
The daily return of a security is the difference between the opening value of the

security and the closing value of the security in the stock market; this is usually a monetary value. Similarly, the monthly return of a security is the difference between the opening value on the first trading day of the month and the closing value on the last trading day of the month.

▶ **Portfolio return**
An aggregation of the return on all securities in a portfolio. Similar to a security return, it can be calculated on a daily or monthly basis.

For the purposes of this chapter, in this case study we will create a portfolio that includes the top 40 companies traded in NASDAQ. Henceforth, the word *portfolio* will refer to a collection of these securities. This portfolio consists of a wide range of securities from IT, healthcare, and retail industries.

The purpose of this case study is to simulate the *value-at-risk* for this portfolio, a statistical technique that is used to measure the level of financial risk for an investment portfolio over a specified period of time. If the value-at-risk is high, investment management should consider optimizing the portfolio. In subsequent sections, we will cover how to optimize the portfolio by maximizing the portfolio return. We will also define the mathematical models and constraints for optimizing the portfolio in the process of solving this problem.

Technical Implementation

This chapter focuses only on the technical implementation of simulating the value-at-risk and optimizing the portfolio return. We will cover how to perform various operations that are needed for this case study in SAP HANA.

6.2   Monte Carlo Simulation of Value-at-Risk

To simulate value-at-risk for the case study, we will use the *Monte Carlo simulation* technique, a popular problem-solving technique for approximating the probability of particular outcomes through multiple simulations using random variables.

In this case study, we are calculating the approximate value of the portfolio return for a future time using multiple trial runs and random variables. Value-at-risk will be the outcome of this statistical approximation for the future return value.

There are different statistical models that can be used for approximating value-at-risk. Here, we will use the GBM model, which uses random variables along with parameters based on the historic performance of a portfolio.

In this section, we will first look at the various random variable generation techniques in SAP HANA. We will then provide insight into the GBM model before moving on to designing logical models in SAP HANA. Finally, we will look at and compare alternative approaches for implementing and simulating value-at-risk.

6.2.1 Random Variable Generation

Randomization is the most important step in calculating value-at-risk outcomes in a Monte Carlo simulation. SAP HANA supports four distinct random distribution sampling techniques to generate random variables through the PAL function `DISTRRANDOM`: uniform, normal, weibull, and gamma.

In this section, we will look at these four random distribution techniques, their equations, parameters, and control tables. Then, to better understand the distribution output of the random variables generated, we will discuss binning functionality.

Random Distribution Techniques

In this section, we will look at the four random distribution techniques.

Uniform

Uniform distribution (also known as *rectangular distribution*) occurs when all intervals are of the same length between each given minimum and maximum value. The number of sampling values in each interval will be uniform. The probability of uniform distribution is constant. SAP HANA uses the uniform distribution function for generating random variables, like the one shown here:

$$f(x) = \begin{cases} \dfrac{1}{b-a} & \text{for } a \le x \le b \\ 0 & \text{for } x < a \text{ or } x > b \end{cases}$$

The distribution control table to generate uniformly distributed random numbers requires minimum and maximum values. Figure 6.1 shows the distribution control table values as an example.

	NAME	VALUE
1	DistributionName	UNIFORM
2	MIN	100
3	MAX	1000

Figure 6.1 Uniform Distribution Control Table

The output of these random variables in a uniform distribution looks as shown in Figure 6.2. The output shows that the number of random variables in each interval is in a similar range.

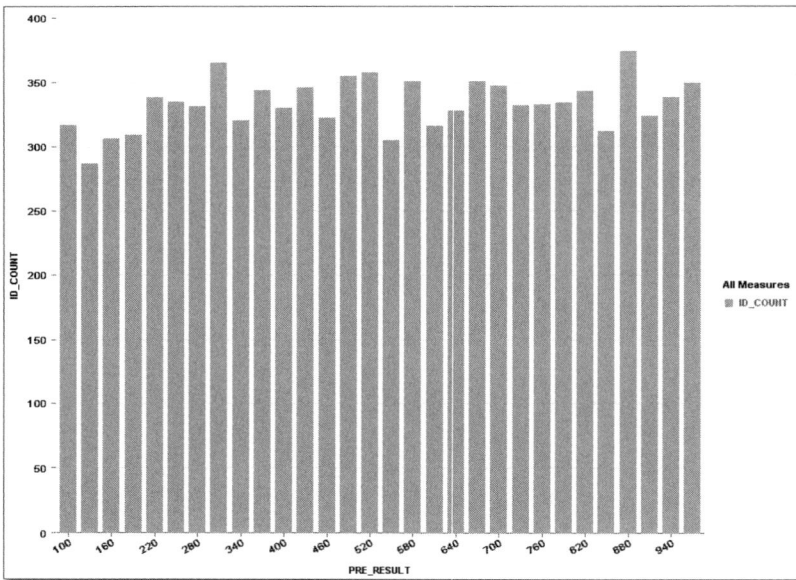

Figure 6.2 Uniform Distribution of Random Numbers

Shape of Distribution

The bars in Figure 6.2 will change with the next random generation. However, although the numbers generated are random, the overall pattern will be same. This is true for all random generation techniques discussed in this chapter.

Normal

A *normal distribution* is defined with a variant of x, a mean of μ and a variance of σ^2. This distribution usually forms a bell shape. An example of a random variable SAP HANA generates with the normal distribution is as follows:

$$f(x, \mu, \sigma) = \frac{1}{\sigma\sqrt{2\pi}} e - \frac{(x-\mu)^2}{2\sigma^2}$$

There are two parameters that control normal distribution random number generation: mean and variance. A mean of 0 and variance of 1 are most commonly used for generating a bell-shaped normal distribution. Figure 6.3 shows the control parameters for the normal distribution.

SELECT TOP 40000 * FROM "MONTECARLO"."PAL_DISTRRANDOM_DISTRPARAM_TBL"

	NAME	VALUE
1	DistributionName	NORMAL
2	MEAN	0
3	VARIANCE	1.0

Figure 6.3 Normal Distribution Generation Control Parameters

By generating a chart from the Figure 6.3 control values, you can see normally distributed random numbers, as shown in Figure 6.4.

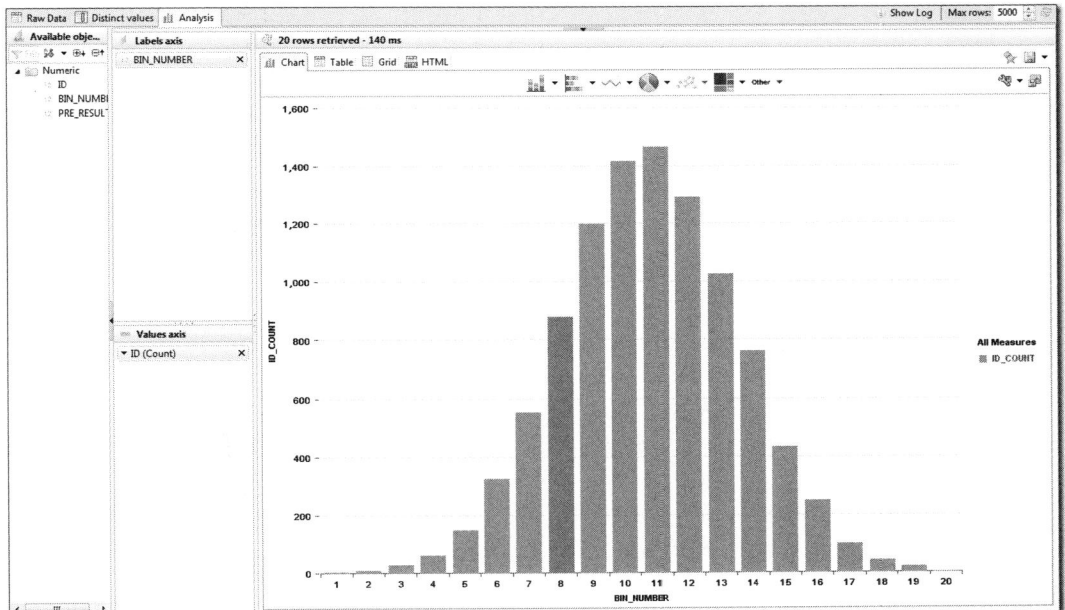

Figure 6.4 Normal Distribution of Random Variables

Most Monte Carlo simulations require the normal distribution of random variables. For such simulations, you want each simulation that is normally distributed to have a mean of 0 and variance of 1.

The bin shown for the normal distribution technique shows the overall random sample distribution to be normal while using normal distribution.

> **Binning**
>
> *Binning* is a way to group number values into small groups or "bins". We will discuss the binning functionality in detail in the Binning section.

Aggregating the random numbers shows a mean of 0 and a variance of 1. This is the technique we will use for the case study.

Weibull

The following equation shows a two-parameter weibull probability density function of a random variable of SAP HANA:

$$f(x; \lambda, k) = \begin{cases} \dfrac{k}{\lambda}(\dfrac{x}{\lambda})k - 1_e - (x/\lambda)^k & x \geq 0 \\ 0 & x < 0 \end{cases}$$

This distribution is used for survival analysis and life distribution analysis. The K parameter effects the shape of the distribution, and λ defines the slope or scale of the distribution. Figure 6.5 shows the weibull distribution input parameters.

	NAME	VALUE
1	DistributionName	WEIBULL
2	SHAPE	2
3	SCALE	200

Figure 6.5 Weibull Distribution Input Parameters

Figure 6.6 shows the weibull distribution generation in a graphical chart after generating random numbers, illustrating the distribution along with binning.

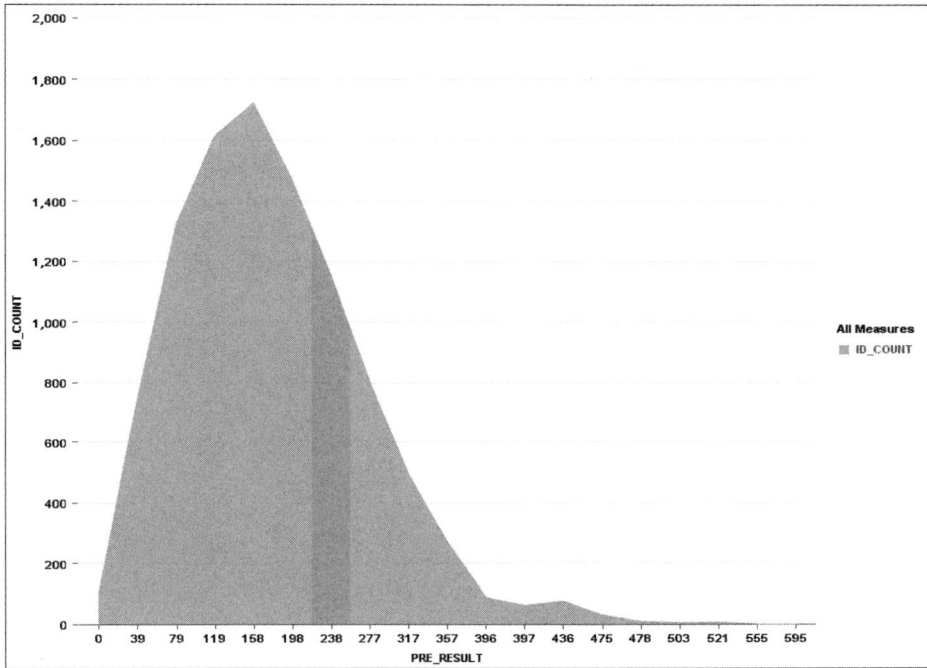

Figure 6.6 Weibull Random Variable Distribution

Gamma

The following equation defines the gamma probability density function with a shape parameter of K and a scale parameter of θ (this is an exponential distribution function):

$$f(x; k, \theta) = \frac{x^{k-1} e^{-\frac{x}{\theta}}}{\theta^k \Gamma(k)} \quad \text{for } x > 0 \text{ and } k, \theta > 0$$

The parameter control table with gamma distribution is shown in Figure 6.7.

	NAME	VALUE
1	DistributionName	GAMMA
2	SHAPE	2
3	SCALE	3

Figure 6.7 Gamma Distribution Parameter Values

The result of these parameters is shown in the distribution table in Figure 6.8.

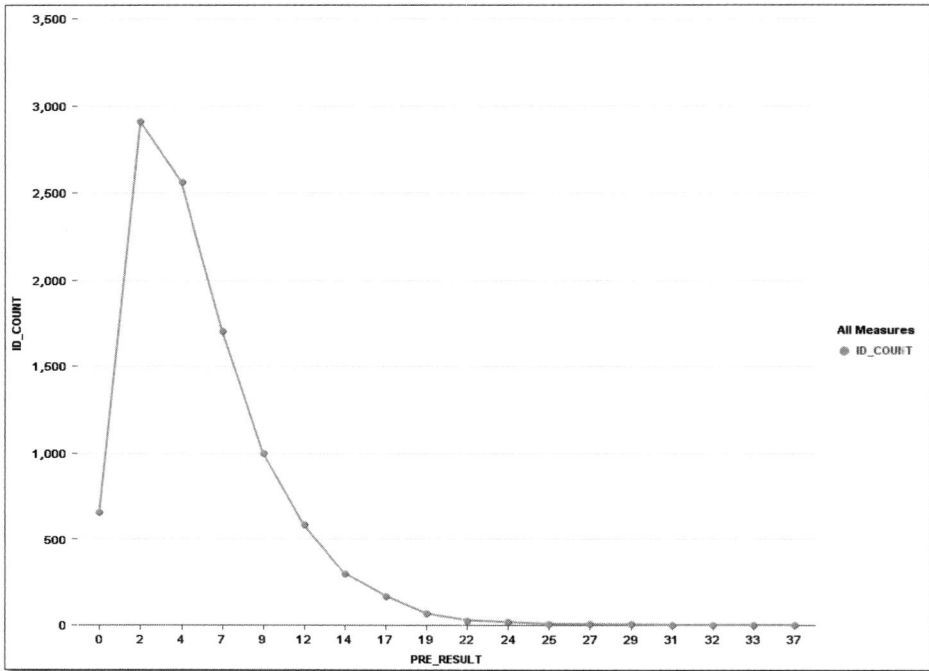

Figure 6.8 Gamma Distribution of Random Variables

As you can see, these four random variable generation techniques produce different distributions based on their parameters.

In the next section, we will look how these results can be understood in SAP HANA.

Binning

It is not easy to understand the distribution of outputs generated by random variable generators by looking directly at the result sets. As an alternative, you can leverage the SAP HANA PAL binning functionality to better understand the distribution. Binning is an effective way to understand the distribution of random variables. All PAL functions are multithreaded and use the processing power of the SAP HANA servers, and using a binning function is an efficient way of manually classifying groups in boilerplate SQL code. You can control the output bins by using various parameters and potentially avoid writing boilerplate code in SQL.

Using the SAP HANA AFL framework, generate a wrapper procedure called BIN- NING_VAR_PROC for the BINNING PAL function and use the output of the random distribution as an input to this procedure to better understand the distribution of random numbers. Listing 6.1 provides common code for generating random distributions and viewing the result after binning.

```
CREATE PROCEDURE MONTECARLO.RANDOM_DISTRIBUTION_BIN (OUT v_
output "MONTECARLO"."PAL_BINNING_RESULT_T")
 LANGUAGE SQLScript READS SQL DATA WITH RESULT VIEW
 MONTECARLO.BIN_DISTRIBUTION AS
BEGIN

 input1= SELECT * from  "MONTECARLO"."PAL_DISTRRANDOM_DISTRPARAM_TBL";
 input2 = SELECT * FROM "MONTECARLO"."PAL_CONTROL_TBL_ANIL";
 CALL "MONTECARLO"."DISTRRANDOM_PROC" (:input1, :input2,  dis_inp);

 bin_input = SELECT "ID", "RANDOM" AS "VAR" FROM :dis_inp;
 control_input = SELECT * FROM  "MONTECARLO"."BIN_PAL_CONTROL_TBL";

 CALL "MONTECARLO"."BINNING_VAR_PROC"(:bin_input, :control_input,
v_output);

 END;
```

Listing 6.1 Random Variable Generation Code

In Listing 6.1, DISTRRANDOM_PROC will generate a distribution as per the control parameter and distribution parameter tables. Use the output of the random generation as an input for the binning function BINNING_VAR_PROC to understand the distribution.

Random Generation Outputs

The figures provided for each of the random generation techniques are outputs of the procedure in Listing 6.1, with different control parameter values for random distributions. The result view analysis in SAP HANA Studio is used to produce Figure 6.2, Figure 6.4, Figure 6.6, and Figure 6.8.

In a control input table for generating random numbers, there are three parameters for generating input numbers:

▶ THREAD_NUMBER

For performance, this displays how many threads to use to generate a distribution.

▶ SEED

Initializes the random generation for pseudo random generation. Here, use 0.

▶ NUM_RANDOM

Indicates the number of random variables to be generated.

Figure 6.9 is an example of a control table for generating random variables.

	NAME	INTARGS	DOUBLEARGS	STRINGARGS
1	THREAD_NUMBER	2	?	?
2	SEED	0	?	?
3	NUM_RANDOM	10,000	?	?

Figure 6.9 Control Table for All Types of Random Sample Distribution

We will use the normal distribution's random variables in the next section for the Monte Carlo simulation, define the GBM model along with random variables, and run simulations for the portfolio return. Based on these simulated outcomes, we will calculate the value-at-risk.

6.2.2 Simulation Model and Process

A randomly distributed process (also referred as a stochastic process) St is said to follow the GBM model if it satisfies the following equation, where Wt is a Brownian motion and σ and μ are constants:

$$dSt = \mu\,Stdt + \sigma\,StdWt$$

The first part ($\mu Stdt$) of this differential equation is referred to as the *drift in time* or *trend*. The second part of the equation ($\sigma StdWt$) is called *random noise* and controls the trajectory of the simulation. Because it is a random approximation in time, this is a Monte Carlo simulation.

Random Numbers in a GBM Model

In a GBM model, the number of random numbers depends on the input parameters of the date you want to know the value-at-risk. It can be 10 days in advance, 180 days in advance, or higher for long-term securities.

The overall process of a value-at-risk simulation is shown in Figure 6.10.

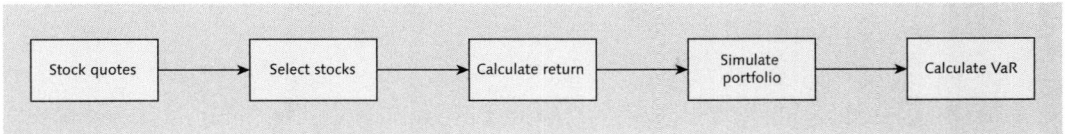

Figure 6.10 Overall Value-At-Risk Simulation Process

We will describe the process seen in Figure 6.10 step by step:

- **Stock quotes**
  In this step, we will discuss the data storage of stock market prices.

- **Select stocks**
  This is the process of creating a portfolio and using that portfolio for a simulation. Because you already have defined a portfolio with the top 40 company securities in it, continue using that portfolio.

- **Calculate return**
  In this step, define the SAP HANA logical model for calculating return.

- **Simulate portfolio**
  In this step, discuss the logic for implementing the simulation model.

- **Calculate value-at-risk**
  In this step, calculate the value-at-risk from the simulation outcomes.

In the following sections, we will implement each of these steps in SAP HANA by creating a stock table to calculate the value-at-risk.

Stock Quotes

Figure 6.11 shows the table definition of a stock quote with a sample stock. This table is populated every day from NASDAQ or similar stock markets using SAP HANA ETL tools.

As previously discussed, a portfolio is combination of various securities, usually diversified with the various stocks of a company and its weights. For this case study, we have uniformly distributed the weights of randomly picked stocks to create a portfolio (see Figure 6.12).

RE	SYMBOL	DATE	12	OPEN	12	HIGH	12	LOW	12	CLOSE	12	VOLUME	12	ADJCLOSE
	ABC	Jun 1, 2000		24.5		25.69		24.12		25.38		2,333,600		5.59
	ABC	Jun 2, 2000		25.38		25.5		24.5		25.25		1,146,800		5.56
	ABC	Jun 5, 2000		25.06		25.06		24.38		24.38		586,000		5.37
	ABC	Jun 6, 2000		24.88		26.44		24.75		26.25		2,472,400		5.78
	ABC	Jun 7, 2000		26.06		26.44		25.25		25.62		974,000		5.65
	ABC	Jun 8, 2000		26		26		24.44		24.81		565,600		5.47
	ABC	Jun 9, 2000		24.62		25.94		24.62		25.75		1,508,400		5.67
	ABC	Jun 12, 2000		25.75		26.88		25.62		26.19		3,944,400		5.77
	ABC	Jun 13, 2000		26.19		29.25		25.88		29.25		2,157,600		6.44
	ABC	Jun 14, 2000		29		29		27.12		27.5		1,719,200		6.06
	ABC	Jun 15, 2000		27.56		29.06		27.56		28.62		927,200		6.31
	ABC	Jun 16, 2000		28.69		29.44		28		29.44		1,119,600		6.49
	ABC	Jun 19, 2000		29.44		30		28.5		28.75		1,278,400		6.33
	ABC	Jun 20, 2000		27.5		29.88		27.5		29.12		1,127,200		6.42

Figure 6.11 Stock Quote Table Structure

	Name	SQL Data Type	Dimension
1	ID	INTEGER	
2	SYMBOL	VARCHAR	10
3	WEIGHT	DECIMAL	10,6

Figure 6.12 Portfolio Definition Structure

Figure 6.12 is populated with a portfolio that consists of up to 40 securities. Initially, you will weight each of these securities in your portfolio as 1/40, or 0.025. Once the initial portfolio is created, you can calculate the portfolio return.

Calculate Return

The *monthly return* of a stock is calculated as the difference between the values of a stock on opening day and on the last day of the month. Figure 6.13 shows a table containing the columns MONTH_LAST and MONTH_FIRST for each month. The difference between these two values for each month is the monthly return.

A portfolio's monthly and daily return is the sum of the monthly and daily returns of all stocks that belong to a portfolio. A calculation view definition that calculates stock returns is depicted in Figure 6.14.

We will use the calculated daily return to determine the mean and standard deviation of the portfolio, which are used as constants in the GBM simulation.

SYMBOL	DATE	OPEN	HIGH	LOW	CLOSE	VOLUME	ADJCLOSE	MONTH_LAST	MONTH_FIRST
ABC	Jun 1, 2000	24.5	25.69	24.12	25.38	2,333,600	5.59	0	24.5
ABC	Jun 2, 2000	25.38	25.5	24.5	25.25	1,146,800	5.56	0	0
ABC	Jun 5, 2000	25.06	25.06	24.38	24.38	586,000	5.37	0	0
ABC	Jun 6, 2000	24.88	26.44	24.75	26.25	2,472,400	5.78	0	0
ABC	Jun 7, 2000	26.06	26.44	25.25	25.62	974,000	5.65	0	0
ABC	Jun 8, 2000	26	26	24.44	24.81	565,600	5.47	0	0
ABC	Jun 9, 2000	24.62	25.94	24.62	25.75	1,508,400	5.67	0	0
ABC	Jun 12, 2000	25.75	26.88	25.62	26.19	3,944,400	5.77	0	0
ABC	Jun 13, 2000	26.19	29.25	25.88	29.25	2,157,600	6.44	0	0
ABC	Jun 14, 2000	29	29	27.12	27.5	1,719,200	6.06	0	0
ABC	Jun 15, 2000	27.56	29.06	27.56	28.62	927,200	6.31	0	0
ABC	Jun 16, 2000	28.69	29.44	28	29.44	1,119,600	6.49	0	0
ABC	Jun 19, 2000	29.44	30	28.5	28.75	1,278,400	6.33	0	0
ABC	Jun 20, 2000	27.5	29.88	27.5	29.12	1,127,200	6.42	0	0
ABC	Jun 21, 2000	28.88	29.94	28.81	29.06	845,600	6.4	0	0
ABC	Jun 22, 2000	29.62	29.62	28.12	28.5	967,600	6.28	0	0
ABC	Jun 23, 2000	28.5	28.56	27.75	28.44	510,800	6.26	0	0
ABC	Jun 26, 2000	28.44	29.94	28.44	29.94	979,600	6.6	0	0
ABC	Jun 27, 2000	29.94	29.94	28.06	28.06	756,800	6.18	0	0
ABC	Jun 28, 2000	28.31	29.69	28.31	29.69	1,800,800	6.54	0	0
ABC	Jun 29, 2000	29.88	32.38	29.88	31.12	2,566,800	6.86	0	0
ABC	Jun 30, 2000	31.25	32.12	31	31.02	1,772,400	6.83	31.02	0
ABC	Jul 3, 2000	31.19	31.19	30.44	30.5	337,600	6.72	0	31.19
ABC	Jul 5, 2000	30.5	31.81	29.81	30.62	1,068,400	6.75	0	0
ABC	Jul 6, 2000	30.81	34	30.75	33.94	2,234,800	7.48	0	0
ABC	Jul 7, 2000	33.94	35	33.88	34.69	1,366,400	7.64	0	0
ABC	Jul 10, 2000	34.56	35.12	34.12	34.75	1,398,000	7.66	0	0
ABC	Jul 11, 2000	34.5	34.56	31.75	32.75	1,802,400	7.22	0	0
ABC	Jul 12, 2000	33.25	33.62	31.19	31.94	960,000	7.04	0	0
ABC	Jul 13, 2000	31.94	31.94	30.75	30.75	554,800	6.77	0	0
ABC	Jul 14, 2000	31	31.62	29	30.44	2,023,200	6.71	0	0
ABC	Jul 17, 2000	30.19	32.56	30.19	30.75	715,600	6.77	0	0

Figure 6.13 Monthly Return of a Security

Type	Name	Aggregation
	SYMBOL	
	YEAR_INT	
	QUARTER_INT	
	MONTH_INT	
	DAY_INT	
	DATE_SQL	
	OPEN	SUM
	HIGH	SUM
	LOW	SUM
	CLOSE	SUM
	VOLUME	SUM
	ADJCLOSE	SUM
	MONTH_LAST	SUM
	MONTH_FIRST	SUM
	MONTHLY_RETURN	SUM
	DAILY_RETURN	SUM
	ID	
	WEIGHT	
	COUNTER	FORMULA

Figure 6.14 Calculation View Definition of Portfolio's Monthly and Daily Returns

Simulate Return

Using the concepts covered in Section 6.1 and Section 6.2.1, Listing 6.2 presents the pseudocode for the Monte Carlo simulation with a GBM model.

```
select round(AVG(A_R),6), round(STDDEV(A_
R),6), count(*), round(STDDEV(A_R)/sqrt(count(*)),6)
  into drift_of_return, stddev_of_return, number_of_time_steps, dt
  from (
  select DATE_SQL, SUM(DAILY_RETURN*WEIGHT) A_R
      from "_SYS_BIC"."montecarlo/AN_STOCK_RETURN"
      where ID = :PORTF_ID
      and DATE_SQL between :BEGIN_DATE and :END_DATE
      group by DATE_SQL
  );

  TOPROWS := TIME_STEPS * SERIES;

  input1 = SELECT * FROM  MONTECARLO.PAL_DISTRRANDOM_DISTRPARAM_TBL;
  input2 = SELECT * FROM MONTECARLO.PAL_CONTROL_TBL
          union
      select 'NUM_RANDOM', :TIME_STEPS, null, null from dummy ;

for k in 1 .. :SERIES do
  CALL MONTECARLO.DISTRRANDOM_PROC(:input1, :input2, v_output);
  eps_list = select top :TIME_STEPS "ID" as row_
id, RANDOM as eps from :v_output;
  insert into MONTECARLO.SIM_LOOP_WORK_TEMP  select :k, 0,  :INIT_
RETURN, :INIT_RETURN, 0 from dummy;
  select 0,0 into t,W from dummy;
  for i in 1 .. :TIME_STEPS do
    select eps into eps from :eps_list where row_id = :i-1;
    dW := stddev_of_return*eps*sqrt(dt);
    t := dt*i;
    W := W + dW;
    insert into MONTECARLO.SIM_LOOP_WORK_TEMP
    select top 1 :k, :i,  RETURN_+RETURN_*(:drift_of_return*:dt+:dW),
        (RETURN_2+RETURN_2*(:drift_of_return*:dt+:dW))*exp((:drift_
of_return*t-0.5*:stddev_of_return*:stddev_of_return*:t) + :W),
        0 from MONTECARLO.SIM_LOOP_WORK_TEMP where SERIES =
 :k order by TIME_STEPS desc;

  end for;
end for;
```

Listing 6.2 Pseudocode for Monte Carlo Simulation

The following are inputs used in Listing 6.2:

▸ **Portfolio ID**
   The portfolio for which you want to simulate the future value-at-risk.

▸ **Date range**
   The daily returns of the stocks selected for a given date range.

▸ **Series**
   The number of required simulations.

▸ **Time steps**
   A future date that requires a value-at-risk to be simulated.

▸ **Reliability**
   The confidence level for the value-at-risk.

▸ **Base return**
   The future value of this base return will be simulated.

In Listing 6.2, the initial query retrieves the primary parameters from the stock market data (i.e., the drift and trend that are used for the GBM simulation). Then, simulation loops deduce the future value of the portfolio.

As shown in Listing 6.2, the Monte Carlo simulation for value-at-risk using the GBM model involves simulating the daily stock value for the nth day in the future for m iterations. Then, the lowest value of the nth day, based on a desired confidence level, is used as the value-at-risk. As discussed earlier, the mean and standard deviation are used as constants for trend/drift in time and random noise (also referred to as *volatility*).

The output of the simulation procedure is shown in Figure 6.15 for the base value of 100 dollars, the number of the simulation as 1, the number of time steps as 5, and a reliability of 0.99.

The output contains the simulation number in the STEPS column. The TIME_STEPS column contains the day from the end-date. The RETURN_ column is the simulated portfolio return. We will use this output to calculate value-at-risk in the next section.

	SERIES	TIME_STEPS	RETURN_
1	1	1	101.30312926464998
2	1	2	93.16376897295272
3	1	3	91.7390942654559
4	1	4	89.27045375761803
5	1	5	84.31623032566077
6	2	1	100.49563071321683
7	2	2	95.06869575252342
8	2	3	90.77150337249485
9	2	4	90.96347338171573
10	2	5	97.51114364672662
11	3	1	102.26613164603624
12	3	2	107.88254521764736
13	3	3	106.65077020960955
14	3	4	111.5850866364025
15	3	5	112.16216990084597
16	4	1	95.17992603929932
17	4	2	96.47981896904626
18	4	3	100.86052511118086
19	4	4	98.63839794455299
20	4	5	99.61374284601386
21	5	1	98.10953183936068
22	5	2	99.27225075530579
23	5	3	94.51896924833203
24	5	4	100.4730504579822
25	5	5	94.99418687529007
26	6	1	105.65275944978909

Figure 6.15 GBM Simulation Output

Calculate Value-At-Risk

Value-at-risk is the max value of the reliability percent record. This can be calculated using simple SQL by selecting the top percentage records of the simulation value for the nth day. Figure 6.16 illustrates how to calculate value-at-risk from a simulation result created in the previous section.

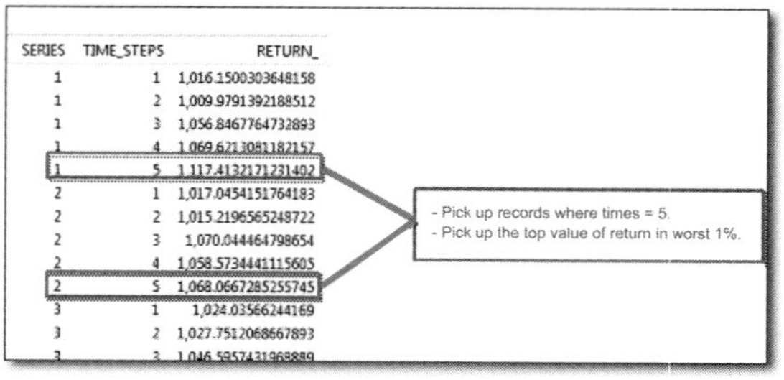

Figure 6.16 Value-at-Risk Calculation

You can calculate the percent of records that need to be considered for a simulation based on the user input. If the reliability input for the procedure is 0.99, that means value-at-risk is of 99% confidence. In this case, choose 1% of the lowest `RETURNS_` of the simulation. The highest value of this 1% record will be determined as the value-at-risk. Remember, you are looking at only the *n*th day of the simulation; all of the lowest value selections are only for that day.

Now that you have calculated value-at-risk for the simulation output, you will want to see the distribution of the simulation itself. You used the binning technique to see the distribution of random variables, and you can effectively use the same technique to understand the distribution of the simulation of `RETURN_OF`. Remember, you are interested in the last day of the simulation.

If you bin the output of the simulated value-at-risk for each of the simulations, the distribution will resemble that shown in Figure 6.17.

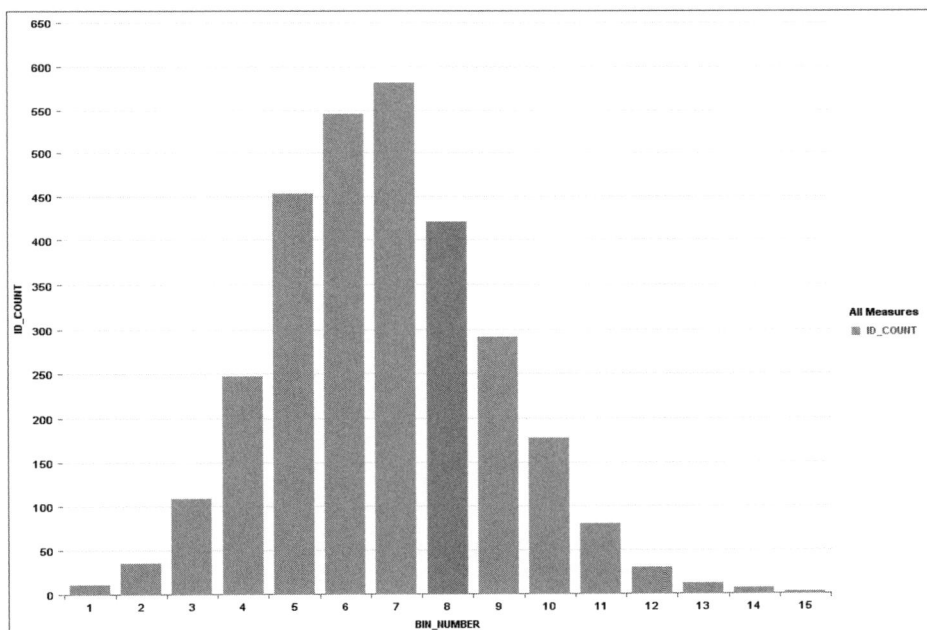

Figure 6.17 Value-at-Risk Simulation Output Distribution

You will notice that the overall simulation is also normally distributed.

One of challenges of pseudocode is that it can be slow due to imperative logic. One way to optimize its performance is to execute the simulation procedure in different connection sessions in parallel. In addition to this option, in the following sections we will try another approach to avoid imperative logic with random distribution.

6.2.3 Avoiding Imperative Logic

Imperative logic in a SQLScript stored procedure prohibits SAP HANA from using its full processing power due to the sequential nature of the execution requirements. Some of the logic can be executed using SQL statements that make use of parallel processing in SAP HANA. Using set theory or thinking in sets is another approach to utilizing parallel computing power through SQL processing.

Looking at Listing 6.2, you can see that there are a couple of loops. The first loop is used for calculating the return for each day. Another loop is used for the number of simulations. We call this technique a *stepwise simulation*, which has a loop simulating each day of a return.

If the number of simulations are large, you can explore generating random distributions once for all simulations and adjust the stepwise processing in the formula for the Monte Carlo simulation. Listing 6.3 is pseudocode for this new logic in which we generate the random variables once for all the simulations. We call this a *non-stepwise technique*.

```
select round(AVG(A_R),6), round(STDDEV(A_
R),6), count(*),  round(STDDEV(A_R)/sqrt(count(*)),6)
  into drift_of_return, stddev_of_return, number_of_time_steps, dt
  from (
  select DATE_SQL, SUM(DAILY_RETURN*WEIGHT) A_R
     from "_SYS_BIC"."montecarlo/AN_STOCK_RETURN"
     where ID = :PORTF_ID
     and DATE_SQL between :BEGIN_DATE and :END_DATE
     group by DATE_SQL
  );

  TOPROWS := TIME_STEPS * SERIES;

  input1 = SELECT * FROM  MONTECARLO.PAL_DISTRRANDOM_DISTRPARAM_TBL;
  input2 = SELECT * FROM MONTECARLO.PAL_CONTROL_TBL
     union
     select 'NUM_RANDOM', :TOPROWS, null, null from dummy ;

  CALL MONTECARLO.DISTRRANDOM_PROC(:input1, :input2, v_output);

  eps_list = select top :TOPROWS "ID" as row_id, CASE WHEN
  MOD("ID"+1,:TIME_STEPS) = 0 THEN :TIME_STEPS ELSE  MOD("ID"+1,
```

```
              :TIME_STEPS) END   AS "times",
              RANDOM as eps, :dt dt, :stddev_of_return sigma,
              :drift_of_return drift_of_return
              from :v_output;

  eps2 = select "times", sigma*eps*sqrt(dt) dW,
         dt*"times" t, sigma*eps*sqrt(dt)*"times" W, sigma, dt,
         row_id, drift_of_return from :eps_list;

  out1 =   select FLOOR((row_id-1)/:TIME_STEPS)+1
           "SERIES",  "times" as "TIME_STEPS",
           (:INIT_RETURN+:INIT_RETURN*(drift_of_return*dt+dW))*exp(
           (drift_of_return*t-0.5*sigma*sigma*t) + W) "RETURN_"
     from :eps2  order by 1;
```

Listing 6.3 GBM without a Loop

In Listing 6.3, the random variables are generated once; the GBM processing is adjusted to cater for the non-stepwise processing required.

Figure 6.18 depicts the overall GBM output without loops.

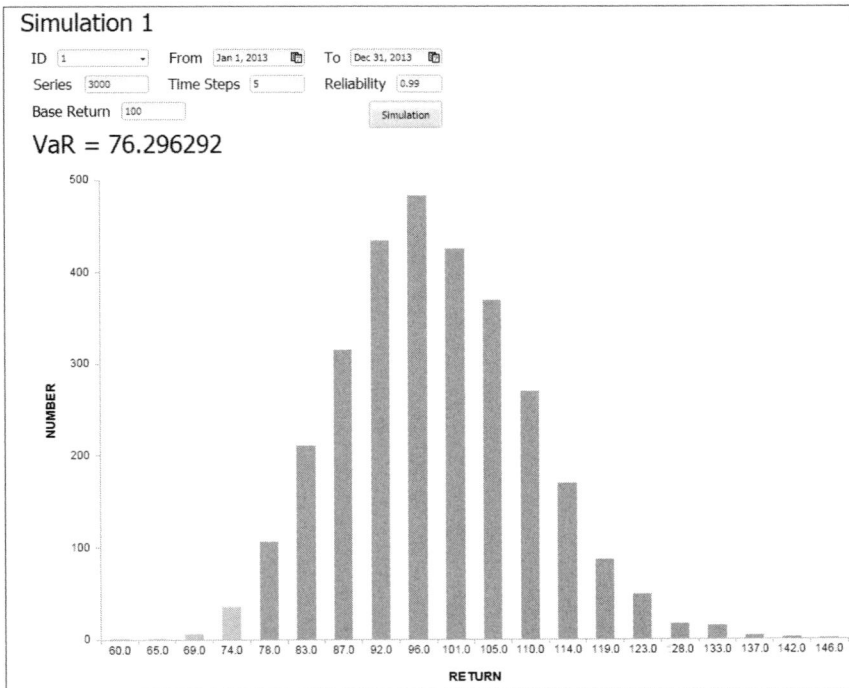

Figure 6.18 Non-Stepwise GBM Output

The output visualization in Figure 6.18 is created using SAP BusinessObjects BI to create visualizations for comparison. The distribution of the simulation in Figure 6.18 is normal. The leftmost four bars in the distribution are the values below and close to value-at-risk; value-at-risk itself is shown in the visualization. The input for the model is taken from the user through the controls.

You can also see a comparison of both stepwise and non-stepwise simulations side by side to observe the differences in calculating value-at-risk. Figure 6.19 shows a comparison of the output of both models.

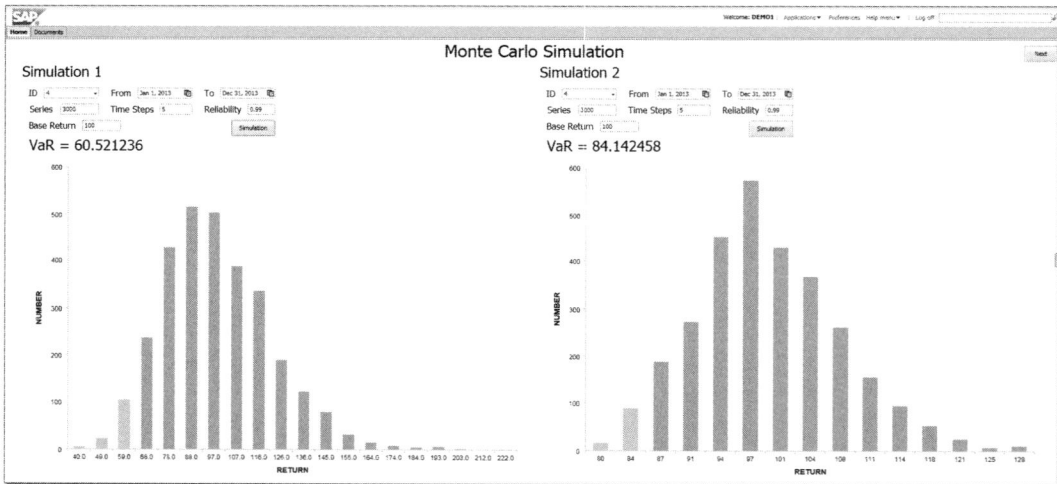

Figure 6.19 Comparison of Stepwise and Non-Stepwise GBM Models

The light gray region indicates that the number of simulated outcomes is less than the value-at-risk. The two charts in Figure 6.19 are for two types of simulations; as noted previously, the random sampling distribution is generated once for the entire simulation and then for each individual simulation. Value-at-risk for each technique is different; the random number being distributed once for each simulation seems to be more realistic than the earlier technique.

Value-at-risk values for each of these models differ by a large amount: 15%. Given that this can be adjusted, there are now two different GBM models: stepwise and non-stepwise (which is without imperative logic). Values of simulated value-at-risk are normal distributions in both simulations, but stepwise is closer to the realistic value and the more preferred method for each simulation.

The next section looks at parallel processing and its performance-enhancing capabilities for imperative logic.

Using Parallel Processing in LLANG

LLANG is strictly for SAP internal use only, and SAP developers can use it only through an approval process. This section is applicable for those qualified developers, and it is only to show possible options in an SAP HANA platform.

In SAP HANA, you can write code in one of the three languages: SQLScript, L, and R. L is closer to the procedural language, with data structures, operations, and functions. L in SAP HANA supports *parallel processing*, which can be used to achieve better performance for imperative logic. Listing 6.4 is the pseudocode for the stepwise logic in LLANG.

```
Void calcVaR( Int32 times_each,  Double drift_of_
return,  Double stddev_of_return,
     Double dt,  Int32 init_return,
   _shared_read PAL_DISTRRANDOM_DISTRPARAM_T input1, _shared_
read PAL_CONTROL_T input2,
          _reset MON_SIM_WORK2_T & monoutput1 )
 {

    PAL_DISTRRANDOM_DISTRPARAM_T read1 = input1.clone();
    PAL_CONTROL_T read2 = input2.clone();
    PAL_DISTRRANDOM_RESULT_T read3;

    Int32 counter = 0;
    Size table_counter = 0z;

    Column<Int32> mon_time =  monoutput1.getColumr<Int32>("TIME_
STEPS");
    Column<Double> mon_return =  monoutput1.getColumn<Double>("RETURN_
2");
    Column<Int32> mon_var_flg =  monoutput1.getColumn<Int32>("VAR_
FLG");
    Column<Double> mon_return_org =
  monoutput1.getColumn<Double>("RETURN_");
    Column<Int32> mon_series =  monoutput1.getColumn<Int32>("SERIES");

    while (counter < times_each) {

      pal::distrRandom(read1, read2, read3);
      Column<Int32` idC = read3.getColumn<Int32>("ID");
      Column<Double> randomC =  read3.getColumn<Double>("RANDOM");
```

```
      Size coutContent = 0z;

      Double w = Double("0");
      Double eps = Double("0");
      Double dW = Double("0");
      Double t = Double("0");
      Double constant = Double("0.5");

      Double rETURN2 = Double(init_return);
      Int32 index1 = 1;
      while ( coutContent < idC.getSize()) {

         eps = randomC[coutContent];
         dW = stddev_of_return * eps * math::sqrt(dt);
            t =  dt * Double(index1);
            w = w + dW;
            Double expInpt = (drift_of_return*t-constant*stddev_of_
return*stddev_of_return*t) + w;
            rETURN2 =   rETURN2+Double(rETURN2)*(drift_of_
return*dt+dW)*math::exp(expInpt);

         mon_time[table_counter] = index1;
         mon_return[table_counter] = rETURN2;
         mon_var_flg[table_counter] = 0;
         mon_return_org[table_counter] = expInpt;
         mon_series[table_counter] = 0;

         coutContent = coutContent.next();
         table_counter = table_counter.next();
         index1 = index1 + 1;
      }

         counter = counter + 1;
      }

   }

_parallel {
         calcVaR( times_each, drift_of_return,  stddev_of_
return, dt, init_return, read1,  read2, montecarlo1);
      calcVaR( times_each, drift_of_return,  stddev_of_
return, dt, init_return, read1,  read2, montecarlo2);
      calcVaR( times_each, drift_of_return,  stddev_of_
return, dt, init_return, read1,  read2, montecarlo3);
      calcVaR( times_each, drift_of_return,  stddev_of_
return, dt, init_return, read1,  read2, montecarlo4);
      calcVaR( times_each, drift_of_return,  stddev_of_
return, dt, init_return, read1,  read2, montecarlo5);
      calcVaR( times_each, drift_of_return,  stddev_of_
return, dt, init_return, read1,  read2, montecarlo6);
```

```
    calcVaR( times_each, drift_of_return,  stddev_of_
return, dt, init_return, read1,  read2, montecarlc7);
    calcVaR( times_each, drift_of_return,  stddev_of_
return, dt, init_return, read1,  read2, montecarlc8);
    calcVaR( times_each, drift_of_return,  stddev_of_
return, dt, init_return, read1,  read2, montecarlc9);
    calcVaR( times_each, drift_of_return,  stddev_of_
return, dt, init_return, read1,  read2, montecarlc10);
    calcVaR( times_each, drift_of_return,  stddev_of_
return, dt, init_return, read1,  read2, montecarlc11);
    calcVaR( times_each, drift_of_return,  stddev_of_
return, dt, init_return, read1,  read2, montecarlc12);
    calcVaR( times_each, drift_of_return,  stddev_of_
return, dt, init_return, read1,  read2, montecarlc13);
    calcVaR( times_each, drift_of_return,  stddev_of_
return, dt, init_return, read1,  read2, montecarlc14);
    calcVaR( times_each, drift_of_return,  stddev_of_
return, dt, init_return, read1,  read2, montecarlc15);
    }
```

Listing 6.4 LLANG Procedure

In Listing 6.4, SAP HANA parallelizes the execution of logic in the `_parallel` block. We have implemented GBM in a `calcVaR` function in a LLANG procedure and called it multiple times in the parallel block (`_parallel`). This enables us to perform a large number of simulations in matter of subseconds. One million Monte Carlo simulations are executed in less than five seconds with this approach.

With this, you have now seen all of the random variable generation techniques in SAP HANA and their use in the Monte Carlo simulation for calculating value-at-risk using the GBM model. You have also seen various alternatives for implementing the simulation and compared the outcomes.

Once an investment manager identifies risk in a portfolio, the next step is to optimize the portfolio for maximize return, which we will cover in the next section.

6.3   Portfolio Optimization

A large number of securities are traded on various bases around the world every day. An *investment portfolio* is a combination of various securities with distributed weights as per diversification rules. Performance of a stock/security is usually measured by the return of a security for a particular period in time until the time in question. The *volatility* of a portfolio is determined by the weighted volatilities of the individual security returns. This volatility is also known as *risk*. The *Sharpe ratio* is defined as the ratio of return to risk. The performance of a portfolio is assessed based on values of the return, risk, and Sharpe ratio. A maximum return with minimal risk is an ideal expectation for an investment in a portfolio. In other words, the higher the Sharpe ratio, the higher the return.

Portfolio optimization is the process of maximizing returns and minimizing risk, or maximizing the Sharpe ratio under specified constraints. One of the critical components for optimizing a portfolio is building a variance-covariance matrix that explains the correlation amongst all the securities in a portfolio. The covariance matrix return, risk, and Sharpe ratio are defined as follows:

- **Return**

  $R(P) = \sum_{i=1}^{n} (W_i * r_i)$, where:

  - W_i is the weight of the *i*th security in a portfolio.

  - r_i is the return on the *i*th security (daily or monthly).

  - R is the return of a portfolio P.

  - n is the number of securities in a portfolio.

- **Risk**

  $\sigma(P) = \sum_{i=1}^{n} \sum_{j=1}^{n} (w_i w_j \sigma_i \sigma_j \rho_{ij})$, where:

  - w_i is the weight of the *i*th security in a portfolio P.

  - w_j is the weight of the *j*th security in a portfolio P.

  - σ_i is the variance of the *i*th security in a portfolio P.

  - σ_j is the variance of the *j*th security in a portfolio P.

  - ρ_{ij} is the covariance of the *i*th and *j*th security in a portfolio P.

- **Sharpe ratio**

  This is the ratio of return to risk. In this example, we will maximize the return using matrix algebra, as explained in the following sections.

Figure 6.20 illustrates the overall process to optimize a portfolio.

We will use the same stock definitions and portfolio and return calculations as introduced previously (see Section 6.2.2). The following sections cover the remaining processes involved.

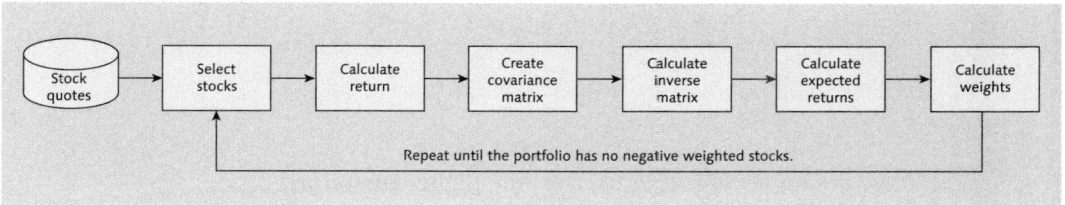

Figure 6.20 Portfolio Optimization Process

6.3.1 Variance-Covariance Matrix

A *variance-covariance matrix* of a portfolio consists of a correlation of each security in a portfolio with others. A variance-covariance matrix can be designed in two ways in SAP HANA: via a matrix structure or a table structure. The following two sections look at each option in detail.

Matrix Structure

As shown in Figure 6.21, a matrix structure is dependent on the number of securities.

	ABC	JP	APP	SAP	IBM
ABC	1	0.5	0.2	0.2	0.6
JP	0.5	1	0.23	0.45	0.64
APP	0.2		1	0.67	0.78
SAP	0.2		0.45	1	0.24
IBM	0.6		0.64	0.78	1

Figure 6.21 Matrix Structure

For the matrix structure table design, if you know the securities of a portfolio beforehand, you can define the physical data model of a table as a matrix structure as shown in Figure 6.21. If you want to be flexible for optimizing and reoptimizing purposes and there are different securities to optimize, consider using SAP HANA flexible tables. A *flexible table* allows you to add columns dynamically. In SAP HANA, you can use the SCHEMA FLEXIBILITY expression for this option and add the columns while performing optimization processes. Listing 6.5 displays the set SQL statements that will define a flexible table.

```
CREATE COLUMN TABLE COVARIANCE(
SECURITY  VARCHAR(15),
SECURITY_A DECIMAL(6,3),
SECURITY_B DECIMAL(6,3)
) WITH SCHEMA FLEXIBILITY;

INSERT INTO MONTECARLO.COVARIANCE VALUES ('SECURITY_A', 0.6, 0.7);
```
Listing 6.5 Flexible Table

With the INSERT statements in Listing 6.6, you can add new columns to this table. The new columns are SECURITY_C and SECURITY_D, with NVARCHAR(5000) for the type.

```
INSERT INTO MONTECARLO.COVARIANCE (SECURITY , SECURITY_A,SECURITY_
B, SECURITY_C) VALUES ('SECURITY_A', 0.6, 0.7, 0.8);
INSERT INTO MONTECARLO.COVARIANCE (SECURITY, SECURITY_A,  SECURITY_
B, SECURITY_C, SECURITY_D) VALUES ('SECURITY_A', 0.6, 0.7, 0.8, TO_
DOUBLE(-0.3));
```
Listing 6.6 Flexible Table Population with New Columns

Irrespective of the value of the new field type, the new column type will be NVARCHAR. This requires changing additional type conversion operations to numeric. In Figure 6.22, the columns inserted with INSERT statements are created with NVARCHAR data types.

	Name	SQL Data Type	Di...	Column Store Data Type	Key	Not Null	Default	Comment
1	SECURITY	VARCHAR	15	STRING				
2	SECURITY_A	DECIMAL	6,3	FIXED				
3	SECURITY_B	DECIMAL	6,3	FIXED				
4	SECURITY_C	NVARCHAR	5000	STRING				
5	SECURITY_D	NVARCHAR	5000	STRING				
6	SECURITY_E	NVARCHAR	5000	STRING				

Figure 6.22 Table Columns with Flexibility Option

For the portfolio, we have considered more than 2,000 securities, but it would be difficult to manage the table structure with so many columns. In such a case, the table structure can be used instead of the matrix structure. The other advantage of a matrix structure is that building a covariance matrix is possible with the SAP HANA PAL multivariate statistics function, MULTIVARSTAT.

Table Structure

A table structure has consistent columns irrespective of the number of securities and grows with the number of rows. In Figure 6.23, note that only a number of rows differ based on the number of securities in the portfolio.

SYMBOL1	SYMBOL2	Variance
Security A (ABC)	SECURITY B (JP)	0.5
Security A (ABC)	SECURITY C(APP)	0.2
Security A (ABC)	SECURITY D (SAP)	0.2
Security A (ABC)	SECURITY E (IBM)	0.6

Figure 6.23 Table Structure

In the next section, we will see how we can implement and populate a covariance matrix in the columnar table structure.

Columnar Table

The columnar structure is easier with respect to maintaining a structure; however, because it is not in a matrix format, you need to rely on low-level data structures of LLANG on SAP HANA or RLANG for the matrix operations. Because SAP HANA supports R integration, it would be simplest to perform some of these activities with R.

Also, it is easier to populate covariance values into a columnar table structure using the following formula. For a calculation, you need to sum the squares of the returns for the two securities and use the correlation calculation formula shown here:

$$f(x, y) = \frac{1}{n}\sum_{i=1}^{n}(x_i y_i) - \bar{x}\bar{y}$$

The SQL query shown in Listing 6.7 will calculate covariance for securities.

```
SELECT ID, RUNID, SYMBOL_A, SYMBOL_B,
          NUM1 as "CORR",
          COMMONSIZE, "TYPE"

    FROM
    (
    SELECT
          :portfId as "ID", :runid as "RUNID", SYMBOL_A, SYMBOL_B,
          round(VAR_A,6) VAR_A, round(VAR_B,6) VAR_B,
          round((psum / n - sum1 /n * sum2 / n), 6) as "NUM1",
```

```
             sqrt((sum1sq - power(sum1, 2.0) / n) * (sum2sq -
 power(sum2, 2.0) / n)) as "NUM2",
             round((((psum - (sum1 * sum2 / n)) /sqrt((sum1sq -
 power(sum1, 2.0) / n) * (sum2sq - power(sum2, 2.0) /
 n))),6) AS "CORR",
             n AS "COMMONSIZE", 'M' as "TYPE"
   FROM
   (
     SELECT
                 n1.SYMBOL AS SYMBOL_A,
                 n2.SYMBOL AS SYMBOL_B,
                 STDDEV(n1.MONTHLY_RETURN) AS "VAR_A",
                 STDDEV(n2.MONTHLY_RETURN) AS "VAR_B",
                 SUM(n1.MONTHLY_RETURN) AS sum1,
                 SUM(n2.MONTHLY_RETURN) AS sum2,
                 SUM(n1.MONTHLY_RETURN * n1.MONTHLY_RETURN) AS sum1sq,
                 SUM(n2.MONTHLY_RETURN * n2.MONTHLY_RETURN) AS sum2sq,
                 SUM(n1.MONTHLY_RETURN * n2.MONTHLY_RETURN) AS psum,
                 COUNT(*) as n

         FROM :portfolio AS n1
     INNER JOIN :portfolio AS n2
     ON
     n1.YEAR_INT = n2.YEAR_INT AND n1.MONTH_INT = n2.MONTH_INT
     GROUP BY
     n1.SYMBOL, n2.SYMBOL
   )
 );
```

Listing 6.7 Calculating Covariance Matrix Using SQL

Covariance Table Data

With a large number of securities in a portfolio and the easy population of cova-riance values, a table structure suits our portfolio optimization. The covariance table structure is shown in Figure 6.24.

	Name	SQL Data Type	Di...	Column Store Data Type	Key	Not Null	Default	Comment
1	ID	INTEGER		INT				
2	RUNID	INTEGER		INT				
3	SYMBOL_A	VARCHAR	10	STRING				
4	SYMBOL_B	VARCHAR	10	STRING				
5	CORR	DOUBLE		DOUBLE				
6	COMMONSIZE	INTEGER		INT				
7	TYPE	VARCHAR	1	STRING				

Figure 6.24 Covariance Table Structure

We will populate the table in Figure 6.24 using the SQL in Listing 6.7 for calculating the correlation factor. Figure 6.25 shows some of the first records of the covariance table.

	ID	RUNID	SYMBOL_A	SYMBOL_B	CORR	COMMONSIZE	TYPE
1	1	1	AFC	A	0.177415	86	M
2	1	1	AFC	AA	0.230146	86	M
3	1	1	AFC	AAN	0.099556	86	M
4	1	1	AFC	AAP	0.02537	86	M
5	1	1	AFC	AAPL	0.097618	86	M
6	1	1	AFC	AAT	0.345488	41	M
7	1	1	AFC	AAV	0.296933	86	M
8	1	1	AFC	AB	0.405309	86	M
9	1	1	AFC	ABB	0.132963	86	M
10	1	1	AFC	ABBV	-0.095...	17	M
11	1	1	AFC	ABC	0.159625	86	M
12	1	1	AFC	ABEV	0.170623	86	M
13	1	1	AFC	ABG	0.10486	86	M
14	1	1	AFC	ABM	0.186007	86	M
15	1	1	AFC	ABR	0.204316	86	M
16	1	1	AFC	ABT	0.160904	86	M
17	1	1	AFC	ABX	-0.019...	86	M
18	1	1	AFC	ACC	0.158136	86	M
19	1	1	AFC	ACCO	0.242504	86	M
20	1	1	AFC	ACE	0.264399	86	M
21	1	1	AFC	ACG	0.332095	86	M
22	1	1	AFC	ACH	0.134006	86	M
23	1	1	AFC	ACI	0.202945	86	M
24	1	1	AFC	ACM	0.150228	85	M
25	1	1	AFC	ACMP	-0.008...	47	M
26	1	1	AFC	ACN	0.143885	86	M
27	1	1	AFC	ACP	0.138973	41	M

Figure 6.25 Sample Output of Covariance Table

The stronger the positive correlation between the two securities, the closer the value of CORR is to 1. Positively correlated stocks exhibit similar upward or downward movements more often than not. Negative correlation is signified by a value closer to -1. This indicates a strong inverse movement between two securities. This information is crucial for the process of optimization and portfolio planning.

Bidirectional Covariance Values

The SQL in Listing 6.7 will populate bidirectional covariance values into the table. You will have two entries for the covariance of securities ABC and C corporation, with SYMBOL_A AS 'ABC' and SYMBOL_B 'C', and another entry with the reverse combination with SYMBOL_A 'C' and SYMBOL_B AS 'ABC'.

Use SAP BusinessObjects BI tools to visualize covariance analysis based on the correlation value. Figure 6.26 shows a visualization for the top positive and negative correlated securities based on the correlation factor.

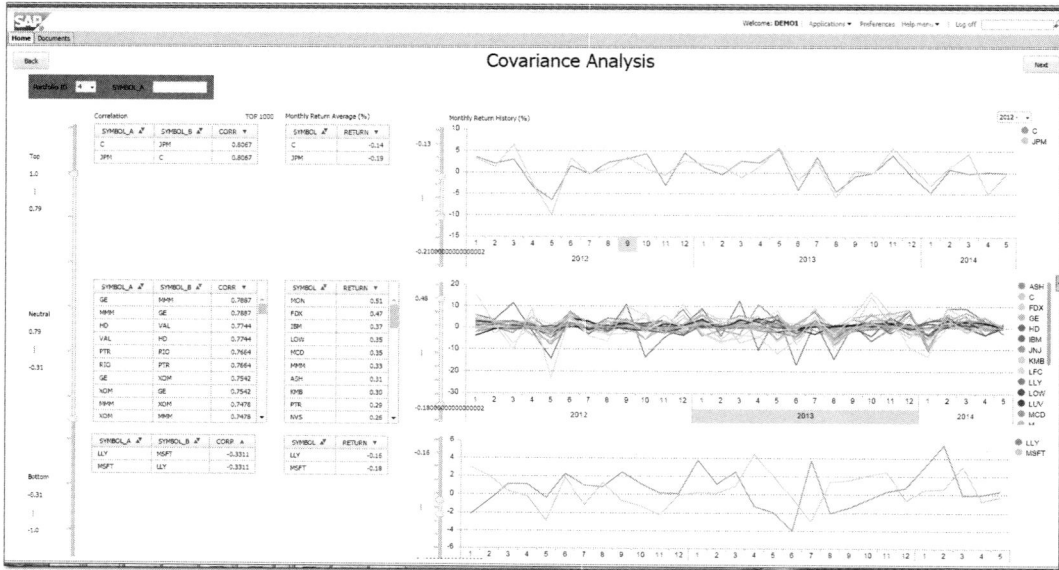

Figure 6.26 Correlated Securities Movement

In Figure 6.26, notice at the top of the image that if the correlation factor is greater than 0.79 (strong positive correlation), the securities have a similar trend of returns. Similarly, negative correlated securities at the bottom of the image exhibit the same pattern.

In this section, we have seen the various options for creating a covariance matrix. We populated the covariance matrix between securities in a portfolio in a tabular format for this case study. We now know how we will use the covariance matrix for maximizing the portfolio return by defining the matrix algebra models in the next section.

6.3.2 Modeling for Optimization Constraints and Equations

Portfolio optimization was proposed in 1970 by Harry Max Markowitz using the covariance matrix and matrix algebra. In the next sections, we will go through the model and how we will derive the equations for optimization execution with an example.

Optimization Model

In this section, we will discuss matrix algebra and derive the optimization equation for maximizing the return.

The following formula (formula 1) is based on the *portfolio optimization theory*:

$$\begin{pmatrix} 2V & R & 1 \\ R & 0 & 0 \\ 1 & 0 & 0 \end{pmatrix} \begin{pmatrix} W \\ \lambda_1 \\ \lambda_2 \end{pmatrix} = \begin{pmatrix} 0 \\ r^* \\ 1 \end{pmatrix} \text{----- (1)}$$

In this example, V stands for variance matrix, W is the weight, R stands for the return, and r^* is the expected return of the portfolio.

You can rewrite this equation for calculating the inverse matrix as follows (formula 2):

$$\begin{pmatrix} 0 & 0 & R \\ 0 & 0 & 1 \\ R & 1 & V \end{pmatrix} \begin{pmatrix} \lambda_1 / 2 \\ \lambda_2 / 2 \\ W \end{pmatrix} = \begin{pmatrix} r^* \\ 1 \\ 0 \end{pmatrix} \text{----- (2)}$$

Finally, let's represent the above equation (2) in a simplified format (formula 3):

(A) x (W) = R*---- (3)

Where A is the return and variance matrix, W is the weight matrix, and R^* is the return matrix.

Let's run through an example of a variance matrix and a return matrix to derive the equations for an optimization based on the preceding simplified formula (3). Let's consider an example of a three-by-three variance matrix V, as shown in Table 6.1.

	Symbol A	Symbol B	Symbol C
Symbol A	0.5	0.2	0.1
Symbol B	0.2	0.6	0.3
Symbol C	0.1	0.3	0.7

Table 6.1 Example Variance Matrix

Similarly, let's consider a return matrix for symbols in V for R, as shown in Table 6.2.

	R
Symbol A	5
Symbol B	4
Symbol C	3

Table 6.2 Return Matrix Example

Using the example V and R matrix, A is as shown in Figure 6.27.

$$A = \begin{pmatrix} 0 & 0 & R \\ 0 & 0 & 1 \\ R & 1 & V \end{pmatrix} =$$

	R	1	Symbol A	Symbol B	Symbol C
R	0	0	5	4	3
1	0	0	1	1	1
Symbol A	5	1	0.5	0.2	0.1
Symbol B	4	1	0.2	0.6	0.3
Symbol C	1	1	0.1	0.3	0.7

Figure 6.27 Matrix Example Including the Returns and Variance Matrix

The inverse matrix of A^{-1} is shown in Figure 6.28.

$$A^{-1} =$$

	R	1	Symbol A	Symbol B	Symbol C
R	-0.25	1.05	0.5	1.29E16	-0.5
1	1.05	.4.72778	-1.61111	0.222222	2.388889
Symbol A	0.5	-1.61111	0.555556	-1.111111	0.555556
Symbol B	1.29E16	0.222222	-1.111111	2.222222	-1.111111
Symbol C	-0.5	2.388889	0.555556	-1.111111	0.555556

Figure 6.28 Inverse Matrix of Example A

Given that the expected return is an input, you can derive the weights from formula 2, as shown in Figure 6.29.

$$\begin{pmatrix} \lambda_1/2 \\ \lambda_2/2 \\ W_1 \\ W_2 \\ W_3 \end{pmatrix} = A^{-1} \begin{pmatrix} r^* \\ 1 \\ 1 \\ 0 \\ 0 \end{pmatrix} = \begin{pmatrix} \text{Weight Parameters} \\ -0.25 & 1.05 & 0.5 & 1.29E-16 & -0.5 \\ 1.05 & -4.72778 & -1.61111 & 0.222222 & 2.388889 \\ 0.5 & -1.61111 & 0.555555 & -1.11111 & 0.555555 \\ 1.29-E16 & 0.222222 & -1.11111 & 0.222222 & -1.11111 \\ -0.5 & 2.388889 & 0.555556 & -1.11111 & 0.555556 \end{pmatrix} \begin{pmatrix} r^* \\ 1 \\ 0 \\ 0 \\ 0 \end{pmatrix}$$

Figure 6.29 Weight Parameters Based on the Inverse Matrix

As shown in the first two columns of Figure 6.29, the inverse matrix will calculate each weight as defined here:

$$W_1 = 0.5 * r^* - 1.611111$$
$$W_2 = (1.29 - E16) * r^* + 0.222222$$
$$W_3 = -0.5 * r^* + 2.388889$$

If the calculated weights W_1, W_2, and W_3 are less than 0, then you need to iterate the process, because you should consider W > 0 as an optimizing constraint.

Once you have the weights calculated for the inverse matrix, write the weights matrix for formula 2 and the variance matrix (V) for formula 1, as follows:

$$W = \begin{pmatrix} W_1 \\ W_2 \end{pmatrix} = \begin{pmatrix} a_1 r^* + b_1 \\ a_2 r^* + b_2 \end{pmatrix}$$

$$V = \begin{pmatrix} \sigma_{11} & \sigma_{12} \\ \sigma_{21} & \sigma_{22} \end{pmatrix}$$

Next, we want to show that the expected return is always between the minimum and maximum of R as follows (you will use this in the Sharpe ratio equation):

$$Return = r^* \, (\min(R) <= \max(R))$$

Now, write the defining formula for risk, which is related to the previous formula:

$$Risk = W^t VW = (a_1 r^* + a_2 r^* + b_2) \begin{pmatrix} \sigma_{11} & \sigma_{12} \\ \sigma_{21} & \sigma_{22} \end{pmatrix} \begin{pmatrix} a_1 r^* + b_1 \\ a_1 r^* + b_2 \end{pmatrix}$$

$$= Ar^{*2} + Br^* + C$$

Once you have defined the risk, you can use the Sharpe ratio equation for optimizing the returns:

$$\text{Sharpe ratio} = \mathit{return} \, / \, \mathit{risk} = \frac{r^*}{Ar^2 + Br^2 + c}$$

The Sharpe ratio equation will be used to optimize returns. As you have seen in this section, in order to optimize the Sharpe ratio, you first need to perform a matrix inversion operation using the covariance matrix built in Section 6.3.1. Then, use the preceding equation for optimization. The next section will cover the inverse matrix.

Inverse Matrix

Now that we have defined the covariance matrix in tabular form in the Covariance Table Data section, you need to transform the data into the matrix form and perform an inverse matrix operation. You will use R to transform and retrieve the inverse matrix.

To begin, define the input table types of an RLANG procedure. Figure 6.30 shows the input table type.

Table Name: R_INPUT_T							Schema: MONTECARLO		Type: Table Type

Columns | Indexes | Further Properties | Runtime Information

	Name	SQL Data Type	Di...	Column Store Data Type	Key	Not Null	Default	Comment
1	SYMBOL_A	VARCHAR	10	STRING				
2	SYMBOL_B	VARCHAR	10	STRING				
3	CORR	DOUBLE		DOUBLE				

Figure 6.30 Inverse Matrix Input Table Type

You only need two output values to optimize the portfolio for each symbol, as explained in the previous section. Figure 6.31 displays the output table type.

Table Name: WEIGHT_PARAMETR_T							Schema: MONTECARLO		Type: Table Type

Columns | Indexes | Further Properties | Runtime Information

	Name	SQL Data Type	Di...	Column Store Data Type	Key	Not Null	Default	Comment
1	SYMBOL	VARCHAR	10	STRING				
2	INVERSE_RETURN	DOUBLE		DOUBLE				
3	INVERSE_ONE	DOUBLE		DOUBLE				

Figure 6.31 Output of Inverse Matrix Procedure

Next, let's look at the RLANG procedure code. Listing 6.8 displays the RLANG procedure that will transform the covariance matrix in the table structure to the matrix structure and calculate the inverse matrix.

```
library(plyr)
library(reshape)
library(reshape2)
library(data.table)
Cov_list<-data.table(covariance_list)
Cov_matrix<-cast(Cov_list, SYMBOL_A ~ SYMBOL_B)
Cov_inverse_matrix<-solve(Cov_matrix)
Cov_inverse_matrix_frame<-  cbind(row.names(Cov_inverse_
matrix),Cov_inverse_matrix[,c(1:2)])
colnames(Cov_inverse_matrix_frame)<-c("SYMBOL","INVERSE_
RETURN","INVERSE_ONE")
result<-as.data.frame(Cov_inverse_matrix_frame)
```

Listing 6.8 Transform the Structure and Perform the Inverse Matrix Operation

The previously mentioned R function `solve` will calculate the inverse of the matrix, and `cast` will transform the function from the table format to the matrix structure. Finally, select the first two values for each security for optimization and send them back to SAP HANA (see Figure 6.32 for the output values of Listing 6.8).

	SYMBOL	INVERSE_RETURN	INVERSE_ONE
1	!1_return	-6.70033858435769	0.046467665430281
2	!2_one	0.0464676654302809	-0.000993027401361245
3	ASH	12.4522627876101	-0.0530019529603186
4	BAC	-3.06998541582984	0.0604207515771895
5	C	0.11581659601597	-0.00604871937950228
6	DOW	-7.73744876952769	0.00189772014744749
7	FDX	13.7880881273532	-0.0147624983138658
8	GE	-10.811743208595	-0.0403812839921442
9	HD	-13.872881074211	0.108868112513957
10	IBM	2.04954375858982	0.128578078799978
11	JNJ	-3.63056121539364	0.0312412428149356
12	JPM	0.995235429875882	-0.0587361376336547
13	KMB	-7.42391464841289	0.385500220558485
14	LFC	-2.61378274141545	-0.0276929400737491
15	LLY	-4.05229405341493	0.0426235758811967
16	LOW	13.8217586047896	-0.0409323639119372
17	LUV	0.949184941742886	-0.000441013224645632
18	LYG	-10.5646024228684	0.0117130978130218
19	MCD	12.2552903891175	-0.0160569121913219
20	MMM	0.273579121652377	0.029106872514646
21	MON	8.99506658753909	-0.041226894393764
22	MRK	3.1347928209447	-0.0122033274380123
23	MSFT	-7.67690594239091	0.0842926487933565
24	NVS	25.7434223479644	0.0889784898750469
25	ORCL	1.77278515775506	0.0322738704272656
26	PFE	-30.3842960485779	0.212004609238737
27	PTR	8.98679203181127	-0.0450463264090583

Figure 6.32 Output of Inverse Matrix for Optimization

Insert the output in Figure 6.32 into the WEIGHT_PARAMETER table, which will be used to calculate the expected result in the next section.

Calculate Expected Return

Next, we will minimize and maximize the return using the derived equation in R by passing the relevant parameters of A, B, and C calculated in SAP HANA and leveraging the optimized function in R to calculate the expected return.

Begin by defining the input table type for the RLANG procedure, as shown in Figure 6.33.

	Name	SQL Data Type	Di...	Column Store Data Type	Key	Not Null	Default	Comment
1	A	DOUBLE		DOUBLE				
2	B	DOUBLE		DOUBLE				
3	C	DOUBLE		DOUBLE				
4	MAX_RETURN	DOUBLE		DOUBLE				
5	MIN_RETURN	DOUBLE		DOUBLE				

Figure 6.33 Input Table Type to Optimize Function

You can then calculate A, B, and C for the model as follows using SAP HANA SQL (see Listing 6.9).

```
select sum(A) as A,sum(B) as B,sum(C) as C,sum(max_return) as MAX_
RETURN,sum(min_return)  as MIN_RETURN from
 (
 select sum(CORR*IR_A*IR_B) as A, sum(CORR*(IR_A*IO_B+IR_B*IO_
A)) as B, sum(CORR*IO_A*IO_B) as C, null as max_return, null as min_
return
 from(
 select M.SYMBOL_A, M.SYMBOL_B, M.CORR as CORR,  WP_A.INVERSE_
RETURN as IR_A, WP_A.INVERSE_ONE as IO_A,  WP_B.INVERSE_RETURN as IR_
B, WP_B.INVERSE_ONE as IO_B
 from "MONTECARLO"."COV_MATRIX_NN" as M
 inner join "MONTECARLO"."WEIGHT_PARAMETR" as WP_A
 on M.SYMBOL_A = WP_A.SYMBOL
 inner join "MONTECARLO"."WEIGHT_PARAMETR" as WP_B
 on M.SYMBOL_B = WP_B.SYMBOL
```

Listing 6.9 Calculation Equation Parameters in SQL

In addition to the Listing 6.9 code, also select the minimum and maximum returns of the securities to pass them as an input to the RLANG procedure. Listing 6.10 is the pseudocode of the RLANG procedure.

```
library(data.table)
p<-data.table(r_input)
A<-p[1,A]
B<-p[1,B]
C<-p[1,C]
max_return<-p[1,MAX_RETURN]
min_return<-p[1,MIN_RETURN]
f<- function(x) x/(A*x^2+B*x+C)
xopt_max<- optimize(f=f,interval=c(min_return,max_return),tol=
0.000001,maximum=T)
xopt_min<- optimize(f=f,interval=c(min_return,max_return),tol=
0.000001)
expected<-matrix(c(xopt_max$maximum,xopt_max$objective,xopt_
min$minimum,xopt_min$objective), nrow=1, ncol=4)
colnames(expected)<-c("OPTIMIZED_EXPECTED_RETURN","OPTIMIZED_
SHARPE_RATIO","MINIMUM_EXPECTED_RETURN","MINIMUM_SHARPE_RATIO")
result<-as.data.frame(expected)
```

Listing 6.10 Optimize the Return

Note that the optimize function definition is defined in the model, which is followed by calling the minimize and maximize optimized functions. The outputs of the optimized functions are maximized and minimized returns with their respective Sharpe ratios.

Redistribute the portfolio by assigning weights, using the maximum expected return OPTIMIZED_EXPECTED_RETURN from the procedure in Listing 6.10 to achieve maximum returns. You will store this output in a table in SAP HANA.

Calculate Weights

As per the model, a new weight can be calculated based on the maximized expected return and the inverse matrix as $a_1 r^* + b_1$ for a security. Use following SQL statements to calculate the same:

```
calculated_weights = select :portfId, :runid, :expected_
return, SYMBOL, INVERSE_RETURN * :expected_return + INVERSE_ONE
 from "MONTECARLO"."WEIGHT_PARAMETER";
```

The output looks like that shown in Figure 6.34 for securities in a portfolio.

	ID	RUNID	EXPECTED_RETURN	SYMBOL	WEIGHT
1	4	150,226,000	0.012173986861577595	!1_return	-0.03510216846381094
2	4	150,226,000	0.012173986861577595	!2_one	-0.00042733065292482203
3	4	150,226,000	0.012173986861577595	ASH	0.09859173061295837
4	4	150,226,000	0.012173986861577595	BAC	0.023046789459642197
5	4	150,226,000	0.012173986861577595	C	-0.0046387696612512205
6	4	150,226,000	0.012173986861577595	DOW	-0.09229787951491233
7	4	150,226,000	0.012173986861577595	FDX	0.15309350539480607
8	4	150,226,000	0.012173986861577595	GE	-0.1720033037643305
9	4	150,226,000	0.012173986861577595	HD	-0.06002015941571617
10	4	150,226,000	0.012173986861577595	IBM	0.15352919758927885
11	4	150,226,000	0.012173986861577595	JNJ	-0.012957161721419759
12	4	150,226,000	0.012173986861577595	JPM	-0.04662015458616918
13	4	150,226,000	0.012173986861577595	KMB	0.29512158116723297
14	4	150,226,000	0.012173986861577595	LFC	-0.05951309682675905
15	4	150,226,000	0.012173986861577595	LLY	-0.006708998684325673
16	4	150,226,000	0.012173986861577595	LOW	0.12733354374666847
17	4	150,226,000	0.012173986861577595	LUV	0.011114351785339557
18	4	150,226,000	0.012173986861577595	LYG	-0.11690023328076896
19	4	150,226,000	0.012173986861577595	MCD	0.13313883199061272
20	4	150,226,000	0.012173986861577595	MMM	0.032437421147243975
21	4	150,226,000	0.012173986861577595	MON	0.06827892806195252
22	4	150,226,000	0.012173986861577595	MRK	0.025959599177936242
23	4	150,226,000	0.012173986861577595	MSFT	-0.0091659032868774
24	4	150,226,000	0.012173986861577595	NVS	0.4023785753112086
25	4	150,226,000	0.012173986861577595	ORCL	0.05385573364617546
26	4	150,226,000	0.012173986861577595	PFE	-0.1578934116549344
27	4	150,226,000	0.012173986861577595	PTR	0.06435876171394232

Figure 6.34 New Weights Calculated

The overall expected return of the portfolio with the new weights calculated in Figure 6.34 can be calculated as shown in Listing 6.11.

```
portfolio_return =
 select :portfId, :runid, :expected_return, var_,  :expected_return/
var_
 from(
   select sum(CORR*WEIGHT_A*WEIGHT_B) as var_
   from (
   select M.CORR as CORR, W_A.WEIGHT as WEIGHT_A, W_
B.WEIGHT as WEIGHT_B
   from "MONTECARLO"."COV_MATRIX_NN" as M
   inner join :calculated_weight as W_A
   on M.SYMBOL_A = W_A.SYMBOL and W_A.ID = :portfId and W_A.RUNID =
 :runid and W_A.EXPECTED_RETURN = :expected_return
   inner join :calculated_weight as W_B
```

```
   on M.SYMBOL_B = W_B.SYMBOL and W_B.ID = :portfId and W_B.RUNID =
:runid and W_B.EXPECTED_RETURN = :expected_return
   )
 );
```

Listing 6.11 Calculating New Weights

The output of Listing 6.11 looks like that shown in Figure 6.35.

	ID	RUNID	EXPECTED_RETURN	VARIANCE_	SHARPERATIC_
1	4	150,226,000	0.012173986861577595	0.0008546639906161394	14.24417899343248⁸

Figure 6.35 New Portfolio Return Based on the New Calculated Weights

In this section, we performed an inverse matrix operation to get the weights for each security. We then derived the optimization equation from the matrix algebra and performed the matrix transformation. Finally, we calculated the maximum expected returns using the optimization function.

We still need to recalculate the portfolio weights until the constraints of optimization are met, which we will cover in the next section.

6.3.3 Executing Optimization Models

One of the constraints of a portfolio is that there should not be any negative weights; that is, weights should be greater than 0.

A new portfolio can be created by removing the negatively weighted securities from recalculated weights and performing the same iterative process of optimizing until you reach a portfolio optimized without negative stocks.

In this example, a portfolio optimization simulation exercise with 2,742 securities is executed 12 times to remove all negative stocks—and finishes in under 10 minutes. Figure 6.36 shows a set of optimal portfolios with a defined level of expected return (known as an efficient frontier) from which the calculated Sharpe ratio and risk derived from the simulation are depicted.

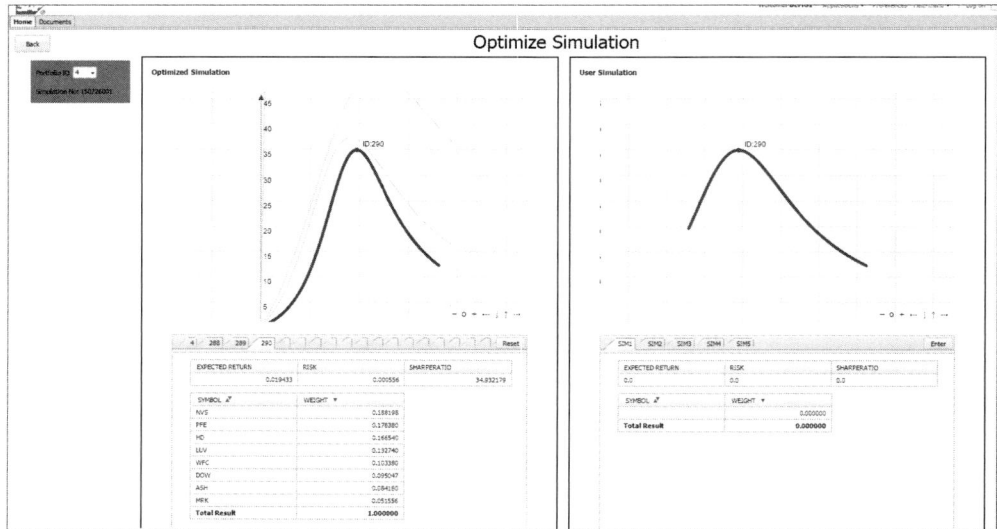

Figure 6.36 Efficient Frontier of Portfolio Optimization

6.4 Summary

In this chapter, we discussed how to perform a Monte Carlo simulation to calculate value-at-risk using a GBM model. During the simulation process, we presented various random variable generation and imperative logic techniques. We also described how to perform matrix algebra based on portfolio optimization in SAP HANA. During this process, we also looked at matrix data design and matrix operations such as the inverse matrix and using optimized functions.

This completes our journey through advanced data modeling in SAP HANA. In this book, we looked at SAP HANA modeling capabilities, how to build complex models for complex logic, and how to scale these models for high performance. Together, we explored how the SAP HANA platform allows us to perform predictive modeling using R and PAL together for predictive models. We concluded the book by looking at a simulation and optimization case study for performing data structure operations in SAP HANA. With this book, you should now be able to model complex logic in SAP HANA, build predictive models with R, PAL, and more, and utilize performance tools to enhance your SAP HANA data models.

The Authors

Anil Babu Ankisettipalli has more than 17 years of experience in developing application and technology software. He has a master's degree in computer applications and extensive knowledge in database technology. Since 2010 he has designed and developed SAP applications and products using predictive analytics, machine learning, and data mining algorithms. For the last few years, Anil has used various data science and big data technologies on the SAP HANA platform to solve critical problems for SAP customers in multiple industries, such as retail, medical, FCMG, and more.

Hansen Chen is an experienced database expert. In 2006, he joined Business Objects in Canada and worked on SAP BusinessObjects Web Intelligence and the semantic layer. After SAP acquired Business Objects, he joined the SAP Strategic Customer Engagements group as a senior specialist in 2011, and worked with customers in co-innovation projects on top of the SAP HANA platform. He has worked with SAP HANA for more than four years, acquiring vast experience and knowledge on SAP HANA modeling and performance tuning topics.

Pranav Wankawala graduated with a degree in computer science, and has more than 13 years of experience in software engineering and developing enterprise applications. Pranav started working with SAP HANA in 2009, when it was still a research project. He designed and architected one of the first SAP products that ran on SAP HANA. Today, he leads a team of highly skilled engineers and technologists that help SAP customers improve their day-to-day business processes by helping them ideate, envision, and renovate their technology landscape using the SAP HANA platform.

Index

T

Interested in reading more?

Please visit our website for all new
book and e-book releases from SAP PRESS.

www.sap-press.com